MOUNTAINEERING
ESSENTIAL SKILLS FOR HIKERS AND CLIMBERS

ALUN RICHARDSON

ILLUSTRATED BY GEORGE MANLEY

Skyhorse Publishing

Skyhorse Publishing books may be purchased in bulk at special discounts for sales promotion, corporate gifts, fund-raising, or educational purposes. Special editions can also be created to specifications. For details, contact the Special Sales Department, Skyhorse Publishing, 555 Eighth Avenue, Suite 903, New York, NY 10018 or info@skyhorsepublishing.com.

www.skyhorsepublishing.com

10 9 8 7 6 5 4 3 2 1

Library of Congress Cataloging-in-Publication Data

Richardson, Alun, 1957-
  Mountaineering : essential skills for hikers and climbers / Alun Richardson ; illustrations by George Manley.
      p. cm.
  Includes index.
  ISBN 978-1-60239-989-1 (pbk. : alk. paper)
  1. Mountaineering. I. Title.
  GV200.R53 2010
  796.52'2--dc22
                              2009050723

Inside photography © Alun Richardson www.freedomphotography.co.uk, excepting those credited throughout the book to John Biggar, the Stefan Doerr Collection, Clive Hebblethwaite, Shaun Hutson, Steve Long, Kristjan Maack, the John Taylor Collection and Mike 'Twid' Turner.
Illustrations © George Manley

Thank you to the Met Office for their permission to reproduce two weather charts on pp. 31 and 160 © Crown Copyright (2008), the Met Office.
Edited by Lucy Beevor
Designed by James Watson

Printed in China

CONTENTS

Alpamayo, Peruvian
Andes

FOREWORD

I first met Alun when I moved to South Wales in the late 70s. At that time he was an academic, working for a PhD in Biochemistry. Climbing was his passion and turned out to be his future career, yet the skills and application of the academic never left him completely and have expressed themselves most recently in this impressive book. He even applies his biochemistry to climbing—such when he talks about coping with fear and why more men than women tend to be thrill seekers!

Alun has learned and retained more than most over his thirty-odd years of rock climbing, mountaineering, and working as a mountain guide all over the world. Sometimes he learned the hard way, which we all know is the most effective way to learn. In this book he passes on all the years of acquired knowledge and wisdom in a novel and very effective way.

I've been climbing a decade longer than Alun yet I learned something new on almost every page and found little to take issue with. It is a booked packed with good advice, whether you're planning a trip to a remote mountain range or heading down to the gear shop, and this advice is put across in a personalized way which makes the book more user-friendly than the usual "textbook." There are anecdotes intermingled with the factual information, and Alun is not afraid to express his opinion even when it challenges conventional wisdom (e.g., "it doesn't matter which way around you hold your ice axe"). Having said this, some of the chapters are little textbooks in themselves, giving as much information as anyone could wish for on subjects such as mountain weather, navigation and cliff rescue.

The end result is one of the most comprehensive and ambitious books about mountaineering ever published, covering just about every aspect of the sport as well as some you will never have associated with mountaineering—such as the hazards of snakes, spiders, and dogs on expeditions, and the correct protocol for shooting a polar bear.

You may never travel and climb as widely as Alun has done. But if you do, I'm confident that time spent reading this book beforehand will help to ensure a safe, healthy, and successful trip.

—Pat Littlejohn, OBE

ACKNOWLEDGMENTS

The ideas in this book are the culmination of 25 years' mountaineering, and there are many people I need to thank.

Alan Dance, Dave Williams, Steve Lewis, Trevor Massiah, Haydn Griffiths, Gary Lewis, Jim Beynon, Andy Long, Twid and Louise Thomas, Graeme Ettle, Pat Littlejohn, Owen Cox, Paul Donnithorne, Stefan Doerr, John Taylor, Tim Jepson, Phil Thomas, and the many Guides, Instructors, and clients that I have spent hours discussing issues and techniques with.

Special thanks must go to Lesley Jones who supported me throughout the project and read it many times; to Clive Hebblethwaite who chewed over many issues with me in a tent and supplied some of the photographs; to Adam Gent who helped me to sort out my muddled thoughts on weather; Dr Jim Duff at www.treksafe.com.au, who helped with medical issues and partner concerns; and to George Manley, whose excellent illustrations help towards making this book both a demonstrative and stunning visual record.

A small army of friends corrected and commented on the text—Matt Spencley, John Biggar, John Taylor, Andy Perkins, Bruce Goodlad, Simon Lowe, Kit Spencer, Adam Gent, Blyth Wright, Ian Parnell, Richard Mansfield, Graeme Ettle, Eric Pirie, and Kit Spencer. Some even posed for photographs—Trevor Massiah, Bas Jongmans, Paul Donnithorne, Clive Hebblethwaite, Sam Ponsford, Chris Trull, Andy Perkins, Bruce Goodlad, Emma Alsford, and Gareth Richardson.

I must also thank the following manufacturers, who generously supported the photo shoots; DMM, Lyon Equipment, Mountain Equipment, Face West, Select Solar, Mammut, and Fritschi.

Thanks too to Rhiannon Richardson and Molly Jones who helped me to sort the text and diagrams, and Robert Foss from A&C Black Publishers, who had the confidence to get behind the book.

Any of the opinions expressed in this book are mine and should not be associated with any of the above people, companies, or organizations.

Everest Base Camp trek

v

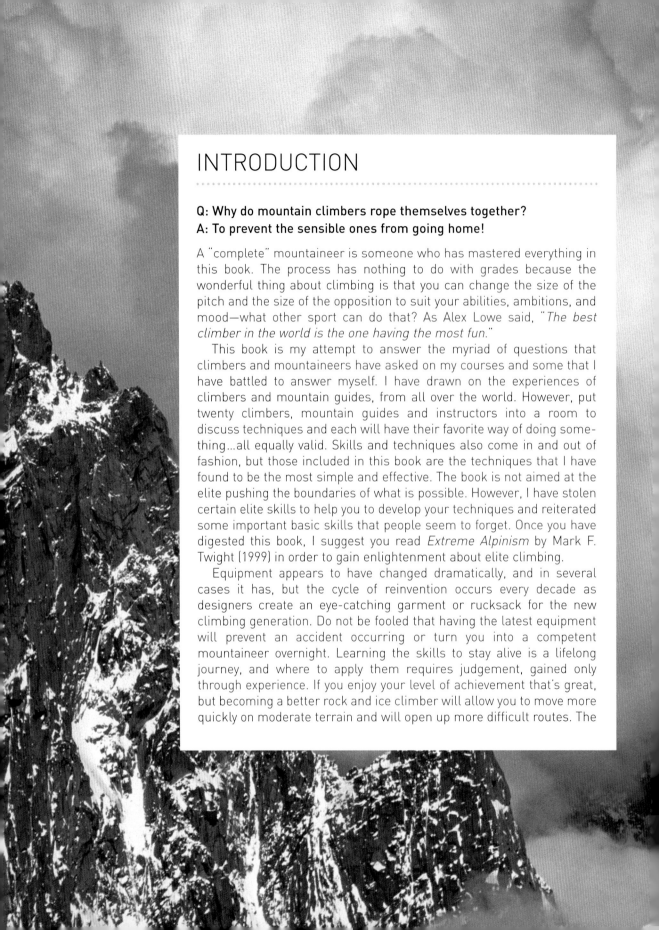

INTRODUCTION

Q: Why do mountain climbers rope themselves together?
A: To prevent the sensible ones from going home!

A "complete" mountaineer is someone who has mastered everything in this book. The process has nothing to do with grades because the wonderful thing about climbing is that you can change the size of the pitch and the size of the opposition to suit your abilities, ambitions, and mood—what other sport can do that? As Alex Lowe said, "*The best climber in the world is the one having the most fun.*"

This book is my attempt to answer the myriad of questions that climbers and mountaineers have asked on my courses and some that I have battled to answer myself. I have drawn on the experiences of climbers and mountain guides, from all over the world. However, put twenty climbers, mountain guides and instructors into a room to discuss techniques and each will have their favorite way of doing something...all equally valid. Skills and techniques also come in and out of fashion, but those included in this book are the techniques that I have found to be the most simple and effective. The book is not aimed at the elite pushing the boundaries of what is possible. However, I have stolen certain elite skills to help you to develop your techniques and reiterated some important basic skills that people seem to forget. Once you have digested this book, I suggest you read *Extreme Alpinism* by Mark F. Twight (1999) in order to gain enlightenment about elite climbing.

Equipment appears to have changed dramatically, and in several cases it has, but the cycle of reinvention occurs every decade as designers create an eye-catching garment or rucksack for the new climbing generation. Do not be fooled that having the latest equipment will prevent an accident occurring or turn you into a competent mountaineer overnight. Learning the skills to stay alive is a lifelong journey, and where to apply them requires judgement, gained only through experience. If you enjoy your level of achievement that's great, but becoming a better rock and ice climber will allow you to move more quickly on moderate terrain and will open up more difficult routes. The chapter on ski mountaineering and snow-shoeing will enable you to travel in the mountains when the snow is too deep to walk and the chapter on lightweight expeditions may give you the confidence to travel further.

There is no doubt that mountaineering and climbing is dangerous, but the rewards are immense. Some of the moments when I have felt most alive have been when working hard to stand on the summit of a mountain. Following the skills and techniques in this book will not remove the hazards, but it may help to reduce the risk. Finally, fame and glory are not the right reasons to climb any mountain—the most stupid statement I have ever heard was, "summit or death, either way I win." The mountains will always be there…will you? We would all be wise to remember the words of Edward Whymper, who was the first person to climb the Matterhorn:

"There have been joys too great to be described in words, and there have been griefs upon which I have not dared to dwell, and with these in mind I say climb if you will, but remember that courage and strength are naught without prudence…Do nothing in haste, look well to each step, and from the beginning think what may be the end." —**Edward Whymper**

ALUN RICHARDSON

For information on guiding and courses by Alun Richardson go to www.alunrichardson.co.uk or www.freedomphotographs.co.uk.

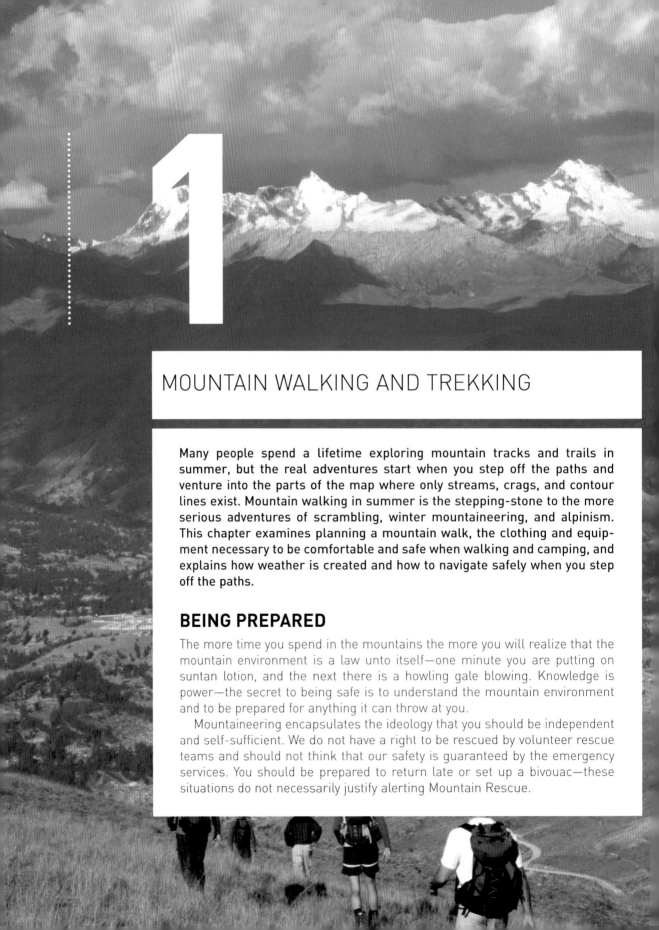

1

MOUNTAIN WALKING AND TREKKING

Many people spend a lifetime exploring mountain tracks and trails in summer, but the real adventures start when you step off the paths and venture into the parts of the map where only streams, crags, and contour lines exist. Mountain walking in summer is the stepping-stone to the more serious adventures of scrambling, winter mountaineering, and alpinism. This chapter examines planning a mountain walk, the clothing and equipment necessary to be comfortable and safe when walking and camping, and explains how weather is created and how to navigate safely when you step off the paths.

BEING PREPARED

The more time you spend in the mountains the more you will realize that the mountain environment is a law unto itself—one minute you are putting on suntan lotion, and the next there is a howling gale blowing. Knowledge is power—the secret to being safe is to understand the mountain environment and to be prepared for anything it can throw at you.

Mountaineering encapsulates the ideology that you should be independent and self-sufficient. We do not have a right to be rescued by volunteer rescue teams and should not think that our safety is guaranteed by the emergency services. You should be prepared to return late or set up a bivouac—these situations do not necessarily justify alerting Mountain Rescue.

Ask yourself:

- Have you packed your back pack with the necessary items?
- What is the weather forecast? Bad weather and poor visibility can dramatically alter estimated times. You can protect yourself against high winds and poor weather by choosing a sheltered route and staying off ridges.
- What route are you taking? What general direction are you heading? Break your route down into smaller legs/sections and create a mental picture of the legs.
- How far is it? How long will it take?
- How steep is the terrain? You may have to zigzag your route for comfort, but will this take longer?
- What is the ground like? Are there boulders, debris, or is there boggy vegetated ground that may slow you down? Can they be avoided?
- Are there any prominent features you will pass on the way, e.g., streams (which can become impassable in heavy rain—see chapter 6, page 282), paths, buildings, valleys, steep hills? Are you going around hills or over them?
- Are there any dangers, for example, steep slopes or hidden cliffs?

As you tackle more difficult routes, the gap between walking and climbing becomes blurred, and you must master the skills of scrambling (see chapter 2).

Trekking in the Alps

WHAT IS A MOUNTAIN?

A mountain is a landform that extends above the surrounding terrain in a limited area. It is generally steeper than a hill, but there is no universally accepted standard definition for the height of a mountain or a hill, although a mountain usually has an identifiable summit.

HOPE FOR THE BEST, PREPARE FOR THE WORST

"We must not think of the things we could do with, but only of the things that we can't do without."

—Jerome K. Jerome
(*Three Men in a Boat*, 1889)

The massive choice of equipment available can make buying gear a nightmare. The best items are not always the most costly and very lightweight options are fine, but only if they are going to work for you. Borrow equipment at first, and when you do buy take your time; read the latest reviews from the experts. The Internet may be cheaper, but there is nothing like handling the gear, so support your local shop (remember to go armed with questions and prior research).

WHICH BOOTS ARE BEST FOR MOUNTAIN WALKING?

A pair of approach shoes or soft fabric boots is fine for treks on simple tracks, but more rugged terrain requires a sturdier mountain walking boot, especially in poor weather. It must be well constructed, water resistant, have an aggressive tread pattern, a medium level of ankle support and, most importantly, the sole should have resistance to twisting (lateral support). Fabric boots are lighter, dry faster, and are cheaper, but check for ankle support and lateral stiffness to get a good grip on wet, grassy slopes.

A good quality leather boot, looked after with a "water proofing" agent, is still the most popular choice with serious mountain walkers, but fabric boots are improving rapidly. GORE-TEX boots are great in hot conditions, but not if it's muddy—then the only boot that is waterproof is a rainboot!

GETTING A GOOD FIT

Comfort and fit is due as much to the socks you use as to the model you choose. Socks should be snug, with a smooth knit, good shape and elasticity, and made of wool or synthetic fibres to draw moisture away. A thin liner and a thicker sock will reduce the chance of blisters. For very wet conditions a GORE-TEX sock worn over a thin liner sock will function like a GORE-TEX boot. Do not roll your socks over the top of your boots or tuck your pants into them as it makes it easier for grit to get in.

Do not hesitate to call Mountain Rescue when it is really needed! (Alan Giles and John Palmer.)

Your feet change shape during the day so try boots on in the afternoon or after exercise. A rough test of fit is to put the boot on un-laced. Push your foot forward until your toes hit the front; you should then be able to squeeze a finger down the back of the heel. Next lace the boots properly by standing up to weight the foot, but not too tightly over the arch—the foot is very sensitive to pressure. A good fit is one where there is no pressure on your toes, you can wiggle them, there is no side-to-side movement of the foot, and your heel does not lift. If in doubt, buy larger.

You can create tension in different parts of the boot by tying a knot at any stage in the lacing then continue to the top. Put both boots on and simulate uphill and downhill walking. Wear a loaded backpack because this will alter the shape of your foot. Finally try male and female versions—you never know!

A good walking boot has lateral resistance and is a stable platform on grassy slopes.

BREAKING BOOTS IN

Performance mountain walking boots are less supple than soft "trail boots" and may require "breaking in" by doing progressively longer walks. It is risky to use new boots for a long trek (see photo on p. 6!).

CARE OF BOOTS

Stuff wet boots loosely with newspaper and leave them to dry in a warm, but not hot, place. Apply waterproofing to clean boots a few days before it is needed, to allow it to soak in, but avoid too much treatment as it can soften the leather.

LOOK AFTER YOUR FEET

Wash your feet every day; use moisturiser to keep them soft and a pumice stone to remove any hard skin. Air them regularly and use powders or antiperspirant to keep them dry and reduce blisters. Cut your nails by following the contour of the nail, so that the nail corner is visible. Cutting too short can cause painful ingrown toenails.

MODIFYING BOOTS

Twenty-five percent (52) of the bones in your body are in your feet. How these bones move in relation to each other has a major effect on comfort, balance, posture, and long-term foot health.

Check how you walk by looking at the soles of an old pair of shoes. If the wear is centralized to the ball of the foot and a small portion of the heel, you

HOW TO WALK!

Pace
Take your time walking and enjoy it. If you can't talk when you walk or keep going for a few hours, then it's too fast. Start slowly, maintain an even pace, and keep something in reserve. Try to walk for at least an hour before stopping for your first rest.

The rest step
Straighten your rear leg between every step so that it is supported by bone, not muscle, and relax the muscles of the forward leg. This momentary rest refreshes the muscle and, because you will perform it thousands of times, its effect over hours of ascent is beneficial. Synchronize your breathing with each step.

Downhill
Tighten your laces, bend your knees, place each foot lightly, using the thigh muscles to absorb the impact. Keep a measured pace and zigzag to shift the strain.

Boulder slopes
Stand in the gaps between stones, rather than on them.

BLISTERS

If your boots fit and they are laced correctly, you wear good socks and you look after your feet, you should never get blisters. If you feel a hot spot, act immediately. Always pop the blister, but do it neatly. Use a sterilized needle and pop several holes in the blister, press it flat and apply a small square of gauze to pad it. Hold the gauze in place with tape as it can be slippery. Bandaids fall off, making a sticky mess at the first moment of perspiration.

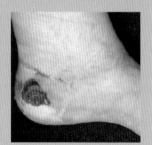

Photo: Kristjan Maack

have a normal amount of foot movement. Some pronation is normal in walking as the foot settles on the ground, but when this type of movement becomes excessive, it can generate pain.

Overpronation ("flat feet") is when there is too much movement of the foot. If you overpronate there will be wear patterns along the inside edges of your shoe. It is a common cause of pain at the heel and throughout the lower extremities. Underpronation (supination) occurs when the foot rolls outwards at the ankle and results in wear along the outer edges. If under or overpronation goes uncorrected, it can also lead to posture and back problems. Orthotic supports, volume adjusters, and stretching can all make your boot more comfortable and ease painful rub points. Insoles also provide extra insulation.

GAITERS

A good quality gaiter should be waterproof. Nylon is cheap, but not breathable, and canvas is durable, but stiff. Elastic or lace bindings under the boot are easy to use, but rubberized or cable straps last longer. Velcro closures are easier to use and keep water out, but a zippered closure with a good storm flap will work better.

Gaiters come in three designs:

- **Low (stop tous)** —Ankle high and cooler, less able to keep rain and snow out, but my choice for most conditions.

- **High** —Calf-high and helpful when you are hiking on wet, muddy trails, wading through streams, or crashing through vegetation.

- **Full, over-the-boot gaiters** —Useful when walking in very wet, boggy terrain because they turn the boot into a rainboot. But they can be too warm, are expensive, and the rubber erodes easily, particularly the instep.

TREKKING POLES

Poles help protect your knees, make crossing streams easier, save you energy, and generally speed you up—but only when they are correctly adjusted!

Love them or hate them, gaiters keep ticks and leeches off your legs, and mud and snow out of your boots.

Keep poles short, so that when you are standing on flat ground your hands are below your navel. Some have a rubber grip below the handle so that on traverses and steep ascents you can grasp the pole lower without having to adjust it. Avoid using the hand loops (even cut them off!), making it easier to jettison the poles should you slip. Do not use poles extended to their limits, and adjust the sections equally to maintain maximum strength.

The advantages of shock-absorbing springs are in doubt; they simply increase the pole weight, length, and cost. Poles made from 7075 aluminium alloy or carbon fiber are stronger. Leave the basket on the pole, otherwise they sink into soft mud. A flick lock, rather than a screw system, is more reliable and enables the poles to be cut shorter to fit inside your backpack more easily.

Two, three, or four section poles are available—the more sections there are the shorter the pole is when collapsed, but more sections means more joints and increases the cost (and weight) of the pole. Dry poles before collapsing, but do not oil the tubes—the joints may never lock firmly again!

Poles do have downsides: they transfer the stresses to your elbows and shoulders, keep your hands full, increase total energy expenditure, and there is evidence that they prevent novices from learning essential balance. I rarely use them on simple walks, but when the going gets tough—especially downhill—they are invaluable.

AVOIDING KNEE INJURIES

Maintain the strength of the muscles supporting the knees, especially the quadriceps, which take some of the load off your joints.

EMERGENCY USE

Placing two or more trekking poles in opposite directions behind the backpacks of two people creates a good system for carrying an injured person off the hill. Wrap duct tape around the poles.

Using trekking poles (Shani Tan, Argentina).

The layering process: base layer, mid-layer, insulating layer, and waterproof layer.

CLOTHING

Mountain weather is fickle: even on sunny days the wind can quickly cool you. To stay warm, stay dry, as wet clothing leads to heat loss through evaporation and impaired insulation. Wearing many thin layers traps heat far more efficiently than one piece of bulky clothing, and allows you to regulate your body temperature and therefore reduce perspiration. Even if you set off in shorts have some layers in your backpack.

The layer of clothing next to the skin (the base layer) should be snug, porous, and made from a performance fabric, such as polypropylene, that wicks perspiration away from your skin to the mid-layer. Merino wool is gaining in popularity because it smells less, absorbs moisture well, is soft, land is biodegradable. It is, however, heavier, slow to dry, and expensive. Avoid cotton, which traps moisture, cooling you.

The mid-layer should be a thicker synthetic fleece to hold heat in, yet should still wick moisture away from the body. The insulating layer can be a thicker fleece or, if you are doubtful about the weather, a lightweight dawn-filled jacket (e.g., Mountain Equipment Trango jacket).

Up to 40 percent of body heat is lost through your head, so carry a hat all year round, and a sun hat is vital.

Gloves are essential. Bulk equals warmth, although you lose dexterity. For more information on duvet jackets, gloves, and sun protection, see chapters 3 and 4.

Wired visor and large enough to fit over a helmet

Toggles tied at both ends

Taped seams

Good storm flap

Mesh-lined chest pocket

Short enough to give freedom of movement

The parts of a good water-proof jacket

WATERPROOF JACKETS

Raincoats form the final layer and are crucial, not only for repelling rain, but also reducing the wind chill. For most of us, the purchase of a jacket represents a significant investment and you get what you pay for...up to a point! Look for lifetime guarantees. Raincoats with zips to attach a fleece on the inside are rarely of any use. Smocks with a long zip are underrated—jackets are commonly either on, with the zip done up, or they are in a backpack. However, smocks are more difficult to get on and off.

MATERIALS

Waterproof fabrics are usually manufactured with coated fabrics or membrane fabrics. Large manufacturers have their own cheaper, lower-performing brands that are often good value and perform well enough for most users.

A non-breathable coated jacket does not allow water in or out. As soon as you start exercising you get damp from sweat. In light rain you may find you are less damp without the jacket than with it! This type of jacket is, therefore, only suitable for short-term, non-strenuous use.

Breathable fabrics use either a microporous membrane laminated to a face fabric, where the pores in the coating are large enough to let water vapor pass through but small enough to keep water droplets out (GORE-TEX), or a coating. Two types of breathable coating exist; microporous, which works like GORE-TEX (Lowe Triplepoint), and hydrophilic (Sympatex), which relies on the chemical and molecular properties of water molecules.

The more active you are, the more breathable the material must be. However, good ventilation and adjusting your layers to reduce sweating is just as important for keeping you dry.

In reality, how well a jacket breathes and keeps out water is down to the design of the jacket and how active you are, rather than the breathability and how much water pressure the material can withstand. Identify the key activity you expect to use your jacket for and buy the most suitable and specific jacket, rather than making a compromised choice to suit a wider range of activities.

Lightweight materials are great when the weather is mostly dry, but if the environment you walk in is often wet, choose heavyweight fabrics. Take any manufacturer's claims of staying dry in torrential rain with a pinch of salt as a fabric's breathability is always compromised when it is wet or dirty. This is why it is important to reproof the outer layer to maintain water beading and cleanliness.

FIT

Your jacket should provide freedom of movement so try it on with the maximum layers you are likely to wear. Reach for the sky—are your wrists and belly exposed or does it pull at the waist and cuffs? Can you see your feet? It should not be too loose because you must build up a water vapor pressure difference between the inside and outside of the jacket to force water vapor out. Waist drawcords help with this process, making your jacket fit more snugly.

WEIGHT

The heavier a jacket is the more durable it is likely to be, but do you really need a ski pass holder, pit zips, or lots of pockets?

HOOD

The attention to detail in the hood will tell you if the jacket is well designed. Hoods that roll away into a zipped pouch are rarely large enough and do not have a stiffened peak or wired visor—essential in the wind. A hood should be large enough to fit a hat or even a climbing helmet underneath it but not flop down over your eyes or obscure your vision when you turn your head. Volume adjusters reduce the hood's size when you are not wearing a hat.

The greatest advance in raincoats came with the development of elastic drawcords on hoods, which are secured at both ends and "lock" with a toggle that can be operated single-handedly. You no longer have to endure them hitting your face in windy conditions.

EXPERT TIP

Owen Samuel, BMG/ IFMGA Guide
owenrichsamuel@ hotmail.com

"When in the mountains, anything on your person that flaps in the wind or dangles past your knees will at some point slap you in the face or trip you over."

ZIPS AND STORM FLAPS

Two-way zips allow you to increase ventilation, put the jacket on in a hurry, and undo it to answer calls of nature!

The zip is a weak point in combating the elements and it should have a Velcro storm flap to prevent water getting through. Uncovered, water-resistant zips on lightweight jackets work well when new, but they are not so durable and do not slide as easily. Pit zips (which vent the upper-arm area) can increase ventilation in extreme situations, but you can achieve the same effect by opening your cuffs, pockets, and neck zip. They can also be difficult to do up while wearing a backpack.

LENGTH

Mid-length jackets protect the waist and thighs when walking, but can restrict movement. Shorter jackets are lighter and less bulky, fit under a harness, and allow greater freedom of movement when scrambling or climbing, but they may expose your back when bending over.

POCKETS

Chest pockets should be mesh-lined, to improve ventilation, and large enough for a map (although this can be cut into smaller sections). An extra mesh pocket on the inside is useful for sunscreen or snacks, etc. If you regularly wear a harness avoid pockets below the waist.

A soft shell. Evaporation uses heat, therefore the more breathable a jacket is the cooler you will feel. (Walker: D. Williams.)

SOFT SHELLS

This garment supposedly provides an outer and insulating layer in one. It is soft to the touch, water resistant, wind resistant, highly breathable, and often stretchable. While not 100 percent waterproof, a soft shell delivers twice the breathability. It does however take a long time to dry out when wet and you will then feel the cold more.

The decision to wear soft shells or conventional clothing depends on the activity. If rain is likely, a conventional waterproof jacket is important, but for aerobic activities in cold, dry, high-activity situations, soft shells may work well.

WATERPROOF OVER-PANTS

Often the discomfort these pants can cause outweighs the protective factor: on a warm, wet day you might not wear them as they make you sweat too much; on a cold, wet day you risk hypothermia if you do not wear them. I carry a lightweight pair in summer and a heavy-duty pair of ski pants for winter conditions. The most important thing is how easy they are to get on and off, plus how far can you lift your leg up in them. Full-length zips make them easier to remove and braces help to stop them sliding down.

CARING FOR JACKETS AND OVER-PANTS

Roll them up to place them in your backpack to keep the membrane flat. Breathable fabrics are treated to make surface water bead up and roll off the garment. This keeps the fabric surface clear so that sweat and body heat can pass through from the inside.

Over time the water-repellent treatment wears off and the garment becomes less effective. Try heating the material with a cool iron or in a tumble dryer, and when this no longer works treat the jacket with a reproofing product.

Dirt and sweat can clog the pores of breathable materials. Most garments are machine washable, but do not use modern detergents, conditioners, or softeners; use pure soap or a specialist cleaning product and check the care label.

SELECTING A BACKPACK

Choosing the correct backpack will depend on what its main use is for. The size is important but so is volume adjustability; an overloaded small pack is as uncomfortable and unstable as a partly full one, especially if you have to hang gear outside.

SIZE

For day-long summer walking a 30 litre (80 gal.) sack should suffice, but 50 litres (13 gal.) is more versatile for multi-day walking between hostels and huts, or winter walking. When camping, you may need 60–70 litres (16–18 gal.). Ensure it supports the load comfortably.

EXTENDABLE LIDS

Extending lids increase the amount you can carry in the main compartment, but make the lid pocket difficult to use. Plus they can flop around when the sack is not full (tuck the lid inside the sack and tuck the connecting straps away).

COMFORT AND FIT

For small sacks and light loads a simple padded back is enough. Most larger sacks have a flat internal frame preventing the backpack from losing its shape and transferring the weight to the top of your buttocks and your hips. Remove the wands from inside your new backpack and get a friend to bend the struts to the shape of your back. Do not sit on your backpack as you may bend the frame.

Most adjustable harness systems allow the shoulder straps to move up and down the frame—if the back length is too long it will transfer the weight to the collarbone. Tensioning straps link the top of the backpack to the top of the shoulder straps and pull the backpack closer to your back to improve stability. Release them when going downhill to keep the backpack upright.

COMPRESSION STRAPS

These reduce the backpack's volume and hold the weight close to the wearer's back for stability. They are also useful for carrying walking and tent poles, sleeping mats, etc. Wand pockets at the base are also useful to attach poles.

On a correctly adjusted or sized backpack the shoulder strap will curve neatly over the shoulder, as shown in the bottom picture.

CHEST AND SHOULDER STRAP

A chest strap that links the shoulder straps will help to locate them correctly over your shoulders, especially when going downhill.

HIP AND WAIST BELTS

A padded hip-belt helps to redistribute a heavy load from your shoulders to your hips. The top of your hip should sit in the middle of the padded belt to transfer the load to the top of the buttocks.

POCKETS

If the backpack has a large pocket, side pockets are unnecessary; they get in the way and usually prevent the usage of compression straps. Bellowed or removable side pockets are a good compromise if you are a side pocket fan.

ZIPS

Backpack with zips give easier access to your gear, and are ideal for trekking where unpacking and packing is a regular occurrence. However, zips do break; take the strain off them with compression straps.

HEAD CLEARANCE

If you regularly wear a helmet ensure the backpack does not prevent you from looking up.

PACKING A BACKPACK

A backpack is never totally waterproof so always store gear in watertight bags. On rough terrain a top-heavy backpack will throw you off balance, so keep the load close to your back and centered between your shoulder blades (see Fig. 1). For skiing, the weight should be even lower and closer to your back to minimize twisting of the shoulders.

FIGURE 1
Packing a backpack

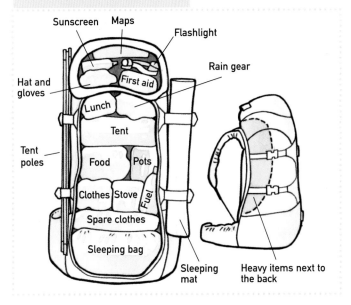

Sunscreen Maps
Flashlight
Rain gear
Hat and gloves
First aid
Lunch
Tent
Tent poles
Food Pots
Clothes Stove Fuel
Spare clothes
Sleeping bag
Sleeping mat
Heavy items next to the back

- Stuff your sleeping bag into the bottom and squeeze in any additional lightweight items you won't need until bedtime.
- Do not waste space: put small items of clothing inside your pots and pack smaller items, such as food, more efficiently in individual units.
- Keep frequently used items at the top.
- Tighten all compression straps to limit any load shifting.
- Carry tent poles vertically, secured on one side of the pack with the ends tucked into a wand pocket at the pack's bottom.
- Do not carry an insulating mat at the top or bottom of the backpack; it will eventually be caught by the wind or get torn, wet, and muddy.

HEAD LAMP

Hand-held flash lights are useless because you often need both hands. Head lamps with LEDs are small, lightweight, and powerful. They produce a brighter, and clearer, high-quality light than standard bulbs, operate in all temperatures, and are virtually unbreakable. Choose an LED model with a zoom facility to throw the beam further. Keep a battery in a pack close to the body in cold conditions. Always carry a spare bulb and battery, or if it is LED, a spare light (see chapter 6, page 331, for information about battery types).

SURVIVAL BAGS

It would be foolish to venture into the mountains without shelter.

FOIL BLANKETS

A waste of time as they flap around and do not keep out the elements.

PLASTIC/FOIL BIVOUAC (BIVVY) BAGS

Lightweight, do not let water in, but can't let water out. Excellent for simple day walks.

WATERPROOF/BREATHABLE BIVVY BAGS

Best for extended use, when combined with a sleeping bag, but they are too expensive to keep for emergencies. Ensure the bivvy bag is large enough for a sleeping bag to expand fully. GORE-TEX Exchange material is more permeable than standard Nexus GORE-TEX. Hooped versions are heavy—a single skin tent is better.

SLEEPING BAG COVERS

Protect your sleeping bag in damp conditions, but don't use them for sleeping outside in the rain.

BLIZZARD BAG

Part bivvy bag, part sleeping bag and available for one, two, or three people, a blizzard bag is a lightweight alternative to a breathable cover and a sleeping bag, and worth considering if you are somewhere where a plastic bag will not do.

GROUP SHELTERS

Very quickly provide warmth and can be used for anything, from simple lunch stops to more serious situations. Available for two or more people, sit together on your backpacks and pull the shelter over the top of you. It is windproof, but not completely waterproof.

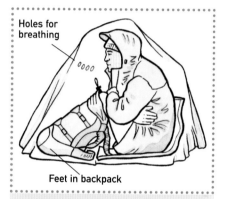

Holes for breathing

Feet in backpack

FIGURE 2
Using an orange plastic bivvy bag— pull it over your head and punch a few breathing holes in it.

A GORE-TEX bivvy bag is essential for extended camping or bivvying in damp conditions. It also makes your sleeping bag warmer.

A group shelter is a must for serious walkers.

TENT FLY SHEETS

Worth considering if you are on a budget, as they can do the same job as a group shelter and are waterproof (although condensation can be a problem). However, tent fly sheets are not as lightweight or the right shape to be used without poles.

FIRST AID

Everyone should have basic first aid training and carry *Pocket First Aid and Wilderness Medicine* by Jim Duff and Peter Gormley (2007) to refer to in a crisis. Pre-assembled kits are convenient, but expensive—it is better to make your own. A basic first aid kit should be able to stop serious bleeding, splint broken limbs, control pain, treat known chronic illnesses, allergies, and conditions.

Adapt your kit for more demanding trips, to the environment you are in, and to suit the number in your group. Pack everything in a small, clear Ortlieb watertight bag. For more information see chapter 6, page 282.

SMALL FIRST AID KIT

Adam Gent says, *"This first aid kit has been designed to cope with as much as possible using as little as possible."*

Accident and casualty cards
Antiseptic wipes
Antihistamine cream
Aspirin
Plastic wrap
Conforming and triangular bandage
Duct tape
Gloves
Glucose tablets
Ibuprofen
Iodine non-adherent and, wound bandages

Scalpel
Bandages
Small flashlight
Resuscitation face shield
Saline solution
Shears (strong scissors)
Steri-strips
Surgical blades
Tweezers
Waterproof pen

CAMPING EQUIPMENT

There are many variations on tent designs, ranging from ultra-lightweight to sturdier mountain designs, and in three- and four-season models.

DOME TENTS

Domes give a lot of sleeping space, but are not as stable as geodesic designs in strong winds.

GEODESIC TENTS

Utilize four or five flexible poles in a self-supporting configuration, so they stand strong in the wind and provide generous interior headroom. Models with the poles running through the inner are roomier. They are also freestanding and my tent of choice.

TUNNEL TENTS
These tents rely on two or three hoops. They are not freestanding and will collapse should the guying fail. They do not cope well in a storm or on snow. They are, however, lightweight.

ULTRA-LIGHTWEIGHT TENTS
Used for extended trekking in remote areas where you must carry everything yourself, they usually have a single hoop or upright pole. They are not freestanding and are often unstable in high winds.

SINGLE SKIN TENTS
Made from one layer of breathable material. They are lightweight and quieter in strong winds, but they are expensive, and the breathability depends on how warm it gets inside. If your sleeping bags are efficient you may find frost on the inside during cold nights. They are not as warm as double skin tents.

MAKING YOUR CHOICE
For valley camping, buy a big tent with an awning to stand and cook in. The perfect mountain tent is spacious yet small, lightweight yet rugged, waterproof yet not flammable due to its coating. When making your choice, consider the following:

- Cheap tents are great for non-serious camping and do the job well, but won't withstand the stresses of a serious trip. UV resistance is also poor, although you can enhance this with a spray coating.
- It must be able to withstand the harshest conditions you might encounter.
- Three-season models are lighter and not as sturdily constructed. They often have netting that allows the elements to blow through in a storm.

A night or two under a tarpaulin in poor weather will convince all but the most hardy that a tent is worth the extra weight. (Clive Hebblethwaite.)

There are still some ultra-lightweight single pole models available, such as the Mountain Hardwear Kiva light.

Tunnel Geodisic large
Dragonfly 2 X T (Mountain Equipment)

Geodisic Hielo (Mountain Equipment)

Lightweight All Ultralight
(Mountain Equipment)

FIGURE 3
Tent designs

- Four-season tents are 10–20 percent heavier (typically due to extra poles), but are tougher in snowstorms, and the fly sheet extends to ground level.
- Ensure you compare like with like as manufacturers include different things in their weights.
- Freestanding tents can be easily moved to shake out debris. Very lightweight tents are rarely freestanding.
- Silicone coated nylon is more expensive than polyester, but is lighter, more durable, and more water repellent throughout its life. Choose it for ground sheets and fly sheets.
- Aluminium poles are much more reliable than fibreglass.
- Tent seams must be sealed.
- If camping on snow, look for snow valances, although they add weight and increase condensation.
- Capacity ratings are optimistic. A two-person tent is a tight squeeze for two large adults and their gear.
- Choose a warm interior color, like yellow, when spending a long time in your tent because it will help you feel warmer and happier.
- Think about the entrances for cooking and storage capacity. Leave backpacks outside in a waterproof bag if the porch is small.
- Look for large storage pockets.
- Look for efficient venting, to reduce condensation, and mosquito netting.

PITCHING A TENT

Practice erecting the tent at home and color code the poles and sleeves for easy identification. If you get confused, just follow the seams. Buy stronger tent pegs as manufacturers' pegs are often inadequate. Close the doors when erecting to ensure correct tensioning, and push the poles, rather than pull them, through the sleeves to prevent separation. If it is windy, put something heavy inside the tent when erecting or dismantling.

If your tent sags after rain do not re-tension the guy lines because it may shrink and rip apart as it dries out. When taking your tent down disassemble the poles from the center to stretch the elastic cord evenly and prolong its life. For camping in winter, see chapter 6, page 282.

CHOOSING A CAMPSITE

Ensure the ground is well drained and sheltered and not easily damaged. Choose previously used, and therefore hardened, areas if possible.

If you have to move stones and clear vegetation, find somewhere else or replace. Use a protective groundsheet on stony ground. Avoid low spots as they are cold, and pitch the entrance away from the prevailing wind.

Camp at least 50m (164ft) from water sources. It may seem idyllic to be close to water, but water attracts mosquitoes and midges, and rivers can flood. Do not dig drainage channels around your tent. In bear territory, hang your food 100m (328ft) from your tent, leave nothing aromatic (including food, toothpaste, lotions) inside nor sweaty items hanging overnight—salt-loving rodents may shred them.

LOOKING AFTER YOUR TENT

Air and dry the tent after every trip to prevent mildew. Do not wash or tumble dry them as this removes the coating. UV light damages tents and although it is not possible to follow some manufacturers' advice, such as taking your tent down then putting it back up at night and pitching it in the shade at altitude, do try to limit exposure to sunlight .

CHOOSING A SLEEPING BAG

Your sleeping bag should be long enough, lightweight, easily compressible, have a hood, a full-length zip, a neck/zip baffle, and be warm enough for the coldest expected temperatures.

To ensure more warmth let the sleeping bag "loft" up before getting into it and use an insulating mat. Exercise and eat something to get warm before getting into your bag. Fill your Nalgene water bottle with hot water and take it to bed (see chapter 6 for camping on snow).

Camping in Nepal

FIGURE 4 Box and sewn-through construction of sleeping bags

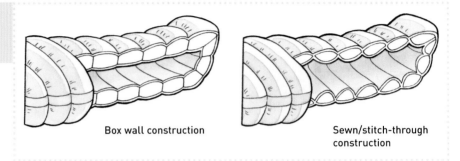

Box wall construction

Sewn/stitch-through construction

Consider the following when making your choice:

- Mummy-style bags insulate more because there are less interior dead areas, but they can be constricting. If you camp only in warm places a rectangular bag is more comfortable.
- There are two methods of constructing sleeping bags—"sewn-through' and "box wall." Sewn-through bags are colder than box-wall construction, but are cheaper.

Despite continued advances in synthetic insulation, down is still the best choice in terms of performance. However it is more expensive and requires specialist cleaning. Down-filled bags are lighter, compress better, and last longer than synthetic versions. The oils in the down help quick recovery and dry as rapidly as synthetic materials, even after a soaking. Advances in down bag covering means that most will cope with condensation and dry much quicker. Materials like Drilite or Pertex Endurance have been specifically developed to provide weatherproof protection to down-filled products. (Use a GORE-TEX bivvy bag if wetness is a problem, and air the bag frequently.)

Synthetic bags are cheaper and provide some insulation, even when wet. Synthetic bags dry out fairly quickly and are non-allergenic, but are heavier and bulkier. They also lose their lofting ability more quickly due to constant compression when packed away.

A good night's sleep is important (Lorenz Frutiger, Swiss IFMGA Guide).

DOWN STRENGTH

The best bags have 95 percent goose down with 5 percent chopped feathers. The down's "fill power" measures how much space a set sample of down occupies in cubic inches, and hence how much insulation it provides for its weight. For example, a 30g (1oz) sample of down with a fill power of 600+ occupies a minimum of 600 cubic inches. Therefore, the higher the fill power, the better the performance of the bag. A 550 fill power is used in mid-range bags; anything over 650 is excellent. (These figures are used in the European fill power test; in the U.S. the figures are higher, but mean the same.)

CARING FOR YOUR SLEEPING BAG

Never leave your sleeping bag damp. Air-dry it every day and after every trip. Stretch it out on a bed or in a dry room until you're sure it's dry and, to prevent the breakdown of the filling, leave it loosely packed. Avoid washing a down sleeping bag as it removes oils—if necessary, use a small amount of down soap, a gentle cycle, and rinse well. Take care with a wet bag—the shell and the baffles can rip. Do not separate the down by hand, but use a tumble dryer with several tennis balls.

INSULATING MATS

You compress a sleeping bag's insulation when you lie on it, so you need a reliable buffer between your bag and the ground. An air mattress is comfortable, but will not insulate you.

Closed-cell foam mat—Made from dense foam filled with closed air cells. Cheap, durable, non-absorbant, won't deflate, and insulate well, depending on thickness. However, they are stiff and uncomfortable. To make it easier to strap to your backpack cut it into convenient strips then stitch and tape them back together.

Self-inflating mat—Expensive, very comfortable, and insulate well, compact when rolled up, but are heavier. They can be punctured, but are repairable (with a proper repair kit), even in remote places. Short versions are fine but your feet get cold. The surface can be slippery with the result that you slide off during the night.

Down-filled mats—Offer the highest degree of insulation available without the bulk or weight, but are by far the most expensive.

CHOOSING A STOVE

Stoves have pros and cons depending on where you will be using them and the length of your trip. I tend to use the MSR Pocket Rocket, which is one of the fastest and lightest gas stoves; the Jet Boil, which is easy to use in poor weather; and the MSR liquid fuel range, which is the most reliable and works well at altitude, but only if you are meticulous about clean fuel.

When choosing a stove, consider the following:

- Is it light and compact? Can it fit in the pan?
- Is it sturdy enough to take the abuse of mountain camping?
- Is it easy to set up, stable on uneven ground, and do pots sit well on the top?
- Which fuel is best for your trip? Consider cost, burn time, availability, and number of people.
- How easy is it to light? Does it require priming? Can it be primed with fuel from the stove itself?
- Will the stove simmer?
- How easy is the stove to maintain in the field? Does it have a windshield?

An easily maintained gasoline stove is noisy, but better on trips of more than a few days, while the convenience of gas is an advantage for overnight trips.

FUELS

Use gasline on longer trips and gas for overnight trips. Gasline stoves generate a lot of heat, but are heavier. Gas stoves are clean and light, but expensive to run and you must dispose of the canisters. Alcohol stoves are safer and more environmentally friendly, but do not burn as hot. Solid fuel stoves are useless and open fires ruin the environment.

The amount of fuel you take depends on your trip. Are you melting snow? Do you need to cook your food or just add water to a pre-cooked meal? As a rough guide use 200ml (702—typically one hour's burning time) for a party of two per day (250ml 8.2 oz.) of melting snow).

Butane, Propane, or Isobutane blend—Expensive, convenient, clean, and easy to light. Burns hot immediately and does not require priming. Easily adjusted for simmering, and cannot easily spill. You must carry and dispose of the canisters. Isobutane works better in cold conditions.

Kerosene—Inexpensive, easy to find throughout the world, and has a high heat output. It does not ignite easily, smells, burns dirty, and spilled fuel evaporates slowly. Priming is required, and it tends to gum up stove parts.

Alcohol—A renewable fuel resource with low volatility, that burns silently. Alcohol-burning stoves have fewer moving parts, decreasing the chance of breakdown. However they have a lower heat output, perform poorly in the cold, and require more fuel, which can be hard to find.

White gas (pure gasoline)—Inexpensive, clean, and easy to light. Spilled fuel evaporates quickly but can also ignite quickly. Use stove fuel to prime it. Difficult to find in third world countries.

Unleaded gasoline—Inexpensive, easy to find throughout the world. Unleaded gasoline burns dirty/sooty and can lead to frequent blockage of the stove jet. An attractive option for traveling in remote areas, but ensure the stove is easily maintained.

Multi-fuel stoves—They cost more than single-fuel models, but if you're visiting a range of destinations, the added flexibility is worth the extra cost.

PERFORMANCE

A stove's performance is typically measured in the boil time for 1l (34 oz.) and can range from two and a half to ten minutes (a good range is three–five minutes). A stove that boils water quickly is likely to work better at higher altitudes and in the cold. The size and material of your pan, and how sheltered you are, also affects the cooking time. At altitude, water boils at a lower temperature, at 3000m (9843ft) food takes almost four times longer to cook and at 7000m (22,966ft) thirteen times longer. Therefore, the most suitable foods at altitude are those that only require warming.

Clean the stove frequently. Keep the fuel warm and pass it through a coffee filter before use. Use a lid, windscreen, and a reflective base, and consider an MSR heat exchanger on trips of more than two days.

To conserve fuel, try the Dutch oven method: bring the food to the boil for about fifteen–thirty seconds, with a lid on. Turn off the stove and keep the pot hot with insulation for about ten–thirty minutes. The food will cook as well as if it was boiling, but you use no fuel in this time. This works well with most foods, although some types of rice can be a bit stubborn.

COOKING IN TENTS
Tent manufacturers tell you never to cook inside your tent because of carbon monoxide poisoning and fires. However, if you need to when camping on snow or in a storm, or to keep the tent warm, remember the following:

- Always start the stove outside the tent.
- Have something ready to smother the flames.
- Check that the vestibule is large enough.
- When you take the stove inside the tent place it on a thin piece of closed cell foam with a stiff foil covering, or a thin piece of wood.
- Ventilate, because carbon monoxide sinks.
- When you have finished cooking put the stove outside in case it leaks.

A "Light My Fire" works even in the wet.

POTS AND PANS
A proper cook set is better in terms of weight and space than a set from home. Aluminium is the lightest, but dents easily; stainless steel is heavier and can scorch the food; titanium is lightweight but expensive.

STAY WELL-FED AND HYDRATED TO KEEP WARM
Staying warm does not only depend on your clothing, but also on your water and energy levels. Smoking also reduces peripheral circulation. Have a good breakfast and maintain your energy levels by eating small amounts of food, such as granola bars, dried fruit, and bananas, every thirty minutes or so. Eat slow-burning carbohydrates, such as peanut butter and honey sandwiches, and if money is not an issue, high-energy gel packets work well when you need energy fast but cannot eat solids (see chapter 6 for further information).

A 5 percent drop in hydration levels can reduce performance by up to 50 percent, due to reduction in blood volume causing your capillaries to shut down. Signs of dehydration are headache, light-headedness, lethargy, and a vague feeling of being unwell. Tea and coffee act as diuretics, but the effect is minimal compared to the amount of fluid you are taking in, although there is some evidence that water absorption is reduced in the intestine. While alcohol is not to be recommended as a rehydration method, moderate intake of less than 4 percent alcohol does not dehydrate you. All three, however, do make you more susceptible to cold in the winter.

Water intake in hot environments should be about 2–3l (8.5–12.5 cups) a day. Carry a maximum of 2l (8.5 cups) and drink plenty two hours before going out and the rest upon return. Hydration bladders are great, but are expensive, freeze in the cold, and tempt you to finish your water too quickly.

A NICE HOT DRINK

Carry a jet boil stove or a Thermos in cold weather, but a warm drink is only psychologically different to a cold one (the energy content keeps you warm, not the heat). However, there is some evidence that warming the liver increases the flushing of toxins caused by exercise from the body.

Is it safe to drink water from a stream? (Lesley Jones.)

WATER FROM STREAMS AND RIVERS

Advice is varied, and it depends on the source of the water. It is probably safe high up in the mountains where there are no animals grazing. Avoid Alpine stream water from glaciers because the tiny mineral particles can upset your digestive system. "Inside Science News Service" reported that water from springs, wells, and long-term ground water is usually pure and wholesome. The Mountaineering Council of Scotland state that mountain streams in the U.K. can be drunk untreated well away from human habitation, but avoid oil-covered peat sources. Treat water if in doubt.

ENERGY AND REHYDRATION DRINKS

Two main factors affect absorption of fluid into the body:

- The speed at which it empties from the stomach. This depends on the carbohydrate content—the higher it is the slower your stomach empties.

- The rate at which it is absorbed through the walls of the small intestine.

"Energy" drinks and fruit juices are not suitable for rehydration because they slow down stomach-emptying and may even draw fluid into the stomach away from the body. Artificial sweeteners also dehydrate you because they draw fluid from the large intestine.

Conversely, salts, especially sodium and potassium, in a drink allow fluid to empty quickly from the stomach and promote absorption from the small intestine, thereby encouraging hydration.

Isotonic sports drinks (in balance with the body's salts) or even better, hypotonic (lower than the body's salts), with a carbohydrate level (complex glucose not pure glucose) of approximately 6 percent are emptied from the stomach at a rate similar to water and may be beneficial if you are walking for hours and cannot eat. However save the extra plastic bottle—a banana and plain water will probably do the same.

Check the additives in sports drinks, because some are dangerous for mountaineering. For example, norepinephrine is a vasoconstrictor (narrows the blood vessels), which is bad in cold climates.

MAKE YOUR OWN

It is easy to make 1l (4 cups) of your own sports drinks at a fraction of the price.

- **Isotonic**—500ml (2 cups) of unsweetened fruit juice and 500ml (2 cups) of water.
- **Hypotonic**—100ml (4 cups) squash, 900ml (1 oz.) of water and a pinch of salt.

THE WEATHER

"Anyone can enjoy a sunny day; it takes a poet to be uplifted in a storm."
—Tristan Jones, weather forecaster

Mountaineers should have enough understanding of the weather to interpret weather maps and forecasts; understand how local conditions and mountains change the weather; and how to blend theory with real life (see also chapters 3 and 4).

To predict weather from charts and jet-stream images on the Internet you will first need to understand how Earth's weather is formed. The global weather system is a massively complex subject, but patterns do exist, allowing us to identify and predict common types of weather behaviour. Weather may be chaotic, but it is not random.

What follows is a greatly simplified picture of weather formation, with apologies to meteorologists.

THE SUN

Weather often results from temperature differences between one place to another. On large scales, temperature differences occur because areas closer to the Equator receive more heat from the Sun than regions closer to the Poles. On local scales, temperature differences occur because different surfaces (such as oceans, forests, ice sheets, or man-made objects) reflect or absorb heat. The white of the snow at the poles reflects 90 percent of the incoming heat energy, while the dark green canopies of the jungles at the Equator absorb the most. If Earth was not tilted we would not have seasons, and without uneven heating the world would be surrounded by an amorphous mass of weather. The differential heating causes local weather effects and more importantly global weather changes.

The heating of Earth causes warm air to rise, which has more energy and becomes less dense (more space between the molecules). The vibrating molecules' energy is eventually lost; it cools, spreads outwards, becomes more dense, and starts to fall.

On a small scale, the rising air causes things like coastal breezes. The global picture of rising and falling air shows that the falling air spreads out at Earth's surface towards the Poles and the Equator. The warm Earth and sea then drive three large cyclical "cells" of rising and falling air—The Hadley, Ferrel, and polar cells (see Fig. 6). It is at the boundaries between these differing "global scale" masses of air that our dramatic weather systems are born.

A cumulonimbus cloud is created by warm air rising, often with devastating results.

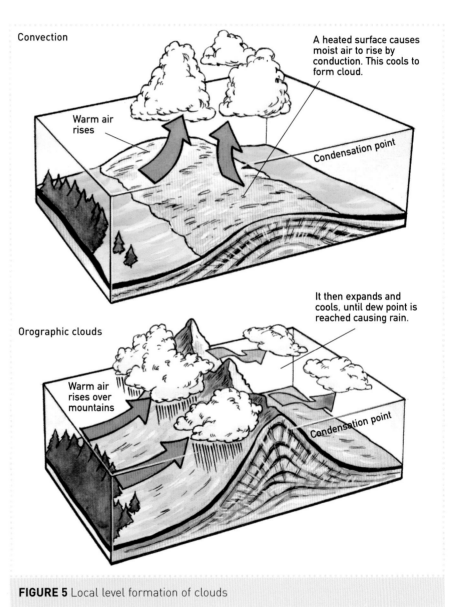

FIGURE 5 Local level formation of clouds

HOW ARE CLOUDS FORMED?

As warm air rises, it takes moisture with it from seas, lakes, and the ground (water molecules fit more easily into the gaps between the air molecules when air is warm). Warm air passing over seas can absorb huge amounts of moisture, which explains why the warm ocean currents circulating Earth affect our global weather picture. As the warm, moist air rises, it cools, the molecules become

When the droplets are heavy enough they fall as rain, or if it is very cold they form snow. Therefore, looking where the air mass is coming from tells you how much moisture it has and whether the air is cold or warm. For example, if the air mass is circulating over southern France, it will be warm and dry.

PRESSURE IN THE AIR

The rising warm air and denser, sinking cold air results in lower and higher pressure air masses or air systems.

A lot of air above us is called **high pressure** and a small amount of air above us is **low pressure**. On top of a mountain, there is less air pressure and the air is therefore less dense, hence cooler, meaning clouds can form. There is not a particular pressure that makes an air mass high or low; it is the relative differences between air masses that count.

Clouds and rain are therefore created through:

At a local level through (see Fig. 5):

- convectional rainfall: heating from below making the warm, moist air rise
- orographic or relief rainfall: air being forced to rise over the land

At a global level through:

- "frontal lifting": when a mass of warm air meets a mass of cold air the warm air is forced up over the boundary, or front, of cold air resulting in cooling, and, hence, clouds.

GLOBAL CIRCULATION AND WEATHER PATTERNS

Localized and global weather patterns are separate, but affect each other to create chaos. To understand why we get large weather systems and frontal lifting we must look at the global circulation of air masses. If the Earth was not spinning, warm air would rise and move northwards, cool, sink, and then move southwards. However, because the Earth is spinning it is deflected, in the Northern Hemisphere, to the right (westwards) of its direction of flow by the Coriolis Effect (see Fig. 7), which is strongest at the Poles. In the Southern Hemisphere the Coriolis Effect turns air the other way. This means that in the polar and Hadley cells (see Fig. 6) the air returning to the Equator at ground level is moving to the right, i.e., westwards to form the **"easterlies."**

The gap between the Hadley and polar cells is the Ferrel cell. Unlike the other cells, it is not a distinct cell (it is thermally inactive). The Ferrel cell has been described as the ball bearing between the Hadley and Polar cells. Because it is an indistinct mass of air, the Ferrel cell is affected more by the general circulation of air around the world than the Coriolis Effect, which means that the air is moving eastwards forming the **"westerlies."**

The polar and Ferrel cells meet not-quite-head-on and are sliding past one another (*see* Fig. 8). The boundary between different air masses is a **front**, in this case the **polar front**. Here a sharp gradient in temperature occurs between the two air masses. The polar front meanders around, breaks up, and sometimes disappears. In winter, it shifts towards the Equator, whereas

WIND DIRECTION

A westerly wind comes in from the west and an easterly wind comes in from the east.

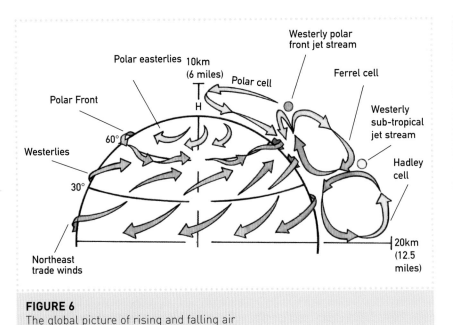

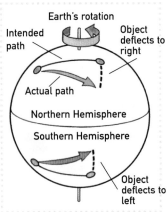

FIGURE 6
The global picture of rising and falling air

FIGURE 7
The Coriolis Effect is caused by Earth's rotation. It is the apparent deflection of moving objects relative to an observer on Earth.

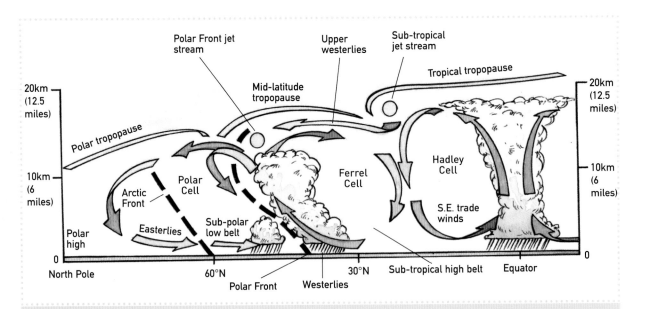

FIGURE 8
The polar front—the stratosphere. Here the air ceases to cool at –50°C (–58°F), becoming almost completely dry. The troposphere is the lowest of Earth's atmospheric layers—it is here "weather" occurs.

in the summer high-pressure systems can dominate as the polar front moves northwards. It is at the boundary between the polar and Ferrel cells that the high winds are at altitude, and the jet streams are created. They are formed by temperature differences in the upper atmosphere, between the cold polar air and the warm tropical air.

This abrupt change in temperature causes a large pressure difference, which forces the air to move eastwards, along with the general circulation of air around Earth. This circulating band is very fast because it has to keep up with the mass of air circulating at the Equator.

Due to the spinning of Earth and the relief of the land, the boundary between the easterlies and westerlies is turbulent and follows a forever-changing wave pattern around Earth (see Fig. 9).

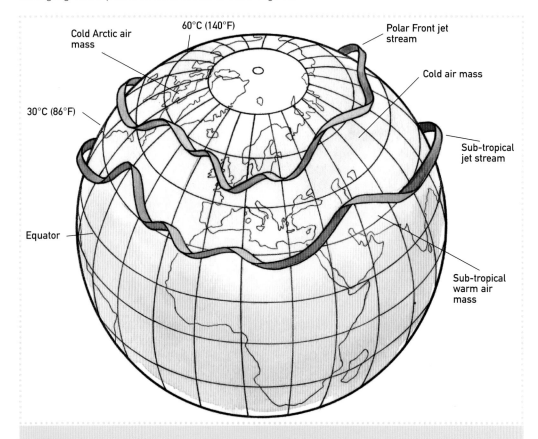

FIGURE 9
The jet stream is a good indicator of the polar front's position. The polar front is not the only boundary between air masses that exists, but it is the one that affects the U.K., Northern U.S., and Canada the most. Go to www.nws.noaa.gov to see interactive forecasts that show the movement of the jet stream and its associated depressions.

THE FORMATION OF DEPRESSIONS AND FRONTS

The movement of the atmosphere, the effect of mountain chains, and the warming of the sea creates great bends (kinks) in the polar front. These act like colossal waves (Rossby waves) migrating from west to east that carry the high and low pressure systems with them. As the warmer air rises up over the denser colder air, the cool air rushes in to fill the void left by the rising air and the wave eventually closes up and disappears. This is the formation and destruction of a **depression**—also called a **low**-pressure system—something which is constantly occurring along the Polar Front.

The latitude of the U.S., Canada, and Britain is such that they are frequently underneath the polar front, which explains our characteristic unsettled weather!

WARM AND COLD FRONTS

In a depression the warm air (which occupies the segment of the ripple pushing up into the boundary) is moving slightly to the east. The surrounding cold air is moving slightly to the west. This sets up an counter-clockwise rotation around the kink. The leading edge of the warm area is the **warm front**, behind it (the back of the kink) is the cold air moving in to fill the space (the **cold front**—see Fig. 10). If a front is "warm" or "cold" (depicted on a weather map by red semi-circles or blue triangles respectively) it describes the condition of the air behind it.

At any front there is invariably rainfall as warm air rises above cold. The warm front is slow moving and the boundary is wide, giving prolonged, increasingly heavy rainfall. Conversely, cold fronts are faster moving (which is why the depression eventually dies out as the "wave" shape closes in and dies) and bring shorter, but significantly heavier rainfall. The warm sector in between is invariably warmer and drier.

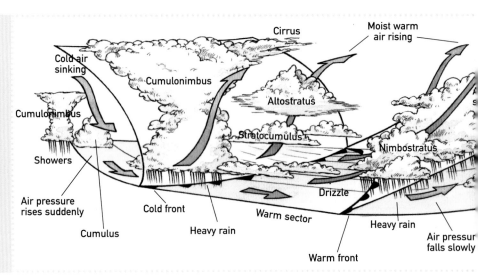

FIGURE 10
A typical depression and associated fronts. As they meet at the polar front, the warmer westerlies rise above the easterlies. Rising moist air cools, forming clouds and possibly rain. This is **frontal rainfall**.

An **occluded front** occurs when a cold front catches up and overtakes a warm front. This causes the warm air to be undercut and lifted up from the surface.

WHAT WEATHER IS CAUSED BY DEPRESSIONS/ FRONTS?

The deeper the depression, the more unsettled and windy the weather. The volume of rain depends on the amount of moisture contained in the air, which depends on the history of the high and the low. Has it traveled over dry land or the sea, and where is it heading? The weather (cloud and precipitation) is not uniformly distributed around a depression. Different parts of it have very different types of weather, which changes as the depression develops. The most significant precipitation occurs along the fronts.

Warm front—As the front approaches, temperatures start to rise, and the pressure falls steadily. Warm fronts progress from thin, high-level cirrus clouds up to 1000km (621 miles) ahead of the surface position to low, dense stratus clouds. The rain can extend 160–320km (99–198 miles) ahead of the front.

In the warm sector—The passage of the front is followed by a rise in temperature and humidity, and a veer in the wind, while the pressure also stabilizes. The amount of cloud falls as they start to thin out. The precipitation also stops, and the weather is generally fine, with a little stratus or stratocumulus.

Cold front—Pressure begins to fall increasingly rapidly as the cold front approaches, but rises steadily as the cold front passes over. The air temperature starts to drop. Large, towering cumulonimbus clouds develop producing heavy downpours of rain and fierce squalls, sometimes with hail and thunder.

After the cold front—There is an end to the heavy rain as the cumulonimbus clouds move away. Barometric pressure continues to rise in a steady fashion.

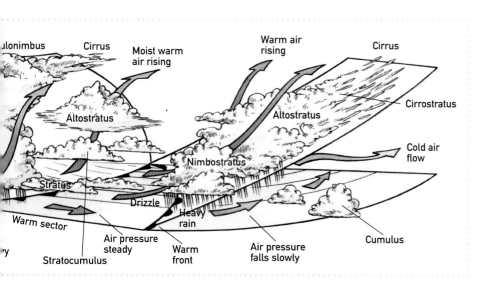

FIGURE 11
Cloud types

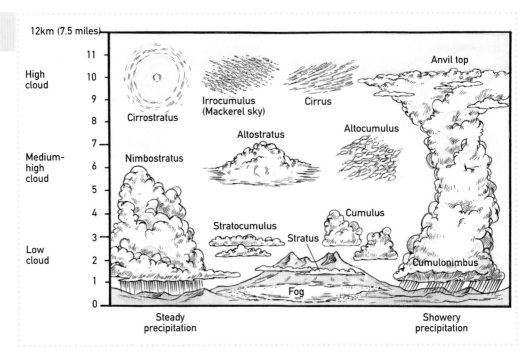

Clouds create the most fascinating shapes. (Cirrus clouds, Argentina.)

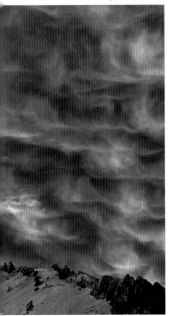

A few showers may occur from some small cumulus clouds, but it is generally fine and cool behind the cold front.

Occluded front—The characteristics of an occlusion are similar to those of a cold front, in that the rain belt is narrow.

ANTICYCLONES OR HIGH PRESSURE

In a depression the air is rising, creating low pressure. Elsewhere, warm air is cooling and falling over a large area (100 sq km/38 sq miles). The falling air creates areas of high pressure called **anticyclones**, which spread outwards in a clockwise direction in the northern hemisphere and an counterclockwise direction in the southern hemisphere.

If rising air cools and forms clouds, it is reasonable to assume that sinking air warms and inhibits cloud formation. Hence anticyclones usually bring prolonged warm, dry, sometimes cloudless or hazy weather in the summer.

Anticyclones are slow-moving and often "sit" over an area that can block the usual repetitive movement of depressions. On a weather chart they are depicted by widespread isobars around an area of high pressure.

When anticyclones form over land, the skies above are often clear. During the summer this means long, sunny days and clear nights. In winter, the longer nights mean that temperatures fall lower, with frost forming, which may persist throughout the day. The fall in temperature overnight and light winds can also lead to fog.

When anticyclones are over the sea (and picking up moisture) the weather can vary from fine and sunny to overcast and cloudy. Cloud may be thick enough to give drizzle and may fall low enough to produce fog. If the moist air is pushed up over mountains, it can rain. This happens most often during spring and is least frequent in autumn.

If the anticyclone extends over both land and sea, cloud and fog can spread across coastal regions, sometimes reaching quite far inland.

THE MOVEMENT OF HIGH- AND LOW-PRESSURE SYSTEMS

Depressions occur in "families," which migrate easterly across the Atlantic along the polar front. Sometimes as many as four or five mature depressions may make their way across the U.K., before a ridge of high pressure builds up to prevent more from advancing over the country. The movement of a depression is not easy to predict but using the following can help:

- Future movement is usually an extension of its previous track.
- They tend to move from areas of increasing pressure to areas of decreasing pressure.
- The center will move parallel to the isobars in the warm sector.
- They tend to move around large stationary high-pressure areas.
- A depression with an occluded front tends to move to the left of its track.
- High-pressure systems have no definite path of travel, and may linger for several days before being pushed away by depressions.

HOW TO INTERPRET WEATHER CHARTS

Isobars—Lines joining areas of equal pressure.

High pressure or anticyclone—A large area of widely spaced isobars, where pressure is higher than surrounding areas.

Low pressure or depression—Often isobars form a distinctive "thumb-print" pattern with low pressure at the center. Winds blow counterclockwise in low-pressure areas, their strength shown by the distance between the isobars. Isobars that are close together mean you can expect strong winds; wider apart means light winds.

Troughs—Elongated extensions of areas of low pressure. They bring similar weather to depressions.

Ridges—Elongated extensions of areas of high pressure. They bring similar weather to anticyclones.

Cols—Area of slack pressure between two anticyclones and/or two depressions.

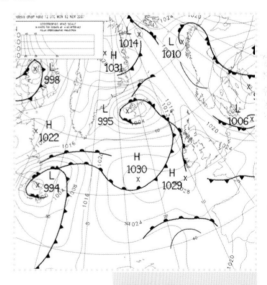

FIGURE 12
A weather (synoptic) chart—always check the date! © Crown Copyright (2008), the Met Office

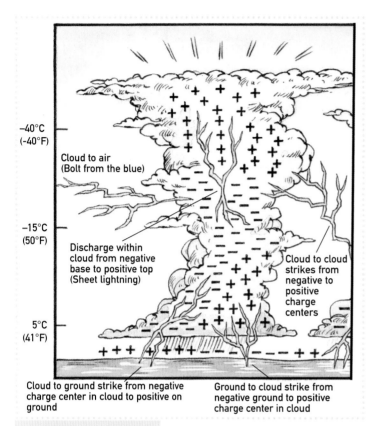

−40°C
(−40°F)

Cloud to air
(Bolt from the blue)

−15°C
(50°F)

Discharge within
cloud from negative
base to positive top
(Sheet lightning)

Cloud to cloud
strikes from
negative to
positive
charge
centers

5°C
(41°F)

Cloud to ground strike from negative
charge center in cloud to positive on
ground

Ground to cloud strike from
negative ground to positive
charge center in cloud

FIGURE 13
A thunderstorm and the
formation of lightning

THUNDERSTORMS

Large cumulonimbus thunderclouds often have hail associated with them. If it's hailing then you are under a thundercloud and, since lightning causes the thunder by the extreme heating and expansion of the air along its path, you had better move downward fast.

Lightning is a large electrical spark caused by the movement of electrons in cumulonimbus clouds. The fact that 90 percent of it travels from cloud to cloud (sheet lightning), means that 10 percent is coming earthwards! It heads earthwards when the electrical differences between the cloud and the ground become large enough.

Lightning can strike up to 50km (31 miles) from its origin. The speed of sound in air is 335m (1009ft) per second, which means that it travels about a kilometre in just over three seconds. To determine the distance in km between the lightning strike hit and your position, count the number of seconds between the lightning flash and the thunder, and divide by three.

Many lightning fatalities are the result not of a direct strike, but of a conductive injury that causes a cardiac arrest, so learn Cardio Pulmonary Resuscitation (CPR) techniques (see p. 219 for avoiding lightning).

HURRICANES

A hurricane is a large rotating storm centered on an area of very low pressure, with strong winds blowing in excess of 116km (72 miles) per hour. The storm may be 10km (6 miles) high and 650km (404 miles) wide. They form when a warm sea heats the air enough for it to rapidly create an area of low pressure. The rising air is replaced by cool air around it and the rotation of Earth causes the rising column to twist. Hurricanes occur in the Atlantic, eastern and western Pacific north of the Equator and off the coast of Australia between July and October, and in the Indian Ocean between November and March. Although the U.K. is not affected by hurricanes it does get the remnants of hurricanes as deep depressions.

MOUNTAINS AND WEATHER

Mountains influence the weather at local, regional, and global levels (the Canadian Rockies are known to create Rossby waves).

At local level, mountains force air to rise and consequently assist the formation of clouds and precipitation. Mountains, therefore, tend to have much wetter climates than the surrounding plains, particularly low-lying areas in the rain shadow, for example, the Scottish Highlands can receive over 250cm (98in) of precipitation every year, while on the east coast, it may not exceed 75cm (30in).

Mountain ranges can dramatically influence global climate. Most airflow in Earth's atmosphere is orientated along east-west trends. Consequently, north-south orientated mountain ranges influence the general circulation. Although some air is forced to rise over mountains, the eastward movement of large air masses are generally deflected by north-south orientated mountain chains. For example, the Rocky Mountains, which stretch along the western side of North America, deflect air to the north, which cools in the polar latitudes before returning south. The colder north-westerly wind influences the climates of the Canadian and U.S. interiors, and winter temperatures are therefore exceedingly low.

Moist air rising over the hills can create its own weather. (North Wales.)

IT GETS COOLER AS YOU GO HIGHER
The average temperatures on higher hills and mountains are lower, the winters are longer, and summers shorter. Temperature usually falls with height, at a set rate (lapse rate) depending on the humidity of the air—the average in the U.K. is a drop in temperature of 2°C per 300m (35.6°F per 984ft).

Wind speed (m/h)	Wind chill temperature (°F)							
	32	−23	−14	5	−4	−13	−22	−31
10	24	13	1	−10	−21	−32	−43	−59
20	20	8	−4	−15	−27	−39	−51	−63
30	18	5	−7	−19	−31	−44	−56	−68
40	−14	3	−9	−22	−34	−47	−39	−72
50	−14	2	−11	−24	−37	−50	−62	−75
60	−13	0	−13	−26	−39	−52	−65	−78

FIGURE 14
Wind chill is the apparent temperature felt on exposed skin due to the combination of air temperature and wind speed. Covering up reduces the effect of wind chill.

A temperature inversion is when there is warmer air above and colder air below.

TEMPERATURE INVERSIONS

As you ascend, the temperature usually decreases, but the opposite can also occur. A temperature inversion occurs when there is warmer air above and colder air below. They form in many ways, but the most common is on still winter evenings when the ground, and the air near the ground, cools quickly. As air is a poor heat conductor, it does not mix with the warmer air above. This inversion will only disappear the following morning, when the sun heats up the ground.

Inversions can also form as the pressure rises. Above high pressure the air is descending and warming up again resulting in a band of warm air above the colder air below. This is frequently seen in the winter months.

LOCALIZED WINDS

Higher ground tends to be windier, which makes for harsher winter weather. Hills often cause cloud to form over them, when winds have to go over them or as they become heated by the sun. As the air descends on the other (lee) side, it becomes compressed, dries and warms, sometimes enough to create a strong, gusty, dry wind. The term Föhn is often used as a generic term for a warm downslope wind, although it does have other local names around the world such as "Chinook" (meaning snow eater) in Colorado, U.S.

Not all downslope winds are warm. Even when air warms as it descends it can still be cooler than the air it is displacing, which results in a biting cold wind. Katabatic winds occur when cold, dense air drains down a mountainside into the valley below, such as the "Mistral" in France.

MOVING OUTSIDE

Contact—A tiny AM radio picks up local stations, even in wilderness.

Look at the sky—The shapes and movements of clouds typically foreshadow changes in the weather such as the arrival of warm fronts and cold fronts. Cold fronts can develop rapidly and move swiftly, causing temperatures to drop, wind directions to shift and barometric pressure to fall.

Get up early—If late-day storms become a pattern during your trip, rise early each day and cover more ground during the day's stable hours.

Altimeters—Use the barometer and thermometer on your altimeter watch to monitor weather changes. Obviously, the air pressure needs to be monitored at the same location in order for any changes to be meaningful. This is easy enough overnight, but if you are leaving camp and returning later it may be worth noting the pressure in the morning and evening to keep an eye on any significant changes (a barometer memory function is useful here).

WEATHER FORECASTS

Forecasting weather is an uncertain science, particularly beyond two or three days. It is largely based upon observations from ships, aircraft, oil rigs, buoys and balloons, satellites, radars, and manned land stations around the world. Computer models use this information to create a weather map and predict the weather.

Weather forecasts are obtained from a number of sources, and each has its pros and cons.

- **National radio and TV forecasts**—Mostly too general and do not tell you what is happening to developing depressions. Informing you that today is "going to be mainly warm and sunny" does not warn you that you have a 70 percent chance of getting wet. Local stations are more precise, and some provide special mountain forecasts, but of course you must be in the area to receive it.

- **Weather maps**—You can take a map with you (warning—that newspapers often use the previous day's weather map).

- **Telephone and fax**—There are many premium rate services that offer you forecasts for the coming week, but you pay by the minute and the cost easily mounts. If you have access to a fax machine, you can get a detailed forecast plus an Atlantic chart from the Met Office in the U.K.

- **Internet**—You can take your time and print out all the information you gather from the Internet, plus you can access web cameras all over the world to witness actual weather as it happens. In the U.K., visit the Met Office and Met Check. In the U.S., visit NOAA.

WATCHING THE WEATHER

You can use your altimeter watch to monitor changes in air pressure by monitoring the altitude reading when you are at a fixed location. A 30m (98ft) increase in altitude roughly equates to a 2mbar drop in air pressure, so, if the altitude reading has gone up by 120m (394ft) overnight, for example, then the air pressure has dropped by around 8mbar, and you would be well advised to keep an eye out for further signs of deterioration in the weather. On the other hand, if the altitude reading has dropped, this means the air pressure is increasing and good weather may be on the way.

I have never been lost, just temporarily displaced!

MOUNTAIN NAVIGATION AND ROUTE FINDING

Simple navigation techniques and route-finding skills allow you to identify the land around you and to choose a good path, avoiding dangers such as cliffs and avalanches. Navigation is easy to learn, but using it under stress is a different matter.

MAPS AND SCALE

A map is simply a scaled down representation of the ground. A large-scale map covers a small ground area, but with lots of detail. A small-scale map shows a larger area, in less detail. Specifically, 1:50,000 will cover four times the area and a 1:40,000 map over two-and-a-half times the area than a 1:25,000 map.

Almost every corner of the globe has been mapped, but the quality varies tremendously. In poorly mapped areas military maps are the best option, but they are not always easily available.

The best large-scale maps in the U.K. are the Ordinance Survey (OS) 1:25,000 Explorer maps—1cm represents 25,000cm or 250m (820 ft) on the ground. Therefore 1km (.02m) on the ground is 4cm (1.57m) on the map (grid lines every 4cm). They are very detailed and have all the features a walker requires.

The best small-scale maps are the 1:50,000 OS Landranger maps—1cm (.39in) represents 500m (.6 mi) on the ground. Therefore 1km is 2cm (.78 in) on the map (grid lines every 2cm). This is better to use for route planning rather than navigating, however, many experienced walkers find them adequate and, since they cover a larger area, long distance walkers need fewer sheets. They are also useful in winter when features on 1:25,000 maps may be obscured by the snow.

Also available in the U.K. are Harvey 1:25,000 and 1:40,000 walkers' maps of some popular upland areas and long distance paths. They place less stress on land ownership boundaries (which obscure OS maps in places) and are therefore very clear. The maps conform to the OS grid and are waterproof.

LOOKING AFTER YOUR MAP

Weatherproof editions are available and they are often more durable, but are bulkier, heavier, and more expensive than paper maps. The best thing to do is remove the cover, cut the map into useable segments and laminate with clear plastic. Carry two maps; a laminated 1:25,000 cut-out of the area with standard approach/descent bearings and distances, etc., written on the back. This easily fits into any pocket and is totally weatherproof. Also carry a 1:50,000 of the whole area, as a back-up.

Clear waterproof map cases are popular, but many make it difficult to read the map and take bearings. Cheap cases can crack and leak; the best and most waterproof are made from a stretchy plastic, e.g., Ortlieb.

DIGITAL MAPS

Often maps are available in digital form and offer many advantages over paper maps. The software packages are initially expensive, but they are in fact cheap when compared to collecting the equivalent paper maps. You are able to:

- view and print maps at different scales
- define your own walking routes by drawing on top of the map or entering a series of grid references
- calculate the length and height profile of defined routes, with estimates of walking time
- share routes with other users or download them from the web.

You are also able to link them with a compatible GPS and/or pocket PC, which allows you to program your GPS with a route in advance, record a route as you walk it and then download it to your home computer. You can then even view a map and route on a pocket PC while walking.

Digital maps can be viewed in 3D form with virtual "walkthroughs." Not only are they fun to watch, but they also give a good illustration of how much ascent is involved in your route. Some systems allow you to scan in your own paper maps, e.g., Fugawi.

READING A MAP

Although a map contains thousands of pieces of information, it cannot always tell you what the terrain is like and how difficult it is to walk on. This information can only be gained through experience, talking to others, and even using aerial photographs. To read a map you must first understand the language it is written in, and then translate that into a 3D image of the real world.

Most maps are incredibly accurate, but they do only show the land at a particular point in time—when it was surveyed. Glaciers retreat, snow covers the ground, and forests are planted, so the more recent your map, the more accurate it is. Most U.K. maps include the same basic features—grid lines, surface features, contour lines, and symbols.

GRID SYSTEM

When the image is taken from the globe and put on a flat sheet, the grid lines are used as reference points. Vertical lines are **lines of longitude** and horizontal lines **lines of latitude**. The U.K. National Grid was devised, based along latitude and longitude, to separate the country into easily map-able sections. Each square is 100km^2 and is given a two-letter code. Each square is then subdivided into 1km^2 grids, which is what you see on U.K. maps (see Fig. 15).

The Grid uses 49° north and 2° west as a starting point. That means at these lines the National Grid (Grid North) matches Earth's

FIGURE 15
Lines of longitude and latitude are used as reference points.

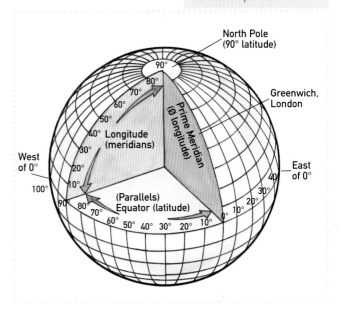

NB	NC	ND		
NG	HH	NJ	NK	
NM	NN	NO		
NR	NS	NT	NU	
	NX	NY	NZ	
	SC	SD	SE	TA
	SH	SJ	SK	TF	TG
SM	SN	SO	SP	TL	TM
SR	SS	ST	SU	TQ	TR
SW	SX	SY	SZ	TV	

FIGURE 16
The National Grid in the U.K.

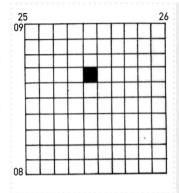

25 26
09

08

FIGURE 17
Read along the eastings and then along the northings to get a grid reference. In this example, 2508 is the four-figure grid reference for the 1km (.6 mi) square. The six-figure grid reference for the marked square is at 254086.

A grid reference should include the two letters of the 100km (62 mi) square before the numbers, leaving no doubt about your location (say, for example, south-west Scotland at grid reference 509582).

lines of latitude and longitude (True North) perfectly. As you move away from these points the match with lines of longitude increases. The vertical grid lines are **eastings** and the horizontal grid lines **northings**. Each grid square has a unique four-figure number associated with it (grid reference). This gives an accurate point of your location. Further subdividing the grid square into 100m (328 ft) squares gives a six-figure grid reference for any location (see Fig. 17).

MEASURING DISTANCE

Each grid square on an OS map represents 1km (.6mi) across and approximately 1.5km (.9mi) diagonally. Use the ruler on the side of your compass and do some simple maths, or use the roamer (see Fig. 20) to convert distances. However, measuring distance from a map is only an estimate because it ignores the ups and downs.

CONTOUR LINES

Contour lines are thin orange or brown lines with numbers on them. They tell us the height above sea level of that position. A single contour line will be at the same height all the way along its length. The map key will tell you the contour interval used—on an OS 1:25,000 map they are 10m (33ft) apart (Harveys 1:25,000 maps have a 15m (49ft) interval).

Understanding the shape of the land by interpreting contour lines is by far the most important map reading skill you can develop. There are four basic principles to reading contours:

1 Contours close together represent steep land.

2 Contours wide apart show flatter land.

3 Contours closing up towards the summit show a concave slope.

4 Contours getting wider towards the summit show a convex slope.

Think of contour lines as high-tide lines, left by the sea as the water level drops (see Fig. 18), or a hill cut into horizontal slices. One point of confusion

WHICH WAY IS UP?

Two things tell us which way the slope runs:

1 The numbers on the contour lines.

2 All streams will join downhill (a confluence), not separate.

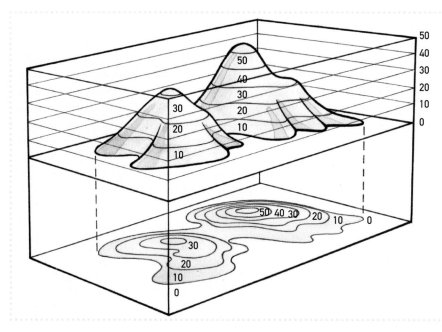

FIGURE 18
Contours are used to show
the shape of the land. They
are typically colored brown,
and rise in 10m (33ft)
increments, although this is
sometimes 5m (16ft). Check
the map key.

is that smaller features can be missed by contour lines yet appear on the ground. A 9m (29ft) high feature can sit between 10m (33ft) contour intervals and may not appear on the map, but if the feature exceeds the contour interval by a meter, it is shown. If the feature is just below the contour line, then it may be shown as a dotted line. The important thing is to try and create

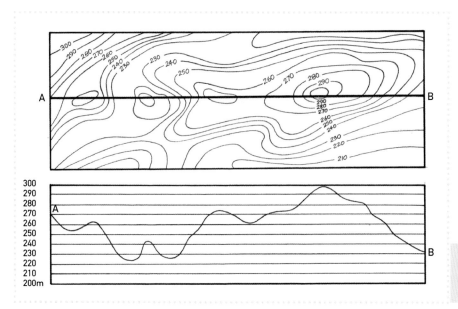

FIGURE 19
Sectional view through
a map

Matching the features on a map to the ground is the first step to becoming a competent navigator.

an overall picture of the land and not to identify each contour line.

MOUNTAIN FEATURES

Many terms such as hill, valley, mountain, and stream are in common use and need no definition, but there are some less common terms, which are not always fully understood:

- **Basin**—area of fairly level ground surrounded, or nearly surrounded, by hills; area drained by a river and its tributaries
- **Cwm/Cirque**—natural amphitheater at the head of a valley
- **Col**—depression between adjacent hills or mountain tops that is easily accessible
- **Crest**—line on a range of hills, or the top of a ridge from which the ground slopes down in opposite directions
- **Gorge**—narrow stream passage between steep, rocky hills; ravine with precipitous sides
- **Knoll/ring contour**—small knob-like hill
- **Left/right bank**—bank of a river or glacier on the left/right facing downstream
- **Plateau**—level elevated region
- **Re-entrant**—very small valley. On the map it usually shows as an indented contour line (or several)

NEGOTIATING SCREE SLOPES

A scree (talus) slope is broken rock that appears at the bottom of crags, mountain cliffs or valley shoulders. Scree can vary from slopes consisting of small stones to large boulders. When you are climbing along mainly boulder-strewn slopes, aim for steady bigger rocks that look like they have been there for a while. Scree with small rocks is easier to walk down than up because it is "soft" and slides with you. The biggest danger is knocking stones on people below you, so ensure that you walk on independent lines or close together.

- **Saddle**—depression on a ridge that is not easily accessible from either side
- **Spur**—ridge running out from a hill or mountain.

THE COMPASS

The compass is a device that, quite simply, shows us where magnetic north is and allows us to find an angle from grid north.

Compasses must have a long enough base plate for taking bearings from the map and fluid to dampen the movement of the needle.

The needle is a magnet—keep it away from metal sources and objects, such as high-tension power lines, which will affect your compass up to 55m (180ft) away, magnetic therapy bands on your wrist and even under-wiring in bras! Some areas of the world have rock types that can create anomalies.

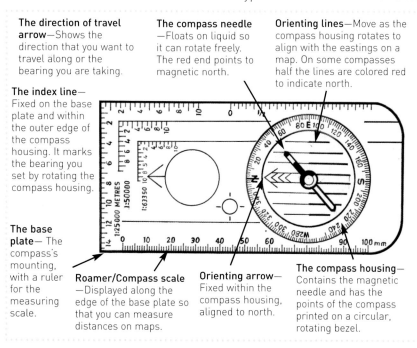

The direction of travel arrow—Shows the direction that you want to travel along or the bearing you are taking.

The compass needle—Floats on liquid so it can rotate freely. The red end points to magnetic north.

Orienting lines—Move as the compass housing rotates to align with the eastings on a map. On some compasses half the lines are colored red to indicate north.

The index line—Fixed on the base plate and within the outer edge of the compass housing. It marks the bearing you set by rotating the compass housing.

The base plate—The compass's mounting, with a ruler for the measuring scale.

Roamer/Compass scale—Displayed along the edge of the base plate so that you can measure distances on maps.

Orienting arrow—Fixed within the compass housing, aligned to north.

The compass housing—Contains the magnetic needle and has the points of the compass printed on a circular, rotating bezel.

FIGURE 20
The parts of a compass

Keep the compass attached by a cord to an upper pocket of your jacket. I am not a fan of having it on the shoulder-strap of the backpack for fear of breaking it. Consider a pouch to keep the base plate in good condition.

GOING NORTH

All maps are set from a line of longitude, where grid north lines up with true north. As one travels east or west from that line of longitude, magnetic north no longer lies perfectly with true north. Since the needle is a magnet it points to magnetic north (see Fig 21). The magnetic variation (declination in the U.S.) is the difference between the two norths, depending on where you are in the world.

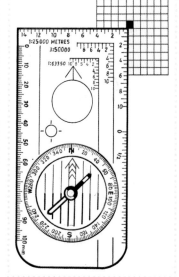

FIGURE 21
Using a compass romer to find a grid reference.

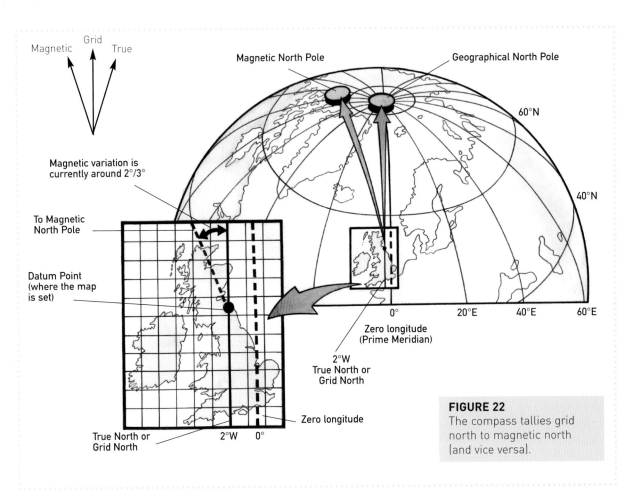

Magnetic   Grid   True

Magnetic variation is
currently around 2°/3°

To Magnetic
North Pole

Datum Point
(where the map
is set)

True North or
Grid North

2°W   0°

Magnetic North Pole

Geographical North Pole

60°N

40°N

0°   20°E   40°E   60°E

Zero longitude
(Prime Meridian)

2°W
True North or
Grid North

Zero longitude

FIGURE 22
The compass tallies grid
north to magnetic north
(and vice versa).

The magnetic variation (which can be east or west of your position) between

BUBBLES

You may find that after
time, and if you go to
altitude, bubbles appear
in the compass housing.
This is nothing to worry
about, unless it affects
the action of the
magnetic needle.

BEARINGS FROM THE EAST AND WEST

East of magnetic north:
- Working map-to-ground—add the degrees
- Working ground-to-map—take away the degrees

West of magnetic north:
- Working map-to-ground—take away the degrees
- Working ground-to-map—add the degrees

grid north and magnetic north is required for taking a bearing. It is usually
given in the map margin, but do not forget to take into account the changes

since the map was produced.

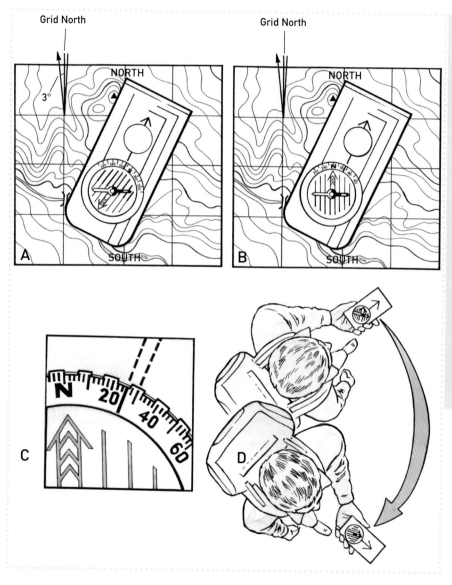

Grid North

Grid North

NORTH

3°

A

SOUTH

NORTH

B

SOUTH

N 20 40 60

C

D

FIGURE 23
Taking a bearing from
the map.
A—Align the compass along
the required route A to B.
B—Holding the compass
firmly in place so as not to
move it on the map, rotate
the compass housing to
align the orienting lines
with north-south on the
map.
C—Rotate the compass
housing to compensate for
magnetic variation.
D—Remove the compass
from the map. Place the
compass flat in the palm of
your hand in front of you.
Turn your whole body (not
just the compass) until the
needle is aligned with the
red north arrow and
proceed following the
direction-of-travel arrow.

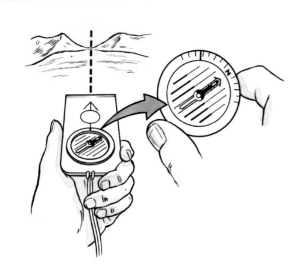

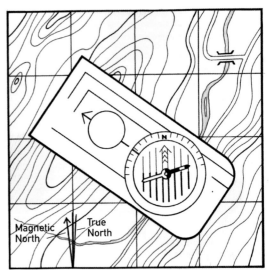

FIGURE 24

Taking a bearing from the ground to the map: point the direction arrow at a feature you can clearly see; twist the compass housing until the north arrow is underneath the magnetic needle. Remove the magnetic variation. Place the compass on the map, ensuring the north arrow is parallel to the line of longitude and is pointing north. Slide the compass into position so that the edge of the compass or a parallel line on the base plate intersect either your position or the feature—whichever is known. Ignore the magnetic needle now, it is always pointing north! Ensure the direction arrow is pointing away from your position or towards the feature.

TAKING A BEARING

NAVIGATING OUTDOORS

The real test of your understanding of the language of the map and how to navigate is when you move outdoors! Route finding and navigation are intertwined yet separate skills. You need to use your eyes and brain to find the best and safest route in the mountains, whereas with navigation the map points us in the general direction, and a map and compass help us when visibility is bad.

SETTING THE MAP

Set the map, identify features on the ground, and rotate the map until everything matches up. For example, you may be at a junction with paths diverging in different directions. Turn the map until it matches the directions of the paths. You now have the map set in the direction you want to go.

Another method when visibility is poor is to use a compass. Place the compass anywhere on the map in any position and simply turn the whole map (not the compass) until the north end of the magnetic compass needle points to the top (north) of the map, and is lined up with the grid lines.

READING THE GROUND

Reading the ground is the art of choosing a route to reduce the ascents and descents and to avoid hazards. It is the skill of moving through difficult terrain by contouring, and avoiding obstacles with minimum effort and maximum speed.

Practice reading the map. Select features on the map and identify them on the ground, and then do the opposite. Identify smaller and smaller features until the map comes alive. This skill will increase your confidence so that you can identify large features quickly and accurately when you really need to.

MENTAL MAPS

You should track your position on the ground while you are walking as much as possible. Create a mental picture of your route and "tick off" features as you pass them; you will then always know where you are. Ask yourself, "Am I traveling on the flat or going uphill or downhill? I have just crossed a stream, where is that on my mental map?" Break the route into smaller "legs" so that your mental map is easier to store.

HAND-RAILING

If you are not sure of your position or want to be sure you reach a certain point, follow a "hand-rail" that will definitely lead you to where you want to be. This could be a stream, a wall, even a ridge or steep slope: keep it on one side of you.

CONTOURING

Beware that there is a tendency to lose height when traversing a slope.

IDENTIFYING YOUR LOCATION

Even the best navigators do not always know exactly where they are in the mountains, but they have a strategy to find out.

- **From the map**—I think I am here on the map. If I am, then I must be able to see the following features identified from the map, e.g., a steep slope in front of me and a ridge to my left. If I cannot see them, I am not where I think I am.

- **From the ground**—I can see features, e.g., a steep slope in front of me, a ridge to my left—where are they on the map? If I can identify them I must be at this location.

- **From a compass bearing**—The mist clears and you want to identify a peak or feature. Hold the compass flat and point the direction of travel arrow at the peak. Turn the

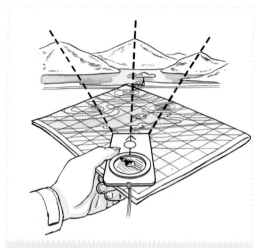

FIGURE 25
Setting the map by rotating it until it matches the ground around you.

Reading the terrain and matching it to what is on your map is fundamental to good navigation.

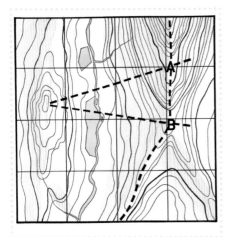

FIGURE 26
Transit lines—are you at A or B?

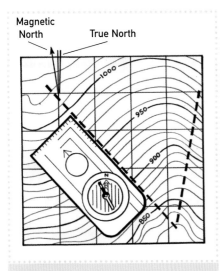

FIGURE 27
Slope aspect

compass housing until the orienting arrow lies underneath the magnetic needle, and the red end of the magnetic needle points to north. Read off the bearing.

- **From transit lines** (see Fig. 26)—You may be descending a ridge and the mist clears. In the distance is the summit of an identifiable peak. Take a bearing on it: lay your compass on the map, the map with one of the long sides at the peak. Move the compass until the orienting lines in the housing are aligned with the grid lines. You must be where the line crosses the ridge. Do not worry about magnetic variation unless it is more than several degrees.

- **From resection**—This is the next step from transit lines and is the process of identifying three features and drawing lines to place you inside a triangle on the map. It is an academic exercise, because when the technique would be useful, i.e., in poor weather, you cannot see enough features to use it!

- **From the slope aspect** (see Fig. 27)—This is useful when you are contouring a mountain rather than going over it or following a plateau rim. To find your approximate position, point the compass in the direction of the fall line (the track a ball would take if you rolled it down the hill). Transfer this bearing to your map. Like a transit you must be close to where that line crosses your contouring route. This method is not that accurate and only eliminates where you are not.

MEASURING DISTANCE ON THE GROUND

We have looked at measuring distance from the map, but how do we know in the dark or mist that we have walked 500m (1640ft)?

PACING

To pace successfully you need to know how many double paces you take for every 100m (328ft). Counting the strides on one leg simply means a smaller number to remember. A person of average height will take approximately 65 double paces every 100m (328 ft). It is vital you work it out for yourself, but walk normally and keep a steady pace. Check your pacing against known distances whenever possible. Your pace may change between the morning, when you are fresh, and the afternoon, as you get more tired.

On steep terrain, or in dense vegetation skip a pace or add a pace now and then, rather than trying to maintain your standard pace. The important thing is to always relate the ground to your paces; if you reach an uphill section that was 200m (656ft) away and you have only walked 150m (492ft) according to your paces, your pacing is wrong!

Horizontal distance (ft)	Speed (mph)				
	1.2	1.9	2.5	3.1	3.7
3281	30	20	15	12	10
2953	27	18	13.5	10.8	9
2625	24	16	12	9.6	8
2297	21	14	10.5	8.4	7
1969	18	12	9	7.2	6
1640	15	10	7.5	6	5
1312	12	8	6	4.8	4
984	9	6	4.5	3.6	3
656	6	4	3	2.4	2
328	3	2	1.5	1.2	1

Vertical height (ft)	Time (mins/seconds)			
33	.45	1.00	1.15	1.30
66	1.30	2.00	2.30	3.00
98	2.15	3.00	3.45	4.30
131	3.00	4.00	5.00	6.00
164	3.45	5.00	6.15	7.30

**FIGURE 28
TIMING CHART**
A to B—Distance 850m (2789ft) = 8 x 12 = 96 = 9.6 minutes. Round off to the nearest half minute = 9.5 minutes. Add half a minute for the extra 50m (164ft) = 10 minutes.
Height gain 130m (427ft) (13 contours, including the one which encloses the 1,083 spot height), 1 minute for every 10m (33ft), or for every contour if using this map = 13 minutes.
Total time from A to B = 10 + 13 = 23 minutes.
Tranter's variation to Naismith takes into account the work rate of the individual, the load carried and fatigue. It is an overcomplicated method of correcting and I have never needed to use it.

TIMING

Working out the time to travel from A to B is easy on the flat, but the ups and downs of the mountains must be accounted for. The Scottish climber, Naismith, created a simple formula that took into account the changes in height while calculating speed over the ground—X km/hr plus half-an-hour for every 300m (924ft) of ascent or 1 minute per 10m (33ft) contour line.

On a descending slope it is assumed that you will be walking faster on shallow slopes, but slower on steeper descents. Therefore, no adjustments are made for descents because it will even out over the day.

Using Naismith's rule we can work out how fast we are walking and how long a leg will take. While timings are useful, do not rely on them to the exclusion of other, more important, things such as what the ground is doing underfoot.

When you have measured how far a route, or leg of a route, is from the map, you can work out how long it will take you to walk it, if you know, or can at least guess, how fast you are walking. At 4km/hr (2 mile/hr), which is an "average" speed for most walkers with a light backpack, it will take you 1.5 minutes to cover 100m (328ft), so a leg of 700m (2297ft) on flat ground should take you 10.5 minutes to walk.

TOGGLES

It is useful to carry toggles on your compass, which you can slide along to keep a record of the number of 100m (328ft) walked.

TAKING AND WALKING ON A BEARING

Earlier we examined taking a bearing from the map. Walking on the bearing is another skill altogether.

- Create a stable platform for the map by kneeling and using the front of your thigh as a table.

- If there is heavy wind or rain, consider getting inside a group shelter to take that crucial bearing.

- In wet conditions it can be hard to line the edge of your compass accurately along your chosen bearing on the map. Try using the long black lines marked inside the base-plate.

- After you have taken your bearing, hold the compass just above waist height with the direction-of-travel arrow pointing forward. Lock your elbow into your side and turn your whole body (not just the compass) to reach the required direction of travel. Hold the compass firm and remove mobile phones, magnetic wristbands, etc.

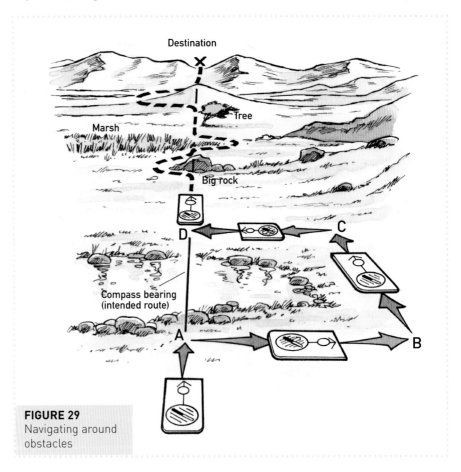

FIGURE 29
Navigating around obstacles

- Following a bearing is laborious on legs longer than 250m (820ft). To make life easier select something in the distance that is on the bearing and walk to it, then check your direction of travel and set off again to a new object.
- Back bearings can also help you check that you are not following a parallel line. Turn and identify an object on the reverse bearing (just match the white needle with the orienting arrow), walk, and after a while turn and check the object is still on the same back bearing.

NAVIGATING AROUND OBSTACLES

On occasion you will come across an unavoidable obstacle that takes you away from your bearing, e.g., a small lake, crevasses. You have two options, depending on visibility:

- Leave a friend behind (use a flashlight if it is dark). Walk around the obstacle, and when you have a back bearing that lines you up, stop and your friend can join you.
- Walk a rectangle around the object (see Fig. 29). At the obstacle make a right/left angled 90° turn (A), walk x paces until you can walk around the obstruction then turn left 90° (B) and walk until you can turn 90° left again and return X paces (C). Now turn back to your original bearing (D). You will be along your original line of travel.

COPING WITH POOR WEATHER

The mist is down, darkness has arrived, you know where you are and where you need to get to, but you cannot see the ground ahead. What do you do? Navigating in poor weather or at night is a real test of how well you understand the language of maps and can apply timing, pacing, and compass-reading techniques to ensure you are walking where you want to go.

Plan your route by breaking it down into shorter, more manageable legs.

- Aim for obvious features such as a definite change in direction or the steepness of a slope.
- Travel along hand-rails.
- Guess time, distance, and direction first, then when you work it out accurately you will spot if you make a mistake.
- Take a bearing on the leg (even pre-plan them and write them down if you are somewhere comfortable).
- Measure the distance.
- Calculate the time taken (4/5/6km/hr (2/3/4 miles) plus 1 minute/ 10m (33ft) contour).

EXPERT TIP

Lorenz Frutiger IFMGA Mountain Guide www.expedition greenland.com

"The story about the tortoise and hare often holds true; a party moving steadily the entire day will be faster than the party that runs between long breaks."

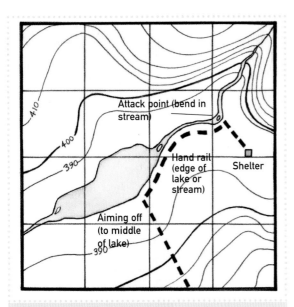

FIGURE 30 Hand railing, attack point, and aiming off

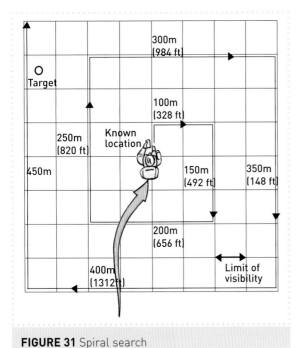

FIGURE 31 Spiral search

- What is the ground going to be like? Are you going uphill or downhill? Are there any identifiable features on the way?
- What if you make an error? Are there any dangers on the route, e.g., a cliff? When battling a strong wind you will inevitably veer away.

If the next place you want to go to is not easily identifiable use the following techniques:

Attack points—Navigate to something obvious or larger that is closer to your indistinct point, like the middle of the lake in Fig. 30.

Aiming off—You may want to find a path that crosses either a wall or a stream. If you navigate directly to it, you may miss it and then you will not know which side of it you are. Therefore, deliberately navigate to one side of it and follow the wall or stream to find the path (see Fig. 30).

Collecting features—To avoid walking too far, use features that tell you when you have passed your destination, e.g., a wall, steep ground—or flat ground.

Use your group—Have a group member out in front, on the bearing, or get one of your friends to check you. Rope up if there is a risk of falling over an edge.

SEARCH AND RELOCATION

If, after following one of the previous techniques and checking your map for obvious features, you cannot find what you are looking for, you must do a systematic search to locate your next point.

There are two types of search you can undertake:

1 **Spiral search**—A good method if you are alone. Use your compass and walk north to the limit of your visibility. Stop and turn 90° to the right and walk twice the limit of your visibility (you will have to pace accurately). Stop again and turn another 90° and walk three times the limit of your visibility. Keep repeating this process with longer legs until you find your checkpoint or object.

2 **Sweep search**—The more people the better for this approach. Space everyone out perpendicular to you but still within sight and sweep backward and forward across the area to be searched until your checkpoint or object is located.

GLOBAL POSITIONING SYSTEM (GPS)

The GPS picks up signals from satellites, calculates your position, and displays it as a latitude and longitude fix to the nearest 1/100th of a minute, or a grid reference, depending on how you have set your GPS. It can do this anywhere on Earth and in any weather, but only when it has a clear view of the sky and can pick up signals from at least three statellites. It also gives direction, the speed you are moving, distance to a location, and even altitude, but vertical accuracy is not as good as an altimeter.

When the system was created, timing errors (selective availability) were inserted into GPS transmissions to limit the accuracy of non-military GPS receivers to about 100m (328ft). This was eliminated in May 2000, but there is still a possibility that the GPS signal will become unavailable in specific regions of the world in future conflicts (a dedicated European GPS system may be online soon).

Like any other measuring device, a GPS is not perfect. Officially, positioning with 95 percent confidence is accurate to better than 20m (66ft), but in effect it is often much better than that.

HOW DOES GPS RELATE TO MAPS?

Using a GPS alone to track your route or follow waypoints is fine. However, when we relate the position given by a GPS to a map a problem arises.

Different countries have their own datums in which their country is mapped, and if your GPS is not set to the right one, it can place you as much as several hundreds of meters off route.

In 1984, a world geodetic survey was published and it is now possible to produce maps and charts of Earth's surface to a common datum, which is abbreviated to WGS84. Many countries are in the process of converting their country's maps and charts to WGS84 datum.

HOW USEFUL IS A GPS?

A GPS can provide very accurate information, but use only as an aid for mountain navigation; traditional map and compass skills still remain the backbone of sound navigation. Relying solely on a GPS would be foolish, considering:

- The batteries could die, just when you need it.
- Even in normal usage, there are still times when GPS can give a bad position without warning.
- Because the satellite paths do not go over the North Pole, users of a GPS in high northern latitudes will receive signals from most satellites at relatively low elevations to the south of them. These may then be obscured by steep ground.
- A confusing signal error may occur if the receiver is close to large, reflective objects such as boulders or cliffs.
- Severe weather conditions can prevent you from operating your GPS—

Study the instructional manual for your model carefully. An excellent resource for novice GPS usage is available on www.Garmin.com

pressing small buttons while wearing gloves or mittens is tricky. It can also be difficult to read the details on the screen in a storm.

However, a GPS can be used as an aid in complex and featureless terrain where traditional map-and-compass navigation is tricky, e.g., crossing ice caps or a poorly mapped area. It can:

- Give a very accurate grid reference of your present location.
- Provide the facility to return to a previous location by marking a "waypoint" at the location, and then using it to return at a later time. A GPS will usually take you to within a few feet of a previously visited location, e.g., a tent. Waypoints are useful because they can be preloaded. They can then be followed back down the hill if the weather is bad, especially useful in snow covered and glaciated terrain.
- Allow you to enter the grid reference of a specific point you want to go to. Do remember: when following a "GO TO" on a GPS receiver, it is very easy to ignore the ground under your feet, to leave the map in your pocket and to forget about the contours. You can easily get into a situation where you are lost, relying solely on only your GPS, and at the mercy of technology!
- It can show you the bearing and distance to the next objective, but this can be depressing! When a GPS unit indicates you are 1.6km (1 mile) from a designated spot, that is an "as the crow flies" mile, not a mountain mile. This can be displayed as a compass-type directional display relative to the current heading, for ease of following a route, but you need to be moving for the device to work out a heading. It is best to switch it on and then use your compass to follow a bearing. Some models incorporate an electronic compass, which will work when stationary.
- Track positions all day and can be used for later comparison with the map.
- Link with digital maps to upload waypoints or routes, email waypoints to friends, and download your track to a map, and vice versa.

A GPS is useful in poorly mapped areas. (Trekking in Peru.)

WHICH GPS SHOULD YOU BUY?

Consider the size of the screen, how easy it is to move between different functions, and how easy it is to put waypoints into the unit, especially with gloves on. Rechargeable units are fine but they are not so useful when in remote places.

ALTIMETER

An altimeter measures atmospheric pressure just like a barometer and turns it into an altitude. Since the weather is caused by high and low pressure systems, you must regularly calibrate the altimeter by setting it when you are at a known elevation. An altimeter can also be used for navigation:

- Knowing your exact altitude can pinpoint your position on large uniform slopes and ridges. Ski mountaineers use altimeters to navigate complex slopes and broad glaciers, but regular calibration is always needed, particularly on shallow ground, because a small change in height may mean a big difference in your position on the ground.
- In poor visibility on a rock climb, altimeters may be more useful than a map.
- Altimeters are particularly useful when accurately following a contour line for any distance.
- They help you descend and ascend to a specific point—note the target altitude from the map but "aim high" when coming down from above and "aim low" when coming up from below. You can even set your altimeter alarm.
- Combined with slope aspect, an altimeter can position you more accurately.
- It can help with planning ahead, e.g., how much height is left to reach a summit or halfway down? Have you reached the summit?
- Monitor your progress through the day—if it has taken an hour to climb the first 400m (1312ft) and you have another 700m (2297ft) to go, then you can expect it to take at least two more hours.

LIMITATIONS AND ACCURACY

The Pressure Graph—Air pressure does not decrease uniformly as you ascend, but altimeters approximate that it does over small ranges. An altimeter calibrated at 1200m (3937ft) in the valley will give significantly less accurate readings than at 3200m (10,499ft). Reset it to a new reference altitude after changes in height of several hundred metres.

Weather changes—Small changes in air pressure significantly alter the altitude reading, so recalibrate every few hours, particularly if there is an active weather system around.

Temperature effects—Temperature has an affect on air pressure—the altimeter therefore uses a list of average air temperatures for different altitudes. The problem is that the air temperature in your location is unlikely to be exactly the world average for that particular altitude. Therefore, regularly set the altitude at known points to minimize any effects. In cold weather (below 15°C (59°F) at sea level/freezing level of 2400m (7874ft)) an altimeter will tend to under-read any altitude changes. Conversely, in hot weather, it will tend to over-read changes. Wearing your altimeter on your wrist should not make a difference to the reading, as the unit will be compensated in order to be able to deal with different operating temperatures.

Wind effects—An increase in wind speed due to air flowing around an object creates a drop in pressure where the wind speed is highest. Conversely, if you set the altimeter out of the wind, and then use it somewhere much windier, it might read too high.

2

ROCK CLIMBING

"Rather than being a risk-taker, I consider myself, and my climbing peers to be risk-controllers, keeping risk at a reasonable level."

—Alex Lowe, one of the world's best climbers

Climbing is a true "sport for all." What other sport allows you to change the size of the opposition, or the size of the pitch, according to how you are feeling? Rock climbing is a technical, physical, and mental game that is subdivided into indoor, sport, traditional, big wall, bouldering, winter, alpine, and expedition climbing. This chapter is concerned with the first five listed and assumes the reader has a basic understanding of climbing. Much of the information contained here is important in understanding the following chapters. (See Appendix, page 355, for grading systems of climbs around the world.)

Rock climbing is hazardous and there are always factors beyond your control, but you can decrease the chance of things going wrong by using common sense; find out the weather forecast, look after your equipment, and check the buckle on your partner's harness, for example. Safe climbing is having an awareness of the hazards and matching your skills and experience to the dangers to decrease the risks. Unfortunately, good judgment only comes with experience and, as Oscar Wilde said, "Experience is simply the name we give our mistakes," so tread very carefully!

Dave Williams abseiling, Riglos, Spain.

FALLING

"Without gravity you wouldn't have a sport."
—Matthew Ketterling, climber

It seems strange to start by talking about the one thing all climbers try not to do—fall off, but if you understand how the forces are generated in a fall, how to lessen them, and how to use climbing equipment so that it does not exceed its limitations, you will be safer. Equipment failure is rare and is usually the result of old age, poor maintenance, or a misunderstanding of its limitations.

IMPACT FORCE (IF)

A 100kg (220 lb) climber hanging on a rope exerts a force of approximately 1kN. A climber who is seconding and falls with a small amount of slack generates about 2-3kN. The amount of energy a falling lead climber generates will depend on their weight and how far they fall (see Fig. 1).

The force reaches a maximum when the rope has stretched fully—this is called the Impact Force (IF). The IF is partly dissipated by dynamic elements in the system; rope fibers stretching, friction over carabiners, the movement of the belayer, knots tightening, rope sliding through the belay device, even runners popping out. The remaining energy is transmitted to the climber, the belayer (or belay anchors if a direct belay is used), and the protection. The bad news is that the same physics allowing a pulley to work mean that the force transmitted to the protection which stopped the climber falling is nearly double what it was (actually 1.66 times when you consider friction loss across the carabiner).

Safety is having an awareness of potential danger. (Beyond The Azimuth E1 5a, Pembrokeshire, U.K.)

THE KILONEWTON

A kiloNewton (kN) is a measurement of force. If you are hanging on a rope the force on the rope in kN is your mass divided by 100 (so a person weighing 80kg (186 lb) creates a force of 0.8kN (1.86 IN).

Climbing is a way of life, in much the same way as following any passion.

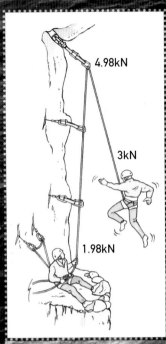

FIGURE 1
The approximate forces on a climber, belayer and carabiner.

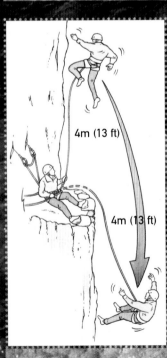

FIGURE 2 Fall factor 2

FALL FACTORS (FF)

It may seem logical that a longer fall will generate a higher IF than a shorter one. In fact, a leader fall of 3m (10ft) can create the same force as a leader fall of 20m (66ft) because in the shorter fall there is less rope to absorb the force created.

The severity of a fall is approximated by the Fall Factor (FF)—the distance fallen divided by the amount of rope paid out—which ranges from zero to two. At zero there is no force on the rope and you have probably hit the ground.

Take the example of a climber 10m (33ft) above the belay. He falls off and travels 20m (66 ft), generating a FF of two (20 divided by 10 (33ft). If the climber had placed a runner at 10m he would only have fallen 10m (33ft), yet there is still 10m (33ft) of rope out and the FF is then one.

ROPES

"Ropes cannot break at the tie in the knot, or at the running belay."
—Pit Scubert, UIAA Safety Commission

Trevor Massiah mid-flight, Pembrokeshire.

The FF is a worse-case scenario because it does not take into account the dynamic components described earlier or the friction created by the rope running through carabiners. An 82kg (181lb) climber theoretically generates 7.46kN in a FF1 and 10.18kN in a FF2. These are the IFs that the climber and the belayer would receive at the end of the fall. The good news is that the dynamic elements described earlier reduce the forces considerably, and in a typical fall (less than FF1) the top runner rarely receives 7kN, at worst an FF2 with a very heavy climber. The maximum force possible is 12kN.

There is, however, a way of generating a FF greater than two by taking the rope in as the climber falls. This reduces the amount of rope available to absorb the fall and increases the forces on the equipment. The opposite is also possible and paying the rope out can reduce the FF, but check the climber is not going to hit anything before doing this.

You should therefore do everything you can to reduce the IF received by the runners. With the exception of micro nuts and very small camming devices, the strength of all climbing equipment exceeds the forces generated in typical climbing falls; breakages are usually due to inappropriate use. If you are using micro gear consider doubling it up to share the load.

CHOOSING CLIMBING EQUIPMENT

"While I never tidy the house all my equipment is totally ordered, classified, and perfectly maintained."

—Philippe Batoux, leading French alpinist

There is not the room to look at every model, but here is some advice to help you make the correct choice.

ROPE
Modern ropes are either dynamic (stretch to absorb forces) for climbing or low stretch (static) for abseiling and ascending. They are available in 50, 60, and 70m (164, 197, and 230 ft) lengths, and in 9.5-11mm single, or 8.2-9mm, half ropes.

Consider the following when buying a rope:

- A 60m (197ft) single rope is best for sport climbing. Falling usually wears out the first 10m (33ft), so longer ropes can be cut and still leave a usable length.

- A 50m (164ft) or 60m (197 ft) single rope is best when you are starting out because it is easier to use.

- Two 50 or 60m (164 or 197 ft) half ropes are better for traditional climbing.

- Ignore the published number of falls a rope can withstand; they all pass a minimum number (five) and the drop test does not simulate real falls.

- A rope with a higher IF is more durable (for indoor and sport climbing), but a rope with a lower IF reduces the force transmitted to the runners, which is better for traditional climbing.

Ropes don't break, they are cut. (The author jumaring.)

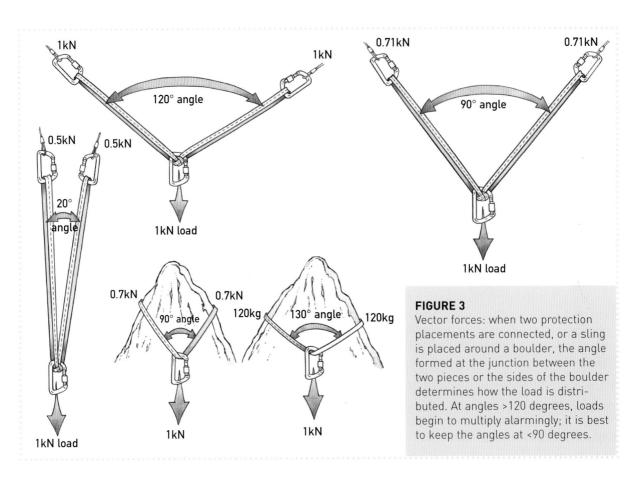

1kN   1kN
120° angle
0.5kN   0.5kN
20° angle
1kN load

1kN load

0.71kN   0.71kN
90° angle
1kN load

0.7kN   0.7kN
90° angle
1kN

120kg   130° angle   120kg
1kN

FIGURE 3
Vector forces: when two protection placements are connected, or a sling is placed around a boulder, the angle formed at the junction between the two pieces or the sides of the boulder determines how the load is distributed. At angles >120 degrees, loads begin to multiply alarmingly; it is best to keep the angles at <90 degrees.

- Thinner ropes stretch more and do not last as long, but they are lighter, easier to clip into protection and have lower IFs.
- The sheath can move over the inner fibers. Zero sheath slippage makes a rope stiffer and more durable, but it is less soft to handle. High sheath slippage makes a rope less durable, but decreases the likelihood of it cutting over a sharp edge (may be important for traditional climbing).
- The weight of a rope is only important on long desperate pitches or when carrying them.
- "Dry coated" ropes are better because wet ropes abrade and stretch more, and when frozen are up to 40 percent weaker and less dynamic.
- Color is a matter of taste, but bare in mind that 30 percent of males are color blind! Two half ropes should be different colors.
- Most ropes have a middle mark. If your rope doesn't, avoid using tape because it catches in belay devices and can damage the rope: use a manufacturer's marker ink (the solvents in other pens may affect the nylon).

LOW STRETCH ROPES

Suitable for abseiling and ascending, low stretch ropes should not be used for climbing (slings are also low stretch, so do not clip into them and climb above them). Under tension low stretch ropes are susceptible to damage from edges, so use rope protectors.

HOW LONG WILL ROPE LAST?

The advice from manufacturers is often misleading. Research by the German Alpine Club (DAV) concluded that a rope used for normal climbing cannot break in a fall. For bottom roping, DAV safely used a rope until the sheath broke or it became too stiff. They did find, however, that a rope's ability to hold a fall over an edge (1-5mm) is dramatically reduced with time. Ropes don't break, they are cut!

A rope used frequently for bottom roping or at a climbing wall should not, therefore, be used for leading where there is a chance of the rope running over an edge due to the increased wear and tear from constant lowering over a carabiner. DAV also concluded that after many small falls a rope should not be used in a situation where an edge fall is likely.

Ultimately, if you don't trust it, get rid of it. Look after ropes, and as they get older or have taken falls, reduce their exposure to sharp edges. Relegate them to top and bottom roping or abseiling where the possible IF is less.

ACCESSORY CORD

These are brightly colored, mostly low stretch, 2-9mm nylon ropes on reel—they should not be used as climbing rope. Instead, accessory cord can be used to make prusik loops, slings (extenders), and as threads for protection.

Accessory cord is also available in Dyneema/Spectra (polyethylene), which is much stronger, more durable, has higher cut resistance, and lower water absorption than nylon. A smaller diameter cord can be used to give the same strength, but it is slippery, has a lower melting point, lower resistance to abrasion, and is more brittle with poor resistance to constant flexing. For making threads and abseil use 7mm Spectra cord, but tie the ends with a triple fisherman's knot, due to the slippery nature of the rope.

CARE OF ROPES AND CORD

Regularly run the rope or cord through your hands, feeling for soft and hard areas, indicating damage. Allow the rope to rest for 15 minutes after a fall, or tie on to the other end so that the stressed end can recover. Keep rope clean and in a bag, as dirt and salt abrade the fibers. Ropes can be washed below 40°C (104°F) with pure soap flakes or a specialist rope cleaner. Add softener to remove salt and chalk. Flake the rope out inside a loosely woven sack, or "daisy chain" it. Rinse well, but do not spin dry; leave in a cool room.

SLINGS AND EXTENDERS

Tape is low stretch and made from 8-26 mm nylon or Dyneema/Spectra. Types of sewn slings available include quick draws, extenders (long quick draws), shock slings, snake slings, and daisy chains.

KINK FREE ROPES

New uncoiled ropes are kink free. To keep them that way, reverse the manufacturer's coiling by inserting your hands through opposite sides of the coils and tip the rope hand-over-hand. Avoid abseiling on a new rope until the sheath and core have settled. Kinks can be removed by running the rope through your hands several times, by hanging it down a cliff, or by "daisy chaining" it (see Fig. 45).

FIGURE 4
Structure of a kernmantel rope. Acids and bleaches damage nylon rope irreparably, yet gasoline, diesel, and oil have minimal affect at normal temperatures.

Slings—one of your strongest bits of kit. **Tape on a reel**—tape (webbing) from a reel is nylon (Dyneema is not sold loose on reels, because of the difficulty of tying an adequate knot) and can be knotted or sewn to create a sling.

Quick draws are short tapes that link crabs together for protection. Extenders come in different lengths and are a vital addition to any climber's rack. The standard "single" extender sling is 60cm (24in), the "double" sling, 120cm (48in) (there is also a 240cm (94in) sling).

Quick draws often have a captive end that holds the crab in place for easier clipping. They are great for sport climbing, but are not versatile enough for traditional climbing—you may find normal extenders better.

"Shock slings" reduce the energy transmitted to protection by rupturing the stitching in a controlled manner, but only in small falls. Snake slings with a sewn loop in either end can be easier to use as a thread, but they are not CE rated. Daisy chains/chicken slings are a loop of webbing sewn into lots of small loops along the sling's length—they are useful as a "cow's tail" and for aid climbing. Avoid clipping into two of the loops, because the stitching only has a 2kN breaking strain.

ROCK SHOES

A good fit that allows you to use your big toe effectively and minimizes foot movement inside the shoe will help you to feel secure on small holds, thereby increasing your confidence.

There are a variety of good rock shoes to choose from. Some are stiff, providing edging ability, and others are flexible, providing better smearing. Climbers have different styles, though, and few climbs have just edges or smears alone.

Unless you are an elite climber, avoid very stiff or very soft boots—one well fitting, allround shoe of moderate stiffness with a thin sole will do. Lace-up versions fit a greater variety of foot types and can be fine tuned, whereas if Velcro versions fit your foot they are easier to pull on and off.

Don't worry about the type of rubber (it's not real rubber anyway)—it doesn't make any difference to most of us.

GETTING A GOOD FIT

A good fit is much more important than the name on the shoe or the shape. Modern, low-stretch materials mean that rock shoes stretch more widthways than lengthways, lined models less than unlined. For today's climber it is unnecessary to endure pain and force your foot into a rock shoe—they will only stretch more! The comfort and fit will depend on whether your big toe or middle toe is the longest. Try many different models, male and female versions, to find the one that best fits your foot.

There are three basic shapes:

Rock boots need not hurt. (The author after a long route in Spain.)

1 **Symmetrical**—The shoe is not bent to the shape of the foot and may be better for those climbers with the second toe the longest.

2 **Asymmetrical**—Modelled on the shape of the foot (the majority of climbers will choose these), suiting those with the big toe the longest.

3 **Active**—These have an extreme asymmetrical shape, with a downward cant to concentrate the load onto the big toe. They are not as comfortable, but provide a more precise feel for top end climbers.

Center the tongue and undo the lacing or Velcro so that your foot can reach the front easily. A well-fitting shoe should be snug and accept your foot without doubling up your toes too much, and will not allow the foot to rotate or the heel to lift. It will allow you to stand on a small edge without excessive strain in your foot and without the shoe deforming. Do not flex the shoe from toe to heel—place it on a hold and flex the ball of the foot backward. It should give with little resistance, like a good running shoe, without the foot moving around. Try the shoes on for a while without socks (only use thin socks when they are for all day use on long routes). If you are using bare feet use foot powder to absorb sweat.

CARE OF ROCK SHOES

Don't leave rock shoes in your backpack for weeks, or in the sun. Rinse them in warm water to remove salt water and dry by stuffing them with paper away from direct heat. Rock boots can be re-soled and re-randed, but re-randing often changes their shape, so try to re-sole them before it is needed.

FEMALE SHOES

Shoes designed for females are narrower, overall volume is lower, and the arches are higher. However, they may also suit many male's feet.

Wear a helmet—the human skull is only capable of withstanding 1000kN without injury. A 5kg (11lb) stone falling 2m (7ft) produces an impact force of 1800kN. The impact of even a small pebble is enough to cause serious injury. (Climber: Lucy Archer.)

SECOND-HAND GEAR

"My general rule is that if there is obvious visual damage—deep scratches or cracks—then the unit should be discarded. If there is no obvious visual damage then I would use the unit."
—Chris Harmston, quality assurance manager for Black Diamond

Nylon gear should always be thrown away when you don't know its history.

HELMETS

With the advent of lightweight helmets, there is no excuse for not wearing one, except on climbing walls and some sport climbs. Comfort is the most important factor when choosing a helmet; if it's not comfortable, you won't wear it.

There are two types; hard shell made from plastic, fibreglass or carbon fiber composites, and injected foam shell. Hard shells are the "classic" mountaineering helmets with a hard shell outer and an inner cradle. The injected foam models are more like cycling helmets, much lighter, but less durable. In general, the new lightweight foam helmets absorb less energy during an impact from above. Where stonefall is common, or when ice climbing, a hard shell is probably better.

FITTING

The helmet should not flop over your eyes or expose the front of the skull when you look up. Consider whether you are likely to wear a balaclava, waterproof hood, a flashlight, or glasses and try the helmet on while wearing your backpack to see if it gets in the way.

CARE OF THE HELMET

Most manufacturers give the lifespan of "plastic" helmets as five years with fiberglass much longer, but regard modern plastic helmets as one-hit wonders. While these seem conservative estimates, it is difficult to assess an ageing helmet's ability to absorb forces by visual inspection.

- Check rivets regularly. Look for deep cracks or chips on fiberglass helmets. If the foam lining is cracked the helmet should be discarded.
- Do not use paint or put stickers on helmets.
- Do not leave plastic helmets in the sun, even though most have UV-resistant shells.
- After exposure to salt water, rinse in fresh water.

HARNESS

For rock climbing a model without leg buckles is fine, but if a harness is also to be used for winter or alpine climbing, adjustable leg loops are essential.

If you wear a backpack when climbing, gear loops attached to the bottom of the waist belt make it easier to clip gear on and off. The waist harness belt must be above the hips and leave at least 10cm (4in) of tail out of the buckle with a variety of clothes. Examine the waist for effectiveness; some collapse very easily and are merely fashion accessories.

Female versions have a larger distance between leg loops and waist belt and a different size relationship between the legs and waist.

FULL BODY HARNESS

These whip the climber upright very quickly and hinder the ability to rotate and pivot during a fall, limiting the chance of your feet and legs absorbing the impact. Full harnesses are only really useful for pregnant women ascending (having less pressure on the stomach) and possibly over large or young climbers with no hip definition.

CARE OF HARNESSES
Manufacturers recommend that harnesses be changed as frequently as a rope—Petzl recommends a life of five years. Regularly check the tie-in loops, buckles, and any sewn joints for wear and tear. Keep harnesses in a bag, and if you don't trust it, replace it.

CARABINERS
In recent years carabiners (crabs or biners) have undergone a period of evolution with ever-lighter and more radical concepts appearing. They come in 10, 11, or 12mm diameter and in cross-section they can be oval, round, T-shaped, or a variation.

There are three points to remember about crabs: the load-bearing portion is the back bar; their strength across the minor axis is considerably lower; and they are only effective with the gate closed.

Some manufacturers make crabs lighter using hot forging to move the metal away from less stress-prone areas. Aluminum's drawback is its softness, which means that crabs can be damaged when clipped through steel bolt hangers and pegs. Steel crabs are heavy and will take a lot of wear and tear, but they are only really useful for the anchor point when bottom roping.

There are different models of harness for sport, traditional, and winter/alpine climbing (Trevor Massiah, The Arrow E156).

OPEN GATE CARABINERS
There are two main shapes that are useful:

1 **Oval**—Useful for aid climbing, because their shape holds etriers and gear in an orderly fashion. Heavier and with a weak gate open strength, they are not suitable for normal climbing.

2 **Asymmetrical D**—The only shape to buy for general use. They are narrower at one end to bring the forces closer to the back bar.

GATE DESIGN
Straight gates are applicable to any climbing situation, but bent gates make clipping into the rope easier. During a fall there is the very small chance of the gate opening due to vibration or banging against the rock. A crab with an open gate is up to 50 percent weaker and can fail completely. Wire gates reduce this problem due to the lower mass of the gate. They are also much lighter, and are better for winter climbing because the gates do not freeze.

METAL TO METAL

Clipping crabs together has been described as playing Russian roulette. The risk is nothing to do with metal to metal interactions, but that, with open gate crabs, they can twist and unclip from each other. Think before you clip, and if the crabs cannot twist it is okay to clip them together.

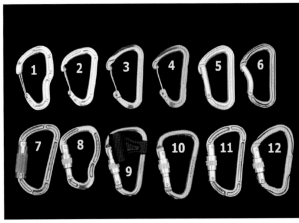

Crabs come in a wide variety of shapes and gate mechanisms each with their pros and cons.
1 DMM Shield;
2 DMM Spectre;
3 DMM Prowire;
4 DMM Livewire;
5 & 6 DMM Shadow;
7 DMM Zodiac Locksafe;
8 DMM Sentinel HMS;
9 DMM Belay Master;
10 DMM Fat Boy;
11 DMM Zodiac;
12 DMM Eclipse

The DMM Revolver crab has a small pulley sitting within the beefed-up bottom part of the carabiner. It is designed to reduce the friction created by the rope running through a carabiner by 30 to 40 percent.

LOCKING CARABINERS

A locking crab is essential where failure of a single crab would be catastrophic, e.g., when abseiling. Useful shapes are oval, offset D, pear shape (HMS), and Klettersteig. The shape of the cross section can affect the operation of some belay devices—round bar is usually better.

- **HMS ('Halb Mastwurf Sicherung' or half-securing knot)**—a large pear-shaped crab, for use with the Italian hitch. You can fit more ropes into it and belay devices work more smoothly with the large end facing the device.
- **Klettersteig**—a large asymmetrical D crab designed specifically for Via Ferratas (Klettersteigs). Sometimes confused with the HMS, it does not work well with an Italian hitch or belay device.

LOCKING GATES

Options are screwgates and auto-twist locks (spring-loaded twist locks). Screwgates have the advantage that they can be operated while wearing gloves. However the gate can unscrew when vibrated and, conversely, can lock up tight.

Auto-twist locks have a spring mechanism to lock the gate automatically, but are difficult to use with gloves. Some designs have a mechanism that locks the gate after it has closed, e.g., a Petzl ball lock. A twist lock is most useful in situations where forgetting to do up your screwgate could be catastrophic, e.g., in an abseil/belay device.

MAILLON RAPIDE

These are not made specifically for climbing, but they are extremely strong and offer a less expensive alternative to steel crabs for permanent lower offs on sport climbs. Beware: there are some maillons available for linking fencing, etc., which are not strong enough for climbing use.

Maillon rapide

CARE OF CRABS

In *Climbing* magazine, Black Diamond stated that, *"if stored in a dry environment (salt water speeds up the oxidation process on aluminum), a crab could last 100 years"..."there is no way to know whether dropped hardware is safe without doing expensive analysis."*

The UIAA recommend 10 years for all metal climbing equipment. Carefully inspect old crabs before using them and, if in doubt, replace them. If you do retain old crabs, e.g., for cleaning crabs on aid pitches, mark them clearly.

If you are active on sea cliffs buy anodized versions and rinse your gear frequently. Sticking gates can be cleaned in kerosene, wiped dry, and then sprayed with silicone.

To release a stuck screwgate undo it under load or use a pair of pliers. If it is stuck due to salt water, soak it in hot water and spray with WD40, but use this sparingly because it attracts dirt.

Crabs frequently clipped into old style bolts and pegs can develop small nicks, so on quick draws use the same crab for clipping into the ropes.

BELAY AND ABSEIL DEVICES

The first belay device was the Sticht plate (1968). There are still some plate devices available, but for most situations tubes are better. Also available are auto-locking belay devices that use a "camming" action to jam the rope and some that use a combination of braking methods.

BELAY TUBES

Belay tubes either grab the rope, or have a smooth action. However, there is no CE test for belay devices and the frictional differences are anecdotal, not hard facts.

Grabbing devices stop the climber more easily, but make paying out the rope more difficult. Those with a smooth action allow the rope to move easily, but require greater vigilance to hold a fall. Even smooth action belay tubes can grab at the rope when it is wet, icy, dirty, or furred up. Models with grooves add friction when holding a fall and abseiling, but do not affect the belaying action.

Most tubes without grooves provide sufficient friction to stop a fall, but also allow one of the half ropes to be pulled through even when the crab is flush against the device. This is useful when you need to give some rope to a climber, but their weight is on the device.

Be aware that when tubes are used with small diameter ropes, vigilance is required to hold a significant fall and abseiling can be harder work. There are some devices available specifically for thinner ropes, e.g., Petzl Reversino.

All belay devices have a smoother action when used with a round bar HMS crab, the wide end closest to the device. They allow double ropes to sit equally over each slot making paying out individual ropes easier.

Belay devices vary from grabbing to smooth.
1 DMM Bug;
2 Petzl Reverso;
3 Petzl Reversino;
4 Wild Country Vario Controller;
5 Wild Country SRC;
6 Magic Plate;
7 Petzl Gri Gri.

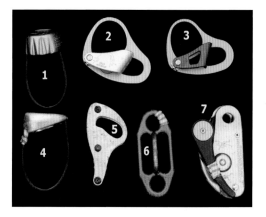

A Grigri is not foolproof!

A Reverso used as an
auto-locking device.
(A: Reverso, B: Reversino.)

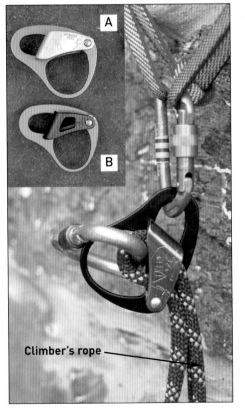

Climber's rope

FIGURE-OF-EIGHT DESCENDER

Outdoor centers use a figure-of-eight descender for abseiling as it lasts longer and dissipates heat more effectively, but it twists the rope. Continental sport climbers also use them for belaying, but there are better and safer devices available.

AUTO-LOCKING BELAY DEVICES

These devices seek to overcome the problem of a belayer not paying attention, e.g., a Petzl GRIGRI or Edelrid Eddy, and they lock automatically. The GRIGRI and Eddy both have a cam like a car seat belt, which pinches the rope when loaded, stopping it immediately. The benefits are three-fold:

1 It takes no strength to hold a fall
2 It stops falls automatically
3 It does not twist the ropes.

The Grigri is standard equipment for sports climbers. However, because it stops a falling climber without any assistance, the temptation is for the belayer to pay less attention. It also takes a high degree of skill to belay a leader using a Grigri.

The GRIGRI and Eddy are not recommended for adventure climbing because they stop the rope without any dynamic element and transfers more of the IF to the protection. They are the heaviest and bulkiest of the belay devices, do not work on icy ropes, and cannot be used with double ropes.

The Eddy has two advantages over the GRIGRI:

1 It can be used with 9–11mm ropes.
2 The lever has to be kept in the center position for lowering. If it is grabbed in a panic, it will lock regardless of the direction in which it is pulled.

However it weighs and costs more than the GRIGRI.

MAGIC PLATES

Magic plates resemble a stretched belay plate and have been superceded by the more versatile Petzl Reverso and Reversino. They can be used for belaying and abseiling, but are particularly valuable as an auto-locking device for bringing up two seconds simultaneously. If one climber falls, the device jams the rope, stopping the fall. It does, however, jam both ropes and the other climber must stop until the fallen climber has recovered. It is also difficult to lower the fallen climber if they cannot get their weight off the rope. Some models are easier to release when loaded.

Magic plates are also difficult to use in an assisted or unassisted hoist, so proceed with caution where falls into space are likely. They are, however, very useful on easier terrain.

OTHER AUTO-LOCKING BELAY DEVICES

The Wild Country SRC uses the trapping action of the connecting HMS in a slot to hold a fall. It is not a true auto-locking device, but it makes it easier to hold a fall, and is more dynamic than other locking devices. Pulling on the narrow end results in a progressive release of the rope, which inspires confidence in novices lowering heavier climbers, and when abseiling. It can only be used with single ropes and should be used with a round bar oval locking crab (HMS do not work well).

The TRE Sirius is an allround auto-locking belay device. It handles double ropes like a normal belay tube and auto-locks like a Grigri. It does take some getting used to and it's not for first timers. It allows you to belay two people simu-climbing, like a Reverso, and release more easily under load. It is a little heavier than a tube device, but has the advantage that to clip the rope into the TRE, you don't have to take it out of the locking crab.

The TRE Sirius is an all-round belay, auto-locking, and abseil device.

WHICH BELAY DEVICE IS BEST?

Tubes —Stop a falling climber when used properly. Find your favorite, but think about the diameter of ropes you frequently use, as some tubes do not accept single ropes. The Petzl Reverso and Reversino are the most versatile. If you want one device for all jobs, use the TRE Sirius.

Auto-locking—The GRIGRI and the Eddy are the best pure auto-locking devices, but the SRC is cheaper and a good alternative for bottom roping with novices (see Belaying, page 78). For bringing two novices up a climb, depending on the diameter of the rope, the Petzl Reverso or Reversino is best.

BOLTS

Bolts are permanently placed into the rock and the crab is clipped on to the hanger. Bolts are often trusted without thought, but they do fail, either by breaking, pulling out of the rock, or destroying the rock around them (a real concern in medium or soft rock). For more information visit www.safeclimbing.com.

REMOVABLE PROTECTION

The development of removable protection has mirrored the advances in climbing standards. These include wedges, hexes, tri cams, sliding nuts, and camming devices. What follows are those you will find on most climbers' harnesses.

WEDGES AND MICRO NUTS

The most popular wedge-shaped nuts (DMM wall nuts) have curved sides to provide more placement options and greater security. When placed and tugged, the curved nut cams on the convex side and rotates into the best position. A further innovation is the use of unequal faces to improve performance in flared cracks—most companies offer this on the narrower faces, e.g., DMM Peenuts.

Bolts are highly controversial in some parts of the world. (Alf Robertson, Right Wall E5 6a, U.K.)

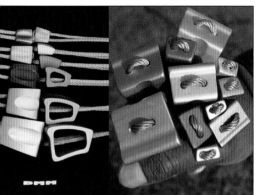

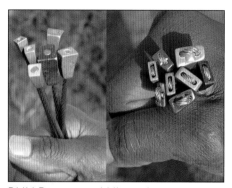

DMM Wall nuts and Wild Country Super-light Rocks above 0.5in. Most wedges are designed with a complementary thickness-to-width ratio, i.e., the wider profile of a Rock 7 is the same as the narrow profile of a Rock 8.

DMM Peenuts and Micro wires

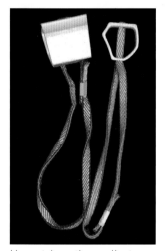

Hexentrics—the earliest camming device

Thicker wire is convenient for placements just out of reach, but may cause the nut to lift out more easily than softer wire.

In hard rock softer micro nuts can deform and pull out, where as in soft rock brass micros have a better bite than harder nuts, which can shear through. Most micro wires fail at the crab end of the wire because their narrow diameter weakens the wire; a 5-10 percent increase in breaking strength has been observed using a 12mm crab as opposed to a 10mm.

HEXENTRICS
These are lighter, less expensive, and offer a stronger placement than moveable camming devices (see Cams below). Hexentrics can be wedged along their widest facet or cammed in four different ways. They have a wire cable or tape attached, or they are bought loose and the accessory cord added. The knot on the accessory cord can be hidden inside larger hexes to prevent it becoming stuck in cracks.

EXPANDABLE TUBES
Uncommon, but consider for climbing long, wide crack pitches. They consist of spring-loaded, telescoping aluminum tubes. Squeezed together, they contract for placement inside cracks or pockets more than 15cm (6in) wide. When released, they expand and hold.

"Big Bro" expandable tubes

TRI CAMS
Specialist camming nut, which works where nothing else can, e.g., in boreholes. Tri cams are used like a wedge or flipped into a camming position for parallel cracks. They are unstable, can fall out if not well-seated, and are sometimes difficult to place with one hand. The smallest sizes are most useful.

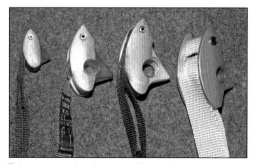

Tri cams work where nothing else can.

SLIDING NUTS

Can be round, flat, or triangular, and some can be separated to form two wedges. They are very strong, easy to use and invaluable for aid climbing and protecting thin, flat cracks, such as those found on slate.

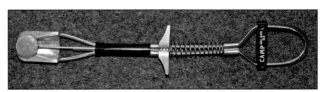

Sliding nuts all work on the same principle—a small spring-loaded wedge slides against the larger, fixed wedge.

SPRING LOADED CAMMING DEVICES (SLCD)

These are also called active camming devices (ACD) or cams. The first prototype was invented by Greg Lowe in 1967. In 1978, the American, Ray Jardine, designed the "Friend," which is one of climbing's greatest inventions. Cams allow the protection of parallel and even flared cracks that were once the preserve of pegs or stacked runners.

Cams sit in a crack, held by the small force generated by the spring. When a force is applied, the cams rotate outwards into the rock. If friction is high enough the device will lock into place. As the crack becomes more flared the forces generated become even greater (depending on the rock type, they can hold in flared cracks of 30 degrees). The large force can make it difficult to recover the device but, more importantly, it can also break the rock.

Cams come as rigid stemmed or cable; center cabled or U-shaped; one axle or two; fat cams or thin cams; three cams or four; matched or offset; bar triggers or rings.

Cam teeth bite through any unstable layer to the rock underneath and grab irregularities in the crack, but they do not work as well on wet limestone or soft calcite layers, or on dirty or lichenous rock. They are most useful in the larger sizes where the camming action is more pronounced. Very small cams have low holding power in less than perfect placements. The smallest cams are designed for aid climbing and not to take leader falls, but many climbers do.

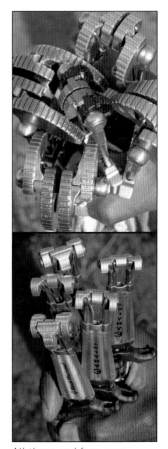

THREE OR FOUR CAMS?

The three cam unit (TCU) fits into slots and narrow peg scars. It is lighter, but has a lower holding power and is less stable—only one cam is in contact with the rock on one side. The smallest cams do not have teeth as that would reduce the contact area. Most climbers use three cam units for aid climbing or thin cracks, and four cams for everything else.

RIGID OR CABLE STEMS?

Rigid stems are more durable, while flexible stems are more useful in horizontal placements. Cable stems fit better in cracks where the crack narrows at the entrance. Models with a single cable stem can be more difficult to place because the cable flexes. Cams using a single finger trigger are difficult to use when climbing with gloves or mittens, but they do allow you to reach further.

CARE

Clean cams regularly; periodically inspect the wire for broken strands; replace tape every few years; wash if exposed to salt water. If a cam does jam,

All three and four cam SLCD units have pros and cons. No one manufacturer has cams to cover all sizes of cracks, so a mixture is inevitable.

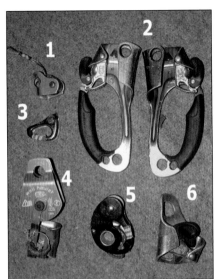

Devices to grip the rope:
1 Wild Country Ropeman Mk11
2 Petzl handled ascenders
3 Petzl Tibloc
4 Petzl wall hauler
5 Petzl mini Traxion
6 Petzl croll chest ascender.

place only the head into boiling water and work until it comes free. Use detergent to get rid of excess oils, let the unit dry, and lubricate sparingly with WD40 oil, graphite, or silicon spray. Check cable cams and sewn slings for wear. Slings can be repaired, wires can be changed, and seized cams can have a new spindle as long as the unit is within its safe working life.

DEVICES FOR CLIMBING A ROPE

Handled ascenders are left- and right-handed devices with a toothed clamp to grip the rope when loaded, preventing it from sliding downward, but still allowing it to be slid upward. The teeth are most important: long, sharp teeth grip frozen and icy ropes but can also damage them. An important safety feature is a hole in the frame that allows the top of the ascender to be clipped around the rope, making it impossible to accidentally pop off.

Wild Country Ropeman ascenders are small and lightweight. Ropeman 1 is for 10-11mm ropes and Ropeman 2 covers ropes from 8.5-11mm. They are excellent for emergencies and grip anything, even though manufacturers give a standard cautionary comment for use on icy or muddy ropes.

Petzl produces the lightest ascending devices—the Tibloc. These work like magic when placed with care, but unless the correct size crab is used, they can damage the rope's sheath.

The Petzl Mini Traxion is a swing-sided, self-jamming pulley used for ascending. It works best when combined with a handled ascender. Do not use it with offset D crabs as it is easily damaged.

Petzl also makes a specific chest ascender (often confused with a normal ascender), called the Croll. The twisted attachment point keeps the device flat against the chest, and the elongated hole attaches to shoulder straps.

DEVICES FOR SOLO CLIMBING (SELF-BELAYING)

There is no one device that is best for self-belaying. Always use a dynamic rope of the correct diameter, and do not allow slack to develop in the system.

SOLOING ALONG A FIXED ROPE
Warning—never use a prusik for this!

- A non-handled ascender, e.g., a Petzl basic.
- Mini Traxion is very smooth and Petzl recommend this for self belaying.
- The Petzl shunt can be used as a self-protection device, but the lever can be inadvertently squeezed on bulges and overhangs. This means it won't grip the rope if you fall, and if something, such as clothing, gets caught in the mechanism it stops working. Petzl issue dire warnings for this (see www.Petzl.com).
- The soloist and solo aid are ideal for self top-roping but they are not CEN tested and are unavailable in Europe (see www.wren.com).

SOLOING WHEN LEADING

Ascenders are not designed for solo climbing. Wren Industries make the Soloist, the Solo Aid, and the Silent Partner. It is important to read the manuals that come with these devices thoroughly!

The Solo Aid—Intended for use by aid climbers, because the rope must be fed through by hand.

The Soloist—Must be used with a chest harness to keep it in correct orientation to catch a fall. Used for both ground-up soloing and top-roped free climbing. However, it will not catch upside down falls or even backward falls.

The Silent Partner—*The* device for many ground-up, roped solo climbers. It incorporates a centrifugal clutch around which a clove hitch is secured. It catches a high fall factor (FF) lead fall, whatever the orientation of the climber. It is very expensive and ineffective for top-rope soloing.

CLIMBING CHALK

Climbing chalk is magnesium carbonate and non-toxic, but chalk particles can transport viruses. To combat the overuse of chalk in climbing walls a chalk ball, a bag of stocking-like material filled with chalk, is used. This can be fitted with a draw cord to make it refillable. If it is cold, put a chemical hand-warmer into your chalk bag. To decrease the environmental impact of white marks some chalk comes in three colors: tan, white, and grey. Another solution to sweaty palms is "Mega Grip," a liquid containing an anti-perspirant and grip enhancers.

KNOTS AND HITCHES

A hitch must be tied around something for it to exist, whereas a knot is tied in the rope itself. Pull them snug, but not over-tight, as the tightening process absorbs energy. Keep them neat for maximum strength.

All knots should be tied to leave a tail at least 10 times as long as the diameter of the rope, e.g., 11cm (4 in) in an 11mm rope. If in doubt, tie an overhand knot in the tail. See pages 72–5 for climbing knots. Practice until you can tie them in the dark and during poor weather.

COMMUNICATION

Shouted instructions can be confusing and misunderstood. There are very few calls you actually need to use—keep them to a minimum so that you can make an educated guess as to what is being shouted. If the crag is crowded, add the person's name. When communication is difficult, use loud whistling. One whistle means that you are safe. Rope tugs can be confusing; just climb when the rope is pulled very tight.

- When the leader has attached to the belay anchors, the shout *"Safe"* informs the second that they no longer have to belay the leader.

"It's aid, it's unsightly, it's been done before without." Remember when chalk was the burning issue of the day and the "Clean Hand Gang" existed?

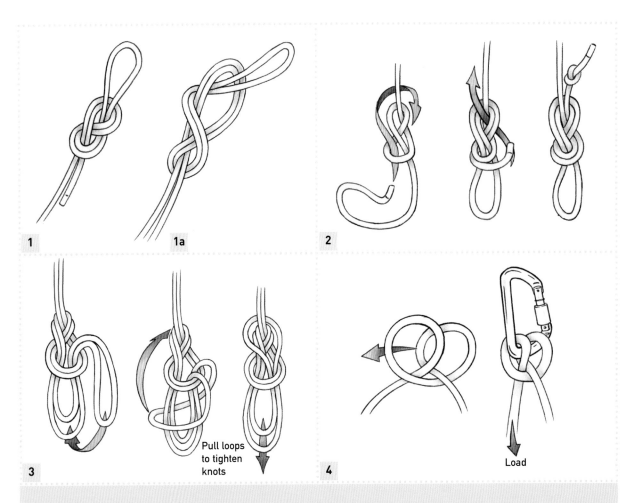

1   **1a**   **2**

3   Pull loops to tighten knots   **4**   Load

FIGURE 5 USEFUL CLIMBING KNOTS

1 **A figure of eight on a bight**, which is difficult to adjust and undo after loading. The figure of nine (1a) takes an extra turn before finishing the knot, which makes it less likely to tighten.

2 **A re-woven figure of eight**. This knot is difficult to untie after loading; easy to see if it is tied incorrectly; does not come loose, and it is good at absorbing the forces generated in a fall. The rewoven overhand creates a smaller knot, but is difficult to untie.

3 **A double figure of eight on a bight (bunny ears)**. Creates two loops adjustable to differing lengths. There is limited use for linking two anchors at a belay. The same knot created with an overhand knot can come undone unless both ends remain clipped.

4 **A clove hitch**. Used for attaching the rope to anchor crabs.

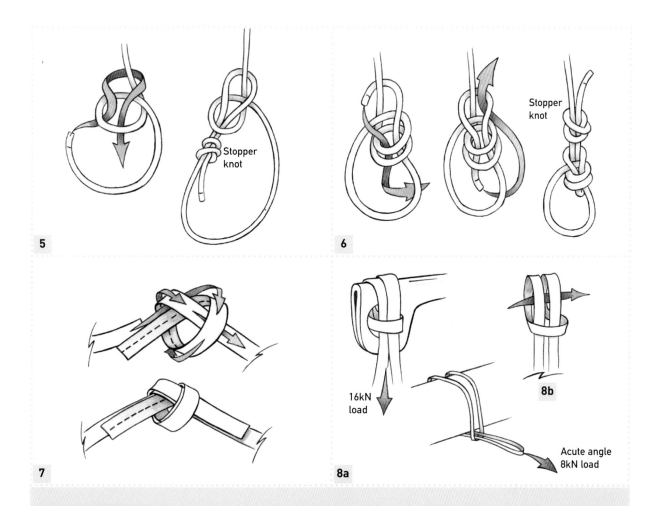

FIGURE 6 USEFUL CLIMBING KNOTS

5 A bowline with a stopper knot.

6 **An improved bowline**. This knot does not untie itself as easily as knot 5.

7 **Tape knot, or water knot**. This is often not used because of the invention of stitched slings. Do not stitch or tape the ends down.

8 **The lark's foot, or girth hitch**, a much misunderstood hitch, even by climbing experts. It is safe and useful for attaching a sling to a harness and tying off a peg, but only when tied without an acute angle created by the sling (8a).

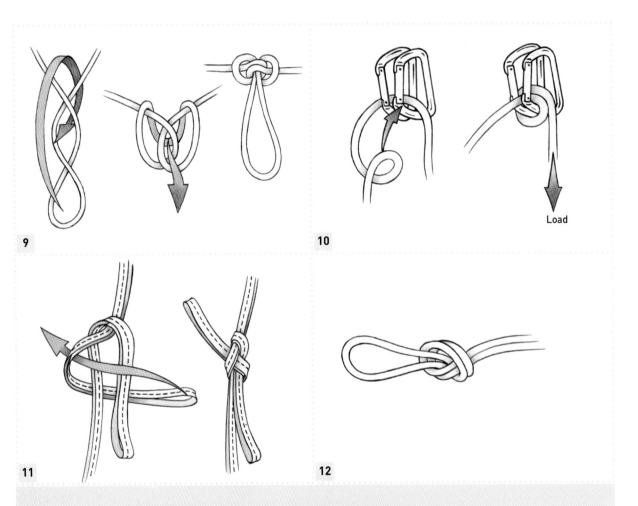

FIGURE 7 USEFUL CLIMBING KNOTS

9   **An alpine butterfly**. This is used for tying into the middle of the rope, for equalising anchors, and for isolating a piece of damaged rope. It has the advantage over the figure of eight and overhand knot in that it directs the force through the knot and doesn't distort it.
10 **A garda/alpine hitch**. This is an auto-locking hitch. Use matching crabs.
11 **A sheet bend**. This is used to create a chest harness called a Parisian baudrier.
12 **An overhand on a bight**. This is used in place of an alpine butterfly or figure of eight. It creates a small loop in a sling or rope, but is difficult to undo after loading unless tied in a bunch of ropes or slings.

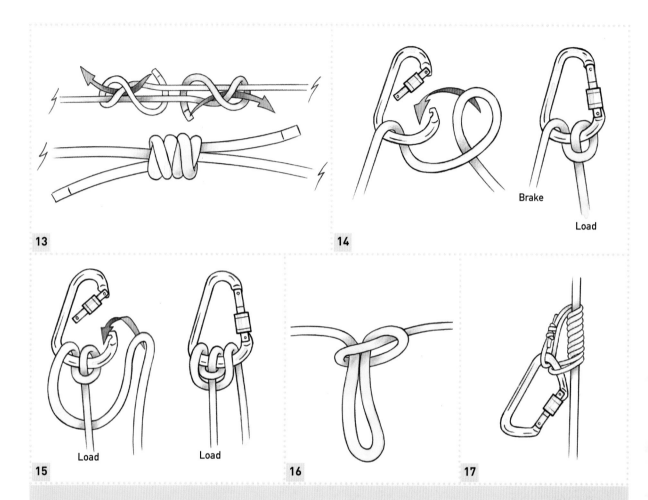

FIGURE 8 USEFUL CLIMBING KNOTS

13 A **double fisherman/grapevine**. This is used for tying two ropes together and the ends of cord together on protection. Ensure that the two portions of the knot fit into each other. A triple fisherman is used for tying Spectra and Dyneema cord.

14 An **Italian hitch/münter hitch**. This is really a half clove hitch, as its German name "halbmastwurf sicherung" (HMS) indicates. It is easy to use with an HMS krag for belaying and lowering moderate loads. Be careful that it does not un-twist the locking gate as the rope moves through the crab.

15 The **super münter hitch** is a beefed up version of the münter hitch with two main advantages—it creates friction, and it reverses the twist in the rope that the standard münter creates. Therefore, the super münter is best used for lowering.

16 The **slippery hitch/mule knot**. This is useful to tie off belay plates as it is easily released.

17 A **French prusik, or marchard hitch**. This is the most useful prusik for protecting abseils (see Rescue section, p. 117–8, for more prusik knots).

OTHER CALLS

- **"Watch me"** ensures the belayer is still alert.
- **"Take in"**—too much slack rope.
- **"Slack"**—more rope is required (avoid "take in slack"—as it can be misheard).
- **"Lower me"** informs the belayer to safely lower you from the belay chain (sport climbing).
- **"Below"**—something has been dislodged, dropped or thrown down. Avoid anything longer.

LEADING A CLIMB

- Leader starts up the cliff, belayed by the second at the base of the cliff.
- Leader reaches the top and attaches to the cliff, i.e., sets up a belay.
- Second removes the rope from the belay device as soon as the leader is safe.
- Leader takes in the slack rope and places it through a belay device, belaying the second up.

- The second removes the rope from the belay device and shouts *"Take in."* The leader can now pull the spare rope up and the second has heard "safe" and taken them off belay.
- When the rope comes tight, the second shouts *"That's me."* This tells the leader that the second is on the end of the rope and the rope is not jammed.
- The leader puts the rope into the belay device, and when he is ready to take responsibility for the second, shouts *"Climb when ready."*
- The second starts to dismantle the anchors if on a multi-pitch climb (and not before) and shouts *"Climbing."*
- The leader acknowledges that they have heard the call by replying *"OK."*

LEADING SINGLE PITCH ROCK CLIMBS

Leading is a physical and mental game of chess as you work your way to the top of the pitch, protecting yourself by clipping bolts or placing protection, belayed by a partner at the bottom.

STAYING SAFE

Learning to lead is an exhilarating yet daunting experience—the following methods are particularly useful for climbers making the transition from indoor walls to the outdoors.

Abseil pre-placement—Abseil down the climb and place protection prior to leading the route.

Bottom rope—Provides protection on your first few forays. Either a third belays it with slack in the system and your climbing rope can be belayed, or your partner belays and your climbing rope just drags behind.

Fixed rope with loops—To simulate a more realistic leading situation tie figure of eight knots or alpine butterflies into an abseil rope every 2m (7ft) with a quick draw attached. Use an alpine or tied off Italian hitch (see Solving problems, page 116), on a ground belay to remove some of the stretch. Climb using one half rope and one single rope. Clip the single rope into the quick draws and the half rope into the protection they have placed. If the route wanders, use intermediate runners to keep the fixed rope in position. If it goes over roofs, fix it below the roof—don't just pass it through a runner.

ORGANIZING CLIMBING GEAR

Sorting climbing gear prior to leading is essential, both to prevent it becoming tangled and to help you to find it easily. Arranging gear on your harness is personal, but here are some ideas:

- Place a maximum eight nuts per crab, doubling them up in size order.
- Distribute protection equally on either side of your harness, unless climbing a layback when you should carry the gear on the side away from the wall.
- Ensure that spare screwgates are not done up.

A TYPICAL RACK

6 quick draws (10 crabs and
    5 short slings)
6 extension slings (10 crabs
    and 5x50cm slings)
2 120cm slings and crabs
2 60cm slings and crabs
2 sets of wires 1-9
1 set of Wild Country
    Rockcentrics 5-9
6 camming devices
2 spare open gate crabs
3 screwgates
2/3 HMS crabs
1 nut key
1 belay device

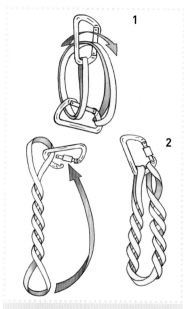

FIGURE 9
Two methods for shortening slings

- Carry several longer extension slings (extenders) on traditional routes to help the rope run in a straight line (see Fig. 25). "Quick draws" are designed for sports routes, which often go in a straight line.

- 60cm (24in) slings can be placed over the head or arm, but are difficult to remove (see Fig. 9 for quick methods of shortening slings).

- Avoid cluttering your harness with knife, jumars, or cleaning rags.

- Carry a nut key—even when leading—for poking nuts into and cleaning dirt out of cracks.

- Use a bandolier (chest sling) when lay-backing to keep gear away from the rock. However, using one on over-hanging routes means that gear hangs behind the body, and on slabs it can obscure the feet. They are useful when swapping leads on multi-pitch climbs, when traversing at sea level (you can jettison the gear should you fall in the sea), or in winter.

TYING INTO A HARNESS

This is a serious business; concentrate and do not be embarrassed to check your partner. Never attach yourself to the rope using a locking crab when leading because a fall can result in cross-loading of the crab's gate. The rewoven figure of eight (see Fig. 10) is the most reliable knot, but a good alternative when sports climbing or at a climbing wall is the improved bowline (see Fig. 6.6), because it is easy to untie after loading.

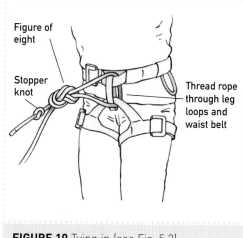

Figure of eight

Stopper knot

Thread rope through leg loops and waist belt

FIGURE 10 Tying in (see Fig. 5.2)

The process

- Take just over an arm's length of rope and tie a single figure of eight.
- Take the end down through the waist belt and leg loops.
- Re-thread the figure of eight to create a fist-sized central loop.
- Tie an overhand knot in the single strand that makes up the tail.
- Finish the knot by tucking the tail back into the knot so you can loosen it.

FIGURE 11 Tying into a chest/body harness
A—A screwgate carabiner on the chest harness allows more freedom of movement.
B—Conventional method. Ensure that the sling from the sit harness is the correct length.

TYING INTO A SIT/CHEST HARNESS COMBINATION

Few climbers use a chest or body harness, but they are useful for small children who have little hip definition (see page 62). A poorly fitted body harness can direct too much force to the back and chest. Fit so that the tie-in point is relatively high (see Fig. 11).

BELAYING A LEAD CLIMBER

A lapse in concentration can lead to painful burns or, worse, a dropped climber, so be vigilant. To belay effectively attach the belay device to the central loop created by tying in (see Fig. 10). Ensure the rope runs cleanly through the belay device without any twists and use an HMS crab, the wide end towards the belay device for a smoother action and improved holding power.

The force the belayer receives in a fall depends on how much friction is created through the protection as the climb meanders up the cliff. It can vary, from the belayer not realising the leader has fallen, to a considerable force slamming the inattentive belayer into the cliff. Usually, the upward movement of the belayer during a fall absorbs some of the force, and having freedom of movement allows the belayer to move out of the way of falling objects. As long as the belayer is attentive there is no need to anchor them to the ground or the cliff, unless one or more of the following apply:

- The leader is more than 50 percent heavier
- The belayer could fall off a drop
- The climb is threatened by waves
- There are boulders to stumble over.

A GOOD BELAYER

A focused belayer, who pre-empts the leader's movements and attempts to clip protection, is invaluable, especially when you are pushing yourself on a climb. Here are tips for better belaying:

- Do not rummage in your backpack or smoke.
- Position yourself close to the cliff to keep the runners in place (see Fig. 25) and to ensure that a fall will not pull you forward.
- Ensure the ropes run cleanly and do not wrap around the leader's legs.
- When the route is running straight up a steep cliff, stand up; it is a more comfortable position to absorb the forces created by a fall.
- Pay out the correct amount of rope so you do not pull the climber backward, but do not give too much rope.
- Keep the ropes tangle-free by loosely feeding them onto the floor with the climber's end on top.
- If the leader falls climbing over an overhang, do not pull the rope tight as it will increase the chance of the leader slamming into the cliff below the overhang.
- Use gloves until the skills have been practised.
- Take the rope in and run backward to save a falling lead climber from hitting the ground. Beware: this reduces the dynamic element of belaying and increases the impact force.

An attentive belayer is worth their weight in gold. (Climber and photo: John Taylor.)

FIGURE 12 Belaying using a belay tube. Always have one hand on the dead rope through-out the changeover.

USING OTHER DEVICES

Belaying with an Italian hitch—The Italian hitch (see Fig. 14) provides sufficient braking power no matter where your hand is. It is useful for direct belaying a second, or indirect belaying a leader, but avoid it when a long leader fall is likely. When used for lowering it kinks the rope; if this is a problem use the super münter hitch (see Fig. 15). The action is the opposite of a belay plate—hands are kept in front of the hitch at all times, but this means that you do not have to be close to it.

Grigri—Any problems arise from its use rather than its design. It is possible to load the rope wrong—don't worry, just use it like a normal belay device. The release arm is an on-off switch, not a gradual release, making it possible to drop the climber if you are not holding the dead rope. When belaying a leader, the rope can jam easily if you don't pay attention. Hold the auto-locking mechanism down with the thumb when paying the rope out (Petzl does not recommend this method).

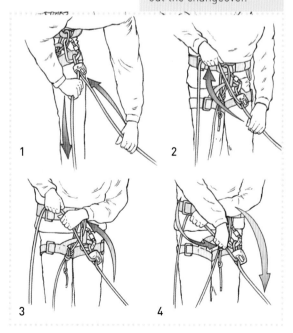

FALLING OBJECTS

Should anything fall down the crag do not look up to see where it is coming from—it may be closer than you think. Instead, when you hear a shout, run towards the cliff. Falling objects usually bounce out from the rock face a few feet.

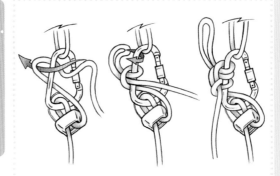

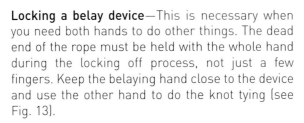

FIGURE 13 Tying off a belay device. The best method is on the back bar, but you can tie off with a slippery hitch in front of the device as for the Italian hitch, but it does obstruct rescue.

THE LIVE AND DEAD ENDS

The "live" end is the active end of the rope. The "dead end" is the end that is not functioning. The rope coming out of the belay device to the climber is the "live" rope; the brake handholds the "dead" rope.

Locking a belay device—This is necessary when you need both hands to do other things. The dead end of the rope must be held with the whole hand during the locking off process, not just a few fingers. Keep the belaying hand close to the device and use the other hand to do the knot tying (see Fig. 13).

Locking an Italian hitch—Pull approximately 60cm (24 in) of rope forward and secure it in front of the hitch with a slippery hitch and a half hitch around the live rope (see Fig. 14).

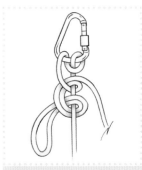

FIGURE 14
Tying off an Italian hitch

BELAYING A SECOND

The ideal belay at the top of a climb puts the belayer sideways to the anchors, with the ropes along one side of the body (see Figs 32–4). To ensure that the brake arm is free to move and lock the belay device, it should be on the same side as the ropes. Belaying is also compromised by a second who climbs too fast.

Waist (hip) belaying—Under no circumstances should this method be used to belay a leader. It may, however, be appropriate when speed is important to belay a second, the loading is low, or there is significant friction elsewhere in the system, e.g., rope runs around a boulder. Gloves and a long-sleeved shirt prevent rope burns. It is difficult to do effectively with double ropes.

The perfect belay for waist belaying is set up with the ropes from the anchors attached to the rear of the harness (see Fig. 15). This allows the belayer to face in the direction of the fall, and the ropes cannot be ripped from behind. When attached to the anchors via the front of the harness, the live rope must be on the same side as the ropes from the anchors, so that a fall twists your body outwards, not inward.

Belaying with a Grigri. Note the use of a crab to add friction during a lower.

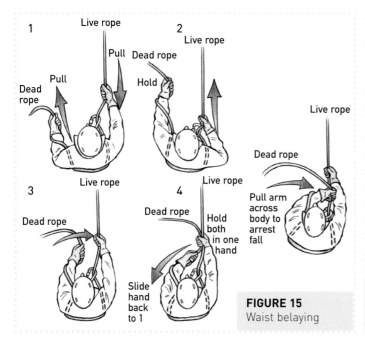

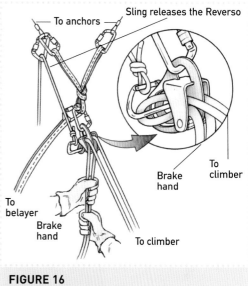

FIGURE 15
Waist belaying

FIGURE 16
Belaying two seconds and releasing a locked Reverso

Belaying two seconds—This is possible using a standard belay device, but it requires dexterity to keep the rope tight on both. Use an auto-blocking device (magic plate or Petzl Reverso) attached directly to the belay, which allows both ropes to lock independently. However, if both or even one climber falls off, it is difficult to lower them and the device must be unlocked or unloaded (see Fig. 16).

Take care using them on overhanging rock where a fall may leave the second in space unable to be lowered. If you are using half rope beware that they stretch more and can deposit the second on a ledge.

DIRECT AND INDIRECT BELAYING

A **direct belay** transmits the forces direct to the belay anchors. The advantage is that the belayer is free to move around, lowering, sorting hoists, and holding a fall are easier. It should, however, not be used to belay a lead climber.

An **indirect belay** transmits the forces to the belay anchors via the belayer, e.g., waist belay. The advantage is that the body absorbs some of the forces and the belayer can feel the climber's movement.

A **semi-direct belay system** is used by most climbers because the forces are transmitted direct to the anchors but, by changing position, the belayer can also absorb the force.

LOWERING

A smooth and steady lower is best. It is easier and more comfortable for the belayer to lower directly from the belay anchors (see Fig. 17). To prevent the possibility of lowering off the end of the rope, tie the end into the anchors.

To lower two climbers simultaneously, tie one climber into the end of the rope and the other into an isolation loop two arm-spans long created using an overhand knot or alpine butterfly.

PLACING PROTECTION

Historically, placing protection was called a "running belay," hence the use of the word "runners" to describe any protection placed by a lead climber.

Choosing the appropriate gear and placing it quickly is an art. Discover what works, and what does not, at ground level before venturing on to a first lead. Be creative, tug them to give you an idea of their holding power, but beware: a tug does not recreate the forces generated in a fall.

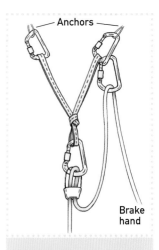

FIGURE 17 Lowering—to make it easier to control the belay device, take the dead rope through a crab above the belay device.

Kitten Claws E35C, Pembroke, U.K. (Climber: Sara Jane Dobner.)

CHOOSING SOUND ROCK

Runner placements are rarely perfect, and choosing sound rock is not easy, especially when leading. Sea cliff limestone and slate have a thin, easily crushed, weathered layer; granite is harder and provides more reliable placements. Scan the rock and look for cracks that create a loose area. If you can, place one hand on the rock and bang it with the palm of the other. If a vibration is felt, try to kick or pull the rock, but take care if you are setting up a belay that the rock does not suddenly come out and disappear over the cliff edge with you hanging on to it. Look for soft rock and crystals inside cracks that can wedge a runner, but snap easily in a fall.

WHEN TO PLACE PROTECTION

Placing protection is not simply choosing the right gear for the right place to stop a fall. There are a number of reasons to place protection:

- To reduce the fall factor
- To keep the rope in as straight a line as possible (see Fig. 25)
- To reduce the length of a fall due to fatigue, loose rock, or a slip
- To help the second follow the route
- To protect the rope from sharp edges or loose rock.

TIPS FOR PLACING PROTECTION

- Identify possible placements before climbing, organizing them on your rack.
- Down-climb if necessary to retrieve protection that may be required higher up.
- The smaller the nut, the larger the force transmitted to the rock. Therefore, place the largest nut that fits properly and ensure that the maximum surface area is in contact with the rock.
- Place protection deep into a crack, as rock is more likely to break on the exterior. However, take care not to embed them so deeply that they cannot be retrieved.
- Think about the consequences of a fall, e.g., will you hit something?
- The distance between runners can increase the higher you climb.
- Do not focus on looking upward; look sideways and downward for placements.
- Do not wait until you need protection, place it when you can. Place before and after the hard moves to protect the second, especially on a traverse.
- What happens if the top piece of protection comes out?
- Do not rely on a single piece of gear unless it is perfect.
- Understand how to place a camming device correctly.
- Be very suspicious of all fixed slings, stakes, pegs, and bolts and replace them even if this requires an abseil beforehand.
- Worry about the quality of the rock, not the strength of the equipment.

Sunny Corner Lane E25C, Carn Barra, U.K. (Climber: Adrian Wilson.)

A sling doubled over a spike and knotted allows the forces generated in a fall to distribute over two strands of the sling.

FIGURE 18 Threads.
Simply thread a sling through the hole and clip with a crab. A better, more difficult way, is to thread a sling through the hole, tie an overhand knot and pull the knot back into the thread tunnel. Any force is then on the knot, and not the rock neck. Do not lark's foot a sling around the neck, because this transmits all the force to the rock neck. Wired runners can also be used as threads.

- Do not blindly trust well-worn runner placements.
- When lay-backing place gear at waist level to avoid becoming pumped.
- Clip bolts when they are at waist level. You are then less likely to fall with a lot of slack rope.
- Double-up small protection pieces.

NATURAL PROTECTION

Nature provides great protection requiring the simplest of equipment.

Spikes and boulders—The strongest way to place a sling is simply to loop it around natural protection, but they can lift off. Rope slings are better on sharp edges, but they can roll off rounded boulders. Roll the sling back and forth to ensure it won't come off the spike. To prevent a sharp edge severing a sling, place the double thickness of the stitched portion over the edge.

To avoid excessive vector forces being created at the edges of the sling, ensure that it is long enough to go around the spike, boulder, or tree, where the angle created in the sling is less than 90 degrees.

Threads—Solid threads can take a pull in any direction making them one of the safest runners (see Fig. 18).

Chockstones—Use a lark's foot to attach to the chockstone. Beware: it may lift out the chockstone or move as you climb past it.

Trees—We should try to avoid trees, but if you do have to use one, ensure it is at least arm thickness, has vigorous growth, and a deep, well-developed root system. Trees and bushes are more brittle after a spell of dry and cold weather. If the tree is used regularly, pad it out, but do not leave the padding in place. Loop a sling around the tree or tie to it using a bowline. Keep the pull close to the ground to decrease leverage.

MAN-MADE PROTECTION

The variety of artificial protection is testament to man's ingenuity.

Nuts and wedges—In theory, the simplest protection after a natural runner.

Hexentrics—More reliable than cams, hexes can also be used sideways as a wedge (see Fig. 19). They fit into pockets and are useful in vertical and horizontal placements. Be careful using them when the crack is inwardly flaring as they may move backward.

Tri-cams—Especially useful in pockets and slots. They take practice to place with one hand and may need a tug to seat them in place. Also used as a wedge.

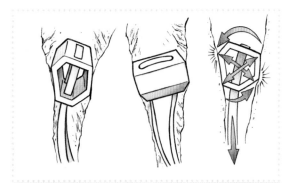

FIGURE 19 Placing hexes. When they twist they cam into place.

Movable camming devices—Their degree of safety can be misleading, because they can also sit in poor placements, held by the small force generated by the spring. It is vital they are placed correctly. See Equipment, page 69, for more information.

TIPS FOR PLACING CAMMING DEVICES

- Cams hold best when all are equally in contact with the rock, they are at 50 percent of their expansion range, and the stem is in line with the direction of any forces applied.
- Take care with cracks that widen as they deepen.
- Avoid cramming a cam into a small placement—it makes them difficult to remove.
- Check the placement of cams after a fall, as they can rotate.
- Horizontal placements are more stable with the wider cams at the base.
- Flexible stemmed cams are better in horizontal placements, because the stem can flex over the rock. However, even flexible cams still work best when aligned in the direction of force.
- In horizontal placements, place rigid stemmed cams so that only a small amount of the bar is showing, or tie them off. Beware of tying off a rigid cam in front of the triggers, because a fall may release the cams. It is better to fit rigid Friends with a second sling through one of the holes designed for making the device lighter (see Fig. 20E).
- They do hold even with just three cams in contact with the rock.

Spring-loaded wedges—Rock n Rollers, Balls, and Sliders work on the stacked wedges idea (see Fig. 21). Owing to a sliding taper, they fit a range of cracks. They work well in narrow, shallow, parallel cracks, but the placement is only as good as the purchase on the rock, and the holding power is reduced when fully extended.

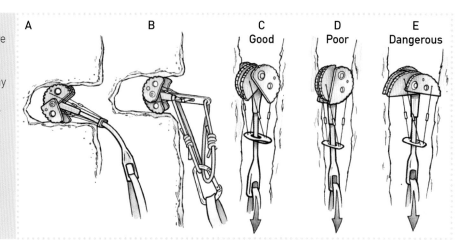

FIGURE 20 Placing SLCDs
A—Flexible SLCDS are more versatile in horizontal placements
B—A tied-off rigid stem may transmit the load to the cams in a more predictable manner, but only when placed correctly.
C—A perfect placement
D—Over-cammed and will be difficult to remove
E—Under-cammed. It is now acting like normal passive protection

A

B

C
Good

D
Poor

E
Dangerous

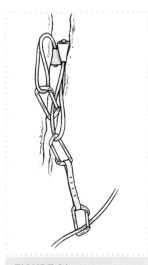

FIGURE 21
Stacked wedges
Nuts place in opposition (stacked wedges) has been superceded by the SLCDs, but may still prove useful. Tug on the one correctly orientated and then clip into it. Clip the two wires together in case the wedge falls out. In large cracks, consider stacking a wedge and a hex, and in desperation a peg and a nut.

SHARING THE LOAD

When each piece of protection is in a poor placement, one stronger piece can be created by connecting them to share the load (see Fig. 22 and 35). If you cannot tie a knot with one hand, use the self-equalizing method described for slings (see Fig. 35), but beware: if one comes out the other will be shock loaded.

MULTIDIRECTIONAL PROTECTION

The force generated by a fall can exert a sideways or outward pull on runners (see Fig. 25). Moving past slings can lift them from marginal spikes; cams can invert and walk sideways; and nuts placed in vertical and horizontal placements can lift out. Protection that takes a pull in any direction is therefore going to be better. Obvious ones are threads, trees, and bolts and, to a lesser degree, pegs, however, multidirectional protection can also be created by linking protection in opposition (see Fig. 22).

Vertical opposition—link one wedge facing down and one facing up.

Horizontal placements—can be linked with a single crab, but this can expose the crab to a dangerous three-way loading.

IMPROVISED PROTECTION

The most versatile "improvised" protection is possibly a jammed knot (see Fig. 23). Tie a knot in a sling, keeping it large and flaccid. In a tight situation try jamming your belay device in a crack!

REMOVING PROTECTION

Avoid tugging them violently, especially micro wires. Loosen with a nut key and remove them the way they went into the rock. Do not move cams back and forth, as they can walk into the crack. If the trigger bar cannot be reached, hook the bar using two wires or a specialist nut key. If the cam has a single finger trigger ring, hook it with the nut key pick. You can also try hooking the holes in the cam itself.

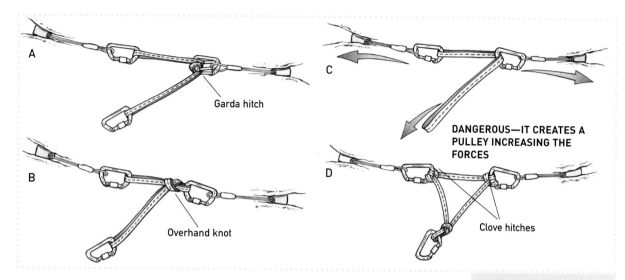

A

Garda hitch

B

Overhand knot

C

DANGEROUS—IT CREATES A
PULLEY INCREASING THE
FORCES

D

Clove hitches

To prevent a piece of gear being dropped, clip the quick draw or extender into the gear loop of the harness before you remove it from the rope. This is particularly useful when sport climbing.

FIGURE 22 Vertical and horizontal multi-directional placements

FIXED PROTECTION
Treat any fixed gear with caution—if you are in any doubt, replace it.

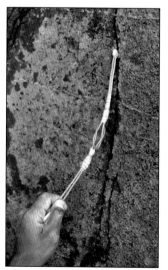

When the placement is out of reach, link two wires together. The stiffness of the wires and size of the nut will dictate how far you can reach.

PEGS
With the advent of modern protection, there is a limited need for pegs, so the art of placing them and assessing their security is disappearing. A perfectly placed peg should slide one-third of the way in before hammering and should go all the way up to the eye when hammered. A well-placed peg should have a resistance that increases as you bang it in, and a rising ringing sound. A dull "clunking" sound usually indicates poor rock, or that the peg is not in contact with the rock. Angle pegs can be overdriven, spreading the sides and reducing their holding power.

FIGURE 23 A knotted sling. Select a nice hourglass constriction in a crack and, using a nut key, poke in the largest knot that will fit and pull down hard to draw the knot up tight. To keep the pull in the right direction when the knot is close to the outside edge of the crack, tie a knot in the strand of sling closest to the cliff.

87

Would you trust your life to this peg?

FIGURE 24
Tying off pegs with a lark's foot, clove hitch, and slipknot

Clove hitch

Trucker hitch

1

2

If you cannot hammer the peg all the way in, stop hammering to avoid loosening the peg. Tie it off using a slipknot, lark's foot, or clove hitch on a sling. The clove hitch will not come off the peg, but it puts the load further away from the rock. The slipknot can come undone, but puts the load closest to the rock.

TIPS FOR PLACING PEGS

- Soft rock requires a soft peg, and hard rock a hard peg. A soft steel peg is better when the crack curves internally.
- The ideal peg placement makes an acute angle between the rock and the direction of the force exerted.
- Bend soft pegs that protrude to decrease the leverage.
- Horizontal placements are always better than vertical ones.
- In a vertical crack, make use of any variations in the rock to hold the piton in place; a narrowing above and below the peg is ideal to prevent the peg pivoting out.
- The eye of the peg is best placed downward, horizontally.
- In roof cracks, place the longest peg possible, with slight horizontal inclination.
- A peg placed in a three-way corner is almost impossible to remove.
- When using angles, place them with three points of contact.

A wire through the eye helps with difficult-to-clip pegs.

TESTING PEGS
Without a hammer it is difficult to test a fixed peg adequately. Try loosely holding a crab with two fingers and tap it on the peg; the sound it makes will indicate whether it is safe.

REMOVING PEGS
Knocking them back and forth will damage the rock, so try gentler blows first. It is better to loosen the peg with predominantly upward blows because then a nut placement is created. However, in practice it is difficult to remove a peg with blows in only one direction. To remove it when it is loose attach a chain of crabs to it and pull outwards.

BOLTS

Beware of any bolt that is set crookedly, wobbles or is in loose or soft rock. Hammering bolts that do not tighten, are in too shallow a hole, or are stripped, will only worsen the situation by bending or cracking the bolt.

Never smash a bolt flat, if it offends you and you need to remove it, pull it out using a thin, flat piton with a 'v' cut into it, and a crow bar. If the bolt breaks, punch the remaining stud as deep as possible. To refill the hole, mix resin with rock dust or use rock-colored cement. To remove glue in bolts, try twisting with a crow bar or cut and punch them in.

ATTACHING THE CLIMBING ROPE

Use a quick draw or an extender to link the rope to runners. They will act as a hinge, preventing the runner lifting out. If you do have to use a single crab on bolts or pegs, use a screwgate. Keep the gates away from edges to prevent the gate being pushed open.

KEEPING THE ROPE IN A STRAIGHT LINE

The only runner that receives a downward force in a fall is the top one; the remainder receive outward pulls towards an imaginary straight line between the belayer and the climber and can be lifted out (*see* Fig. 25). Also consider the effect that a falling second will have on the equipment, especially when traversing (*see* Fig. 26). Maintaining a straight also reduces rope drag (friction) and allows the full length of the rope to absorb the forces in a fall more effectively (*see* Fig. 27).

Use longer slings to straighten the rope and, when possible, the first runner should be able to take an outward or upward pull. In addition to extending the runners to keep the rope in a straight line, the belayer should stand close to the cliff.

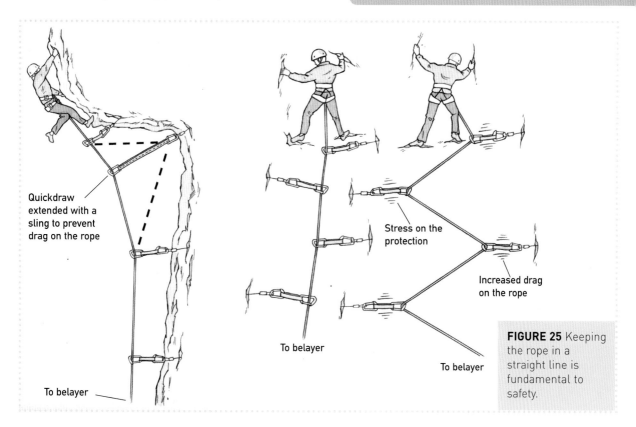

Quickdraw extended with a sling to prevent drag on the rope

To belayer

Stress on the protection

Increased drag on the rope

To belayer

To belayer

FIGURE 25 Keeping the rope in a straight line is fundamental to safety.

FIGURE 26 Take care if the route moves diagonally upward at the end of a traverse, or even on a vertical pitch. If the seconder falls during the traverse, the ropes can saw along rock edges cutting the ropes.

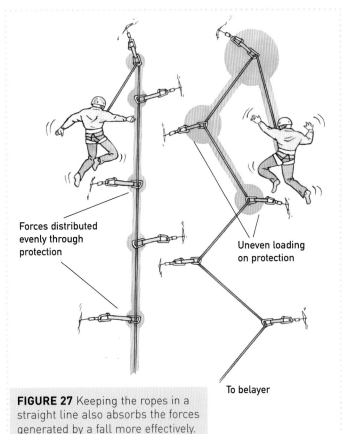

Forces distributed evenly through protection

Uneven loading on protection

To belayer

FIGURE 27 Keeping the ropes in a straight line also absorbs the forces generated by a fall more effectively.

Extend runners with a sling or another wire to prevent the crab breaking over an edge.

CLIPPING THE ROPE INTO A QUICK DRAW

There are two ways of clipping the rope into a crab depending on the direction it is facing and which hand you are using (*see* Fig. 28). The rope should pass from the back of the crab and out to the climber, not the other way as in Fig. 29. This may prevent the rope unclipping from a crab in a fall.

When climbing diagonally, the gate of the crab must always be away from the direction the climber is heading (*see* Fig. 29).

LOOK AFTER THE SECOND ON TRAVERSES

Protect the hard moves before and after the crux. This is because the second climber invariably removes the runner before making the difficult moves and then faces the prospect of a big swing. Also consider placing protection for the second on vertical pitches that have a gradual or subtle traverse. If the second falls off they may swing to the side and on to steeper or overhanging ground.

CLIMBING WITH TWO SECONDS

You can bring two seconds up a pitch, tied to the same single rope. The first is tied into the rope normally, then 2/3 arms spans away attach the second climber using an alpine butterfly on a long loop. If you do this you can clip into runners as normal. However, if each second is tied into a separate rope use the method in Fig. 30 or ask the climber ascending first to clip the following climber's rope into vital pieces. Take care belaying climbers on one half rope, because there is a lot of stretch.

USING TWO HALF ROPES (DOUBLE ROPE TECHNIQUE)

On more difficult climbs or when the route wanders, double ropes have advantages. Double rope technique involves clipping one rope into one series of runners, and the other into another series parallel to the first (see Fig. 31).

Advantages of double ropes:

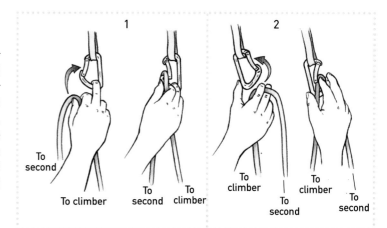

FIGURE 28 Two methods of clipping the rope
1 Hold the crab with the second or middle finger and clip the rope using thumb and index finger.
2 Hold the crab with the thumb and clip the rope with the index and second finger.

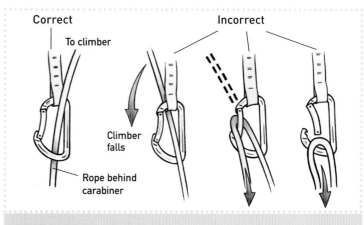

FIGURE 29
Back clipping—the wrong way to clip a rope into a crab!

- Each rope runs in a straighter line through the protection. This advantage is lost if the ropes are crossed.

- When a climber using a single rope pulls the rope to clip into a runner above their head, they momentarily increase the potential distance they could fall. Alternately clipping double ropes into protection reduces the length of a fall should you fail to clip the next piece of protection.

- They reduce the chances of complete rope failure in a fall.

Dream of White Horses,
HVS North Wales.
(Climber: Bill Beynon.)

FIGURE 30
Clipping gear when
climbing with two
seconds on separate
ropes

- They reduce the amount of rope needed at belays as each rope can be used for a separate anchor attachment.
- If the belayer is paying attention to both ropes the impact is distributed between two runners and two ropes.
- On some traverses the leader can clip one rope into the runners then, as long as the belay is above the traverse, the other rope can protect the second along the traverse.
- Double ropes give the option of a longer abseil.

Disadvantages:

- Two ropes weigh more.
- Belaying a lead climber is more difficult as the belayer must take in and pay out ropes simultaneously.

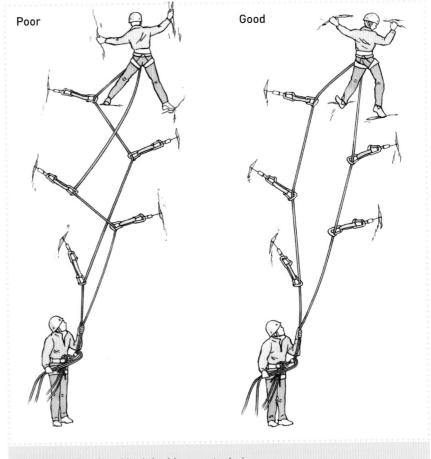

FIGURE 31 Good and bad double rope technique

SECURING YOURSELF TO THE CLIFF (CREATING A BELAY)

At the top of a climb the leader must place anchors and create a belay to bring up the second. The simplest systems for creating a belay are the best.

All belays should have the following features:

Solid anchors—Two anchors are normally a minimum but more may be required if the runners are poor. Give each anchor point a mark from one to five, where five is superb. Your belay should add up to ten, i.e., two superb anchors is enough.

Equalize the anchors—The belay should utilize all the anchors. If part of the belay fails the remainder of the anchors take the load with no movement of the belayer.

Independent anchors—Place anchors in separate sections of the cliff. Two nuts placed in the same crack are in effect a single anchor point; if the crack expands, both come out.

Tight rope—Keep the ropes taut to stop you disappearing over the edge. Rope stretched when the anchors are far apart may deposit the belayer over the edge.

Stand or sit?—Consider sitting down when the anchors are below shoulder height because you can be pulled to your knees and will then let go of the rope. The disadvantage of sitting is that it is more difficult to give assistance to a struggling second.

Communication—Easier when the second is visible.

Direction of forces—Consider the direction a fall will pull you in. Equalize the anchors so that a fall does not pull the belayer sideways or upward.

What if?—Finally, ask "what happens if the climber falls?" If the answer is nothing, then the belay is good. If the answer is anything else, look again.

Double rope technique has some important advantages for traditional climbing. (Lucky Strike E2 5b, Pembrokeshire, U.K.)

LOCKING OR OPEN GATE CRABS—DOES IT MATTER?

When the consequence of the rope coming out of the crab is catastrophic, a screwgate crab must be used, e.g., all attachments to the harness or single anchor points. The chance of the rope coming out of the crab on anchor placements is extremely small, especially when a clove hitch is used and you remain tight on your belay, open gates are then usually adequate. Screwgates are, however, advisable on all top and bottom rope belays because the movement of the system can cause the rope to fall out of an open gate crab.

Avoid carrying a mixture of twistlock and screwgate crabs because it is easy to forget that you have a mixture and not to do up the screwgates.

ATTACHING THE ROPE TO ANCHORS

Figs 32–4 show a variety of simple methods. They all rely on the principle of creating V's between the harness and the anchors and can be mixed and matched.

CREATING A BELAY WHEN THE ANCHORS ARE A LONG WAY FROM THE CLIFF EDGE

Untie from the rope and tie the end of the rope to the anchors. To equalize more than one anchor, use slings (see Fig. 35), a figure of eight on a bight (bunny knot), or an alpine butterfly. Return to within a foot or two of the cliff edge and attach the rope to your harness using a double figure of eight and a screwgate crab. Beware that when the belay is a long way back there is a lot of stretch in the rope that could deposit you over the edge if the second falls off.

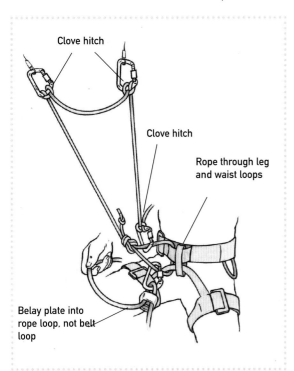

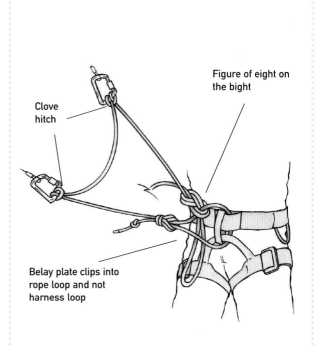

FIGURE 32 Creating a belay when the anchors are within arm's reach, or there is limited rope available. Estimate how far away the cliff edge is and tie clove hitches directly to the anchors. Link the rope to the central loop with a clove hitch on an HMS crab (this is difficult to adjust if you cannot reach the anchors).

FIGURE 33 Instead of clove hitches on an HMS crab, tie directly into the central loop with a figure of eight knot or two half hitches. Take a step towards the anchors before tying the knot to equalize the tension.

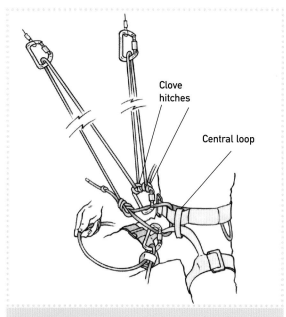

FIGURE 34 Creating a belay when the anchors are not close to the cliff edge. Pass the rope through all the anchor crabs. Take the loop(s) of rope between the anchors and move to the edge. Attach a clove hitch to each rope and clip to the central loop with an HMS crab. All the adjustments are at the harness, avoiding constant walking back and forth adjusting knots, but it uses a lot of rope.

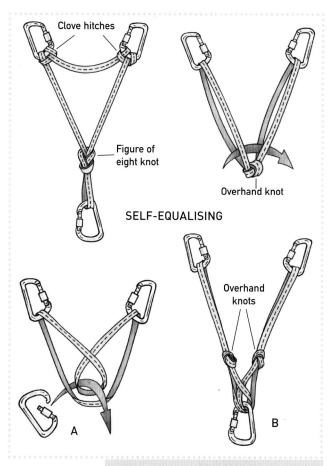

ABSEILING

Abseil is a German word meaning "on rope." In French, it is rappel, meaning "to recall."

RIGGING THE ROPE

The same principles apply when setting up an abseil station as they do for creating a normal belay: solid, independent, and equalized anchors. Whether the rope is fixed or retrievable, i.e., pulled down the cliff to be used for climbing, dictates the rigging method used (see Figs 36 and 37).

Make the belay station high so that "take off" and rope retrieval is easier. Choose steep routes, because easy angled routes provide more opportunities for the rope to snag. Avoid loose rock and use a rope protector on sharp edges. Check that harnesses are buckled correctly and tuck away hair, clothing, and straps.

FIGURE 35
Equalization of anchors to a single point with slings. To share the forces among the anchors, or to save rope when the anchors are far apart, it may be necessary to equalize them with slings. The "self-equalizing" system (A) is only used when the anchors are strong and solid and is used where the belayer needs to move around a lot, but this is rare. The downside of self-equalization is that if one anchor fails, the other anchor is shock loaded. Placing knots in the sling (B) can reduce the shock loading, but this defeats the aim of the self-equalizing system.

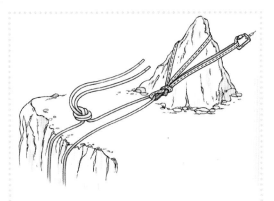

FIGURE 36 Joining ropes for abseiling. The ropes can be pulled down and used to climb with or for the next abseil. Equalize the anchors with a separate short section of rope or slings. Put the abseil rope through the sling(s) or clip into them using a crab. It is easier to pull the ropes down when they are exiting on the outside of the sling.

JOINING THE ROPES

The best method for joining ropes is an overhand knot (leaving 45cm/18in of tail), pulled tight (see Fig. 36). As it rolls over an edge it is less likely to become snagged. Do not be tempted to use a figure of eight knot as it can invert, but if you are nervous about using a single overhand knot tie two very close together.

THROWING THE ROPE DOWN

Make sure there is no one below and check the ropes reach the bottom. If the length of the abseil is unknown, tie a knot in the end of the rope. To prevent double ropes becoming tangled, tie knots in each rope—a figure of eight in the rope to be pulled, and an overhand in the other. If the rope touches the bottom, do not tie knots in the ends because they increase the chance of it becoming trapped under a boulder.

Throw the rope down by layering the rope, doubled, across your hands (lap coiling) with decreasing sized layers. Grasp the middle and throw these down, then do the same with the end of the rope. When it is windy, take the rope down loosely fed into a backpack or create a large loop by tying an overhand knot and daisy chain the rope around the loop; this keeps the rope weighted throughout the throw.

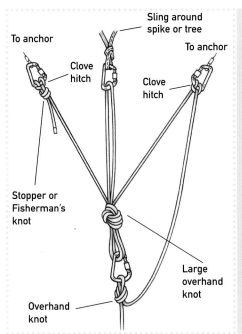

FIGURE 37 A fixed abseil station. The rope cannot be pulled down the cliff. Attach it using a clove hitch (for easy adjustment) to one anchor, then pass it through the other anchors and pull the rope between them to create V's. Tension the rope in the direction of the abseil and tie an overhand knot into the rope loops. Clove-hitch it to the final anchor. Tie a figure of eight or nine in the rope to go over the cliff edge and clip the remainder into the overhand knot using a locking crab. If the full length of the rope is required for the abseil, equalize the anchors with a separate length (rigging rope) or slings, and attach the abseil rope to it.

SLIDING DOWN THE ROPE

The forces exerted when abseiling are low, but a bouncing abseiler can cut or abrade the rope. The ideal body position is 55 degrees to the cliff with the feet apart, knees flexed, and heels on the rock. To pass overhangs flex the knees on the lip, push outwards, and slide quickly down the rope. Alternatively, sit sideways and drop over the lip. The upper hand guides the rope and the bottom hand controls the rate of descent.

To increase friction should you be abseiling on a thin rope, attach the device to the rope using two HMS crabs or use the system in Fig. 38.

PROTECTING AN ABSEIL

The simplest method is to hold the rope at the bottom of the abseil (not directly underneath in case rocks fall). If the abseiler lets go of the rope you can pull the rope tightly, slowing their rate of descent.

The following methods have been criticised by some cavers and John Long in his series *How to Climb* (Falcon Guides), but used correctly they definitely improve safety without having to carry extra hardwear. However, do not trust them implicitly, and set them up so that the prusik cannot jam in the device.

- Attach a French prusik from a leg loop to the rope below the abseil device—the abseil device takes the load should you need to stop, not the prusik. Take care that the prusik does not reach the abseil device.

- To use two hands on the abseil route, extend the abseil device away from the abseil loop with an extender and two screwgate crabs, then attach a French prusik from the abseil loop to below the abseil device. Although popular, it is possible for the quick draw to release the prusik on vertical abseils, it puts the device closer to helmet straps and hair, and it can make going over the edge more difficult.

- It is much easier to abseil past a knot when the prusik is above the abseil device and more appropriate when abseiling with an Italian hitch.

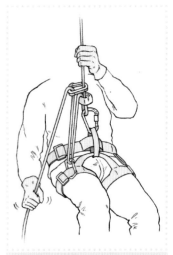

FIGURE 38
Increasing the friction when using a thin rope

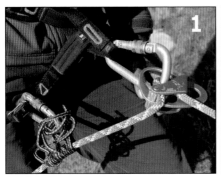

Protecting an abseil with a prusik: **1** Prusik attached to leg loop, **2** Abseil device extended from the harness.

Stopping mid-abseil

STOPPING MID-ABSEIL

If you have to stop mid-abseil and need both hands, do not rely solely on the French prusik to hold you. Take the rope around your waist and wrap it around a leg (see photo opposite) or tie it off in front of the abseil device with two half hitches.

RETRIEVING AN ABSEIL ROPE

Do not stand directly underneath the abseil, move to the side. Separate and untangle the ropes before pulling them down, remove any knots, and make sure you are pulling the correct one! To remember which rope to pull and to remove twists, clip an extender from the harness to the rope to be pulled as you abseil. Check before the last person abseils that the ropes will come down and that they are not going to become jammed in a crack. If the rope is difficult to move, extend the abseil station. Pull ropes running through a sling slowly, otherwise glazing damage can occur to the rope.

If the rope remains stuck, try pulling at a different angle or pull heavily on both and then release the one you do not want to pull; the recoil of the un-weighted rope may free it. Finally get more people to pull. If the rope remains stuck and both ends of the rope are at the bottom ascend up on both ropes. If one end has disappeared part way up the rock you can rope solo back to the anchors (see Rescues, page 127).

MULTI-PITCH CLIMBING

Think of multi-pitch routes as a lot of single pitches stacked on top of each other and they become less intimidating. Carry extra equipment, because some will be left at the belay. On remote routes consider carrying a small bag with a first aid kit, some snacks, a small bivvy bag, a flashlight, and possibly shoes for the descent. Alternatively carry a small first aid kit taped under your helmet.

CREATING A BELAY ON MULTI-PITCH ROUTES

The same principles as for a single pitch climb apply. Solid rock, equalized and independent anchors, tight on the belay. Can you see the climber? Is it best to sit or stand? What if? You must also consider the forces that a leader falling on the next pitch will create. The movement of the belayer upward absorbs some of the force. However, it may be prudent to prevent an upward pull if there is a roof or rock spike above. Whether a direct or indirect belay is used depends on the difficulty of the climb, the terrain, and whether you are swapping leads.

Single point anchor—An alternative to attach to belay anchors is to equalize them to a single point using slings and attach your climbing rope to the slings via a clove hitch (see Fig. 35). This single anchor point can then be used to direct or semi-direct belay a second. It becomes easy to clip the second into the belay without having to swap ropes around.

Eating a whole elephant is a daunting proposition, so do it in tiny bits. Think about each pitch not the whole route. (Arc en Ciel, Saleve, France.)

Swapping ropes when the belay has been set up using rope—On reaching the belay stance, the lead climber attaches the ropes to the anchors. If the second is not leading the next pitch, take their ropes underneath and through the middle of each anchor rope and into the anchor's crab. Alternatively clip another crab into the protection underneath the existing crabs. The leader's ropes will then be on top when leaving the stance.

Hanging stance—May be required on a steep climb or at the base of a sea cliff. Do not struggle with one hand; instead clip into a good anchor and take tension on it while you create the belay. Equalize the anchors to a single point using slings to move changing ropes more easily. To belay a second, clip their rope through a belay anchor or a separate runner above you. To avoid twisting the rope ensure that this crab is perpendicular to the rock.

STORING THE ROPES
A few seconds spent sorting the ropes will save time on the next pitch.

- Place the rope where it will cleanly feed to the belay device.
- Ensure the lead climber's ropes do not run over other ropes.
- Pull the ropes through so the leader's end is on top.
- On a hanging or restricted stance, lay the climbing ropes across your anchor ropes, a rock spike or slings with progressively shorter loops. Attach loops of rope to an HMS crab using a "truckers" hitch.
- When abseiling into a small or a hanging stance, e.g., just above the sea, store the climbing rope in a light rope bag or a backpack. Ensure both lead ends are at the top of the pile and the second's ends are also handy.

On a hanging or restricted stance, lay the climbing ropes across your anchor ropes. (Climber: Babs Jongmans.)

MULTI-PITCH ABSEILING

When the route down is not obvious, save time by lowering someone to check it—if it is incorrect, belay them back up.

Repeated abseils down a long climb require you to be organized and have a method for rapidly attaching yourself and your partner to each belay. Achieve this by lark's footing a sling to the abseil loop on your harness and tying a few knots to create attachment points along its length—a "cow's tail." Then attach your abseil device to the first loop on the cow's tail or into your harness abseil loop.

The first person abseils protected by a Prusik. When the belay is reached, they attach to it via the cow's tail, remove the belay device, and tie the ends into the belay. Finally, they protect the second by holding on to the ropes. When the second has arrived they pull the ropes down feeding the one being pulled through the belay ready for the next abseil. If it is windy take the ropes down, loosely fed into a backpack that is hung from the abseil device.

A multi-pitch belay. To prevent the possibility of a FF2 on to the belay on the next pitch, place a runner immediately after leaving the belay, irrespective of the difficulties. If you can't find a runner, clip an extender into one of the anchor points, but remember the force on that runner is almost doubled. (Climbers: M. Rose and S. Quinton.)

Runner placed before leaving the belay

Rope in a backpack

EMERGENCY DEVICES FOR ABSEILING

If you have only one device between two, pull the belay device back up after the first has abseiled or create a carabiner brake (see Fig. 39). Always use two opposing open gate crabs to create the platform (the collars on locking crabs can obstruct) and attach the crabs to your harness with a locking crab. If this does not create enough friction, set up another carabiner brake and link the two together using a wired nut. Ensure the rope passes over the back bar of the crab and not the gate. An Italian hitch can be used, but it twists the rope. If you have to use it with double ropes, put the Italian hitches on separate crabs and extend one away from the other. If this method is used the person with the abseil device should go last to remove the kinks.

FIGURE 39
Using crabs to create a carabiner brake

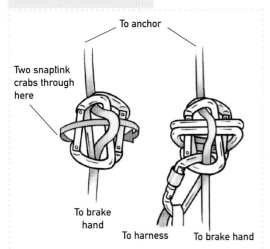

To anchor

Two snaplink crabs through here

To brake hand

To harness

To brake hand

ABSEILING WITH DIFFERENT DIAMETER ROPES

Some longer routes are climbed using a single rope with the second dragging a 7-9mm rope for abseiling. Be aware that the thinner rope stretches more and travels through the device faster. To avoid a disaster, make sure the thicker rope goes through the abseil anchor and that the bottom ends of the rope are tied together. Alternatively use the following technique.

ABSEILING ON A DAMAGED ROPE

When one rope has been damaged (isolate the damage with an overhand knot or alpine butterfly), abseil on the good rope and use the damaged one to pull the ropes down (see Fig. 40a). This method can also be used for abseiling with a Grigri, as well as for abseiling on a thin and thick rope. Take great care pulling the ropes down; should they become jammed, you will have to use the damaged rope or the thin line to climb back up the cliff.

ABSEILING PAST A KNOT

Occasionally two ropes are joined for accessing a big sea cliff, or to escape from a route (see Fig. 42). To pass the knot it is essential that the French prusik is above the abseil device and on an extender (but within reach). When you are close to the knot, stop and put your weight on to the French prusik; remove your belay plate and replace it below the knot. Release the French prusik so that your weight comes onto the belay device (take care that the prusik does not come up against the knot). If you cannot release it, stand in a prusik placed between the abseil device and the knot, and release the stuck one.

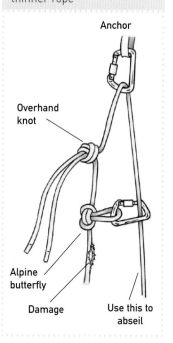

FIGURE 40
Abseiling on a damaged or thinner rope

Anchor

Overhand knot

Alpine butterfly

Damage

Use this to abseil

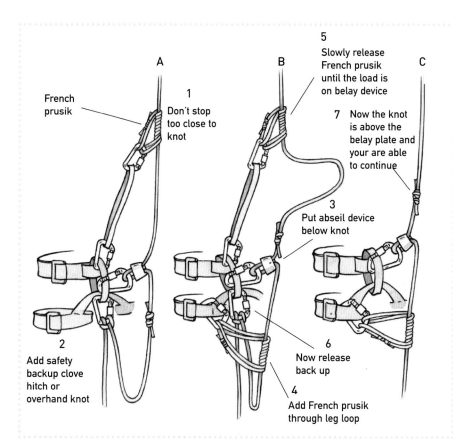

A

French prusik

1
Don't stop too close to knot

2
Add safety backup clove hitch or overhand knot

B

5
Slowly release French prusik until the load is on belay device

3
Put abseil device below knot

6
Now release back up

4
Add French prusik through leg loop

C

7
Now the knot is above the belay plate and your are able to continue

FIGURE 41
Abseiling past a knot (numbers 1–7 show the correct chronological order of this process)

CONSIDERATIONS FOR SPORT CLIMBING

Sport climbs are the ultimate convenience climbs—pre-placed bolts and an anchor point at the top of the climb from which to lower off mean that all you require to climb are 12-15 quick draws and a single 60m (197ft) rope.

FALLING OFF AND GETTING BACK TO THE ROCK

Sport climbing allows you to push your limits in relative safety, but this means you are more likely to fall. When the leader can reach the rope running to the belayer, pull down on it and pulley yourself back to your high point as the belayer takes in the slack rope.

When the leader is hanging in space, use the strenuous technique "snapping." It requires good teamwork—the leader pulls up on their rope and lets go; the belayer simultaneously takes in. The belayer should sit on the rope. As the climber releases the rope the belayer sits further down, takes in as he stands and repeats the process.

THE ART OF FALLING

Falling correctly needs practice and can improve your short-term confidence to climb away from runners, but it is debatable whether practising falling off will remove your long-term fear of it. It is however, useful to take a quick fall on a route that you are about to attempt if nervousness is a problem.

Sport climbs are the ultimate convenience climbs. (Photo: Mike "Twid" Turner. Climber: Glenda Huxter.)

Fifty years ago a leader fall was a serious proposition, but more reliable equipment means that climbers frequently fall off and live to tell the tale. (Climber: Trevor Massiah.)

To save your rope, practice falling at the top of a climb, which leaves more rope to absorb the forces causing less wear on your rope.

A calm, supple body is less susceptible to injury so fall gracefully, in control, facing the rock, and avoiding tumbling. If you fall on a slab, slide down on your feet, pushing away with the hands. Keep your legs bent and apart to act as shock absorbers. Do not freeze up or go limp. Keep the rope running cleanly; a rope wrapped around a leg can tip you upside down. Grabbing the rope as you fly past can result in rope burns, but once you are comfortable with falling off, hold the rope in front of you to stabilize the landing.

LOWERING OFF A SPORT CLIMB

Most sports routes have a "lower off" at the top, consisting of two bolts and possibly a linking chain or sling (see Fig. 42). If the lower off is a sling, do not—under any circumstances—lower from the sling itself, but use a crab. Before climbing, ensure there is enough rope to lower back down, tie a knot in the end, or tie the belayer into the rope. If you have not left enough rope to lower, tie another rope to it and bypass the knot using a second belay device (still on the original belayer's harness). This is easier if there is a third person to help or the lead climber can take their weight off the rope.

When the climb is so steep that you cannot easily retrieve the quick draws, clip one from your harness to the climbing rope to remain closer to the cliff. Be careful removing the last quick draws, because you could take your belayer with you as you swing out. If you need maximum rope length to lower, clip into the bolts using two quick draws from the abseil loop, or a single sling and a screwgate crab. Take a few meters of slack and attach to your harness using a clove hitch. Untie from the end of the rope and thread it through a lower off point. Re-tie into the end and detach the rope from your harness. Take the tension on the rope, checking everything is correct and your belayer is awake, then remove the quick draws or sling and be lowered down.

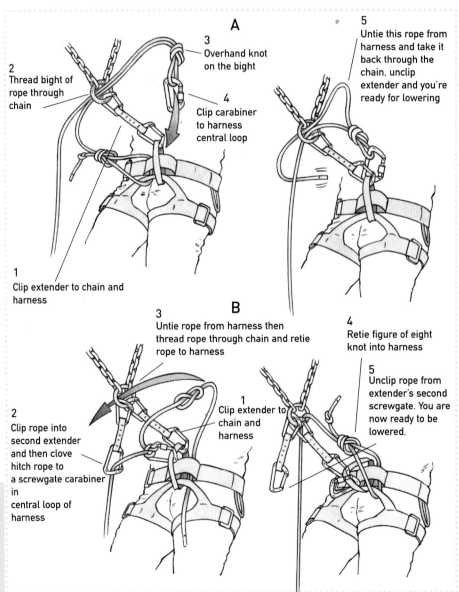

A

3
Overhand knot on the bight

2
Thread bight of rope through chain

4
Clip carabiner to harness central loop

5
Untie this rope from harness and take it back through the chain, unclip extender and you're ready for lowering

1
Clip extender to chain and harness

B

3
Untie rope from harness then thread rope through chain and retie rope to harness

4
Retie figure of eight knot into harness

2
Clip rope into second extender and then clove hitch rope to a screwgate carabiner in central loop of harness

1
Clip extender to chain and harness

5
Unclip rope from extender's second screwgate. You are now ready to be lowered.

FIGURE 42
Two methods for lowering from a sports climbs (the numbers 1–5 show the correct chronological order for each method)

CONSIDERATIONS FOR BOTTOM ROPING

Here the rope runs through a belay station at the top of the cliff, and back to the bottom where the climber and the belayer are situated. The climber ascends the route to the attachment point and is lowered back to the ground. This method is commonly used for practicing a climb, and for novices.

The same factors regarding belays apply to the setting up of a bottom rope, i.e., solid rock, equalized and independent anchors, and direction of pull. Avoid cams, because the weighting and un-weighting of the rope may cause them to walk deeper into cracks (see Fig. 43).

The attachment point for the climbing rope should be two locking crabs, with their gates pointing downward (vibrations can undo the gates), and in the same direction. Twin crabs are not for safety, but to reduce rope wear by increasing the diameter that the rope is running over.

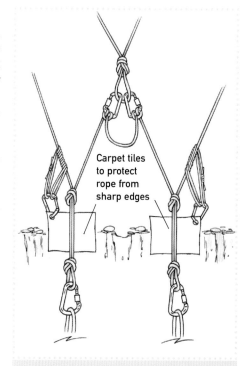

Carpet tiles to protect rope from sharp edges

FIGURE 43

A hitching rail creates a flexible attachment system. A pre-stretched rope reduces wear and tear on edges. Clove hitches on the central anchors provide independent adjustments of the ropes. The attachment rope for the climbing rope must be over the edge.

Bottom roping is a great way to start climbing.

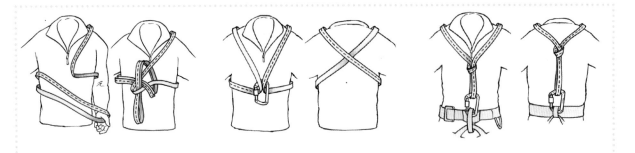

FIGURE 44
An improvised chest harness

OTHER CONSIDERATIONS
Below are a few techniques that do not fit into other categories.

IMPROVISED CHEST HARNESSES
With large or small people, or when wearing a large backpack, there is a possibility that the sit harness could end up around the knees, or you could end upside down after a fall. When either a full body harness or a chest harness is not available, you can create a chest harness using a sling (see Fig. 44).

COILING ROPES
Daisy chaining and lap coiling are the preferred methods for coiling ropes because they reduce kinks (see Fig. 45). The circular mountaineer's coil introduces kinks into the rope, but when divided between two people it can be used to carry an injured person.

FIGURE 45
Lap coiling and daisy chaining

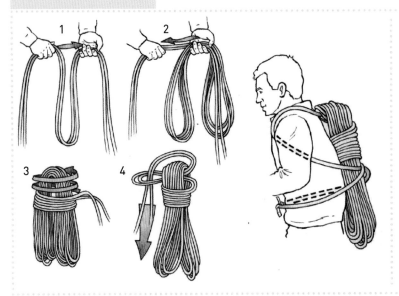

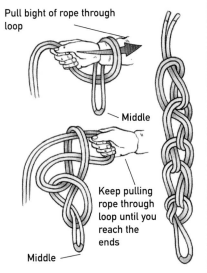

SCRAMBLING

Scrambling is the link between mountain walking and rock climbing. It is potentially a very hazardous activity involving efficient movement in exposed terrain. It is the ultimate test of the "what if?" question: what is the probability of a fall and what are the consequences? If your answer is something other than "nothing will happen," then choose the fastest and most appropriate course of action to avoid an accident. The efficient scrambler is someone who can choose the correct technique at any given moment and change between options quickly.

Scrambling is excellent preparation for alpine climbing, whatever grade you climb. You must make judgements continuously, not only about the terrain ahead, but also about both your ability and your partners'. Safety often hinges on good communication between the team.

Scrambling takes place away from paths and rock walls, in secluded places that are often sanctuaries for rare plants and animals. You must therefore give great thought to every footstep and leave the delicate plant life alone.

EQUIPMENT

The scramble's grade (see Appendix, page 355) dictates the amount of equipment carried. This varies, from a 30m (98ft) single rope tied around the waist, a sling, and an HMS crab, to a full rock climbing rack and a 50m (164ft) single rope. Scrambling terrain is often on wet and dirty rock, therefore, good footwear is essential—a fairly stiff boot with no lateral twist. Leather gloves will improve your grip on the rope when moving together and short roping scrambles.

> **A CLIMBING RACK FOR DIFFICULT SCRAMBLES**
>
> One set of nuts
> Hexs 4-8
> Friends 1,2,3
> 2 240cm slings
> 2 120 slings
> 4 extenders
> 4 screwgate crabs
> 2 HMS crabs

A scramble is what a rock climber would call easy climbing ground. (M. Rose)

STAYING SAFE

A variety of rope-work techniques and skills are required to make scrambling a fluid progression up the route. Those used will depend on the type of terrain covered. Within a single scramble they will range from specific rock climbing skills to shortening the rope between you and your partner for moving together. It is common for two or three scramblers to be attached to one rope.

SCRAMBLING TERRAIN

Techniques are divided into the different standards of terrain encountered on a scramble.

WALKING TERRAIN

Ask yourself, "What are the consequences of a fall and what is the terrain like ahead? Is there more walking after the difficult step or do I need to put a rope on? Do I need to get harnesses out or can I just attach the rope around the waist? What are mine and my partner's abilities? Are we both stable on our feet? Are we climbers or walkers?" Your answers to these questions should tell you if you can enter the next terrain.

EASY CLIMBING TERRAIN

This terrain throws up many difficult and exposed steps where a slip is serious and spotting is no longer effective. You must start to use the rope and adopt a technique commonly called "short roping." Short roping is moving together unencumbered by protection on easy climbing ground. As soon as you are on

Walking terrain—a rope is not required, but you must be able to "spot" each other on a difficult step.

Easy climbing terrain—spotting alone is not enough. (Climbers: D. Williams and T. Massiah.)

ground that you would rather pitch, but decide to move on together and place protection, it becomes simu-climbing (see Alpinism, page 212).

Short roping helps to prevent falls happening and is the transition between walking and rock climbing. Moving together using short roping requires fluency, concentration, and a good body stance. It is a difficult skill to do smoothly and safely, and practice on non-dangerous terrain is essential. To the uninitiated it may seem dangerous to tie yourself to others, but to an experienced practitioner it improves safety. It requires the leader to be in position at all times, ready to hold a slip. If the leader is unstable or unbalanced, your partner(s) must either be stationary or on non-slip ground.

ATTACHING TO THE ROPE

The number of people on one rope depends on the terrain, weather conditions, size and weight, and skill and experience, although generally three is the maximum.

The most versatile method is for the most experienced scrambler to tie into the rope and take chest coils (see Fig. 46), leaving two or three arm lengths to the next scrambler. The last scrambler ties into the end of the rope and takes a coil around their chest to allow for extension on difficult sections. The second scrambler is attached two arm spans in front of the rear scrambler via a loop created using an alpine butterfly or an overhand knot. Tie the second scrambler into the rope loop using a rewoven overhand knot. This method of attaching two scramblers allows tension to be given to them individually or together.

An alternative method of using the rope is the "V" attachment—each scrambler attached to an end. It is easier to maintain tension on individual scramblers and can also be used in descent. Problems can occur when descending broken ground, as the scramblers must take different lines to avoid any rope obstruction. It is also more difficult to use when traversing.

Attaching two people to the rope. (1) Alpine butterfly and re-threaded overhand. (2) Normal tie-in. (D. Williams and T. Massiah).

FIGURE 46
Shortening the rope

SHORTENING THE ROPE

The full length of the rope is rarely required for scrambling—tie into the end and coil the excess around your chest (see Fig. 46). Tie the coils off; don't just drape them over your head. Make them long enough to reach 10cm (4in) above the top of your harness and remember to wear coils on the outside of your backpack to enable you to drop them quickly. Taking three separate sets of coils allow you to drop one without the bother of retying the remaining coils (the disadvantage of this is the number of knots at your waist).

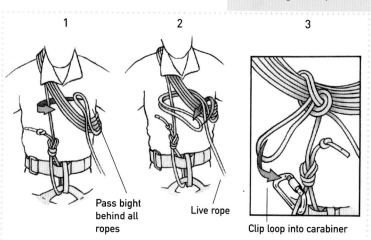

1   2   3

Pass bight behind all ropes

Live rope

Clip loop into carabiner

HOLDING THE ROPE

When moving together, the leader has to hold the rope leading to the scramblers behind, adjusting the tension continuously to keep the rope taut. There are a number of methods:

No coils in your hand—When holding the rope on its own, always have the hand with the little finger closest to the downhill scramblers. It is possible to tie a slipknot in the rope, and hold the rope just in front of the hitch (it is easily removed). This is useful when it is cold or for those with small hands.

Coils in your hand -Take coils in one hand and lock them off by taking the final loop around the rear of the coils and into the hand (see bottom photos), or lap the rope across the palm with one final twist.

Both of these methods allow the other hand to be free, but do not allow the coils to be released under tension.

Holding the rope with a slipknot

Holding the rope without coils. (Climbers: D. Williams and T. Messiah.)

Locking coils

Using both hands—Take the coils in one hand, but hold the rope to the climbers in the other. In this way the tension can always be released if a direct belay is required. The disadvantage is that both hands are occupied.

MOVING TOGETHER/SHORT ROPING

At all times ask, "Can I hold my partner should they slip?" If you cannot hold them, do something about it! If there are three people, place the weakest member next to the leader, and try to always be above them.

On traverses, carry the rope in the downhill hand and stay directly above your partner whenever possible. The leader should be on the uphill side of the rope, and for the rope running from the last scrambler to be on the downhill side of the next scrambler.

When there are two scramblers behind you on a traverse, hold the rope between them. If you cannot be above them, then stay as close together as the terrain allows.

When you come to a section where you or your partner cannot maintain a stable base, stop. Climb over the difficulty and then continue as before. Do not run out long lengths of rope unless you are going to set up a belay, because communication becomes difficult and there is more stretch in the rope.

The following practices minimise the chances of being pulled off-balance:

- Keep your movements regular.
- Keep your arm slightly bent to act as a clutch and absorb some of the initial force in a slip.
- When this is not possible, take the rope in and pay it out as your pace varies.
- Be alert for spikes and boulders around which to loop the rope.
- Look ahead for problem steps and possible belays.

MORE DIFFICULT CLIMBING TERRAIN

You are now no longer confident a slip can be held while moving together, and the consequences of a fall are serious.

The first step is to attach the scramblers to the rock—by wrapping the rope around a boulder, draping the rope between the scramblers over a spike, or clipping the rope between them into a belay. The leader then climbs the pitch, belayed or not, placing protection if needed. Once the leader has climbed the difficult pitch, the seconds must be belayed up the climb. This can vary from a full rock climbing belay (usually a direct one) to a braced stance (see Belays, below). When the section is long or the consequences of a fall are more serious, e.g., a fall would leave the seconds hanging in space, consider placing runners in the pitch, even if the leader does not need them.

When traveling together on an easy ridge, the last climber on the rope can take a few coils in their hands. This gives them a few seconds' thought before deciding which side of the ridge to step if someone falls. You may need to lengthen the rope between the climbers. When the ridge becomes more difficult it is more appropriate to pitch it, or to move together with runners between the leader and climbers.

BELAYS

When choosing a belay try to match the seriousness of the situation to the type of belay used and the distance the climbers are away from you. Apply the same factors for selecting anchors and creating a belay as you would when rock climbing—solid anchors, the direction of forces, tension on the belay, and your ability to communicate with the climbers.

More difficult scrambling terrain. (Climbers: D. Williams and T. Massiah.)

BELAYS ONLY REQUIRING THE ROPE

The following techniques are useful, but if there is a chance the scramblers may have to be lowered back down, swing into space, or may both slip at the same time, do not use them:

- Braced behind a boulder—if the boulder is low down, sit behind it and use a waist belay.
- Direct belay—simply pull the rope around a spike or boulder. Whether you will need to be attached depends on the size of the stance.
- Use a combination belay—take the rope around a boulder and waist belay.

BELAYS WHEN A FALL IS SERIOUS

The size of the stance determines whether you are also attached to the belay.

- Place a sling through a thread, or over a spike/boulder, and direct belay to it using an Italian hitch or Reverso.
- Place runner(s), equalize them with slings, and direct belay to it using an Italian hitch or Reverso.

It is often difficult to determine how the force created in a fall will be transmitted to the belay/belayer, especially on a ridge, because the climber may

Above: Waist belaying braced behind a boulder—this method is not to be used when there is a chance of a serious fall.
Left: Direct belay on a flake—again, this is not suitable when there is a chance of a serious fall. (Climber: T. Massiah.)

slip and pendulum sideways. If there is a traverse ensure you are above it, that you have placed runners to protect it, or that there are boulders and spikes to catch a falling climber.

When the climbers arrive at the stance attach them individually via a locking crab, or by clipping the rope between them into the belay or over a spike to counterbalance them.

DESCENDING

The method you use depends on the size and experience of the scramblers plus the steepness and condition of the descent. This may vary, from moving together to a reversal of rock climbing to abseiling. Choose the easiest line for the leader to protect the scrambler below (this may not necessarily be the same as the easiest line for the scramblers). Decide whether you can hold a slip, need to lower the lead scramblers down the section, or even to abseil. Inform the lead scramblers as often as necessary when you want them to stop for you to place your feet on difficult ground. Ensure you maintain rope tension. If the ground is difficult, place runners to protect the rear scrambler.

Down climbing facing in, feels secure, but the terrain below looks harder than it is. Facing out is faster, but less secure. (1) Using natural terrain. (2) Placing a runner.

VIA FERRATA

Lliterally translated this means "iron way," or "climbing-path" from the German version Klettersteig. Via ferrata are mountain routes equipped with fixed cables, ladders, and bridges. They break just about every rule of aesthetic mountaineering, but they provide an opportunity to move through spectacular and often extremely exposed alpine scenery with minimal equipment. They are popular all over Europe, and vary from a few cables to help walkers ascend a steep section of rock, to complete walkways and ladders.

Routes are generally technically straightforward for a competent climber, but they are steep, exposed, and can be very strenuous—you may even come across snow on some! It may be appropriate for some parties to carry a rope, to be able to direct belay nervous partners or set up a pulley system for tired partners.

In the Dolomite Mountains, Italy, routes are graded according to their difficulty. Grade one usually involves nothing more than an assisted walk; grade five demands serious climbing skills. Another grading system uses a number (1 to 5) indicating the technical difficulty and a letter (A, B, or C) indicating the overall commitment and seriousness

Are Via ferrata safe? As with all in-situ equipment don't blindly trust any of the metal. Take a look at www.viaferrata.org.

ARE VIA FERRATA SAFE?

There are some dangers that cannot be avoided:

- Loose rock
- Corroded or missing ladder rungs or fixings—test suspicious rungs before placing all of your weight on to them
- Damaged wire ropes—wear tough gloves to protect your hands.
- Protection on older routes—ask locals, or consider carrying a rope and some climbing gear
- The weather—carry waterproof clothing if rain is likely
- Lightning—in a thunderstorm get away from iron ladders and wire ropes—this may mean abseiling off!

EQUIPMENT

A helmet is advisable, footwear should not be soft-soled, gloves are useful, and a harness and shock absorbing system are vital. Take a sweater, first aid kit, water, and a flashlight.

There are no circumstances in which you should attempt a Via ferrata using climbing slings without a KISA (Kinetic Impact Shock Absorber), as a fall can shock-load the slings beyond their breaking strength (see Fig 47).

There are a number of shock absorbers on the market, produced by Mammut, Camp, and Petzl. They comprise a length of dynamic rope threaded through a KISA, which leads to a rope or tape Y, with a Klettersteig carabiner at the end of each arm. They offer protection if both arms of the lanyard are clipped into the cable. Older metal shock absorbers suffer from a major limitation—it is essential to be clipped into one arm only if you fall. If both arms are clipped on to the cable and you fall, the energy absorber won't work. If using this type, take extra care when moving past an intermediate anchor point.

Some lanyards also have a short third arm, which allows you to rest on steep sections. Check there is a "K" in a circle on the spine of the crab—if there is an "H" in a circle, it is an HMS carabiner for belaying and is not designed for Via ferrata use. Most modern lanyards are lark's footed on to the abseil loop of the harness.

TECHNIQUE

The basic technique for using the shock absorber is outlined in Fig. 47. Both carabiners should be attached to the cable at all times unless you are

A Petzl Scorpio Vertigo KISA—you should never attempt a Via ferrata without one.

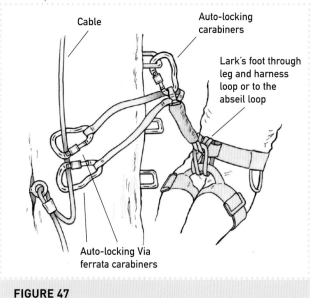

Cable

Auto-locking carabiners

Lark's foot through leg and harness loop or to the abseil loop

Auto-locking Via ferrata carabiners

FIGURE 47
Basic technique for Via ferrata

passing an anchor point. If you fall on a horizontal section, you won't go anywhere. If you fall on a vertical or diagonal section, you will slide down to the last anchor! The "shock absorber" will keep you, the rope, and the cable from receiving too great a shock. If you become tired take a rest using a shorter sling and carabiner lark's footed on to your harness.

SOLVING PROBLEMS—RESCUES

First aid is life saving when administered during the first hour; your rescue skills may help prevent a disaster. The cliff environment is always changing and the belays are never the same, so following procedures like a fire drill will not always work. The following rescue scenarios and their solutions are examples of the tools, rather than the only way, to solve a problem. These techniques are seldom used and regular practice is important to maintain efficiency. For simplicity, all the rescues are described using a single rope; double ropes can make a rescue easier, but they are a lot thinner, stretch more, and prusiks don't grip them as efficiently. A knife is not usually necessary, but rope tangles can occur so carry one, even if it is only for cutting slings to use as abseil tat. Instructors working with groups of young people should refer to *Rock Climbing for Instructors* (2001), by the author.

ACCIDENT AVOIDANCE

Any rescue will be easier by considering the following:

- Everyone should know what to do if they lose contact with the rock.
- Choose stances that allow communication.
- Extend runners to reduce friction.
- Pitches that end with loose rock put the second at greater risk.
- Maintain your climbing and rescue equipment in good condition.
- Keep the rope(s) tidy.
- Create a simple belay and belay diligently.
- Remove all jewelery.
- Have first aid training.

AT THE BELAY

Ensure that you arrive at belays with enough equipment to carry out a rescue—two or three prusiks, a long sling, and several crabs and extenders should be enough. Belay anchors equalized to a single point will make life simpler in a rescue. Alternatively, take the second's rope through a high crab when you think they may fall off—this allows a pulley system to be set up easily, but it does make an assisted hoist more difficult, and the fallen climber will only be on one runner.

PRUSIK CORD

- 1.3m of 5 or 6mm soft kernmantle cord is best. Thinner cord will melt, but thicker cord will not grip the rope in wet conditions.
- New cord is slippery, so carefully roll it around on the floor to "rough it up."
- The ideal number of prusik loops is three, but two will suffice.
- Shorter prusiks maintain the tension on the rope better than longer ones. Elongate them with a sling.
- Tie prusiks with a double fisherman's or an overhand knot pulled firmly.

WARNING

A loaded rope is cut very easily; when practicing, consider using a separate rope to protect the victim.

IN AN ACCIDENT

An accident will not become a tragedy if the question, "What happens if?" is asked at every stage. Tie off the belay plate, take a deep breath, and stay calm. Look, listen, shout for help if necessary, and think carefully. Can you rescue the victim while attached to the belay? Is the injured climber conscious? Do you need to give first aid? Is it quicker to go for help? Are there any climbers on an adjacent route? It is always quicker and easier to descend rather than ascend with a victim, even if it means tying two ropes together and coming back another day to retrieve them.

TOOLS

PRUSIK KNOTS

Prusik knots are friction hitches that grip the rope. There are many useful variations:

- **The Klemheist is difficult to release under load, but grips the rope well** (see Fig. 48). It is used when failure to grip the rope is disastrous. It is not easily released when a climber's weight is on it.

- **The French prusik can be released under load** (autoblocs—see Fig. 49). These are essential for many rescues, but use with care because they can release very easily.

- **The Mariner hitch is a prusik that can be untied when loaded** (see Fig. 50).

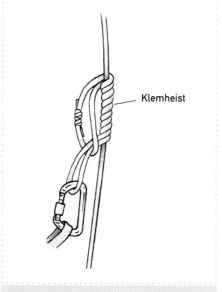

Klemheist

FIGURE 48 The Klemheist. More turns increase the grip. It can be tied using cord or tape.

FIGURE 49
French prusik (marchard knot). To release it when loaded, push firmly on the end of the hitch furthest from the crab (do not pull the whole hitch). It can release if you grab hold of it.

FIGURE 50 Mariner hitch— a useful hitch for lowering someone past a knot when two ropes have been tied together. It can come undone if the tension is removed.

MECHANICAL DEVICES

Handled ascenders are essential for ascending long distances, but they are too big and heavy to be useful in rescues. The lightweight Wild Country Ropeman ascenders are becoming as much a part of climbing equipment as a nut key. However, mechanical devices have a major downside; they cannot be easily released under load, therefore ensure any ascender is not pushed hard up against any knot.

DESCENDING AND ASCENDING THE ROPE

Rapid descent of a rope is essential to reach an injured climber. Your strength, agility, and arm length dictate the distance between the prusik or ascender and your harness. Find out what this is before an accident!

With all methods (see Figs 51–3) of ascending it is prudent to attach the rope into your harness at frequent intervals, using a clove hitch or a figure of eight via a screwgate crab.

PRUSIKING DOWN A ROPE

This is the reverse of ascending, and although it requires practice, it is not described here.

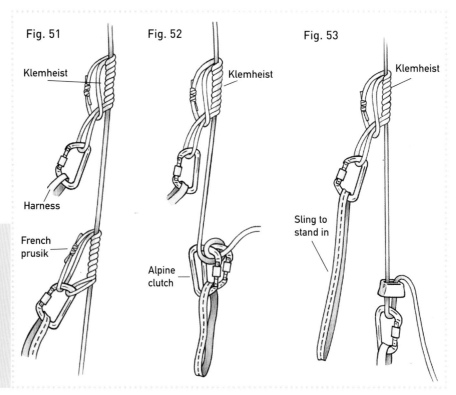

Fig. 51

Klemheist

Harness

French prusik

Fig. 52

Klemheist

Alpine clutch

Fig. 53

Klemheist

Sling to stand in

FIGURE 51 Klemheist and French prusik combination. The French prusik allows ease of foot movement.
FIGURE 52 The Alpine clutch and French combination.
FIGURE 53 Using a single friction hitch.

ABSEILING AND RE-ASCENDING

Abseiling is normally protected with a French prusik below the device. However, if you have to descend to an injured climber and re-ascend to the belay, it is best to abseil with a Klemheist attached above the abseil device. This makes it simple to remove the abseil device and attach a French prusik or garda hitch for the foot to ascend (see Figs 51 and 52).

SOLVING PROBLEMS—HOISTING

Hoisting is physically demanding and hard on your back so avoid it if you can, and never hoist without a pulley system. The practical efficiency of hoists is lower than the theoretical efficiency due to rope stretch and friction. If the second cannot unclip from the runners as they are hoisted, you will have to abseil and remove them beforehand.

SOLVING PROBLEMS—WITHOUT LEAVING THE BELAY

Figs 54–63 examine rescues where you do not leave the belay, all started off by tying off the belay device.

THE IN-SITU ASSISTED HOIST (Fig. 54)

The climber in difficulty can assist by pulling on a loop of their climbing rope. However, this system is limited by several factors; does the loop of rope reach the fallen climber? Are they within sight? Can the victim hear, understand, and carry out instructions? It is important that clear instructions are given about which rope to pull down on.

This is a strenuous method on steep rock. If a rest is required push the French prusik forward so that height gained is not lost. Once the climber has regained the rock, revert to normal belaying mode.

THE IN-SITU COUNTERBALANCE HOIST (Fig. 55)

The advantages of this hoist are that it works well on restricted stances, it is faster than any other method, and, if you must go to the victim, it is simple to change to a counterbalance abseil. However, it is only easily accomplished when the anchors are brought to a single point with a sling. The following is one possible solution to this situation:

Step 1 Attach a French prusik from the live rope to the anchors (if this cannot be done, attach a Klemheist to all the anchor ropes and link the French to this). Then transfer the load from the belay plate to the prusik.

Step 2 Put a screwgate crab on to the anchor.

Step 3 Pull a bight of rope from between the prusik and belay plate (leave the plate in place) and clip it into the screwgate crab. You are now in a counterbalance.

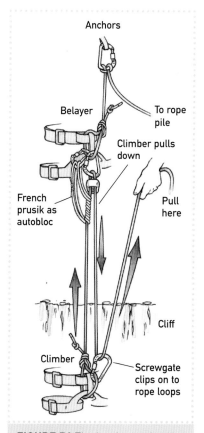

ALPINE CLUTCH

The alpine clutch is mainly used when there is a shortage of prusik loops. When used as part of a pulley system, it generates friction, reducing overall efficiency. It is difficult to release and lower a climber. It can be freed by clipping a rope between the original crabs, and pulling downward.

Anchors

Belayer

To rope pile

Climber pulls down

French prusik as autobloc

Pull here

Cliff

Climber

Screwgate clips on to rope loops

FIGURE 54 The in-situ assisted hoist

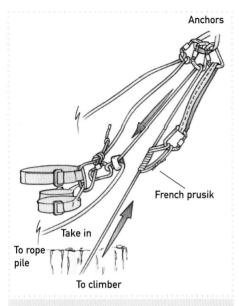

FIGURE 55
The in-situ counterbalance hoist

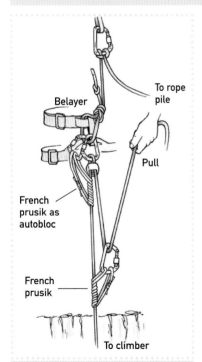

FIGURE 56
The in-situ unassisted hoist

Step 4 Lengthen your tie-in point to the anchor to give yourself enough room to move. Work yourself up the rope towards the anchors, leaning back to take the strain.

Step 5 Pull up on the live rope—if the climber decides to help, you may shoot backward!

THE IN-SITU UNASSISTED HOIST [Fig. 56]

The in-situ unassisted hoist, or "Z pulley," is used when the fallen climber cannot assist you. It is only useful when over a short distance.

This pulley has a 3:1 advantage, i.e., for every 3m (10 ft) pulled the victim gains 1m (3 ft). Note: the use of two crabs or a pulley on the lower prusik will reduce friction. When the bottom prusik reaches the belay device push it down the rope. To avoid losing precious height gained, push the upper French prusik down before taking the load.

AN IN-SITU RESCUE OF A CLIMBER ON A TRAVERSE [Fig. 57]

Belays at the end of traverses are not usually good at directing the forces to the belay. Add anchors to better direct the forces.

The following is one possible solution to this situation:

Step 1 Attach a French prusik from the belay or central loop to the loaded rope.

Step 2 Throw a loop of rope or the end of the rope, if available, to the victim to clip into the belay loop of their harness. This rope can then be attached to an Italian hitch.

Step 3 With or without the help of the victim, lower the loaded rope and pull the victim to below the belay.

Step 4 The victim may be able to climb to the belay. If the climber is hanging free, it is necessary to create a hoist.

Step 5 Retrieve the runners from the traverse. The easiest way is to be belayed along the traverse and back to the belay.

ESCAPE FROM THE BELAY

If the rope cannot be thrown to the climber or they are unconscious, you will have to escape the belay and go to them. This is more serious and care must be exercised to protect the rescuer and the victim—if the rescuer is injured there can be no rescue.

The simplest way to escape is to remove your harness, if it is not required.

To simplify rescues keep the belay anchors within reach. When you cannot reach the anchors, consider tying an alpine butterfly close to your central loop and use that as the belay loop. This allows you to easily and rapidly untie from the rope (see Fig. 58).

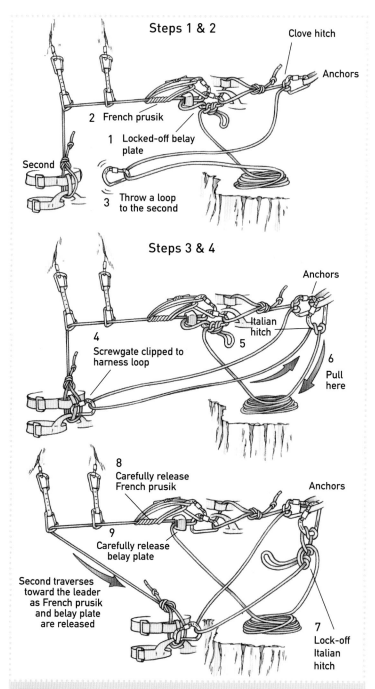

Steps 1 & 2

Clove hitch

Anchors

2 French prusik

1 Locked-off belay plate

Second

3 Throw a loop to the second

Steps 3 & 4

Anchors

Italian hitch

4 Screwgate clipped to harness loop

5

6 Pull here

8 Carefully release French prusik

Anchors

9 Carefully release belay plate

Second traverses toward the leader as French prusik and belay plate are released

7 Lock-off Italian hitch

FIGURE 57
In-situ rescue of a climber on a traverse (the numbers 1–9 show the chronological order for this process)

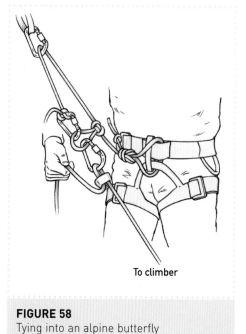

To climber

FIGURE 58
Tying into an alpine butterfly

IF THE BELAY IS SET-UP USING THE CLIMBING ROPE

Step 1 Lock-off the belay plate

Step 2 If the existing belay plate is not created from slings make a single-point belay using slings.

Step 3 Place a French prusik in front of the belay device and attach it to the new sling belay. If only one solid anchor can be reached use it, but improve it as soon as you can. If the anchor is suspect treat the belay as though you cannot reach it.

Step 4 Release the live rope slowly on to the French prusik. Remove the belay device and re-tie the rope into the sling belay using a tied-off Italian hitch.

Step 5 Clip into the belay using a cow's tail and remove the climbing rope.

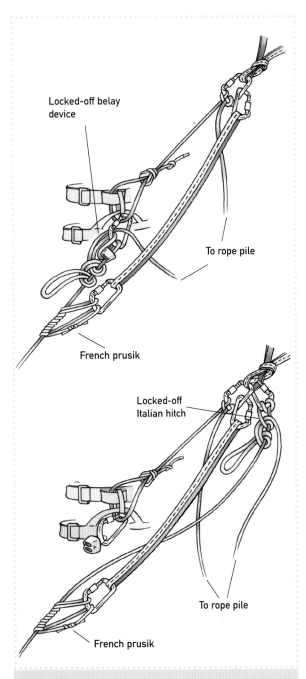

Locked-off belay device

To rope pile

French prusik

Locked-off Italian hitch

To rope pile

French prusik

FIGURE 59
Escape when belay anchors are within reach and set up with the climbing rope.

WHEN THE BELAY ANCHORS ARE WITHIN REACH

If you are using a direct belay created using slings, use the following method:

Step 1 Place a cow's tail on the harness and clip into the sling belay.

Step 2 Untie from the rope and release it from the belay.

WHEN THE BELAY ANCHORS ARE OUT OF REACH

Step 1 Attach a French prusik from the live rope to a Klemheist on all of the anchor ropes created with a 240cm sling with as many turns around the rope as possible (see Fig. 60).

Step 2 Lower the load onto the French prusik.

Step 3 Remove the belay plate and untie (protect yourself with a sling if necessary) from the rope. Leave any knots tied in the end of the rope in place.

There are now two options depending on whether you need all the rope to effect a rescue:

Option 1: You need the full length of the rope

Step 4 Set up another belay from the same anchors using slings.

Step 5 Attach the live rope to the sling belay with a tied off Italian hitch.

Step 6 Release the French prusik and lower the live rope onto the tied off Italian hitch.

Step 7 Remove the rope creating the belay.

Option 2: You don't need the full length of the rope

Step 4 Tie a knot in the anchor ropes below the Klemheist and attach the live rope to the knot with a tied off Italian hitch. If you cannot tie all the ropes together tie a knot in the rope you were attached to and attach the live ropes to the Klemheist.

Step 6 Release the French prusik and lower the live rope onto the tied off Italian hitch

ASSESSING THE SITUATION

What you do after escaping from the belay will depend on how it was set up, how injured the climber is, and how much is left of the climb. The following options are available:

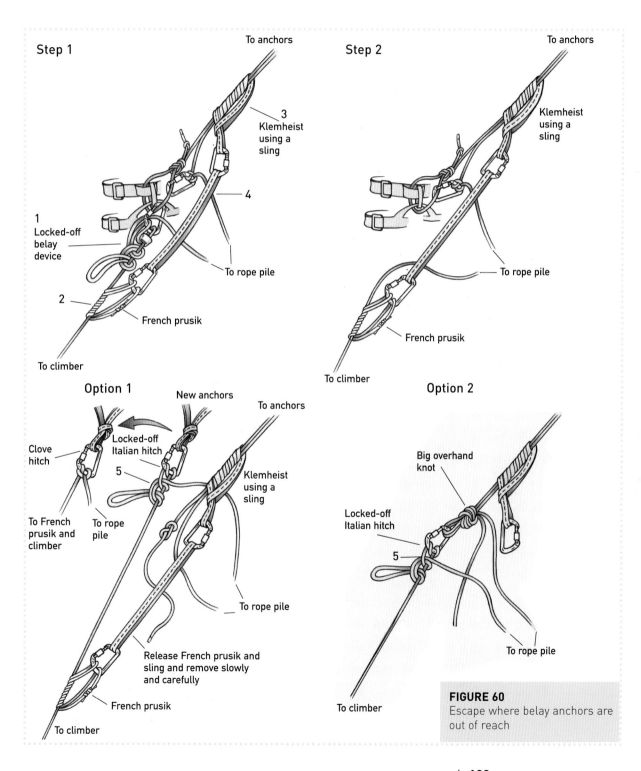

Step 1

To anchors

3
Klemheist using a sling

4

1
Locked-off belay device

2

French prusik

To rope pile

To climber

Step 2

To anchors

Klemheist using a sling

To rope pile

French prusik

To climber

Option 1

New anchors

Clove hitch

Locked-off Italian hitch

5

To French prusik and climber

To rope pile

To anchors

Klemheist using a sling

To rope pile

Release French prusik and sling and remove slowly and carefully

French prusik

To climber

Option 2

Big overhand knot

Locked-off Italian hitch

5

To rope pile

To climber

FIGURE 60
Escape where belay anchors are out of reach

123

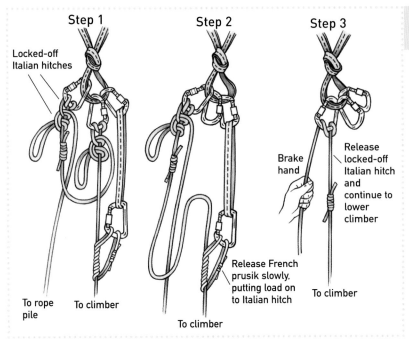

Step 1

Locked-off
Italian hitches

To rope
pile

To climber

Step 2

Release French
prusik slowly,
putting load on
to Italian hitch

To climber

Step 3

Brake
hand

Release
locked-off
Italian hitch
and
continue to
lower
climber

To climber

FIGURE 61
Passing a knot on a lower

LOWER THE INJURED CLIMBER

If the ground is less than 50m (164 ft) away, lower the victim to the ground. The rescuer can abseil and retrieve the rope later. Two ropes allow a longer lower, but require you to pass a knot during the lower (see Fig. 61).

Step 1 When the knot comes 1m (3 ft) away from the belay device attach a French prusik in front of the belay device and link it to the belay via a tied off Italian hitch.

Step 2 Lower the weight on to the French prusik and tie off the spare rope to the belay.

Step 3 Remove the belay device and replace it behind the knot, and then release the French prusik.

LOWER/COUNTERBALANCE ABSEIL

Counterbalance abseils are complex and can go badly wrong if you run out of rope and cannot reach the climber. In that case, abseil until you can create a new belay, attach the climber's rope to the new belay, then transfer the rope to the new belay and continue abseiling.

Step 1 Lower the injured climber almost half a rope length or one rope-length if two ropes are available.

Step 2 Place a French prusik on to the live rope (A).

Step 3 Remove the Italian hitch and replace the rope through the crab. Attach the abseil device from the instructor's harness to the dead rope. The instructor's weight counterbalances the climber (B).

Step 4 Transfer the French prusik from the live rope to protect the abseil (B).

If there is a big weight difference between the climbers, the Italian hitch can be left on the belay. Remember to tie a knot in the end of the abseil rope.

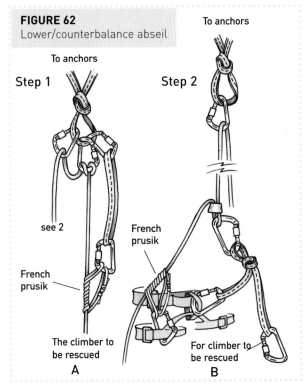

FIGURE 62
Lower/counterbalance abseil

To anchors

Step 1

To anchors

Step 2

see 2

French
prusik

French
prusik

The climber to
be rescued

French
prusik

For climber to
be rescued

A

B

RESCUING AN INJURED CLIMBER ON A TRAVERSE

If the victim cannot be reached with a rope (as in Fig. 57), escape the system. Protect yourself across the traverse, preferably with a mechanical ascender or two cow's tails.

Step 1 Escape the belay and traverse the rope until above the climber, preferably with a mechanical ascender or two cow's tails.

Step 2 Set up a new belay.

Step 3 Transfer the loaded rope to the belay.

Once you are above the victim, set up a new belay, transfer them to it, return to your belay, dismantle it, and rope solo to the new belay. Then hoist or descend.

HOISTING

When descending is not an option, hoist the injured climber onto the belay stance (remember runners must be removed before an injured climber can be hoisted). Once out of the system it is much easier to create an efficient pulley. The actual hoist is the same as shown in Fig. 56.

Step 1 Place a French prusik in front of the tied-off Italian hitch and attach it to a crab in the belay.

Step 2 Remove the Italian hitch and put the rope through a Klemheist in front of the French prusik.

Step 3 Attach the dead rope to the Klemheist via two crabs or, even better, a pulley to reduce friction. Pull. If the climber is difficult to hoist, try attaching the rope to your harness with an Italian hitch and use your leg muscles to pull.

When resting, or moving the lower prusik back down the rope, always push the prusik forward so that you do not lose any height gained.

IMPROVING THE EFFICIENCY OF THE HOIST

The pulley system gives a theoretical physical advantage of 3:1. In reality this may not be enough if the person is heavy or there is friction. There are many ways of increasing the efficiency of a pulley (Fig. 63 shows two methods), but in reality increasing it beyond 6:1 makes any rescue such a slow proposition that it is not worth consideration.

ASSISTED ABSEIL

Once the injured climber has either been lowered or hoisted onto the belay stance you may want to abseil with them. Fig. 62 (B) shows the set up.

REMOVING THE WEIGHT FROM A ROPE TO UNTIE THE VICTIM

To transfer a climber dangling on a rope to a new belay, attach them to the belay and use the method in Fig. 64 (see page 126).

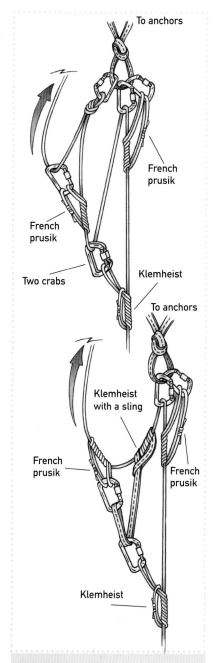

FIGURE 63
Two methods of improving the physical advantage of a hoist (A uses the rope and B uses a sling).

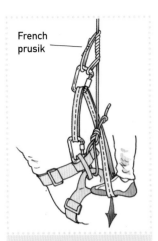

FIGURE 64
Removing a victim's
weight from the rope

French
prusik

FIGURE 65 Rescuing an
injured lead climber

RESCUING AN INJURED LEAD CLIMBER

Before attempting any rescue of a lead climber the security of the top anchor
must be beyond question (see Fig. 65).

Step 1 Create a solid ground anchor and attach to it using an Italian hitch.

Step 2 Escape the belay.

Step 3 Ascend to the injured climber. Because the rope is tensioned it is not
possible to use back-up knots. Therefore, use two Klemheists attached to
your waist. Unclip any anchors, but do not remove them; clip them into the
rope below you.

Step 4 Reinforce the top anchor or create a new anchor.

Step 5 Clip the injured climber to the new anchors using a mariner knot or an
Italian hitch tied off. If necessary attach a chest harness to the climber.

Step 6 Connect the rope you have ascended to the anchors.

Step 7 Descend and remove the bottom anchors.

Step 8 Ascend back to the anchors removing any gear on the way.

You now have a number of options:

Option 1: Lower the climber to the ground.

Option 2: Solo climb out and get help or hoist the climber.

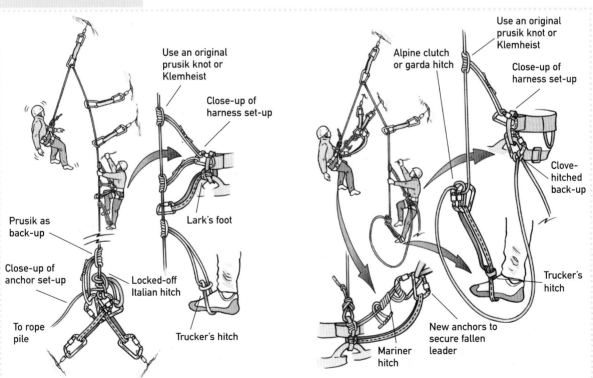

Use an original
prusik knot or
Klemheist

Close-up of
harness set-up

Prusik as
back-up

Lark's foot

Close-up of
anchor set-up

Locked-off
Italian hitch

To rope
pile

Trucker's hitch

Alpine clutch
or garda hitch

Use an original
prusik knot or
Klemheist

Close-up of
harness set-up

Clove-
hitched
back-up

Trucker's
hitch

Mariner
hitch

New anchors to
secure fallen
leader

SOLO CLIMBING

If the accident has occurred close to the top of the crag the quickest option may be to go to the top and get help. Rope soloing is the safest method to get out, but enough rope is needed to reach the top of the crag. The same system is used whether aid climbing or free climbing (see Fig. 66).

Step 1 Set up an upward pulling anchor and tie the rope into it with a double figure of eight or figure of nine knot.

Step 2 Tie into the other end of the rope.

Step 3 From the anchor, take 4m (13ft) of rope, tie a figure of eight knot, and clip it into your harness with a screwgate crab.

Step 4 Take 2m (7ft) of rope from the upward pulling anchor and tie a clove hitch.

Step 5 As you climb, clip the rope below your clove hitch into the placements.

Step 6 When you reach the clove hitch, readjust it to pay out the amount of slack you are comfortable with.

Step 7 When the clove hitch meets the figure of eight take a new 4m (13ft) and attach it to your harness then undo the original figure of eight. Continue climbing as before.

Clove hitch

Fig. 8.13 knot

To anchors

FIGURE 66
Solo climbing

AID CLIMBING

Aid climbing is simply pulling on gear rather than the rock. There are two methods:

1 Clean aid climbing using the placements found on a normal free climbing rack, maybe with the exception of sky-hooks and hand-placed pegs.

2 Full aid climbing using pegs, bolts, and a variety of other equipment that has to be hammered into the rock. Modern climbers do all they can to minimize using full aid climbing because it is time consuming and damages the rock.

EQUIPMENT FOR AID CLIMBING

This is not dissimilar to that found on any climber's rack, with a few additions and adaptations and a lot more of it.

Bandolier or chest rack—Bandoliers can get in the way; a proper chest racking system is worth the money.

Bolts—See Equipment, page 67.

Copper heads (Mashies)—Lumps of soft metal, usually aluminum or copper, that are smashed into shallow irregularities in the rock.

Cheater stick—A long sling with a thin piece of wood placed into it and taped up. Used for placing out-of-reach gear.

The author aid climbing in 210N National Park, U.S.

You will need a lot of gear to aid climb a big wall.

Daisy chains—Connect each etrier to your harness, connect you to a belay, and for many other jobs. They should be a minimum of an arm's span after lark's footing to your harness, and should preferably be different colors.

Etriers/aiders—Four- or five-rung webbing ladders. To get the correct length, hold the top at full arm's span and you should comfortably get your foot into the bottom rung. Different colors make it easier to select them among a background of colorful tapes and gear. A grab loop on the top will protect your hands from the punishment of grabbing crabs.

Fifi hooks—Sometimes attached to the top of each etrier, via a short sling, to enable easy retrieval of the etrier from below. However, they can unclip and notchless open-gate crabs are recommended for novices. A fifi hook or crab is also attached to your harness for easy resting.

Footwear—Choose a shoe with a stiffish, sticky mid-sole and a protective rand.

Harness—Plenty of gear loops and a haul loop on the rear. It needs to be comfortable, but less so if you carry a belay seat.

Helmet—Wear one!

Crabs—Any will do, but oval crabs don't shift on equipment when loaded.

Mechanical (handled) ascenders—Essential for serious ascending.

Pegs—Modern camming devices have largely removed the need for pegs, but this does mean that the ability to place them is disappearing. Most modern pegs are made from "hard" chrome-molybdenum steel, which has a better holding power, but cheaper soft steel pegs may still be found. Rust-free titanium pegs are available from Eastern European countries, but they only last for one or two placements. Pegs can be divided into two types:

1 Blades—Flat, with either a welded eye attached or a bent section with a hole. They come in various lengths and widths: "Lost arrows" and "Kingpins"; knife blades; The RURP (Realised Ultimate Reality Piton); and bird beaks. The thinner blades are for body weight loading only.
   The RURP is a paper-thin rectangle of metal with a cable attached. They have been superceded by bird beaks—2-4cm (0.8–1.6in) pieces of steel with a protruding, downward pointing blade at one end. On harder aid routes they are vital for thin cracks and you should carry at least a dozen.

2 Angles are bent to form a "V" profile. They come in a wide variety of sizes, from 1.5cm to 15cm "Bongs." "Z pitons" or "Leepers" fill the dimensions of large arrows up to standard angle. The extra bend provides greater grip and surface contact than conventional angles, which is important on soft rock and allows stacking of pegs (see Fig. 68).

Pegs can be divided into two types, blades and angles.

Peg hammers—A flat hammer for placing pegs and a blunt pick for removing them. Wooden shafts absorb vibration.

Protection—A wider variety of nuts and camming devices than normal is required and some cracks will require lots of the same size. Micro and small cams are required for peg scars. Sliding nuts are also very useful.

Ropes—Aid climbing is hard on ropes so they must be in good condition. A 50-60m (164–197ft) 11mm rope is best with a spare 11mm dynamic rope towed as a haul line and for abseiling (a dynamic is preferable in case the lead rope is damaged).

Sky hooks—Hard, steel hooks in a variety of shapes to grip ledges and holes. The Black Diamond Talons have three different hooks built into a tripod-style tool, essentially giving you doubles when you carry two of them. Attach the sling so that the lower end of the hook is pulled into the rock (see Fig. 67).

FIGURE 67
Black Diamond sky hook

Slings—Carry short 10-20cm (4–8in) slings (hero loops) attached to any fixed gear to save carrying extra crabs and allow maximum height to be gained with each step. Slings are also needed to "tie off" pegs that are not fully driven in. Carry plenty of medium and long slings for extending the rope over roofs.

Zip line—Some climbers use an additional "zip line"—a 7-9mm rope for hauling equipment, water, or food in the middle of an aid pitch. The zip line is then used to pull the haul line up the pitch.

Miscellaneous—Nut keys, sturdy enough to be hammered; a sack hauler; knee pads; and fingerless leather gloves. Two-way radios avoid shouting.

PLACING AIDING GEAR

To reduce the amount of gear carried, reach as high as possible to place each one. You may be able to carry less gear by reaching down to remove pieces from below as equipment runs out (back cleaning). If you do, leave every other piece in place just in case a piece fails as you stand up. Switching from aid climbing to free climbing is a mentally difficult adjustment, so do not be tempted to do it too soon.

USING SKY HOOKS

Carry sky hooks on the rear of your harness, as they are easily tangled in other gear, and don't carry them on one crab as they can be dropped. Start hooking from a solid runner and clip a crab full of hooks to each aider to minimize the chances of dropping them. Do not bounce test hook placements, as they can bend or snap the rock. Keep your weight on the lower hook as you transfer to the new hook otherwise it may pop off.

Sky hooks can come off or break small edges and pop out of old bolt holes. Prevent this by taping them down to stay in place. Try to avoid hammering sky hooks into bolt holes, because it increases the chance of them coming out and damages the hole for future placements. Because of the likelihood of placements coming out, wear safety glasses.

EXPERT TIP

Mike 'Twid' Turner
BMG/IFMGA guide
Twid turner@aol.com
www.sheersummits.com

"Many experienced rock climbers give up on the first day of a big wall. Ascending and basic aid climbing should be second nature before heading off. Try a one day route first and give yourself a large margin for completion."

It is often said that the three attributes of a good aid and big waller are a high pain threshold, a bad memory, and…I have forgotten the third. (Climber: Paul Donnithorne.)

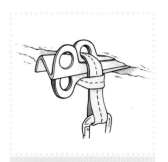

FIGURE 68
Stacked pegs using a leeper

PLACING PEGS

See also page 89. There are some peculiarities that must be mastered for aid climbing:

- Excessive hammering wastes energy; balance how well the pegs are embedded against how difficult it is to remove them.
- Learn the variety of ways to stack pegs.
- Stacked pegs are easily lost; clip them together with a sling before hammering (see Fig. 68).
- Stack blades back to back (see Fig. 68).
- Avoid stacking angles one on top of another (unless the inside one is much smaller), as they are difficult to separate. Stack them facing each other.
- Z pitons are very useful for stacking.
- Pegs can be placed alongside a nut. Clip the wedge to the peg. Whether you weight the peg or the wedge depends on the placement.

USING MASHIES

Place a mashey (piton) as you would a chock (wedge) and then hammer it using either the pick of the hammer, a blunt peg, or a blunt chisel. Start with an "X" pattern using angled strokes, then pound the right and left sides. To test the placement hit the bottom and top at a slight upward and downward angle. If the head rotates, do it again. If you smell a metallic odor it means the mashey has cracked. Check the rock immediately next to the placement. If the edges of the head are separated from the rock, it is suspect. If you come across one without the telltale crisscross pattern, be cautious.

LEADING AN AID PITCH

Approach an aid climb as you would a free climb: plan ahead for good placements and rests, reduce rope drag, etc. Rack up precisely:

- Have three or four pitons per crab on one side and clean gear on the other.
- Keep your hammer accessible, even if you do not think you will need it.
- Keep your ascenders handy—you never know when you may be left hanging in space.
- Aid climbing an overhang creates its own difficulties, but a daisy chain enables you to hang from your harness in a stable position. A chest harness may be useful when the overhang approaches horizontal.

There are many variations on a theme, but here is one basic system (see Fig. 69).

Step 1 Place an aid piece at the furthest point you can reach.

Step 2 Clip in two crabs separately (the second takes the climbing rope). If you have placed a peg, put a small sling (hero loop) on to it and then clip the two crabs into the sling. Do not yet clip the climbing rope into the piece unless the placement you are standing on is poor and the higher piece is more solid.

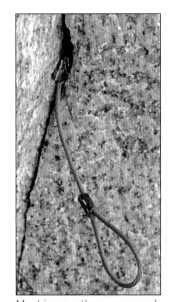

Mashies are the preserve of the hardened aid climber—on moderate routes you are more likely to come across one in-situ than you are to place one.

Step 3 Clip an etrier to the crab. Test the piece with a gentle one footed hop or, if it is poor, ease from one etrier to the other slowly. If it is very steep you can clip yourself into the daisy chain via the fifi hook.

Step 4 Remove your second etrier from the lower piece and clip it into the same crab.

Step 5 Move onto the etriers fully and clip your fifi hook into the new piece or to your daisy chain.

Step 6 Clip in the climbing rope.

Step 7 Stand as high as you can and repeat.

HIGH STEPPING

See Fig. 70. To reach as far as you can often involves moving onto the top step of an etrier. The process is unnerving, but is made easier if there are handholds or the rock is easy-angled. Maintain body tension at all times on steep/ overhanging rock. The strain on your body can be taken by the daisy chain, but the resulting upward pull increases the chance of the aid piece coming out.

RESTING

Move one leg and bend it close beneath you—your bottom is then on the calf of the bent leg. Asking the belayer to take the rope simply increases the forces on the placement.

TESTING DUBIOUS PLACEMENTS

- Ease on to it—slowly ease your weight off the present piece and on to the next piece, hoping it will hold full body weight.

- Shock-test—bounce your weight on the next piece (with the aiders and daisy clipped in), slowly at first, and gradually building up to forces exceeding body weight. The skill is in preventing the present piece from getting shock-loaded if the tested piece does pull. Testing in the middle of a string of marginal placements is one of the scariest parts of aid climbing. Do not shock-test sky hooks.

- Funkness device—this is a short length of cable that is clipped to the piece and jerked with a hammer clipped to the other end. These generate amazing amounts of force and may ruin a piece—use them carefully.

CREATING A BELAY STANCE

This requires a lot of thought, especially when sack hauling. It is best to create a separate single point belay for the ascending rope and the hauling rope.

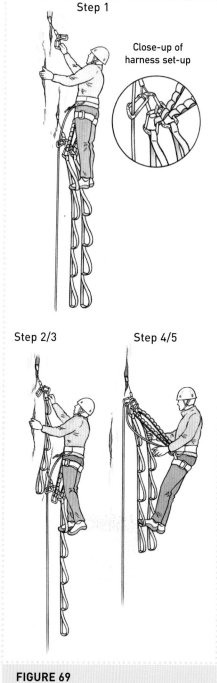

FIGURE 69
Leading an aid climb

Step 1

Close-up of harness set-up

Step 2/3

Step 4/5

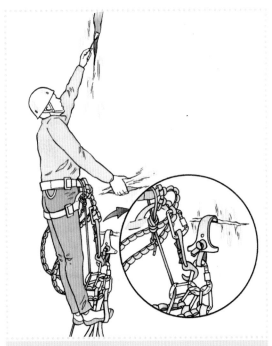

FIGURE 70 High stepping

TENSION TRAVERSES AND PENDULUMS

When the gap is small, the lead climber simply uses tension from the rope to reach another crack or hold. When the gap is greater, the leader must place a solid runner as high as possible. From this they are lowered down just enough to run across the cliff to the next crack. Longer pendulums can be abseiled with the leader still belayed on the climbing rope. The abseil rope can then be left for the second to use. This method obviously requires an extra rope.

Once the new crack has been gained, climb as high as possible before placing any protection. The higher you are before clipping the climbing rope, the easier and safer it is for the second to follow.

The difficult part of a pendulum falls to the second. If it is a short pendulum you may be able to simply unclip and swing across. When it is longer lower yourself across until the lead rope can take your weight.

Clip into the pendulum point using a daisy chain. For a short pendulum, pass a bight of rope through the protection you are lowering from and either clip it into your harness or hold on tightly. Take as much slack rope as you can until it is tight on you. Attach your ascender to the rope you want to eventually ascend and lower yourself across. Once your weight is on the lead rope you can retrieve the double strand and continue up the pitch.

If there is not enough rope you will have to untie and put a single strand of rope through the crab you are leaving behind. If the pendulum is very large an extra rope will make life easier for the second.

To anchor   Pendulum anchor

Jumars (ascender) attached to harness

Remaining section of rope

FIGURE 71
Seconding a pendulum

The difficult part of a pendulum falls to the second. (Climber: T. Massiah.)

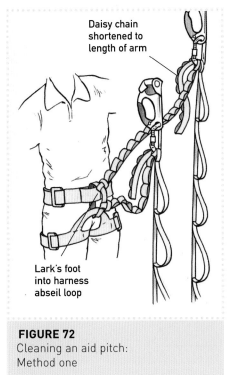

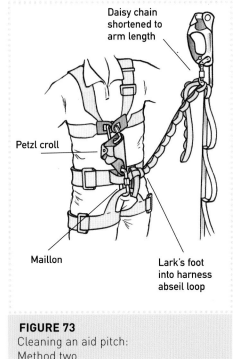

FIGURE 72
Cleaning an aid pitch:
Method one

FIGURE 73
Cleaning an aid pitch:
Method two

ASCENDING/CLEANING AN AID PITCH

Unless the pitch is very short, ascending the rope is faster than aiding. Aiding, however, is better on traverses where ascending would pull outwards on the aid placements. Follow the same sequence as the leader, but remove the climbing rope before stepping on to the etriers.

For longer pitches, ascend the rope by one of three methods:

METHOD ONE
(See Fig. 72.) Connect ascenders to daisy chains, so that the top ascender can just be reached by a full arm extension. The daisy chain to the bottom ascender is slightly shorter. Place the ascender of your dominant hand on top.

METHOD TWO
(See Fig. 73.) A Petzl Croll ascender is attached to a chest harness using a semi-circular Maillon and a smaller, oval Maillon.

METHOD THREE
Set up the ascenders for your arm length with slings, not etriers.

Ascending is faster than aiding a pitch.
(Climber: Louise Thomas.)

GENERAL ADVICE FOR ASCENDING

- As you remove gear rack it tidily.

- Keep your movements smooth and let your legs do the work.

- Attach a double figure of eight knot to your harness every 6-7m (20–23ft) in case the ascender fails.

- When bypassing a knot, clip a third sling above it before detaching etriers.

- Traverses are best aided across (sliding the ascenders ahead of you, but not weighted), because of the potential pendulums between pieces when ascending. If the rope traverses a short distance or runs diagonally, clip a crab from the rear of the ascender to the rope to prevent it popping off. It is important to tie off the climbing rope to your harness frequently.

- If there is a long span of rope between placements on a traverse, lower yourself across. Thread a sling through the pendulum point and then thread a bight of rope from the harness through the sling. Clip this to a locking crab on your harness belay loop. Pull up the slack so that your weight is transferred onto the bight. Unclip the lead rope from the pendulum point and strip the crabs from the anchor. Lower yourself back into jumaring line. Unclip the bight of rope from your harness and pull it through the pendulum point.

- Mashies are best left in place, but tug them a few times if you need to remove them and inspect each one carefully before using again. If the wire is stripped from the mashey, take the time to clean the head from the crack so others can use the placement.

- When you remove gear, clip into it with an old sling so you do not lose it. Sitting in pegs as you hit them can also help to remove the pegs.

FIXING ROPES

Fixed ropes are often used when you reach a bivvy ledge and want to climb a few pitches more. The ropes are fixed to allow you to reach your high point the next day. Use a figure of nine knot on the anchor, because it is easier to undo. To prevent the rope being blown around, pull it taut and anchor it at the bottom—it can be loosened for ascending. Static ropes make the best fixed ropes, but they may not be available (see Fixed lines, chapter 6, page 349).

The most important thing to consider when using dynamic ropes is the sawing action over edges or roofs. To overcome this, pad edges with a rope protector, backpack, or duct tape. You can also direct the rope away from sharp edges, or allow climbers to ascend the same rope by placing intermediate anchors between the main ones (see

FIGURE 74
Fixing ropes

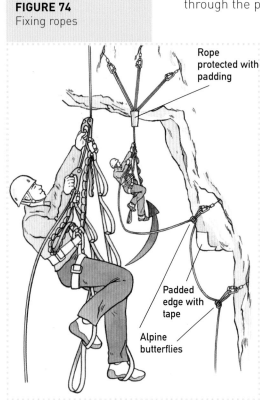

Rope protected with padding

Padded edge with tape

Alpine butterflies

Fig. 74). Use an alpine butterfly to tie into the intermediate anchors. If the fixed ropes are tight and do not allow someone ascending to tie-off at regular intervals, place a French prusik above the mechanical ascender and clip it into your harness.

TACKLING BIG WALLS

"Physically, big walling is like being whipped with rusty chains, all day, lying face down on hot asphalt... Mentally, big walling is like being insane, except worse, since you are aware of your insanity."
—Paul Brunner, big wall climber

Big walling used to be synonymous with aid climbing, but many big walls are now climbed totally free.

Big walls are within the grasp of moderate climbers with good rope-work techniques, free climbing, and aiding skills. They are really more a test of your engineering skills, mental stamina, and physical endurance. A big waller should be aware of how the environment changes—the rock, weather, their partner, etc. Determination is vital. You will invent reasons for not being there and for getting off quickly. My advice is to stick with it for the first day or two and think only of the day ahead and not the next few days.

Master the basics on smaller crags, making placements, aiding efficiently, setting up belays, ascending, cleaning, organizing the rack. Then move on to hauling and using a portaledge (see page 136).

HAUL BAGS AND HAULING

Using anything other than a manufactured haul bag is taking a huge risk, as it could fall apart. Alternatively, you could fashion a homemade haul bag from a large, blue barrel (drill holes in the bottom to let water out); this system is very tough, but difficult to carry around. Manufactured haul bags are incredibly tough and have a removable carrying system for when not hauling. Get the largest you can, as it can then be used on short or multi-day routes. Attach a 2m (7ft) length of rope to one of the haul loops, making it easier to attach to a belay. Off-set haul loops help to get into the bag when it is hanging, but you can attach to the separate haul bag loops with two knots. A 100-150 litre (26–400 pt) bag will do for a two- or three-person team on a moderate two- or three-day wall, e.g., The Nose. Pack it carefully to stop anything protruding—line it with sleeping mats.

Cover the knot with a plastic bottle and attach a Petzl swivel if you are concerned about the rope twisting. It is better to use twistlocks and

The Nose El Capitan. At 5.9 C1 it sounds easy, but it's not, and the failure rate is high.

BASIC BIG WALL CLIMBING

1 Climber A leads, climber B belays.

2 Climber A finishes pitch, sets up new belay, prepares to haul.

3 Climber B releases haul bag from his belay, climber A hauls it.

4 Climber B cleans pitch.

5 It may be faster to climb in batches of six pitches.

The most efficient group for batch leading is a party of three. Climber A leads, climber B belays and hauls, and climber C cleans.

an alpine butterfly or figure of nine to tie in.

If you are also hauling a portaledge or another light bag, hang it off the bottom of the haul bag.

Hauling heavy bags can damage your back. To haul from a ledge, attach a Petzl sack hauler or mini traxion to the belay (often a separate belay from the ascending rope), and use your body as a counterweight to haul (see Fig. 75). You can also use a Yosemite hoist (see Fig. 76). The steeper the route, the easier it is to sack haul. It may be a good idea for the second to ascend alongside the haul bag to clear any jams.

PORTALEDGES

Portaledges are folding stretchers suspended by straps from a single point. They are available in single or double sizes.

During a storm anchor each corner of the bottom of your ledge via a single anchor point to prevent it flying away from the wall. A separate rain fly, which clips into the same single suspension point, provides rain cover. Hang your haul bags underneath the ledge, and stop flapping in bad weather with a flexible tent pole placed inside.

A double is easier to set up than trying to string up two singles off one anchor, and is lighter than two singles, warmer, and more psychologically

It is useful for the second to ascend next to the haul bag. (Climber: Paul Donnithorne.)

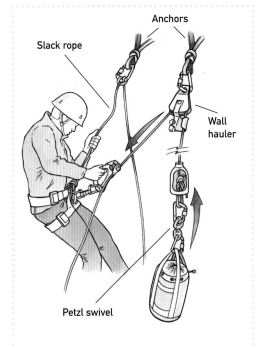

FIGURE 75
A counterbalance hoist

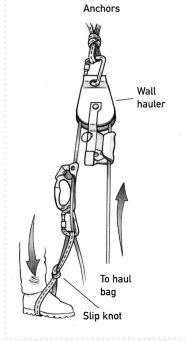

FIGURE 76
A Yosemite hoist

comforting (although not quite as comfortable).

FOOD AND COOKING

Carry antiseptic gel to clean your hands. Avoid foods that are breakable, soft, or that go bad in warm weather. Unlike alpine climbing, you don't have to worry too much about weight, so why not pack a special treat (see chapter 6 for more on food)?

Carry 4-5l (8–10pt) of water per day in plastic bottles, plus half a litre (1 pt) spare. If bottles are not carried in a separate haul bag, tape them up. Big walling in summer can be done without a stove. Portaledge cooking is risky because there is nowhere to run! Clip your stove to an independent piece of gear situated near the ledge, but not with nylon cord.

For alpine big wall climbing a stove is mandatory for melting snow. A butane canister hanging stove is best, as it is easier to maintain and operate. A heat exchanger will help the stove to operate efficiently in cold weather—wrap a piece of copper tubing around your canister, with one end passing through the flame; this will heat up the canister and pressurize the contents. After coiling the heat exchanger around the canister, wrap it in aluminum foil and slip the whole fuel assembly into a custom-made, duct tape covered foam Cozie. This insulates the heat exchanger (making it more efficient), and prevents it from melting gear. On average two people melting snow will burn through at least one 225g butane canister/day. If you're only heating the occasional pan of water, a canister might last two days.

It is possible to use liquid fuel stoves but great care must be taken.

GOING TO THE BATHROOM

Urinate into a clearly labeled bottle. Do your business into a paper bag; airplane sick bags or plastic grocery bags are great but ensure they are biodegradable. Put the bags into a poop tube with cat litter. The poop tube is made of 10–15cm (4-6in) PVC tubing, with a sealed end at the bottom and a screw top at the other end. The top has a loop attaching it to the body of the tube, so you cannot lose it. Put it in the haul bag or clip it with a crab below the bag.

Women may find the Freshette from Sani-Fem helpful (a funnel with an extendible nozzle, thus allowing you to

A separate rain fly, which clips into the same single suspension point, provides rain cover. (Photo: Twid Turner. Climber: Louise Thomas.)

A belay seat is essential on anything more than a one day climb. (Zion National Park, U.S.)

137

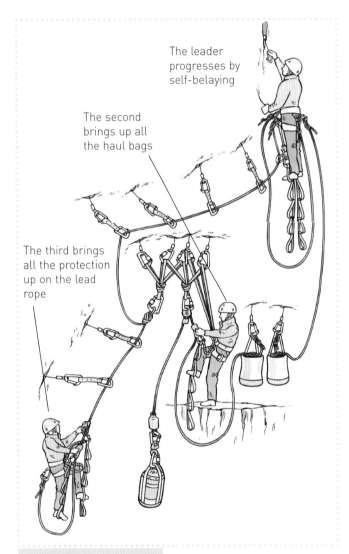

The leader progresses by self-belaying

The second brings up all the haul bags

The third brings all the protection up on the lead rope

FIGURE 77 Block leading

Not all walls require porta-ledges and you can go alpine style, sleeping on ledges or even using a hammock. (Climber: Paul Donnithorne.)

pee standing up).

BLOCK LEADING

To improve speed on big walls, the experienced team will use a technique where each leader will lead multiple pitches in a row, called block leading (see Fig. 77). This system can be used on both aid and free routes to move faster and reduce the amount of time that a leader is waiting at a belay. The best number for block leading is a party of three. The first climber leads, the second belays and hauls, and the third cleans the previous pitch.

All three climbers start at the belay. The leader climbs (dragging a zip line) and when he reaches the belay, he pulls up the haul line and fixes it to the belay. The leader then pulls up the slack in the lead line, fixes it to the belay, and continues up to the next pitch using self-belaying techniques—usually clove hitches. He climbs until he runs out of rope or gear, or is put on belay after the pitch below has been cleaned. A zip line is necessary so he can pull up the gear cleaned from the previous pitch.

Once the haul line is fixed, the second ascends without cleaning the pitch. When the second reaches the anchor, he sets up the hauling system so that the third climber can release the haul bag. The second starts hauling and the third climber cleans the pitch. Once climber three arrives, he puts the leader back on a normal belay and the leader pulls up the cleaned gear and continues his block as the third belays and the second hauls. The process is then repeated.

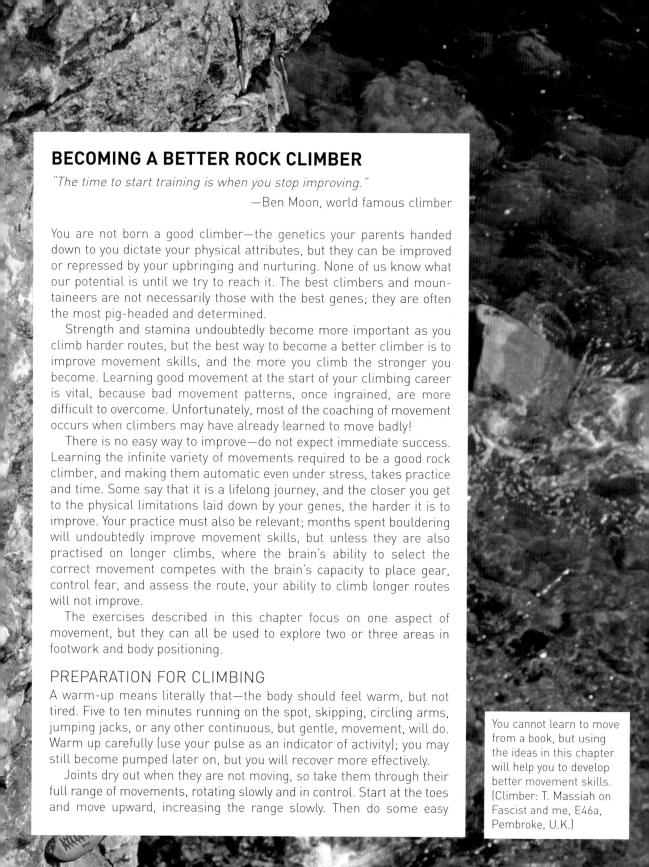

BECOMING A BETTER ROCK CLIMBER

"The time to start training is when you stop improving."

—Ben Moon, world famous climber

You are not born a good climber—the genetics your parents handed down to you dictate your physical attributes, but they can be improved or repressed by your upbringing and nurturing. None of us know what our potential is until we try to reach it. The best climbers and mountaineers are not necessarily those with the best genes; they are often the most pig-headed and determined.

Strength and stamina undoubtedly become more important as you climb harder routes, but the best way to become a better climber is to improve movement skills, and the more you climb the stronger you become. Learning good movement at the start of your climbing career is vital, because bad movement patterns, once ingrained, are more difficult to overcome. Unfortunately, most of the coaching of movement occurs when climbers may have already learned to move badly!

There is no easy way to improve—do not expect immediate success. Learning the infinite variety of movements required to be a good rock climber, and making them automatic even under stress, takes practice and time. Some say that it is a lifelong journey, and the closer you get to the physical limitations laid down by your genes, the harder it is to improve. Your practice must also be relevant; months spent bouldering will undoubtedly improve movement skills, but unless they are also practised on longer climbs, where the brain's ability to select the correct movement competes with the brain's capacity to place gear, control fear, and assess the route, your ability to climb longer routes will not improve.

The exercises described in this chapter focus on one aspect of movement, but they can all be used to explore two or three areas in footwork and body positioning.

PREPARATION FOR CLIMBING

A warm-up means literally that—the body should feel warm, but not tired. Five to ten minutes running on the spot, skipping, circling arms, jumping jacks, or any other continuous, but gentle, movement, will do. Warm up carefully (use your pulse as an indicator of activity); you may still become pumped later on, but you will recover more effectively.

Joints dry out when they are not moving, so take them through their full range of movements, rotating slowly and in control. Start at the toes and move upward, increasing the range slowly. Then do some easy

You cannot learn to move from a book, but using the ideas in this chapter will help you to develop better movement skills. (Climber: T. Massiah on Fascist and me, E46a, Pembroke, U.K.)

The predictable style of climbing will make you good at movement on climbing walls, but not necessarily outdoors. (Climber: Mike Rose.)

THE BENEFITS OF LEARNING GOOD MOVEMENT

- Your foot and body movements become more accurate.
- Good, correct movements become more consistent.
- Less energy is used.
- You will be able to anticipate movements ahead.
- Your confidence will grow.
- You will climb harder routes with ease and in style.

climbing to wake up the brain muscle links and concentrate on the movement techniques described below. Without warming up, your performance will be poor and may even result in injury—if you are young, your tendons have not fully developed; if you are older, your tendons and ligaments are more brittle.

POST-CLIMBING

At the end of a climbing session it is just as important to warm down by repeating the process outlined for warming up. Warming down removes toxins from the body that have built up during exercise and will help to reduce any aches and pains caused by stressing the muscles. Flexibility training can be introduced at this point.

WHERE TO LEARN MOVEMENT

Climbing is an open skill and not a closed skill like a golf swing; you are trying to introduce rules for movement that the brain can select automatically, even under stress. Do not practice the following exercises when you are at your limit, for example when leading a route.

Learning movement is best done in an environment where you feel safe and your subconscious can focus. The best climbers practice on a variety of rock types, however, climbing walls can be used effectively, as long as you understand the disadvantages:

- You will become good at movement on climbing walls, but not necessarily outdoors.
- Modern climbing walls rarely have the features found on outside climbs, such as jam cracks, arêtes, and corners.
- Learning movement on moderately angled rock is effective for learning good technique for steep rock, but the opposite is not necessarily true—very few walls are easy angled.
- Poor route-setters often design routes so that "ape index" (the relationship between arm span and body height) is the limiting factor to success.
- Reaching the top often depends more on your levels of strength and endurance, requiring only a small repertoire of movement skills.

Climbers moving from indoors to outside are strong, but are often limited by the subtle techniques needed to climb on real rock and are poor at finding resting positions.

Spotters should continually examine the climber's trajectory; are they coming feet-first or back-first? Watch their hips and back, not their fingers—a fall can happen very quickly.

SPOTTING

Spotting is the ability to limit injury to a falling climber while bouldering. Spotters do not catch falling climbers; they steer them to the best landing, slow them down, and minimize the number of body parts hitting the ground. The size and skill of the spotter, the landing quality, plus the height above the ground all determine the seriousness of the "boulder problem." Big people are the best spotters, but are the hardest to spot; consider using two spotters if the climber is large. Bouldering mats, when positioned correctly, can help to prevent injury, but they may tempt you to climb higher.

When the boulder problem is steep it is more effective to grab the sides of the climber's back just below the armpits and swing them back to a feet-first landing. On steep, high problems spot the climber's hips and steer them to a feet-first landing, but do not grab them too low causing them to topple backward. The falling climber must try to keep their limbs relaxed and land feet-first.

ADVICE FOR SPOTTING

- Prevent finger injuries—do not wear a climbing harness.
- Remove all jewelery.
- Stand in a karate or boxing stance, braced and ready to support a falling climber.
- Keep your arms at the ready, not by your side.
- Keep your arms close to the climber.
- Keep your fingers together so that they are not bent back.

IT'S ALL IN THE HIPS!

To become a good rock climber you must first learn to dance. Ask most climbers what the most important part of the body for climbing is and most will answer legs or feet. In reality you have four limbs equally capable of pushing and pulling, but it is your hips that allow you to position all the other parts so that you can use them effectively. If you only have the time to improve flexibility in one part of your body, make sure it is your hips.

The main job of your arms and fingers is to hold your body in position, while your hips place your center of gravity (COG) in the best position for your legs and feet to push you up the cliff.

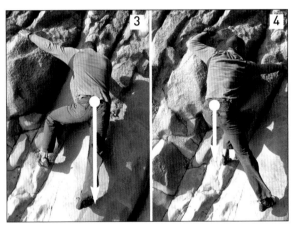

GENERAL EXERCISES

These exercises help you to become aware of your body. Get a partner or use a video camera to tell if you have mastered a move.

Move your hips—Try to take each limb off the wall while adjusting your hips to stay in balance. Then try removing combinations of two limbs.

Use a balance beam—Try it 0.5m (2ft) off the ground—bend, twist, turn sideways, dip your upper body, and move your hips around. Use your leg like an outrigger, forward, backward, and sideways. Close your eyes and feel the pressure in your legs and feet.

Climb smoothly—If you are snatching for footholds or handholds have you successfully transferred your COG and found the most stable position for your body? Compare climbing slowly and gracefully like a ballerina with climbing like a gorilla.

Study the rock—Design your own boulder problems. Mark the holds with a stick of chalk and let your partner try it.

(Top) To free a limb to move easily you must first put your COG in a balanced position by moving your hips (**1**, **2**), lift the now-free leg (**3**) and then transfer your hips over the new foot placement (**4**).

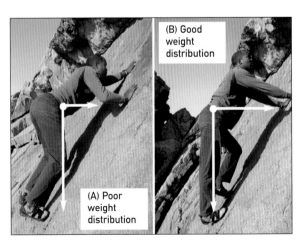

(B) Good weight distribution

(A) Poor weight distribution

(Bottom) On easier angled climbs keep your hips out from the rock (B) and don't stretch for handholds (A)...use your feet to gain height.

CENTER OF GRAVITY (COG)

The exact position of your center of gravity depends on your build. For adult males, it is about 2.5cm (1in) above their navel, and slightly lower in women. Differences in its position, and the length of your limbs, means that everyone has a unique way of climbing. This is why it is difficult to teach someone to climb by forcing them to use particular holds that may not suit their body shape or limb-length. Climbing is about allowing the rock to dictate the movements you make, not the reverse.

OVER-EXTENDING/OVER-STRETCHING

Novices stretch to reach the largest handholds with the result that they become over-extended, can't see their feet, and can't move without hanging on.

- Imagine there is a line drawn at head height. Climb, but your hands must not be taken above the line. This will force you to use your feet and not overstretch.
- Move your feet twice before your hands. Notice how moving the feet higher enables you to reach further. Your body may end up in a "frogged" position or you will discover turning sideways.

Squat and use your legs to push rather than pulling with your arms. **1** Move your hips over one leg; **2** Squat on to a straight arm; **3** Place the foot on to a new foothold; **4** Drive upward with the lower leg and move your hip over it.

When it is difficult to move your hips you can use your hand to act like a third leg and push downward. This will free the leg to move. (Photo: Stefan Doerr Collection. Climber: Stefan Doerr.)

There are many ways to use your feet—edging (top) and smearing.

EFFICIENT FEET

Precise and accurate foot placements are vital for efficient climbing. There are two ways to use your feet:

EDGING

Practice using the inside and outside edge of the toe area of your foot on small holds. Keep the foot still and use the ankle as a hinge to prevent the upper body moving. When using the outside edge, imagine your toes are being curled over the foothold. Do not place your foot deep into large holes; this will only force the lower leg outward, upsetting balance.

SMEARING

Place as much rubber as possible in contact with the rock, even on vertical walls. The steeper the rock, the more your hips must move away from the rock to direct the forces to your feet, or the harder your feet must push.

Where to smear and edge—Examine the rock in detail and try to stand on the smallest smears and edges you can find.

Precision footwork—Climb slowly, with no noise. Noisy footwork indicates that you are not climbing with precision. To improve precision, hover your foot over each hold for a few seconds before placing it. Place your foot on a hold, remove it, and try to reposition it with your eyes closed.

Think before you move—Do not move your feet until you know where you have found the best foot placement. To practice this, don't reposition your foot once you have placed it on a hold.

Use your feet creatively. (Climber: Clive Hebblethwaite.)

Research has shown that good climbers look at their feet more than 70 percent of the time.

HOW TO TRANSFER YOUR WEIGHT (ROCK OVERS)

Small steps are usually better, but sometimes a high step on to a new foothold is necessary (see 3 and 4 in photo on p. 143). Place your foot on to the best part of the hold and smoothly move your hip over it. Your trailing leg may leave the rock completely; let it hang in whichever position keeps you in balance ready for the next move (see Flagging, page 149). Rock overs highlight the importance of climbing smoothly and completing each move until your center of gravity is transferred completely over the new foot.

USE YOUR FEET IMAGINATIVELY

On steep and overhanging routes, take the strain off the arms with your feet. Lock your toes in a horizontal crack, weight the heel, and jam it in place. Place your foot sideways in a wider crack. Hook toes under a roof or in a horizontal break to hold the body in place. Use your heel to hook holds. This is a way of using your foot as an extra hand above or to the side. You will find that having good core body strength is important for all these maneuver.

HAND AND FINGER HOLDS

There are broadly four ways to use finger holds depending on their size, position and shape. On narrow holds keep your fingers together; if there is not room for all of them, give priority to the stronger middle and ring finger and curl the others up to optimize the muscle/tendon system (see jamming on page 152).

1 **The open hand (extended) grip**—The least stressful on joints and tendons, but the most strenuous to use. It allows you to reach further and is often used on rounded holds, layaways, and undercut moves.

2 **The open crimp**—The second finger joints are bent at 90 degrees and the thumb is redundant.

3 **The closed crimp**—The thumb is used to back-up the next two fingers. It concentrates the forces to the tips, making it useful on very tiny holds. Keep the thumb close to the rock to reduce leverage. It is the easiest way to damage your fingers, because the second joint is contracted to its limit (consider taping your fingers).

4 **The pinch grip**—Use as much of the thumb as possible and keep your palm close to the rock to reduce leverage.

USING YOUR HANDS

- Climb routes using one type of handhold only.
- Gripping the rock too hard is common. Climb a route then repeat it, applying the minimum of pressure to the holds.

HOLDS

Search the rock and discover the following holds:

- Jug—The biggest holds, often in-cut
- Side pulls—A hold where you must pull sideways
- Slopers—Large, rounded holds
- Undercuts—A hold facing upside down.

A sloper hold—to use this hold the rest of your body must be in position to allow you to pull on it.

Open-hand grip

Open crimp—often combined with pinching with the thumb

Closed crimp

Pinch grip

Classic layback positions occur in cracks, corners, and on arêtes, but they can be found whenever you use side-pull holds. (Climbers: J. Horscroft and C. Bannister.)

USING OPPOSING PRESSURE TO YOUR ADVANTAGE

The structure of the rock dictates how your body can use holds. For example, a crack in a corner may be difficult to climb facing straight on, so it may be easier to twist the body sideways, use the edge of the crack for your hands, and place your feet on the wall making up the corner (laybacking). These body positions involve the whole body, and not just the feet or hands in isolation.

LAYBACK/LIEBACK

Laybacking relies on technique mixed with strength and determination. Difficult laybacks require a keen awareness of hip positioning to prevent the body swinging away from the rock. Heel hooking on arêtes and holds can help to keep your COG in the correct place.

Use an arête or a line of side-pulls and laybacks. Keep your feet low, push with your feet, and pull with your hands. The steeper the rock, the higher your feet must be, but the more strenuous it is. Keep your arms straight. The hand nearest the rock is usually the highest. The hands and feet can be shuffled or leap-frogged, but generally crossing over hands or feet transfers more weight to the arms.

BRIDGING

This uses the legs in opposition. It can turn a strenuous position into a resting position. When the rock is blank, the only thing that may be keeping you in place is pressure through your feet and your arms. Bridge a corner without using footholds, then try the opposite bridge with no handholds, then try to do it without hands or feet on positive holds.

CHIMNEYING

A chimney is a crack big enough for the body to fit into. The hands are used to push the back away and up, but not too far, or the feet may skid away.

Bridging can turn a strenuous position into a rest. (Climber: S. Lewis on Profit of Doom, E46b, Curbar, U.K.)

FINGER TAPING TO PREVENT INJURIES

Finger taping is best done using rings of 0.75 or 0.5in tape on either side of the joints. The "X" method adds support over more of the finger. Take a turn around the base of the finger, then cross under the finger and take a turn around the middle of the finger. Cross back and take another turn. The tension will dictate the amount of bend in the finger.

MANTLESHELF

This is the ability to gain a ledge, where there are no holds above it, with poise and grace.

Select the best part of a very large hold or the top of a boulder. Walk your feet up until your arms are almost straight. Step up and place one foot on to the mantle. Turn one or both hands inward to push and balance upward. It is usually better to push down with the hand opposite the raised foot. Work towards narrower and narrower ledges.

SIDE PULLS AND UNDERCLINGS

Holds are not always horizontal—sidepull or undercling holds are often missed. Undercling holds allow the feet to be moved higher, enabling you to reach further. The left/right rule of flagging (see page 148) is essential for performing side pull and undercling movements effectively, because you must use the outside edge of the foot opposite the handhold you are using. This allows the hip opposite the pulling hand to twist into the wall.

Practice climbing using exclusively left or right side pulls or underclings.

GASTON OR COMICI

In the same genre as a side pull, this can be done with one or both hands. With both hands in a crack or on two holds, they pull in opposite directions to each other as if you are trying to open a lift door. Moving from this position usually requires leaning your hips to one side. The opposite can also be done by pulling or squeezing both sides of a large block. Try climbing using this technique on some or all of the holds—move your COG around over your feet to find the least stressful position.

WHEN THE ROCK IS STEEPER

A good climber tries to find the best body position for gravity to force the foot to stay in place. What may seem like poor footwork may actually be poor hip positioning. The steeper the rock, the more important the hips become.

Mantleshelf or grovel, it's your choice!

Side pulls are often missed when you are starting out.

Chimneying

Gaston/Comici technique

The steeper the rock, the more important it is to use your hips effectively. (Stefan Doerr frogging to keep his hips closer to the rock.)

Ways to keep your hips closer to the wall:

1 When your hips are not close to the wall your weight is on your arms;

2 Spread your legs (frogging) to bring your COG over your feet or

3 Twist using inside and outside edging.

The left/right rule. On steep walls a straight-on position means that the body wants to pivot when you remove a hand. To prevent this, twist your hips into the wall and work in a diagonal.

MOVE YOUR HIPS IN AND OUT

On vertical rock, bring your hips out when you move your feet and back in when you move your hands.

As the rock steepens your body must twist to reach handholds. Twisting forces you to either swap feet or swivel them on a hold:

- **Swap feet**—Most easily done with your hips out from the rock. Place the big toe of the upper foot a few millimeters above the big toe of the lower foot. Do not jump your foot; instead move your lower foot off the foothold and drop the upper foot on to the now vacant hold. To make this easier gently rise your body at precisely the same time as you move your lower foot.

- **Swivel your feet**—Swivelling the foot from the outside to the inside edge without removing the foot from the hold requires a subtle unweighting just prior to swivelling the foot.

THE LEFT/RIGHT RULE

On steep walls, adopting a straight-on position means that gravity forces the body to pivot—to prevent this, twist your hips into the wall and work in a diagonal. It is more stable and creates a strength advantage when combined with twist locking, because it brings the chest muscles into play.

On a steep wall try moving left arm and left leg then right arm and right leg, then try a diagonal combination—imagine the diagonal limbs are joined by a piece of elastic; as one limb moves, the opposite moves with it. Using left and right sides of the body requires you to twist your hips and to use the outside and inside edges of the feet. Many of the movements that follow all use this fundamental rule.

TWIST LOCKS

Combining twisting the hips with the left/right rule creates a very strong and stable position. Twist into a left-arm lock off standing on the outside edge of the right foot; the body will then face left. The other foot may be inside flagging, or even just dangling in space. Vary the position of your head and see what effect it has. Twisting also allows you to reach further—the longest reach is possible with the hand opposite the foot you are standing on. Letting the spare foot come off can also extend the reach.

FLAGGING, BACK STEPPING, AND KNEE DROPPING (EGYPTIANS)

Back stepping, knee dropping, and flagging may already have appeared as you learn to twist and use the left/right rule.

- **Flagging**—Swapping feet can often be counterproductive in the sequence of moves you want to make. When only one arm and leg is in contact with the rock the other leg can be used as a counterbalance, akin to the outrigger on boats. It can be done with the leg behind, in front, or straight out at the back. The flagging foot does not have to be placed on a hold, but try to keep it in contact with the rock whenever possible. Inside flagging uses a twist lock. It can also be used to avoid switching feet on an insecure foothold. Flagging behind stabilizes the body when it is trying to untwist (barn door).
- On a steep route try to take both left-hand and foot off the rock. The only way to prevent a barn door is to flag the foot or to use the left/right rule.
- Climb a straight line of small side pull holds without using rock overs. Move up and down, adjusting the flagged leg to find the best position for the counterbalance.
- **Back stepping**—Twisting the hips can be taken further by using this variation on bridging. It is usually combined with a side pull. Attain a bridged position between two holds on a wall, rotate sideways, and step the outside edge of the foot on to a hold behind you. Keep your weight over the new hold and use the arm on the same side of the body as the back-stepped foot to reach.
- **Knee drops**—These are a more extreme form of the back step. Drop your knee and torso so the rear knee bends downward. The aim is to keep your weight over the foot that has been back-stepped by placing the dropped knee under your buttocks. This allows you to squat and keep your arms straight, thereby securing a rest position. If the back-stepped

Outside flagging. (Climber: John Taylor.)

Inside flagging—often combined with a twist lock. (Climber: Claire Carlisle.)

149

Back stepping and knee dropping.
(Climber: Clive Hebblethwaite.)

hold is high, lift your foot on to it from a face-on, bridged position, then pivot your feet to face away from it. A combination of twist lock and drop knee is a very stable position.

RESTING

The first rule is to down climb to a rest spot then work out the moves, rather than become pumped hanging on at the crux. Learning to rest will improve your confidence.

Efficient rest positions depend on three factors:

- Body position—keep your center of gravity over your feet.
- Fitness—the ability of the body to avoid the dreaded pump.
- State of mind—how many times have you been "gripped" while placing a runner only to find you are relaxed as soon as it is in place?

USE THE WHOLE OF YOUR BODY

As the rock becomes steeper, keep your hips into the rock and over your feet.

RESTING YOUR ARMS

To allow the blood to flow to your hands more easily, keep your arms low using side pulls or undercuts. If your arms are above head-height grip the rock with minimal force. Keep your arms straight ("monkey hanging") by bridging or sinking into "a squat" (frogging) or twist and knee drop.

A knee bar can allow you to take both hands off the rock. (Climber: John Taylor. Photo: John Taylor Collection.)

USING THE BODY FOR WEDGING AND HOOKING

- Place your backside on a hold.
- Hook your chin over an edge.
- Use your hand as a third foothold.
- A toe hook can help you maintain balance and keep your weight over your feet.
- Use a "thumb catch" by laying or hooking the thumb over an edge and wriggling the fingers.
- Lay the forearm across a hold.
- On small edges, alternate fingers and hands on the hold.
- "Match" hands on the holds by making space between the fingers for the other hand.
- In a corner, stem out and push your chest into the corner.
- "Chicken wing" by putting arms or elbows against the walls.
- Use knee bars by jamming a knee against a hold or roof and pushing with the foot to wedge it in place.

Straight arms can also be used when moving, but only when the holds are large enough.

- Shout "stop" while your partner is climbing, and they must find a rest position and hold it for fifteen seconds. Limit the number of times "stop" can be called.
- Try climbing with straight arms. Using the arms as a lever and the shoulder as a hinge, push with the legs—as the hips are rolled towards the straight arm the body twists and increases the reach.
- Do a circuit on a wall and return to a rest spot to de-pump. Repeat three-five times.

BREATHING/SHAKING OUT

Breathe slowly and deeply when resting and breathe out when you are making a strenuous move, just as weightlifters do. If your arms are pumped, hold them low to allow the blood to drain the lactic acid away, then shake them high and let them gently drop. Stretch the forearms out by pushing your palm against a hold.

DYNAMIC MOVEMENTS (DYNOS)

So far I have isolated climbing movements, but climbing is about flowing and using momentum to climb without pauses. A Dyno is a controlled dash for a hold.

Bend the knees and sink down. Breathe out as you push up. On over-hanging walls keep your arms straight, but on less steep walls pull with your arms as you move upward to keep your hips into the wall. Don't bounce: crouch once and then do it. Before Dynoing consider which hand is doing the holding and which hand the propelling. Try to grasp the hold at the highest point of the movement when the body is motionless (the "dead point"). Climb using one arm, or climb an easy route without pausing between moves.

You are using fewer muscles when your arms are straight. (Climber: Andy Cave on Tippler E156, U.K.)

Climbing is about flowing, but there are times when you may need momentum to "snatch" for a higher hold. (Climber: S. Doerr.)

CLIMBING CRACKS

Crack climbing is all about size and can feel unnatural and even painful when done poorly; tape your hands and fingers to avoid injury.

HAND SEQUENCE

With all jams it is the torquing action of the hand or finger as it tries to untwist that helps it remain in place. Jamming face cracks requires one hand to cross over the other. Jamming corner cracks requires the

Jamming face cracks requires one hand to cross over the other. (Climber: P. Donnithorne, Zion National Park.)

hands to be shuffled, because the body can't be twisted side to side as easily. Which hand stays on top depends on which shoulder is against the rock. Shuffling is rarely used in straight finger cracks, because it feels more secure to alternately place one above the other.

FINGER JAMMING

When using both hands in a crack, put the top hand in the thumbs down position; the lower hand can be thumbs up or down. Placing the thumb downward puts leverage and torque into the jam, which increases as the body moves higher. However, the thumb-upward method of jamming allows a further reach to be made for the next placement.

When fingers go into the crack but the hand is too big, try placing all the fingers in the crack and the thumb downward against the wall (a thumb sprag). A harder, but less tiring, technique is to place the thumb in the crack and wedge the finger next to the thumb.

HAND JAMMING

These begin when the crack is wide enough for the hand to slide in as far as the wrist; the thumb can be up or down depending on the crack. Push the fingers and the palm of the hand against one side of the crack and the knuckles against the other side; the hand will jam. As the crack widens, place the thumb into the palm of the hand giving it more bulk. When it gets too wide, form your hand into a fist shape and jam this in place. There are a number of methods of fist jamming, each depending on whether the thumb is placed outside the fingers like a boxer or inside the hand. A hand jam placed with your thumb up can be turned into an undercut for long reaches.

To finger jam, insert the fingers, thumb upward or downward (ideally above a narrowing in the crack) and wedge the knuckles in place. The thumb is being used to press against the crack—a sprag.

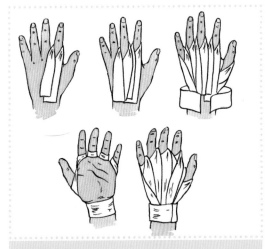

FIGURE 78
When hand jamming many pitches, a tape glove will protect your hands.

Hand jams start when the hand can slide in as far as the wrist and end as a fist jam as the crack widens.

USING YOUR FEET IN CRACKS

On pure crack climbs your feet may be twisted and contorted so they also cam in the crack. A few short movements are better than one long one.

OFF-WIDTHS

Off-widths are full body jams, and the aim is to use the arms and legs to apply pressure to opposite sides of the crack. Stick an arm in until it is a little past the shoulder, and then bend at the elbow, pressing the palm against one side and the elbow and shoulder against the other. This can be further adapted by lifting the elbow upward until it becomes a good resting position. In all of these the outside arm pulls on the outside edge of the crack at neck level.

To prevent your arms becoming pumped do not to let them get too high above the head. The legs can be jammed by locking a foot against one wall and the knee against the other or, if it is small enough, by jamming the heel and toe into the crack. If the crack is too wide for heel/toe jamming, try a T stack, with one foot sideways. The most important thing about off-widths is to maintain a rhythm and use momentum gained from the push or pull to initiate the next.

Off-widths are often a struggle. (Climber: T. Massiah.)

READING MOVES

Technical ability has been correlated to how well a climber remembers the moves and the order made on a climb that they have just completed.

- Think about the route—Identify the holds and how to use them. If the holds are small, try to imagine that they are huge.

- Try to remember what you did—Use a video to see if you did the move in the way you thought you would.

- A fun exercise that helps you and your partner to read, remember, and identify moves is for one to use three handholds and step off. Your partner uses those three and then you add three more, ad infinitum.

- Practice speedy decision-making (stress proofing) by pointing out the holds your partner can use just before they move (an extendable ski pole is useful). You can use this exercise to specifically train feet or hands, pointing out which hand or foot to move. Try to create moves that work on your weakness.

Learning to rest will improve your confidence. (Climber: John Taylor. Photo: John Taylor Collection.)

Being scared is not the problem; how you cope with fear is (the author).

THE MENTAL GAME

Climbing is a physical and mental game of chess, yet training the mind has lagged far behind the development of training a climber's body.

WHY ARE SOME PEOPLE MORE CAPABLE OF TAKING RISKS

"As far as I'm concerned, if someone eliminates the mental part of climbing, then we might as well all go play miniature golf."

—Greg Opland, climber

Whether you are "risk aversive" or a "risk seeker" is dependent upon the levels and balance of chemicals within your brain. These include neurotransmitters, hormones such as testosterone, and the "reward" chemicals (endorphins), which are released when you experience something thrilling.

The amount and balance of these chemicals varies according to your age and gender and explains why some men seek more thrills than most women. Most men have lower levels of the "inhibitory" neurotransmitter serotonin, higher levels of the "excitatory" neurotransmitter dopamine, and higher levels of testosterone, associated with a competitive drive. Different people will feel comfortable in different situations, so pitch the climb at the right level when climbing with a novice if you want them to continue.

COPING WITH FEAR

Fear floods the body with adrenaline and other hormones, in preparation for either a fight or an escape. After your stress level has gone past a certain point, composure cannot be regained straightaway, so you must do everything you can to avoid reaching that point! Under stress we lose access to all but our most ingrained movement rules, and if they are poor, your climbing can go badly very quickly.

The mental side of climbing has long been appreciated but, like many other aspects of climbing performance, it is believed there is little you can do to improve it. You may never be able to have the mental control of a top climber, largely because of influences on you as you grow up and partly due to factors predetermined by your genes, but there are things you can do to lessen the adverse affects of anxiety on your climbing. If you can release tension through relaxation, focusing, and improving self-belief, the "fight or flight" mechanism can be channeled into your climbing and you can enter what some climbers call "the zone"; that moment when you are aware of nothing but the movement.

USING IMAGERY TO IMPROVE YOUR MOVEMENT SKILLS

Studies have demonstrated that the brain is not always capable of distinguishing between something that actually happened and something that was imagined. When you imagine a movement, electrical impulses travel to the muscles that movement requires, providing "kinaesthetic" feedback. Picturing yourself executing a perfect performance can therefore help your brain to enhance that skill.

The use of mental training and, in particular, imagery is the single most important characteristic that sporting champions have over their less successful competitors, so practice it.

Imagery is not daydreaming about the great climbs you want to do. It takes time to become good at imagery, so do not be dismayed if you lose concentration after one movement. Experienced climbers will find it more beneficial than novices because they have clearer images to follow, but it is still a useful skill to practice when starting out. It is also helpful when you have to have an enforced break from climbing, maybe due to injury.

Relax and imagine yourself either by looking through your eyes and seeing yourself doing it or by imagining someone else doing it. Try to imagine scenes in explicit detail, e.g., crabs clinking. Where will your hands go? Which way will your body shift? Feel yourself doing the moves. Use photographs or video to improve the mental picture you have of yourself climbing.

Be realistic; it is no good imagining yourself climbing the hardest route in the world, just picture yourself climbing at your best. Above all, create positive images of yourself dealing with problems on a climb; eliminate images of failure and don't let any negative thoughts enter your head. Work daily to change negative images to positive ones. Lots of five or ten minute sessions are best. Enjoy it—if you are bored, stop.

Relaxation is a mental withdrawal from climbing.

RELAXATION

You will climb better when you are relaxed. It is different from focusing (concentration), which is a withdrawal of attention from factors not relevant. The problem with relaxation is that you may be waiting for something to happen, but in fact you are trying to enter the "no mind" zone.

There are two levels of relaxation—total and momentary—and these depend on how much time you spend relaxing. Relax totally after, rather than before, a climb.

Most techniques of meditative relaxation slow down the metabolism and calm you by occupying the mind with something simple. Here is one method: go to a quiet place with no distractions. You can reach a deeper relaxation by lying down, but this may remove some of the alertness you need to climb and should be kept until after climbing. Take each muscle group in sequence, and tense and then release it. Be aware of the difference in tension.

FOCUSING

When we are under stress one of the body's natural safety mechanisms is to narrow attention to what is perceived as essential for survival. In climbing, this can have unfortunate consequences: we tend to become obsessed with handholds instead of footholds and style deteriorates; we narrow our focus to holds immediately in front of us and fail to see crucial holds on the periphery.

Focusing may help you to distance yourself from worries beyond your control; learn to put aside distractions and stay with the present.

Practice on easy climbs by focusing on one aspect of movement such as hand placements, using the minimum of grip. If your attention wanders, refocus. Try to take thirty seconds over each movement. In time you will be able to transfer your focus between different tasks; this can make concentrating easier when you get into difficulties on a climb.

TALKING POSITIVELY

Self-belief is thinking you can do what you have set out to do. When you think about insecurity, who is watching you, or the consequences of a fall, performance is compromised. Negative thoughts increase muscle tension. Become aware of your thoughts while climbing, because it is possible to train them to be more positive, allowing you to focus and relax.

Instead of fighting fear it may help to go through everything that can go wrong and develop an answer for each of them. Psyche up by imagining how it feels to stand at the top of the route; relax your muscles. Talk to yourself inwardly or outwardly this is used by many climbers without realizing.

Positive self-talk or affirmations reinforce a positive image, e.g., "I can get up this route," "the crux is hard, but it's well protected," "I've climbed much harder on a top rope."

Negative self-talk has a negative effect on self-image and climbing ability, e.g., "It's too hard," "The crux is steep and I may not get protection in," "I found an easier route than this a few months ago." Friends can help by saying things like "you can climb it" rather than "give it a go," which gives an opt out.

WHAT CAN YOU DO WHEN YOU FEEL THE PANIC RISING?

When fear becomes too much, try a technique stolen from martial arts called centering. Close your eyes and relax for a few moments, take a deep breath and focus on the middle of your forehead. Breathe out slowly. Feel this focus travel down the body to just below your navel. Hold this sensation for as long as possible. If you add a positive statement to this, and smile, it may help see you through the moment of panic. It can be done before or during a climb.

The simplest advice for staying calm is to breathe, and keep breathing evenly through moves. If you hold your breath you will be tense and your muscles will not be getting the oxygen they need. Just like weight training, exhale as you make the moves. If you can control your breathing, you can control your heart rate, which can then control the higher-level functions of the brain. When in doubt, breathe out because erratic breathing can induce panic.

Concentrating on something other than the fear may help your climbing. Have a statement to focus your mind on a particular aspect of climbing, e.g., silent climbing—use your feet or grip less to help you to calm down and grip the rock less. You can also try to relax on the route—close your eyes, breathe, and transport yourself to a desert island or somewhere quiet.

Break the route into sections or islands of retreat. (Climbers: Anne May and Guy Wilson.)

Relax and create a positive image of yourself climbing the route. (Climber: John Taylor.)

NON-SPECIFIC ADVICE FOR STAYING CALM

- The worst fear is the unknown. Start by knowing the climbing environment, gradually increasing your experience and knowledge.
- Understand rope-work; how to escape from a route; how to survive a storm and avoid avalanches.
- Start on easy routes—top-rope or abseil it first.
- Slow everything down, including putting your boots and harness on.
- Climb with someone you trust and who encourages you.
- Don't venture on your hardest lead when you're not happy.
- Fool yourself and climb as if the holds are big.
- Expect success.
- Plan ahead and rehearse the moves—break the route into sections.
- Strive for elegance.
- Become calm at rests.
- Double your runners up.
- Down climb if in trouble.
- Listen to your inner voice.
- Breathe in a controlled manner.

Remember the words of Alex Lowe: "The best climber in the world is the one having the most fun!" (Climber: Steve Lewis.)

3

WINTER MOUNTAINEERING

"Constant vigilance keeps people alive."

—Mark Twight, *Extreme Alpinism* (1999)

On a cold clear day, with firm snow, winter mountaineering can be safer than in summer, because the walking is easier and stone fall is less. However, it can all change in a few hours. Gale-force winds, blizzards, zero visibility, avalanches, and the numbing cold will soon sap your reserves.

Winter starts to arrive as the sun drops on the horizon and earth is warmed less effectively. In the Northern Hemisphere this allows the Polar Front to move south bringing colder air from the Arctic. From autumn, well into spring, the battle between the warmer moist air to the south and the colder drier air to the north produces the winter storms that bring the snow.

The low-pressure gradient within winter storms is often large and creates strong winds of 160kph (99.4mph) plus. Winds, especially gusts of 70kph (43.5mph) and above, are difficult to walk in. The wind above 800m (2625ft), especially in Scotland, is at least double the strength at sea level. The wind chill factor can make it feel even colder: +5°C (41°F) in a 50-kph (30-mph) wind can feel like –12°C (10.4°F) on exposed flesh.

Aanoch Eagach
traverse, Glencoe,
Scotland

SNOW, ICE, AND AVALANCHES

When the temperature of a cloud falls below 0°C (32°F), tiny particles, such as bits of clay, encourage water to turn into ice crystals that then grow into snowflakes.

A snowflake is a number of snow crystals, which have joined together as they fall through air that is close to freezing. When the temperature is ideal for stickiness, and the wind is light enough not to break them up, the flakes can grow very large.

Varying temperature, moisture, and wind conditions favor crystal growth in different ways:

- Columns—new snow crystals in a six-sided hollow or solid prism.

- Long, thin needles.

- Plates—thin, usually hexagonal crystals. Plates may not bond well to one another and can cause a weak layer in the snow for long periods of time.

- Stellar crystals—the classic star-shaped snowflake.

- Graupel (soft hail)—rounded particles are formed when the air contains water droplets which freeze to crystals.

- Ice pellets—may form when rain falls though a very cold air mass.

The three attributes of a good winter mountaineer: **(1)** High pain threshold, **(2)** Bad memory, **(3)** I forget the third (Photo: Clive Hebblethwaite).

RISING AIR CREATES THE WINTER WEATHER

FRONTAL LIFT

As a storm develops, warm, moist air is lifted over cold air. This rising air cools, forming clouds, rain, or snow. The warmer the air, the more moisture it contains, the faster it rises and cools, the greater the snowfall. Therefore, air masses originating in warmer areas, such as the Atlantic and Pacific Oceans, have a tendency for greater snowfall. However, just because a cloud contains snow does not mean that it will land as snow. Rain, freezing rain, sleet, and snow can all fall on the same place as the front moves overhead:

- When the warm air extends to ground level, the snow melts and falls as rain (most winter rain is melted snow).

- If the band of cold air is relatively thin and the ground is below freezing, the falling rain cools and turns into ice when it hits something, causing freezing rain.

- When the layer of cold air is thick enough, the falling rain freezes into ice pellets. If the snow can fall all, or most, of the way through cold air, it falls as snow. At very cold temperatures, snowflakes do not form and the snow mostly comprises snow crystals.

- If the snowflakes fall and rise again, they melt and refreeze forming hailstones. When snow falls through moist air it becomes coated with a layer of ice. Convective winds then blow the precipitation back up into the cloud, where it falls through the moist air, and grows in size with an additional layer. This is a form of hail.
- Sleet is a soft, melted snowflake that has refrozen.

OROGRAPHIC LIFT

Although frontal lifting is a major cause of storms in summer, in winter the mountains themselves have a major effect. As a storm front, or even just moist air, reaches the mountains it is forced upward (orographic lift). The resulting cooling forms precipitation and—if cold enough—snow. The rate of lifting depends on the steepness of the mountains, and is greater when the air mass hits the mountains straight on.

PREDICTING SNOW STORMS

To identify possible snow storms, look for the path of the depression and its associated fronts:

- Is it traveling from and over cold areas and can it pick up moisture?
- Is the air dry and cold? Since water vapor is needed to make clouds and snow, cold air will tend to produce lighter snow than warmer air. In general, the heaviest snow usually falls when the temperature is only slightly below freezing, or even above freezing at ground level.
- Is the air mass hitting the mountains straight on?

COLD CLEAR SPELLS

High pressure established over Northern Europe or the United States during winter can bring a spell of cold easterly or northerly air streams to the U.K. or U.S. The clear skies, settled conditions, and light winds associated with high pressure allow heat to be lost from the surface of the Earth. The temperature then falls overnight, leading to air or ground frosts. Light winds, along with falling temperatures, also encourage fog to form, which can linger into the morning and clear slowly.

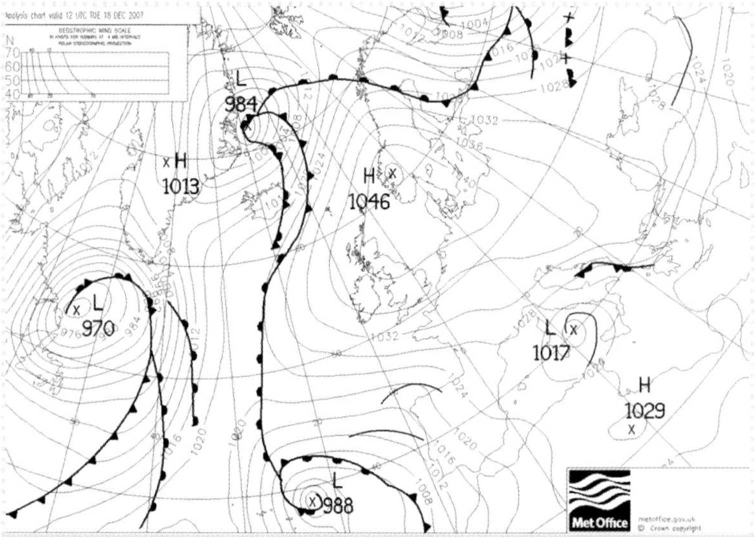

FIGURE 1
A winter weather map © Crown Copyright (2008), the Met Office. In this example, the U.K. is experiencing sunshine and light winds from an anticyclone. A developing polar low north of Iceland will bring freshening easterlies, cold polar air, and some snow from the moisture it picks up over the sea.

SNOW ON THE GROUND

Snow on the ground undergoes cycles of change (metamorphism) unless it is –40°C (–40°F) or less. Ice (from crystal surfaces) changes into water vapor, which moves through the snowpack from warm to colder areas and is deposited as ice on other grain surfaces. Water vapor also moves at the crystal level from the points to the hollows, so that the points become blunt and the hollows fill, affecting the structure and stability of the snowpack.

The difference in snow temperature from the bottom to the top of the snowpack, and more importantly in individual layers, dictates the rate of vapor transfer and is called the temperature gradient. The temperature at ground level is always 0°C (32°F), therefore, the lower the air temperature and the thinner the layer or snowpack, the greater the temperature gradient.

Anything between 5–10°C/m (41–50°F/m) is a moderate gradient and anything below that is a weak gradient. Extreme temperature gradients of 50–60°C/m (122–40°F/m) over short sections of the snowpack are not uncommon in Scotland. Strong temperature gradients promote greater vapor movement than weak gradients.

The depth of snow, aspect of the slope and the air temperature all affect the temperature gradient. The changes in the snowpack do not occur in isolation and are complicated by further snowfall. This results in layering of the snowpack, with the associated danger of avalanches.

ROUNDING/SNOW STABILISATION

If the temperature gradient within a layer or the whole snowpack is weak (usually when the outside temperatures are moderate or the snowpack is deep) "rounding" dominates (see Fig. 3). This breaks down the snow crystals and stabilizes the snowpack (Equilibrium Metamorphism). At snow temperatures close to 0°C (32°F) the change is rapid; the snow layers consolidate and become denser, stronger, and more stable in a relatively short period of time. To assess when the snow has become stable, consider how quickly rounding is taking place. Tony Daffern (*Avalanche Safety for Skiers and Climbers*, 1999) states that small sluffs from steep ground and snow falling off trees may be indicators that rounding is taking place, but there are exceptions to every rule! The process of stabilization of the lower layers is speeded up by the weight of further snowfall.

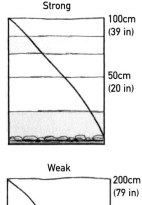
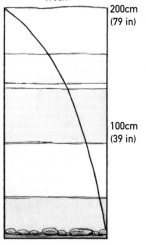

FIGURE 2
Strong and moderate temperature gradients throughout the snowpack. A large temperature gradient promotes faceting. A weak temperature gradient promotes rounding.

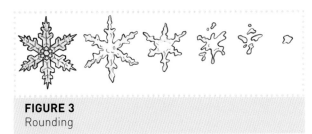

FIGURE 3
Rounding

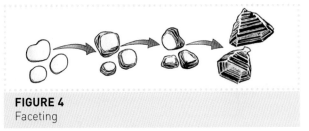

FIGURE 4
Faceting

FACETING

If a strong temperature gradient occurs, a process called faceting (Kinetic Metamorphism) dominates (see Fig. 4), where rounded snow crystals are transformed into angular shaped crystals. These crystals do not bond well to each other and form weak layers. As the vapor moves from crystals in the lower layers to crystals in the layers above, the crystals will eventually develop into a cup-shaped crystal called "depth hoar."

Faceting is faster when the snowpack is loose and there are crusts present, which stop the vapor escaping. Faceted grains and depth hoar will persist in the snowpack for some time and can cause cycles of avalanche activity for the rest of the winter and even into the spring or, in some cases, summer. According to *Avalanche Accidents in Canada* (Geldsetzer & Jamieson, 1999), faceted grains and surface hoar are the weak layers in the failure plane in 78 percent of fatal accidents.

MELT-FREEZE METAMORPHISM

This is when the snowpack becomes wet and refreezes during the night. As the melt-freeze continues, water evaporates from the snowpack and grains of snow fuse to form larger grains, to the point where water can percolate through the snow (from surface melting, rain and ground water drainage), forming loose packed grains called "sugar" or "corn" snow. Melt-freeze can also lubricate layers adjacent to the ground and cause wet slab avalanches.

A warm, dry wind rapidly accelerates the loss of water from the snowpack and the formation of sugar snow.

OTHER FORMS OF SNOW

Rime (hoar in Scotland)—A weak, dull, white, dense deposit formed by super-cooled water droplets freezing on objects exposed to the wind.

Surface or Hoar Frost—Forms on the surface of snow when there is a clear sky with high humidity and little or no wind. These crystals sparkle on trees and on the snow surface after a clear, cold night. Once buried under a new snow layer they can be difficult to detect and very dangerous.

Powder snow—Light, fluffy, newly fallen snow.

Corn snow—Coarse, round crystals formed when surface layers melt and refreeze for several days.

Crust—Forms when melted water on the surface freezes. If the source of heat is the sun, it is called Sun Crust.

Sun cups—A pit in a snowfield, which resembles a cup and is caused by differential melting as the sun moves. They can become very deep when dirt trapped in the hollows absorbs more heat.

Nieves penitents—A tall, sometimes curving, column of ice or compacted snow found at high altitudes and created by deep sun cups.

Cornices collapse easily when they get heavy! (Aanoch Dubh, Scotland.)

Sastrugi—Wind erodes the snow leaving various shapes, such as wave-like sastrugi.

Cornices—An overhanging mass of snow formed on the leesides of ridges by wind action.

ICE

If the ground is dry and cold, not much ice will form. A series of melt-freezes are required to release the water. Because snow melts more easily than ice, the next freeze will make the ice grow, but the snow disappear.

Several forms of ice can be differentiated depending on their source:

White ice—Melt-freeze of hard firn or neve snow. The best ice to climb, but rarely forms on steep cliffs above 70°.

Blue ice—More dense and watery than white ice, developed from water drainage and snowfall, which sticks to it giving it its plastic nature.

Water ice—Icicles from water flow. Transparent, hard, and brittle.

Verglass—Formed by freezing rain or freezing of surface trickles. It is rock hard.

Ice crust—Melt-freeze of surface snow. Very brittle.

AVALANCHES

"Telling skiers about danger is a little like trying to teach safe sex to adolescents—they will try it anyway."

—Henry Schniewind, avalanche expert

Experienced winter mountaineers seem to have an instinctive feeling for avalanche conditions. In reality, they are combining their knowledge of the previous day's weather and the information from the avalanche report, with the conditions they meet when climbing. This expertise is only achieved by experiencing winter in all its guises, but some principles will help. See also page 256 for avalanches when ski mountaineering.

WHAT IS AN AVALANCHE?

Each time snow falls or is blown by the wind it creates a new layer. After the snow has landed, each layer undergoes changes caused by temperature variations, wind, and pressure. This results in different types of avalanche (see Fig. 5).

Wave-like sastrugi

REDUCING YOUR CHANCE OF BEING AVALANCHED

- Avalanches occur whenever snow is lying on a slope of sufficient angle, but mostly 30–45°.
- It does not have to be snowing for slopes to become avalanche prone.
- Ninety percent of the time victims, or members of their party, trigger avalanches.
- If you are buried there is a high chance you will die.
- It is not just large slopes and large amounts of snow that should concern you; small patches of snow on a climb or ridge can slide, taking you with them. A small depth of snow in a large gully can slide and create a lot of snow at the bottom of the gully. Avalanches from ice routes above can pour down on an otherwise seemingly safe ice climb.

A slab avalanche. Avalanches can occur whenever there is snow on the ground.

Figure 5 Avalanche categories

A full-depth avalanche occurs when the whole snow cover slides on to the ground (see sideview right).

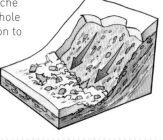

A smooth surface for an avalanche to slide on

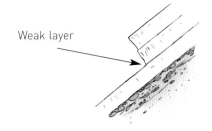

A flowing wet avalanche. Whether an avalanche is defined as wet or dry will depend on the moisture content.

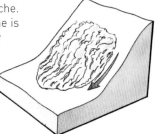

A surface avalanche occurs when one layer slides on to another.

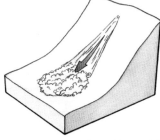

An airborne powder avalanche occurs when it reaches 65kph (40.4mph).

A loose snow avalanche starts from a single point.

A slab avalanche occurs when an area of more bonded snow slides off the surface below (see sideview right).

Weak layer

WHAT CREATES AVALANCHE CONDITIONS?

Weather is the most important factor. It deposits new snow, creates the wind that can redistribute the snow on to new slopes and, combined with temperature fluctuations and gravity, it causes the changes in the snowpack.

Effect of temperature—See Melt-freeze metamorphism, page 162.

Effect of wind—Even on a clear day the wind can rapidly redistribute snow on to lee slopes forming a dangerous layer called "wind slab." The wind pressure can also stabilize other slopes by aiding evaporation. When wind blows over a mountain top, the leeward side experiences top-loading. When the wind blows over a ridge that leads up the mountain it may cause cross-loading. The effects of cross-loading are subtle, usually more difficult to spot, and less stable.

Heavy snowfall—Eighty percent of avalanches happen during or soon after heavy snowfall due to the extra weight of fresh snow and the difference between its consistency and the layer below.

Rain—In the short term this can cause instability through additional loading and possible lubrication of lower layers, but when the snowpack refreezes it can also help to stabilize it. See Melt-freeze metamorphism and rounding, pages 161–2.

PREDICTING AVALANCHE CONDITIONS

AT HOME

Study the previous day's weather to predict the amount of snow that may have fallen, where the wind may have redistributed it, and whether it is thawing. Look at the avalanche report, but remember it is a prediction made by experts in previous days and should be adapted according to the conditions you meet on the mountain.

FROM THE VALLEY

As soon as you leave your car you should start questioning the predictions you made at home.

- Can you see any avalanche activity, especially on slopes with the same aspect as those on your journey?
- From where has the wind been blowing? Does snow being blown from the ridges indicate the current wind direction? Where is the snow accumulating?
- How much has it snowed? A build-up of more than 2cm (0.8in) per hour of new snow can produce unstable conditions and more than 30cm (11.8in) continuous snow is hazardous. Are slopes loaded with fresh or drifted snow?

Remember: you must make your own avalanche assessment on the climb

Rime builds in the direction the wind blows

DURING THE WALK/CLIMB

- Continue to look for signs of where the wind has been blowing—is it a local wind created by the mountain and different to the weather forecast?
- Look for sastrugi or parallel etching, where the steep edge faces the direction from where the wind was blowing, and rime, which builds in the direction of the wind. Look for cornice build-up.
- Feel for changes in the consistency of the snow under foot. Is cracking of the surface an indication of slab? Settling of the snowpack is due to the presence of slab—the harder the slab the more it will settle. Hard slab does not sparkle but has a velvety texture and a dull, matte color. Are small slabs releasing easily as you cross small safe slopes?
- Is there a sudden temperature rise? Is the sun just catching the top of the crag? Carry a thermometer on your backpack to spot temperature inversions.
- Do you feel unsafe? The gut instinct of the experienced mountaineer should not be underestimated; it usually means your subconscious has spotted something.

AVOIDING AVALANCHE-PRONE SLOPES

You can travel in the mountains without ever standing on a potential avalanche slope by choosing a route that keeps to gentle slopes or defined ridges and avoids lee slopes, plateau rims, and open slopes. When choosing where to travel consider the following:

- **What is the angle of the slope?** Statistically most large slab avalanches occur on slopes between 30 and 45°, but this statistic may be misleading because these are the angles that most walkers and skiers travel on. Snow slides off slopes above 60°, but unstable slopes just below this may release very easily.

- **What surface is the snow resting on?** Smooth ground is more likely to result in full-depth avalanches whereas rough ground, or large boulders, will tend to anchor the base layers in position. However, once the boulders are covered, surface avalanche can continue unhindered. Trees and rocks that stick up through the snowpack can help to hold it in place, but the trees must be quite substantial to anchor the slab.

Wind and snow blowing off the ridge can indicate where slab avalanches are likely to be forming. (Photo: Clive Hebblethwaite).

WHAT IS THE SHAPE OF THE SLOPE?

Convex slopes are more hazardous because the point of maximum convexity is a frequent site of tension fracture (see Fig. 6).

WHAT IS THE ORIENTATION OF THE SLOPE TO THE SUN?

During cloudy periods there is little difference between sunny and shady slopes, but when it is sunny:

- North-facing slopes receive little sun, stay cold, and can extend the period of avalanche danger. This is also where the best climbing conditions exist.
- South-facing slopes are warmer, but can develop thin crusts that increase the chances of a weak layer.
- East-facing slopes catch the sun in the colder morning therefore melting slowly.
- West-facing slopes catch the sun in the warmer afternoons and produce more wet avalanches (along with south-facing slopes).

CORNICES

A collapsing cornice can trigger an avalanche. Cornices can be collapsed by the weight of climbers or when warm weather or rain makes them denser. Climbing below cornices should be avoided during a heavy thaw or sudden temperature rise, and twenty-four to forty-eight hours after snowstorms or heavy drifting. Also take care walking above them (see Fig. 7).

WHAT IS THE ORIENTATION OF THE SLOPE TO THE WIND?

Lee slopes, including the sheltered side of ridges and plateau rims, become loaded with snow after a storm or heavy drifting. Ridges are safer. The crests of mountain ridges are usually protected from avalanches, and ribs and buttresses provide rock belays to provide security. However, even small avalanches can take you off your feet and down a cliff on to steeper ground. Travel on the windward side of ridges to avoid wind-blown snow and cornices. Gullies (couloirs) are natural

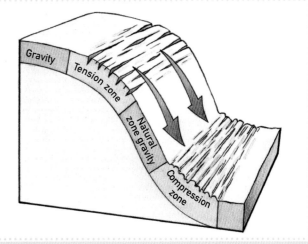

FIGURE 6
Convex slopes are most hazardous.

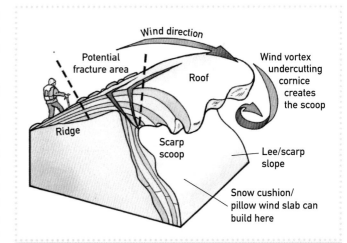

FIGURE 7
The fracture line on a cornice is a long way from the edge!

accumulation zones for slab avalanches and should be avoided when the avalanche risk is high or it is thawing and cornice collapse is possible. Look above you—it is often these slopes that are triggered, which then swoop down on to the slope you are on. Beware of blind faith. Tracks on the slope do not mean it is safe, even if you safely crossed it earlier in the day.

ASSESSING A SUSPECT SLOPE

"Remember this, my friends, the avalanche does not know that you are an expert."

—Andre Roche, snow scientist

Suspect slopes can be partially evaluated by digging a snow pit on smaller, safe slopes of similar orientation and altitude to the main slope. You will need to extrapolate for situations higher up, e.g., below cornices, where surface slab layers may be much thicker. Assessing a slope is not an exact science and even experts get it wrong.

Dig several pits rather than analyze one in depth. Use an avalanche probe to find a representative place with average depth. Dig a snow pit 1m (3.3ft) wide to the first thick layer of old refrozen snow, or 1.5–2m (4.9–6.6ft) deep (no deeper because it is rare for humans to trigger avalanches deeper than this depth).

Smooth the vertical back wall of the pit, feeling for any changes, and then probe with a finger or fist all the way down to assess the hardness of the layers. Look for the weakest layer and try to estimate how well it is bonded to adjacent layers. If you find any of the below it may be a dangerous weakness in the snowpack:

- Adjacent layers of differing hardness
- Very soft layers (fist penetrates easily)
- Water drops squeezed out of a snowball made from any layer
- Layers of ice or loose, uncohesive grains
- Layers of graupel—these act like a layer of ball bearings
- Feathery or faceted crystals
- Air space.

You should also make a judgment on bonding within the layer. Is it going to break up easily or is the whole layer bonded and will the whole slope slide?

HARDNESS OF THE SNOW

1 is hard, 5 is soft

5 Gloved fist penetrates
4 Four gloved fingers penetrate
3 One gloved finger penetrates
2 Pick of an ice axe penetrates
1 Knife penetrates

SHOVEL TEST

The shovel test judges the cohesiveness of layers (see Fig. 8). It must be practiced over many years to the point where you build up a feeling for the stability of layers. Most beginners tend to overrate the danger. A potential problem is that you are removing the weight of snow from the layer each time you dig, and it is difficult to assess the influence of this factor. Because of the small sample size, you need to do many tests to get a true feel for the stability of the snow.

Having made the snow pit observations, isolate a wedge-shaped block, cutting down to the top of the next identified layer. Cut behind the column to below the suspect layer (not the whole column). Insert the shovel (see right) and pull straight out; don't lever on the shovel. Do this for each suspect layer in your pit. You are looking for smooth, straight shears that pop out easily. Try to rank them as easy, moderate, hard, and so on. If a block slides during cutting then there is obviously a weak layer. If the block slides off with pressure from the shovel—and it must be a clean smooth shear to mean anything—and there is 15cm (6in) or more snow on top, then turn each block upside down to identify which weak layer was involved.

QUICK PITS

As you climb, dig snow stances, cut steps or create a belay (see page 197). Check on the surface layers with your ice axe.

TRAVELING ON A POTENTIAL AVALANCHE SLOPE

It is rarely essential to negotiate an avalanche-prone slope, but if you do have to proceed consider the following:

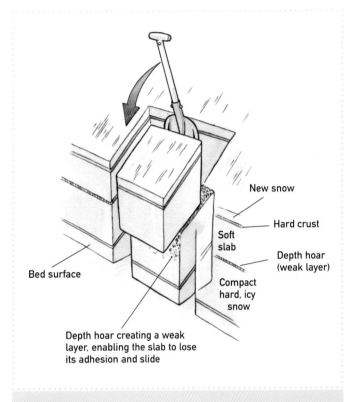

New snow

Hard crust

Soft slab

Depth hoar (weak layer)

Bed surface

Compact hard, icy snow

Depth hoar creating a weak layer, enabling the slab to lose its adhesion and slide

FIGURE 8
The cohesiveness of the layers can also be judged using the shovel test.

- Belay someone down the slope to check it out. Are you going to be swept over a cliff, or will it pile up at the bottom?

- What will happen should the slope avalanche, ie., is the snow bonded?

- What is the depth of snow?

- Is it likely to be a slab or loose snow avalanche?

- Zip up, wrap a scarf round your mouth and nose, and wear a hat.

- Take your hands out of leashes on poles and ice axes.

- Carry avalanche transceivers, a probe, and a shovel.

- Direct descent or ascent of a potential avalanche slope is safer than traversing.

- Cross or descend one at a time—the rest of the party should watch closely.

- Cross or descend in the same track.

- It is possible to trigger avalanches from below a slope?

EXPERT TIP

Blyth Wright SAIS
Co-ordinator
Co-ordinator@SAIS.gov.uk

"All the world's avalanche forecasts in two web sites!"

www.sais.gov.uk
www.avalanche-center.org

WHAT TO DO WHEN CAUGHT IN AN AVALANCHE

If the unthinkable happens, fight for your life! If you are not close to the surface and you have not created an air space, your chances of survival are going to be slim.

- Delay the avalanche taking you by plunging your axe into the snow. This may help to keep you near the top of the slide.
- Shout.
- Run to the side, or jump up-slope above the fracture.
- If the slab is hard try to remain on top of a block.
- Get rid of poles and skis, but recent evidence suggests that wearing a backpack increases your surface area and keeps you higher in the avalanche.
- Try to roll like a log, off the debris.
- Swimming motions are rumored to help.
- As the avalanche slows, make a desperate effort to get to the surface, or at least get a hand through.
- Push the snow away from your face and try to maintain an air space.
- Take and hold a deep breath at the last moment to maintain space for chest expansion.
- Try to avoid panic and conserve your energy. Your companions will be searching for you.

Mountain walkers and climbers rarely wear avalanche transceivers, or carry shovels and a probe, yet digging with your hands is slow and strenuous.

RESCUING AN AVALANCHE VICTIM

A buried victim has an 80 percent chance of survival if they have an air space, are no deeper than 2m (6ft), and they are located within fifteen minutes. Survival chances then decline to 40 percent after one hour and 20 percent the hour after that. Someone who is buried deeper than 2m (6.6ft) has an almost zero chance of survival:

- Check for further avalanche danger and post a lookout.
- Mark the point of entry and the point where the victim was last seen.
- Make a quick search of the debris, looking for signs and sounds.
- Probe the most likely burial spots—pay particular attention to shallow depressions in the slope and around rocks and trees.
- Make a systematic search, probing the debris with axes or poles.
- Send for help.
- Do not give up—the longest someone has survived is twenty-two hours.

COLD INJURIES

The cold and wind make winter mountaineering extremely serious.

HYPOTHERMIA

Hypothermia is the lowering of the body's core temperature and is exacerbated by cold air, wet clothing, tiredness, low energy levels, and dehydration. Prevention is better than cure, so eat, drink, wear layers, and stay dry.

Hypothermic people do not generally notice the symptoms, so it is important for others in the group to spot the signs. Hypothermia affects people in different ways and no one symptom is reliable, but these are indications:

- Feeling cold.
- Mild shivering and cold hands or feet do not indicate you are severely hypothermic, but that your body is trying to generate heat to warm yourself.
- Uncontrolled shivering means that you are hypothermic.
- A lack of shivering does not mean you are not hypothermic, since this can be a symptom of severe hypothermia.
- Cold hands and feet indicate your body is fighting the cold by reducing the flow of blood to the extremities to maintain the body's core temperature.
- Muscles are stiff, weak, and less responsive.
- Mental disorientation, inappropriate behavior and slurred speech, which means that accidents are more likely.
- Armpits feel cold.

Mild hypothermia—Uncontrollable shivering, loss of coordination, or slurring of words.

Severe hypothermia—A further deterioration of mental status to unresponsiveness. The trunk will feel cold to the touch and the body may be

WARNING

Frostbite can be avoided, even at extremes of altitude, temperature, and fatigue. Keep your limbs dry, wear adequate clothing, carry spare gloves and dry socks, and don't wear your boots too tight. Carelessness is often a major factor, as is becoming dehydrated; smoking and caffeine do not help.

Severe frostbite can be avoided if you are careful. (The progression of frostbite. Photo: Shaun Hutson.)

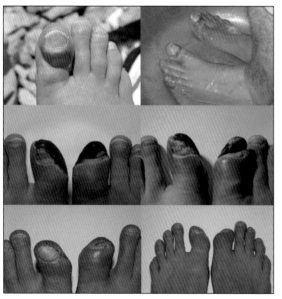

rigid. In severe cases, pulse and respiration may be absent, but the patient should not be considered dead until re-warming has been accomplished.

Treatment—Stop and warm the person, put them in dry clothes and a hat, and protect them from the elements and further heat loss. Put them in a sleeping bag protected from the ground (having someone else in the sleeping bag may not be as beneficial as previously thought). Other heat sources, such as a fire, can be helpful. The skin warms up before the core, so the victim may feel better before they are ready to move. Exercise will not help, because they have depleted their energy reserves so much that they cannot even shiver.

FROSTBITE

All winter climbers have suffered from numb feet or hands, maybe for hours at a time, with no ill effects. It is important, however, to realize that below –10°C (–14°F), any tissue that feels numb for more than a few minutes can become frozen. It rarely occurs above –10°C (–14°F), without wind chill. In the early stages of frostbite (frost nip), in the unthawed state, the skin is yellow-grey, painless, numb, and leathery to the touch. If you feel numbness in your extremities, and the temperature is low, flex your fingers and toes, stamp your feet, clap your hands or place them somewhere warm such as your armpits or groin. This will bring feeling back to the limbs, accompanied by painful "hot aches," or "screaming barfies," as the warm blood defrosts the nerve endings.

Frostnip can be reversed if treated in time, but in deep frostbite, the tissue is hard, white, and obviously frozen. It can be stabilized, but will not heal properly until you have sought medical help. It is better to move for six hours with frozen feet to a place of safety than to thaw the feet at a high camp. Walking on vulnerable and inflamed thawed tissue will result in further damage.

If you cannot reach medical help, once you have reached safety start to re-warm the limbs by immersion in hot water (39–42°C/102–7°F) for periods of twenty minutes, moving fingers and toes if possible. Do not knock or rub the frozen tissue. Avoid smoking (nicotine contracts blood vessels), but alcohol may be helpful (it dilates blood vessels)—but only when the victim is not hypothermic.

By far the most important treatment after re-warming is to keep the skin as clean as possible to avoid any infection. After thawing, separate fingers and toes and wrap them in clean bandages. The victim must not use the thawed tissue, which may require them to be fed and even helped to use the toilet. If a hot water container is not available, warm the affected parts in a warm sleeping bag (or on the abdomen, groin, or armpits) for several hours. Give oxygen if it is available.

Several hours after thawing the tissue will swell, and during the first two days giant blisters form. Do not puncture them; they will settle during the first week leaving tissue that is discolored, and possibly gangrenous, shrunken, and black. If the frostbite is superficial, new pink skin will appear beneath the discolored tissue. If it is deep, the end of a toe or finger will gradually fall off— an unsightly, but usually painless, process. It is extremely difficult to predict the outcome in the first few weeks after frostbite and remarkable recoveries do occur. Surgery is usually best avoided, until it is clear that there is no other alternative.

WINTER ROUTE FINDING AND NAVIGATION

The skills for navigating in winter are the same as for navigating in summer, but the weather is worse; it is cold, gloves get in the way, the daylight hours are shorter, and avalanches and cornices must be avoided. Walking on a bearing and pacing must be spot on, because there are fewer features, and you may even be crawling on your hands and knees!

Carry a spare map, compass, and a reliable flashlight with spare batteries and bulbs. A 1:50,000 map can sometimes be better for winter navigation, because the detail on a 1:25,000 map is often obscured by snow. However, a 1:25,000 map shows more detail for complex route finding. It is also easier to take accurate bearings. Add a few notes inside your map case, with crucial compass bearings, distances, altitudes, pacing, and timings for each navigation leg.

When conditions are difficult it is important to have a robust strategy:

- Use linear features, but beware that new fences, ski tows, etc., can confuse the issue.

GOGGLES

Always carry anti-fog goggles in a rigid case (to avoid scratching or breaking). They are invaluable when trying to map read and navigate with hail being flung at your face.

Anti-fog goggles are invaluable when navigating through hail. (Photo: Clive Hebblethwaite.)

When conditions are difficult, it is important to have a good strategy for navigation. (Photo: Clive Hebblethwaite.)

- Sometimes in intermittent poor visibility it may be easier to follow features that are hazardous, such as a cliff edge, where cornices may be impossible to see. If you do take these routes, rope-up at a safe distance (15–20m/49–66ft) and walk parallel to, but away from, the edge.
- Understand attack points and aiming off.
- Mentally tick-off obvious features as you pass them and think carefully about collecting features that will stop you overshooting your target.
- Beware of following footprints; they should be regarded as a morale booster and abandoned if their direction does not fit the compass bearing.
- Be careful near streams and boulders—you can break through the snow.
- Accurate timing is difficult in winter because of the fluctuating snow conditions, but still use it to establish that you may have walked too far.
- Pacing is also difficult when the snow conditions are changeable. You should understand what is happening to the ground and always relate it to your pacing.
- Slope aspect removes whole sections of the hillside where you are not. Throw snowballs down the slope; this could help you to identify the fall line. If they disappear, stop!
- Do not navigate too complicated areas—instead, head for obvious changes in slope direction and angle.

WHITEOUT CONDITIONS

Whiteout occurs when the horizon and the ground merge into one due to cloud and snow. Add strong winds and darkness and it can be a frightening and bewildering experience. Distances, slope angles, directions, and speeds become impossible to judge. To stay calm, plan your route, identify hazards, measure compass bearings and write them down, and navigate to obvious safe features from the comfort of your shelter. If you do change your plan, write it down so you can match the ground to the map or backtrack later.

It is easy to drift off your bearing, especially in a strong wind or when following a sloping traverse where there is always the tendency to drift downhill. To avoid this, send one person following a bearing in front of the main navigator. As soon as the lead person begins to drift to the left or the right, the navigator can shout instructions to bring them back on course. Use the altimeter, and GPS if you have one, but remember: strong winds can affect the altimeter and cliffs can cause errors in the GPS signal.

OUTRIGGERS

A useful method for finding narrow valleys is to walk in line as if conducting a sweep search, with the main navigator in the middle. A relative rise or fall in the heads indicates the shape of your slope, i.e., at the bottom of a narrow valley the people on either side will be above the navigator.

PUTTING IT ALL TOGETHER

A 2003 review showed that of over a thousand rescues in Scotland, navigation, bad planning, and poor timing were the three big causes of accidents. Another factor identified is different aspirations and abilities within groups leading to poor decisions.

Good planning combined with observations on the hill will help to make a great winter day in the mountains safer:

- Get the current and previous day's weather forecast and an avalanche report.
- Plan where you are going according to the weather and avalanche report.
- Prepare food and drink and pack your backpack the night before.
- Let someone know where you are going. The effectiveness of mountain rescue teams is improved if a reasonably accurate description of your plans is available.

Good snow conditions make traveling in the mountains faster and safer, and poor snow makes it frustrating and dangerous. If you are heading out in poor snow, minimize danger by choosing a good route before going out. Draw arrows on the map showing the prevailing weather conditions to help you determine potential avalanche-prone slopes, deep snow, and cornices.

- Think about the direction of the sun—in the Northern Hemisphere, south and west slopes catch the afternoon sun and consolidate more quickly.
- Dirty snow consolidates quicker than clean snow.
- Beware of hidden holes next to trees, rocks, and rivers.
- Ridges are not the place to be in a storm, as cornices form on them. They are, however, a good choice when the snow is deep or avalanches have been predicted.
- Do not be afraid to turn back.

EMERGENCY SHELTERS AND SNOW HOLES

"Mountaineers should be independent, self-reliant, and able to look after themselves."
- Mountaineering Council of Scotland

It is your responsibility to be prepared for anything the mountains can throw at you. Returning late or being stranded over night does not justify alerting the mountain rescue services. Things do go wrong, so you should be prepared to spend the night out at least once in your winter mountaineering career. Digging a snow hole allows you to survive. Snow holes vary from one dug for survival to one in which you can several nights, or even weeks. They are

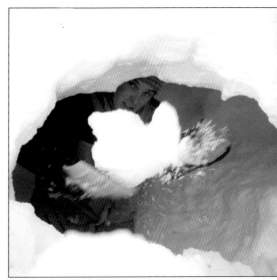

Digging a snow hole is wet work, so take a few layers off and put waterproofs on. (Climber: Dave Williams.)

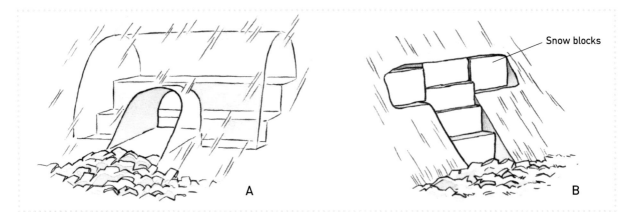

Snow blocks

A

B

FIGURE 9
Two types of survival
shelter

stronger in a storm than tents or a bivvy bag, which must be continually dug out. They are also less cold than outside. Find somewhere free of avalanche danger such as snowdrifts in rivers (but take care not to fall through) and near ridges. Arrange the entrance so that it is on the leeward side of a slope to give protection from the wind, but beware that more snow will collect there.

It is difficult to dig a snow hole with an ice axe, so carry a small metal shovel the same size as your backpack. To lessen the chances of breaking your shovel keep the shaft short and do not lever back on the handle.

Digging in snow is a wet and tiring job so wear full waterproofs, but remove layers so that you have a dry set for when you finish digging. Work in turns so that none of you become too hot or too cold. An insulating mat will keep your knees warm and a plastic bivvy bag makes it easier to pull snow from inside the shelter. The softer the snow, the thicker the walls need to be. A plastic sheet on the floor is useful. Keep a shovel inside and mark the hole with wands or blocks so you do not step through the roof.

Smooth the inner walls to stop drips and take care cooking or using candles, as ventilation is usually poor. A ventilation hole must be poked into the roof for airflow. Keeping a ski stick in this hole and shaking it every so often will keep the hole open.

TYPES OF SNOW SHELTERS:

A survival shelter (see Fig. 9)—In an emergency, dig into a snow bank or a drift to create a compartment large enough for you to at least sit upright (see Fig. 9B). Sit on ropes or your backpack or, using the pad from it, loosen your boots and put your feet into the backpack. When you cannot find a slope to dig into, dig a trench deep and long enough for you to lie in comfortably. Line the bottom with insulating material. The roof can be made of ski poles and covered with a bivvy bag and loose snow or blocks of hard pack snow. Dig a tunnel in from the side and plug it with snow.

A snow cave (see Fig. 10)—This is just a snow hole with more thought put into it. Dig the entrance so that the door is below the sitting level.

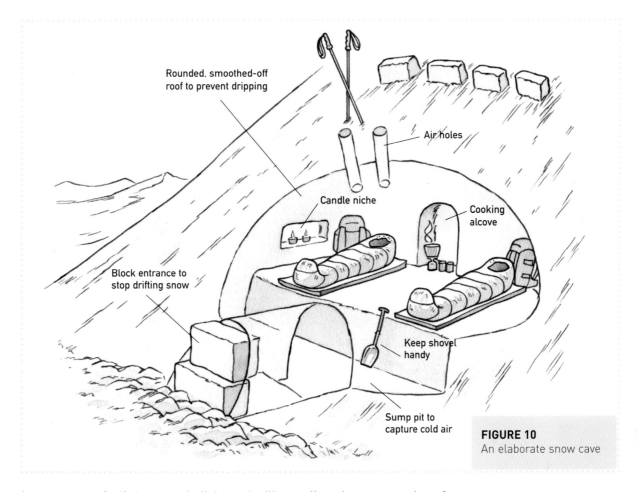

Rounded, smoothed-off
roof to prevent dripping

Air holes

Candle niche

Cooking
alcove

Block entrance to
stop drifting snow

Keep shovel
handy

Sump pit to
capture cold air

FIGURE 10
An elaborate snow cave

A snow mound—If the snow is light and will not allow the construction of a snow hole by digging, make a snow mound shelter (Quinzee). Pile loose snow up, but do not compact it. When the mound is high enough (this depends on the consistency of the snow), allow it to compact naturally over one–two hours. After compaction, dig towards the middle (a ski pole left in the middle can help to prevent you digging too far) and then outwards to create a circle. Install a vent in the roof.

EQUIPMENT TO KEEP YOU WARM

I have never failed on a route because of my clothing, but I have certainly had a more miserable time as my feet and hands have become cold or the draw-cord of my waterproof jacket has whipped me in the face. The secret to enjoying winter mountaineering and ice climbing is to pay attention to the simple things, such as removing metal piercings and adjusting your layers.

A warm drink is only psychologically different to a cold one; it is the energy content that keeps you warm. (The excellent Jet Boil Stove.)

The basic principle is to climb cool and belay warm. Try to stay dry at all costs, even if it means moving more slowly! This is particularly important for those that have more body fat, a slower metabolism, and slower circulation, because they warm up slower and cool down faster, plus a lower metabolism means there is less heat to dry out base layers. Long pitches can save time, but when the weather is nasty or cold, shorter pitches will help to keep everyone warmer.

FUEL TO STAY WARM

Staying warm does not only depend on your clothing; you should also keep your energy levels up. Eat a big breakfast and snack every thirty minutes. Slow-burning carbohydrates, such as peanut butter or honey sandwiches, are best and Gel packets work well on winter routes. Do not smoke and have plenty of fluids, because dehydration causes the capillaries in the fingers to shut down. Carry a jet boil stove or Thermos. To make your Thermos go further, fill your mug with packed snow and melt it with the warm drink.

KEEPING YOUR BODY WARM

See also Chapter 1. A base layer and mid-layer fleece with a waterproof over the top is usually enough when walking, but vary them to reduce sweating. When you reach your climb, or part way through the day, change into a dry base layer. Carry extra warm clothing for when you stop moving and put an extra layer on before you are really cold. Ensure there is enough room to move in your waterproof jacket and pants or SA, and to put another layer on underneath (but not too loose, as cold air exchanges easily with the warm air inside). Cuffs and openings must keep the snow out and be easy to adjust with gloves on. A large hood is essential to pull over the top of your helmet or fleece hat, and all the zip toggles must have a tag large enough to grab hold of with gloves on. Legs radiate less heat and sweat less, so good, well-fitting pants are important. Wear Long Johns underneath a thinner pair of pants.

Removing your waterproof to add a layer when you are wearing a harness is a problem—instead, try layering on top with a synthetic high loft insulated jacket (belay jacket) such as the Mountain Equipment Trango Jacket.

The secret to enjoying winter mountaineering and ice climbing is to pay attention to the simple things. (Climber: John Husband.)

PROTECTING HANDS

Keep your core temperature up and your hands dry (do not put wet hands into gloves). The wrist has the third highest heat loss of the body, so ensure your layers are long enough and make some fleece wrist-overs. Carry a waterproof shell glove or mittens and lots of thin and thick gloves with sticky palms. Change them whenever they are wet and your hands cold (a new pair for every pitch when climbing). Avoid gloves with a floating liner because they are difficult to get on and off, and carry a pair of fleece mittens that are easily accessible at belays and for when it is really cold. Attach gloves to your wrist by a keeper cord.

If you are doing a lot of walking with your hand on top of your axe consider taping a piece of thin closed-cell foam over the top. Do not grip your ski poles or axe handle too tightly and keep "hand warmer" packets handy for putting into your gloves, and even your boots, or carry a charcoal warmer in your pocket. Do not blow on your fingers or into your gloves as it will only make them damp.

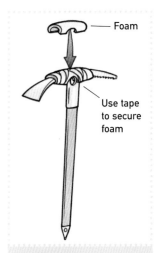

FIGURE 11
Tape thin closed-cell foam over the top of your ice axe to protect you from the cold.

KEEPING YOUR HEAD WARM

Wear a fleece hat, balaclava, or even a neoprene beanie under your helmet. A fleece neck gaiter or a fleece jacket with a hood will seal your neck and prevent heat loss during long belays.

LOOKING AFTER YOUR FEET

Your feet have little muscle bulk and it is much easier to keep them warm than to warm them up. On long belays, avoid standing on snow, weight your feet equally, and stamp your feet when they start to chill. Try to minimize the body closing down the extremities by dressing according to the route and climate, and don't scrimp on leg protection.

Wear warm boots and keep your feet dry, even if it means changing your socks during the day. Wear gaiters. Foot powder with aluminum hydroxide can help to reduce perspiration. For information on vapor barrier liners see Lightweight expeditions (page 340).

OTHER EQUIPMENT

BACKPACKS

A 45–55l (10.2gal) backpack is big enough for extra clothing, hats, gloves, bivvy bag, etc. All that is needed is a simple tube-shape with a lid or pocket and compression straps. You do not need crampon pockets and ice axe tubes, etc., because they add weight and get caught on everything when climbing. A removeable padded, lightweight waist belt is best for climbing.

EYE PROTECTION

Snow reflects a lot of the sun; even when it is not shining, the sun's glare can be intense. Take sunglasses and goggles for navigating in a blizzard.

A sturdy pair of boots with room for your toes to wriggle is essential for warmth and stability in snow.

HELMETS

Ensure your balaclava or fleece hat can fit underneath the helmet and that it has an attachment for a flashlight. Because of the amount of falling ice in winter a classic style helmet may be better than a foam one.

HARNESS

Ensure it will fit over all your clothing and that you can go to the bathroom wearing it.

SKI POLES

They are better than an ice axe on easy, angled safe ground. Buy a pair that can collapse small enough to fit inside your backpack (see Chapter 1).

BOOTS

For climbing mixed routes in less than arctic conditions, leather boots provide a more precise feel. However, plastic boots are warmer, provide greater support for ice climbing, and are more waterproof. The downside is that they are mostly heavier and less sensitive. One problem with plastic boots is that the shells cover two size ranges, with the inner thicker to pad out the smaller size. Over time the inner collapses and can make the fit poor.

Insulating insoles can help to reduce heat loss through the sole, but ensure they are not too large, thus cutting off the blood circulation to your toes. In general, the harder the climbing becomes, the lighter and more closely fitting the boot must be. This is because calf pump can originate from your heel rising up the back of the boot.

Boots suitable for winter use will be stiffer and have a sharp edge to the sole for edging in snow. Plastic boots are best if you are also camping because the inners can be removed and brought inside to stop them freezing.

To make the issue of boot/crampon compatibility more straightforward, boots and crampons can be graded according to their basic design and intended use. However, not all manufacturers follow the system designed by Scarpa (see Fig. 12 opposite).

Boot compatibility

Graded B0 to B3, dependent on the stiffness of the sole and the support provided by the uppers:

B0—Flexible walking boots. Contrary to popular views crampons can be put on them, but not for use on hard snow or ice.

B1—Stiff mountain walking boots suitable for occasional use with C1 crampons only.

B2—Very stiff mountaineering boots, suitable for use with C1 or C2 crampons only.

B3—Fully rigid, winter climbing and mountaineering boots suitable for use with C1, C2, or C3 crampons.

CRAMPONS

Oscar Eckstein started the ice revolution in 1908 with his 10 point crampons, freeing climbers from banging nails into their boots. In the 1930s, Laurent Grivel added front points. Thirty years later crampons were made rigid, enabling climbers to stand on front points only.

Crampons and boots make an integral unit. Using the wrong type of crampon on the wrong type of boot can break it or cause it to fall off the boot. Modern hard mixed climbers use a boot with a bolt-on crampon (called a "fruit boot" in Canada)—if you climb M12 you will know all about them. They are graded C1 to C3, depending on their attachment method and flexibility, but there are some models that seem to fit somewhere between C2 and C3.

A good general mountaineering crampon will do a better job on waterfall ice than a waterfall ice crampon will do in the mountains!

Crampon compatability

C1—Lightweight articulated or flexible walking crampons with simple straps. Most commonly 10 point (2 front and 8 bottom). They are light, simple, and a good choice for occasional use (low-angle snow, glacier crossing).

C2—Articulated or flexible step-in crampons attached with a heel clip and toe strap. Most commonly 12 point (4 front and 8 bottom). They give the best balance between ease of attachment, walking comfort, and climbing performance. They are a good choice for general mountaineering and low- to mid-grade climbs.

C3—Stiffer, or even fully rigid, crampons (although the latter are becoming rarer) attached with a heel clip and toe bail. They usually have 12 or more points, and adjustable front points (mono or dual). The best choice for pure ice and climbing performance, but a pain for general mountaineering/walking.

TERRAIN	CRAMPON			BOOT		
Low-level walking	C1	C2		B1	B2	B3
Mountaineering						
Snow routes Grades 1–2						
Snow routes Grade 3 up			C3			
Buttress climbing						
Mixed climbing and ice-fall climbing						

FIGURE 12 Crampon/boot compatibility table

CRAMPONS

When buying crampons, always take your boots with you and try the crampons in the store. They are all slightly different—some suit narrower boots, some suit boots with a thicker sole, some will not fit boots with too much of a "rocker" (curved section of the sole). For those of you with narrow feet, avoid crampons that have a wide spread between the front points and check the length of the points...they may be too long.

THE FRONT POINTS

These should stick out by 25–35mm (0.98–1.4in). Front points that are drooped and the second row angled forward are more suited to ice climbing. The angled second points reduce calf strain by resting against the ice. Downward facing second points facilitate a more ergonomic walking motion.

Horizontal front points are more versatile and work better than vertical ones for pure ice climbing, and two are better than one. Vertical front points tend to come out of the ice easier when the heel is raised. However, vertical mono points do provide more precision and are the best choice for very steep, hard ice and mixed ground. But, if the route is predominantly firm snow or ice, stick with two.

SHARPENING CRAMPON POINTS

Sharpen the points with a hand file, not a grinder—the heat generated will make the points very brittle. For moderate winter mountaineering, sharpening your front points once a season may be enough, leaving the rest of the points as they are. For harder routes, the sharpness and length of your front and secondary points becomes more important and you will need to re-file them more frequently. A modular design allows you to replace just the front points once they become too short.

Vertical technical points do not need to be razor sharp like a pick, but should have a point so that you can stand on the smallest edges, and not a rounded blunt tip.

CRAMPON ATTACHMENT

There are three main attachment systems:

Strap on—These may be useful in exceptional circumstances because they will fit any boot, but they can restrict blood flow and are difficult to put on. They have been superceded by a plastic heel cup and plastic front bail and are found on most C1 crampons. They will fit on to boots without a heel and toe lip.

Step-in—A wire toe bail fits over the boot welt and a heel tension lever snaps into place on the heel welt. An ankle strap is also typically part of the system. It is a secure system for plastic boots and leather boots with plastic soles that have deep notches on toes and heels. However, without the proper boots, you risk losing a crampon in mid-climb. Correctly fitted, these are fast, vibration free, and easy to use but, for most climbers, a mixed binding is better, because they are easier to put on when your boots are iced up and safer as the welt wears out.

Mixed—Simple and efficient and suitable for most things. The heel attaches with a lever similar to step-in bindings. The toes, however, attach with a strap and a ring or a plastic bail at the front. Because they do not require significant notches at the toes, these bindings can be used with lighter mountaineering boots, without heavy welts, and are used by most climbers, except specialist steep waterfall ice climbers.

DAMAGE TO ROPES

Contrary to popular belief, the UIAA found that standing on a rope in the snow with crampons doesn't damage the rope, nor does standing on it on rock or with a 75kg (165lb) body weight. In a further test, crampon points were forced right through the rope with no occurrence of strength reduction or damage.

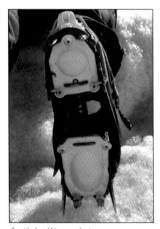

Anti-balling plates are essential to prevent the build-up of snow on the underside of crampons. The traditional remedy is to tap your crampons with your ice axe, but this is awkward, time consuming, and distracting.

TIPS FOR FITTING AND USING CRAMPONS

- The sole of your boot should match the shape of the crampon, without any large gaps.
- A correctly adjusted crampon should remain attached to the boot with the straps and clips undone.
- Put crampons in a crampon bag and carry them inside your pack.
- Trim the straps to a sensible length—long, dangling straps can get caught on the other crampon, but allow enough for gaiters.
- Check all boots and screws are tight, that straps are not cut or damaged, and that there are no cracks in the linking bar or crampon itself.
- If you forget anti-balling plates, use a plastic bag and tape, but do not expect it to last very long.
- Carry some plastic ties, a strap, some cord, and a small nut and bolt to repair crampons.

CHOOSING AN ICE AXE

Your ice axe acts as a walking stick, a self belay in the event of a slip occurring, and a brake if a slip turns into a slide. It can cut steps, bucket seats, snow bollards, large steps for resting or organizing equipment, pits for checking snow profiles, emergency shelters, and can act as a buried axe belay. It is used for climbing ice, hard snow, frozen turf, or even rock. No other piece of winter equipment—and the skill to use it—is more important.

Most axes can perform most of the above tasks, but no single design will perform all the functions equally well. An axe that is a convenient length for walking will be awkward to climb with, and a pick set at a shallow angle for an efficient self-arrest will not perform so well when climbing. How an axe feels is important—if it is not a comfortable fit in your hand or if it does not have a nice swing, then there will be little incentive to have it ready to use. Make sure the shaft is small enough for you to grip it with gloves on.

RATINGS AND STANDARDS

There are two CE marks (European standard—see www.theuiaa.org for details) for ice axes:

- B-rated (Basic) axes—intended for hill walking and glacier walking. They have shafts strong enough to use as a belay anchor.
- T-rated (Technical) tools—intended for climbing and mountaineering. They are 30–40 percent stronger to allow for more extreme use and abuse (such as torquing the picks into cracks).

Picks also have B and T ratings. T-rated picks are thicker to withstand the side-to-side stress test. However, they are not as good for penetrating ice. Whichever you use, it is very difficult to break an ice pick.

Climber: Anna Williams

WALKING AXE

Predominantly for use as a walking stick on flat or easy angle slopes, to arrest a fall, climb grade 1 gullies, and occasionally to cut steps.

Shaft—The length of an ice axe for general use has generated quite a debate over the last few years. The steeper the slope, the more experienced you are, and the more proficient you are on crampons, the shorter the axe can be. It does, of course, depend on the length of your arms and how tall you are—60–70cm (24–28 in) is a good place to start. Longer axes are unwieldy and get in the way if the slope does become steep, but are the best for walking on easier angled slopes.

Weight—Lightweight and B-rated is enough.

The head—Consisting of the pick and the adze, this should be a one-piece construction, with a gentle curve. If the curve of the head is too flat, it is unstable when self-arresting and climbing; if it is too steep, it will tend to snatch and can be wrenched out of the hand. The adze should be a good size, slightly scooped, and at an angle that continues the curve from the pick. The hole in the center of the head is for the attachment of a leash.

The spike—A long, sharp spike is hard to hold if you ice-axe arrest.

GENERAL MOUNTAINEERING AXES

A general mountaineering axe is a balance between performance for walking and low-grade climbs (up to grade 3/4) or winter scrambles. It should be well balanced and have a natural easy swing.

The shaft—A length of 60cm (24in) is a good place to start. It is usually straight, but gently curved models have a better swing, although on easy angled slopes (less than 60°) they have no advantage. A recent design improvement is the hand rest at the base of the shaft; it makes gripping easier and helps to prevent you banging your knuckles against the ice. The hand rest does not appreciatively affect plunging the axe into the snow. Ensure the shaft's diameter is small enough for you to hold with gloves on. Some ultra-lightweight models do not have a spike, which is not a problem in hard firm snow, but they can become blocked and do not work well in ice.

Weight and strength—The axe will be T-rated and have a stronger construction overall to make it versatile and durable. Light is right, but ultra-light axes are not as good at penetrating hard snow. A rubber grip on the shaft will keep your hands warmer, dampen vibration, and help you grip the axe, but it can hinder plunging into hard snow.

The head—A more curved pick gives better hooking, but should not be too steep otherwise it may snatch during self-arrest. The adze may be larger, but it must still follow the curve of the head, for easier step cutting and digging.

TECHNICAL AXES AND HAMMERS

These range from axes designed for all round mixed and ice climbing, to specific steep ice and technical mixed axes. Radical steep ice axes (leashed or leashless) make climbing very steep icefalls or technical mixed terrain much easier. However, on the average Scottish or Alpine route, every part of the axe is used, and radical features found on steep ice fall axes, such as grip rests, triggers, and strange shaft shapes, are sometimes more of a hindrance than a help. General technical tools are robust simpler axes, made for taking a lot of punishment.

Shaft—This is usually 55cm (22in) long with a bend or a curve to allow easier placement on bulges and to reduce the bruising of knuckles. If you are into hard mixed or waterfall a radical curve will clear bulges easily, but is generally less balanced. A radical curve may compromise your safety on Alpine routes, especially on descent, and may make it more difficult to create an ice axe belay.

A dry, fresh snow ski wax will make the shaft on less technical tools stickier, giving greater grip.

Leashless tool handles currently come in two varieties—competition-inspired handles with an upper and lower ergonomic grip, and more classically shaped axes with a "horn" at the base to support the hand. Both types can often be fitted with a "trigger finger"—a smaller horn that can either be used to create a higher grip position on the axe or as additional support for one of the fingers when holding the main grip. The comp-style axes are most effective on very steep ground where much of one's bodyweight must be supported by the upper body. Well-fitting gloves are essential to maintain good contact with leashless tools.

Weight and strength—Technical axes are available with B- or T-rated picks. T-rated are heavier duty and better suited to mixed climbing. B-rated are slimmer, allowing them to penetrate ice with minimal shattering, making them a better option for pure ice climbing. Heavy axes penetrate better on new brittle ice.

The Cirque and Raptor—general mountaineering axes from DMM.

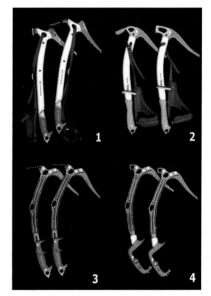

A selection of technical tools. Most climbers use a pair from the same manufacturer, as each manufacturer's axe has a different balance and swing. A pair consists of a hammer (for knocking in pegs) and an adze. They are ideal for climbs of grade 3 and above. (1) DMM Superfly, (2) Petzl Aztar, (3) DMM Rebel (4), DMM Anarchist.

Leashless climbing has advantages, but with thick mittens they are a hindrance.

Head—There are three main pick designs—straight, classic, and reverse curve, but most modern technical tools have the reverse pick. Some have removable picks that can be changed from classic to reverse picks and from ice to mixed, but it is usually only possible beforehand and only with the same manufacturer's pick. The classic pick is best for general mountaineering because the balance is better, but a reverse curved pick makes for better hooking on mixed climbs and ice penetration, and easier removal from steep ice. The adze will be more curved and steeply drooped for hooking and torquing. For pure ice climbing two hammers may prove more useful, but if it is your only set of tools get an adze on one of them.

AXE LEASHES

If dropping your axe is a real possibility, and subsequent retrieval difficult, use a leash. They are useful for step cutting and front pointing. However, they are a hindrance as you zigzag up or down slopes, changing your axe from hand to hand. Attach the leash to the head with a lark's foot knot to make it easy to remove and replace. Avoid leashes that slide up and down the axe on a runner, because they put the leash close to your crampons when not in use.

For the majority of climbers, leashes are important to take some of the strain off the hands, reduce the chances of dropping the axe and, should your feet lose their placement, they may prevent a big fall.

Leashes fall into two categories—**fixed** and **clip**. Fixed leashes are cheaper and lighter. "Clipper" leashes allow quick and easy removal from an axe when needed for those who do not like axes dangling from wrists when they place gear or want to play with leashless climbing. They allow a more ergonomic cuff design and your hand does not have to be removed to place protection.

The leash should be the correct length—too long and it will not take any weight, too short and it will restrict your swing. As a rough guide, hook the wrist-support on to the spike of the axe and shorten the leash until it is tight. Put your gloved hand into the wrist loop and hang from the axe; your little finger should be level with the bottom of the grip/top of spike.

CLIMBING LEASHLESS

Early pioneers climbed leashless and it has recently come into vogue again, evolving from competition ice climbing and very hard mixed routes where leashes restrict some advanced techniques. Leashless tools enable you to shake out more often and, with two grips on the shaft, they make it easier to transfer hands, rest and de-pump. Another advantage to leashless climbing is that hands tend to get less cold as blood can flow more easily to the fingers.

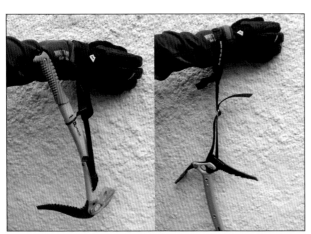

For mixed climbing, the axe should dangle out of the way, but for ice climbing the pivot point should be further along the shaft so that you can easily grab the shaft.

Climbing leashless is an increasingly popular system on continental icefalls and high standard mixed routes, and we will see more climbers using it, but it is mainly experienced climbers on high standard mixed and steep ice routes.

When you climb with thick mittens and your grip gets iced up a leash is very useful. Climbing leashless is a hindrance on routes where a lot of clearing of snow and digging is required. A good alternative is to attach the axes via elastic to your waist (lanyard). They don't get in the way when putting in an ice screw and cannot be dropped. The lanyard can, however, become tangled. You could also try climbing with a leash on just one axe.

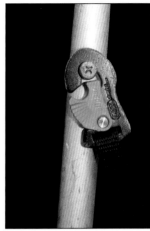

A removable leash system from Petzl

HOW SHARP SHOULD AN ICE AXE BE?

Sharp points save energy. A blunt pick must strike harder to penetrate and can cause the ice to fracture, however this does depend on the temperature of the ice—the warmer the ice the greater the ability to absorb the shock. Even on mixed ground a sharp pick is crucial to penetrate thin dribbles and seams of ice and rock cracks. Beware though, when searching blind for the next mixed hold a razor-sharp pick will often catch on features that won't hold body weight—it is thus better to slightly "dampen" even the most extreme picks. However, for the majority of mixed climbers operating at a more normal level a moderately sharp pick is probably best.

The pick must be filed so that the tip hits the ice first and it can be re-filed until about 2cm (0.78in) of the pick has disappeared. Make a master trace on paper of the pick when you buy the axe so you can file it to match. File with the grain of the metal, not backward and forward, and avoid using anything that will heat up the pick and destroy its hardness.

CHANGING THE MANUFACTURER'S PICK SHAPE

Radical refinement of some picks (see Fig. 13) will improve penetration and holding power on thin ice and make removing it a lot easier, but it may make any warranties obsolete. However, when filed aggressively, a radical point is easily bent and, once gone, it is not possible to create a new one as there's not enough metal left. Such picks are most useful where the pick is placed (rather than hit) against rock features. Unless you are climbing very high grades keep to the manufacturer's pick shape.

Changing the pick shape basically involves reducing the surface area of the tip of the pick:

- Blunt the teeth close to the shaft.
- Slightly round off the sharp edges from the entire underside teeth and sharpen the top edge of the pick.
- Increase the angle of the first tooth so that it hooks better on thin ice and small edges.
- For mixed climbing, file some teeth into the top of the pick to help with Steiner moves.

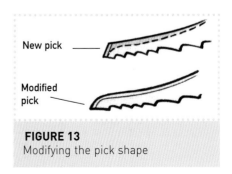

New pick

Modified pick

FIGURE 13
Modifying the pick shape

Leaning into the slope will force your foot off the holds—stay upright, whatever the steepness.

Slice steps—swing from the knee and let the weight of your boot do the work.

WALKING ON SNOW

USING SKI POLES

Those with a big basket are better for balance when carrying a load on flat or low angled snow, but they are not a substitute for an ice axe. If you are carrying an ice axe and a pole do not put your hand through the pole's leash; you may need to discard it quickly to use your ice axe.

CRAMPONS

If it is safer to have crampons on, why travel without them? They are heavy and slow you down by 10–15 percent, so when the snow conditions and terrain allow, leave them off. Put crampons on before you need them, only taking them off if the walking is easier without; safety is not compromised and you will not have to put them back on five minutes later.

KICKING STEPS WITHOUT CRAMPONS

Swing from the knee and let the weight of your boot do the work—snow should fly upward. There are two basic techniques. The uphill edge of your boot can cut across the slope (slice step) or you can kick directly into the snow (pigeon hole step). Keep steps evenly spaced and try to incline them inward to create a platform for your foot. It is important for the followers to also kick in and not just stand in your steps. To change directions thrust the shaft of your axe into the snow and kick a large enough step for both feet, then change direction and continue.

DESCENDING

The mark of a confident winter walker or climber is the ability to descend quickly and safely. The slice step can be used in descent without crampons, but on steeper slopes the following are better:

The plunge step—When the snow is soft stand upright facing outward. Step forward (lean down the fall line), keeping your knee straight, but not locked (the firmer the snow the straighter your leg), plunge your heel into the snow. Maintain momentum and repeat. If the snow is too solid to plunge step you should have crampons on. Hold the axe in the cane position and plunge it co-ordinated with one leg.

The plunge step forces your body weight through the straightened leg.

Down climb—Use this when the slope is too steep to plunge step, yet the snow is soft enough not to need crampons. Turn and face into the slope and kick deep steps, placing the axe firmly into the snow.

GLISSADING

It is fast, easy to do, and exhilarating, but also highly dangerous. Control your speed, look ahead for stones, and do not attempt it when you cannot see the bottom of the slope. If you are wearing crampons remove them or just walk down.

Sitting glissade—This works best on soft snow. To maintain control, run the spike of the axe like a rudder along the snow to one side.

Standing glissade—Crouch with slightly bent knees and spread your arms out for stability. Bring your weight from your heels to the entire foot, and off you go. Control your speed by digging your heels in. An axe and/or ski pole can be used to the side of you to control speed and in readiness to arrest a slip.

WALKING WITH CRAMPONS

To put on your crampons, make a good platform in the snow and ensure your boots and crampons are clear of snow.

FLAT-FOOTING

Edging the foot into a slope only uses one row of points. It is more efficient and safer to roll your ankle and use all the downward facing crampon points. If you find this difficult, your boots may be too stiff, your ankles inflexible, or you are not shifting your center of gravity (COG) over each foot before moving the other. Try undoing the top lacing on your boot to make it easier.

- On lower-angled snow or ice firmly plant all the downward facing points into the slope and walk up with your legs slightly apart. Avoid stamping or dragging your feet.
- As the angle increases, spread your feet and walk like a duck.
- As the angle increases further, walk diagonally, with your toes pointing across the slope or even downhill. Eventually you will have to sidestep up the slope by planting your uphill foot firmly, then swing your lower foot well forward of the upper foot to plant it higher. Take care not to catch your crampon points, gaiter, or crampon straps.
- When descending, point your toes down the slope, flex at the knees and hips, keep your feet apart, and do not dig your heel in—the rear points do not work like the heel of a boot. If you cannot place all your points in, turn around and front point down.

Flat footing uses all the downward facing spikes on your crampons.

Walking like a duck lessens the strain on your ankles.

Walking diagonally requires rhythm and balance. You must swing your leg well in front of the other one.

Point your toes like a Viennese horse to get all the crampon points into the slope.

FRONT POINTING
Only the front-facing crampon points are used. It is the most direct way to ascend a steep slope, but the hardest on your calf muscles (see Ice climbing, page 202).

COMBINATION/AMERICAN TECHNIQUE
On moderately steep snow/ice, try to mix front pointing with flat footing.

USING AN ICE AXE
"To the experienced winter walker, the ice-axe becomes so trusted a friend that it seems like an extra limb." —Martin Moran, BMG/IFMGA Guide

CARRYING YOUR ICE AXE
The purpose-built carriers on the back of your backpack are not the best place to carry an ice axe; it is difficult to keep the sharp points away from other people and it is not easily accessible. Instead, use the compression straps down the side of your backpack (you can even tuck the picks under the lid). As you enter snowy or icy terrain it is better to have your axe ready to hand by tucking it down the back of your backpack (see photo below right).

HOLDING AN ICE AXE
Always wear gloves and keep the axe in the uphill hand. It does not matter whether you hold the pick forward or backward. Holding the pick forward makes it easier to stab quickly into hard snow should you slip, while holding it backward makes it marginally quicker to use in self-arrest.

Place the axe under your shoulder strap—pick upward—and lift it over your shoulder.

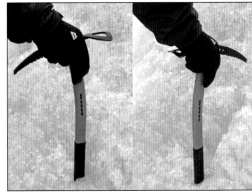

Pick forward or back—contrary to accepted wisdom it does not matter.

The cane or self-belay position (see Fig. 14)—Hold the axe head, spike downward. If you slip, push the axe into the snow and grasp the axe shaft with the other hand to reduce leverage. If that fails, revert to ice axe arrest position.

Cross-body position—A secure position when the slope is steep. As the angle steepens stand upright and do not lean into the slope. Turn your body sideways to the slope, grasp the axe by the head in your downhill hand, and plant the spike across your body into the slope. The cross-body position helps you to stay upright.

Banister technique—Used when descending on ice. Plant the pick as far below you as possible and lift gently; the axe will lock in place. As you descend, slide your hand along the shaft to the head then remove and repeat.

For steeper snow or ice (45° plus) use front pointing combined with:

- **Low and high dagger**—The low dagger position is useful on moderately steep hard snow or soft ice. Face the ice and hold the axe by the head at the adze. Push the pick into the slope at about waist or chest level. The high dagger is used on steeper slopes. Wrap your hand under the head of the axe with the pick facing into the slope.

- **The anchor position**—This position is used on steep ice and snow. It is really front pointing, using your ice axe above your head (see Front pointing, page 204). The anchor position provides more security on short sections of steep snow. Hold the axe near the bottom of the shaft. Swing it to set the pick into the ice (see page 203). Now, front-point your feet upward and move both hands progressively up the axe shaft. Eventually, you

FIGURE 14
Self-belay should be your first line of defence if you slip.

The cross-body position helps you to stand upright on steeper ground.

The bannister technique can give you extra security when descending a steep step.

The low and high dagger is a comfortable way to hold the ice axe on steeper terrain.

Cutting steps in descent.

will reach the dagger position. Step up into a dagger grip so that it is easier to remove—do not remove it too soon. Place the axe again. When ice is very steep, use two tools.

CUTTING STEPS

Useful when a patch of very hard snow is encountered. Even if you are wearing crampons the odd step cut with an axe helps on hard snow or ice, or if someone has a broken crampon.

The most popular way is to cut "slash steps" (a leash may help to support your hand). When ascending diagonally, stand in balance with the axe in your uphill hand and swing your axe like a pendulum from the shoulder until the adze makes contact with the snow. With successive swings, slice out a step across the fall line of the slope and incline slightly inward. To change direction, cut a step large enough for both feet and swap your axe over to the other hand. When traveling horizontally, keep the steps in line, making it easier for the person following.

In descent, hold the axe in the downhill hand, place a hand on your knee to maintain balance, and slash steps.

FIGURE 15 Ice axe arrest
A Hold the axe at 45° across the chest with the adze in the crook of the shoulder. One hand holds the head and the other covers the spike. The break position—turn your head away from the head of the axe. Lift your feet off the snow. Lift the spike upward to force the pick into the snow. If the axe is ripped away, relocate it in the above position and repeat.
B Should you fall head-first, place the pick into the snow to the side of you then pivot around it and resume the break position.
C Should you fall on your back headfirst put the axe out at waist level and pivot around until in the break position.

A

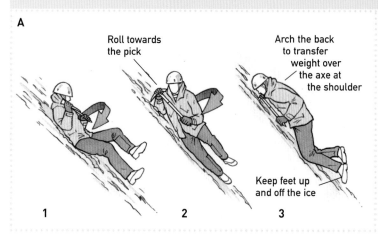

Roll towards the pick

Arch the back to transfer weight over the axe at the shoulder

Keep feet up and off the ice

1   2   3

B

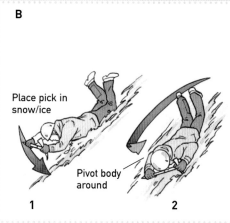

Place pick in snow/ice

Pivot body around

1   2

SELF-ARREST

(See Fig. 15 opposite and below.) This has saved lives, but practice stopping slips before required by plunging the shaft into the snow (self belay) if it is soft enough, or the pick if it is harder, and then you won't have to use it! If you gather speed, you will have to use the pick or the adze for self-arrest technique, but it is difficult to do on ice, hard snow, or very soft snow, where you are most likely to slip. Should you slip without crampons on or an ice axe in hand, roll and push away from the snow on to hands and toes.

Practice on a slope with a safe run-out, without crampons, but with a helmet. Try rolling into it, sliding on your back head-first.

MOVING TOGETHER ON SNOW

"No one route is worth my life, but the mountains are essential to my life."
—Will Gadd, ice climber

Moving together on snow is quick, but requires experience and judgment. (Climbers: Clive Hebblethwaite and Chris Trull.)

Whenever you put a rope on ask yourself: is it increasing your safety? There are two reasons for putting a rope on: to stop you or your partner from falling off something and to stop you falling down something.

Rope-up when the climbing is easy—do not teeter on a steep slope sorting out gear and putting your crampons on. The technique of moving together will depend on the terrain.

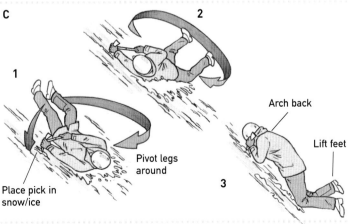

C

1 Place pick in snow/ice

2 Pivot legs around

3 Arch back — Lift feet

On horizontal snow crests carry hand coils to give yourself time to react should someone fall off.

On exposed mixed ridges place protection—you never know when you may slip.

OPEN SNOW SLOPE

Ask yourself—if putting the rope on does not make you safer, why do it? The rope should be short—1.5–2m (5–7ft)—and tight between climbers (no hand coils). This is a fast method, but you must both be wary of a slip. It can sometimes provide an illusion of safety and you may be better running the rope out to a quick snow belay or soloing! See more on shortening the rope in Glacier crossing and Scrambling (page 236).

HORIZONTAL SNOW CRESTS

You should be 5–10m (16–33ft) apart with 0.5m (1.6ft) of coils in each climber's hand, that can be dropped should a climber slip (shout, because the other climber may be looking at their feet). The other climber must then step or jump down to the opposite side, to counterbalance the fallen climber. If there are spikes and boulders, drop the hand coils and weave in and out using these natural features as belays. The strongest climber should be at the back. It is also possible to shorten the rope and for each climber to walk along either side of the ridge, but soft snow can make this difficult.

STEEP MIXED RIDGES

You should be at least be 5–15m (17–49ft) apart with the rope clipped into runners.

SHORT, MIXED STEPS

Spotting is difficult and dangerous because of the number of spikes that will fly towards you. Use direct belays whenever possible to minimize delays (see Scrambling, page 111).

LONGER STEPS

Use techniques akin to rock climbing where the leader is belayed and the belayer anchored; again, direct belaying will speed things up.

USING SHORT ROPING

Short roping has a place in your repertoire when the uphill climber is more experienced and can pull the lower climber back into balance should they slip. Although it can also be used in ascent, it is faster to run the rope out and belay the less-experienced climber up the slope, or to climb with a short section of rope tight between them.

SHORT ROPING ON DESCENT

This technique only protects the lower climber, and without considerable practice it can compromise the safety of the team. It may be safer to solo and then at least only one of you falls. The distance between climbers should be as short as possible.

Short roping requires constant vigilance to do it well.

STEEPER CLIMBING

"Stupidity and blind faith are a short-term asset (it's often been said that to be a good ice climber you need your brains removed) but ultimately it will leave you in big trouble."

—Rich Cross, IFMGA Mountain Guide

A good winter climber is someone who has prepared his or her gear, they look after their hands and feet, and retreat when the conditions are not good. (See Appendix for the grading of winter climbs, page 358).

The rope-work techniques used on winter climbs are largely the same as you would use in summer rock climbing, with the exception that you must do everything wearing gloves and with snow pouring down your neck!

PROTECTING WINTER CLIMBS

The best ice climbing protection is rock-climbing gear, because it is more reliable and quicker to place than ice protection. Having said that, many ice routes require at least eight screws: three for a belay, two as runners, and three for the next belay.

Because protection is often hammered into icy cracks you may prefer to have a dedicated winter rack, rather than your rock climbing rack. Old style hexes are great; some climbers drill holes in them to reduce the weight and to help them to bite in icy placements. Thread them with 5.5mm (0.22in) Dyneema cord so that the knot can be tied inside the hex.

Cams are of limited use in icy cracks (tri cams work better), but still carry a few. Pegs are essential when nuts will not fit (thread them with short loops of 4mm (0.15in) cord to make racking easier). When you are carrying two sets of wires, rack them separately on two crabs; if you drop a set you will still have the full range. Spray-paint your gear in different colors for easy identification.

South Gully, Creag Meagaidh, Scotland. Climber: John Husband.

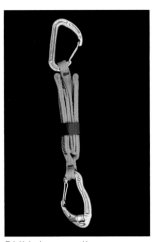

DMM rip stop sling

Clive Hebblethwaite MIC
clive.hebblethwaite@ntlworld.com

"It's a myth that belays in winter are always poor. It's just that it takes more persistence to say, 'No, that won't do,' and to clear some more snow or ice. Save time by looking generally in a few places first before deciding which place to focus your efforts, but don't over focus!"

SHOCK SLINGS

See photo opposite. These reduce the IF by rupturing the stitching in a controlled manner. They may be helpful on marginal gear, such as ice screws, but their usefulness is limited to short falls (5 m/16.4 ft) and a Fall Factor (FF) 0.5. An equivalent amount of energy is reduced if you reverse 1m (3.3 ft) before falling off or the belayer pays out a little rope as you fall (see Forces, page 55).

FINDING PROTECTION IN MIXED GROUND

Experience will tell you where it is worth spending time clearing snow and where it is better to climb on.

- Never pass good runners; you may never know where the next one will be.
- Use 60m (197ft) ropes to allow you to go that bit further.
- Look for signs—has anyone been digging there before?
- Look for old pegs, cracks, shattered rock, etc.
  - Dig for proper cracks, and move on rather than persevere with blind corners.
  - Use ice screws, even if they are poor, to help keep rock protection in place.

CARRYING PROTECTION

If you are not wearing a backpack, a bandolier or a lightweight chest harness is better, but on steeper climbs gear can then hang behind you and be difficult to reach. Rack ice screws higher on the chest for icefall climbing so that you can see them. When you are wearing a backpack, hang gear from the shoulder straps or dedicated gear racks on the shoulder straps or waist belt. You can make your own with some 6mm (0.24in) cord and clear plastic tubing—experiment with the best place to hang it from your own backpack.

ICE SCREW CARRIERS

Several firms produce specialist ice screw racks. Look for one which is easy to use while wearing gloves and that keeps bulk to a minimum.

ROPES

They should be dry-treated 50–60m (164–197ft) or even 70m (230ft) on some long ice pitches. Most climbers use double or half ropes for winter climbing because the routes wander, the impact force is less and abseiling is easier. However, because it is lighter and when there is little drag, such as an ice climb, a single rope with a thinner abseil line dragged behind the second is useful (see Alpine climbing, page 243).

SNOW ANCHORS

The most important thing to realize about snow anchors is that their strength will depend on the consistency of the snow and the surface area of the object buried; in powder snow nothing will hold. Some of the anchors below are too time-consuming to be used as runners during a climb and are likely only to be used for creating a belay.

BURIED AXE

Radically curved ice axes may compromise the holding power in uncertain snow conditions. Dig a clean slot using the adze in undisturbed snow, perpendicular to the direction of loading; the front load wall of the slot should incline slightly to help stop the axe lifting. Next cut a narrow slot using the spike, just big enough for a sling to fit into and at the same depth as the ice axe slot, which will prevent the axe being lifted out. Attach a sling with a clove hitch or girth hitch at a point on the axe that ensures the surface area is the same on both sides of the sling. Do not use the balance point as it invariably pulls through at the head end. Firmly place the axe, pick downward, into the snow. Driving another axe or ski pole, just back from vertical, through the sling in front of the horizontal axe will reinforce the anchor (see Figs 16 and 17).

SNOW STAKE

These can be placed upright in very firm snow or buried like an axe when the snow is softer. If you can push it in by hand it is unlikely to be secure. A T-shaped profile is the strongest and may have better holding power in softer snow than a buried axe belay. On steep slopes stakes should be placed at approximately 45° from the direction of pull; on gentler slopes the angle can be less.

DEADMAN OR SNOW FLUKE

This is a specially shaped aluminum plate with a metal cable attached, useful as a belay anchor and as a runner. They are best in slush or moist and heavy snow. A deadman or snow fluke is best placed at about 40° from the direction of pull with a deep slot to allow the cable to run directly to the belayer. However, great care must be taken to ensure that you dig deep enough and that there are no hard layers to deflect the deadman.

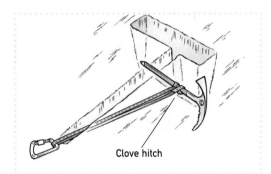

FIGURE 16
A buried ice axe belay

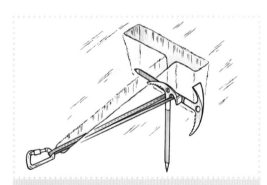

FIGURE 17
A reinforced axe anchor

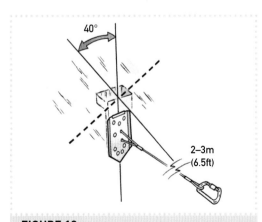

FIGURE 18
The correct placement of a deadman

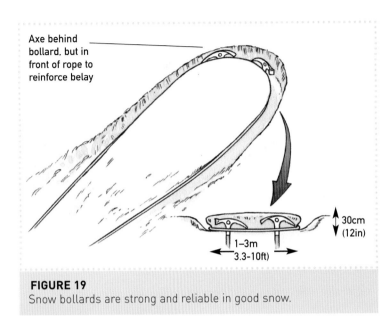

Axe behind bollard, but in front of rope to reinforce belay

30cm (12in)

1–3m
3.3–10ft)

FIGURE 19
Snow bollards are strong and reliable in good snow.

SNOW BOLLARD

The bollard should be horseshoe-shaped, not tear-dropped, to keep as much snow in the anchor as possible. The bollard can be padded with cardboard, clothing or ice axes to stop the rope cutting through the snow. If it is used as an abseil anchor, the ice axes and padding can be removed when the last person abseils.

ICE ANCHORS

NATURAL ANCHORS

On waterfall ice, sturdy ice columns can be threaded with a sling. Cracks between the ice and rock can be used by clove hitching an ice screw with Dyneema cord (take care that the threads can cut a nylon sling) and placing it in the crack at 90° to create a chockstone.

ICE HOOKS

Ice hooks, e.g., DMM Bulldog, fit in places where nuts and pegs will not: they can be placed in rock cracks, turf, between ice features, such as icicles, or into old tool placement holes; but their holding power is always questionable. A stubby screw in thin ice or an angle peg in an ice choked crack will, however, be stronger. Some ice climbers advocate using them on free hanging ice pillars because they will come out if the pillar collapses.

For mixed climbing, the standard ice hook is too long, so you will have to modify an existing design. Some climbers recommend shortening the hook by half and reshaping the pick to resemble your ice axe pick. If it matches the shape, and if your pick finds a tight spot, you can place your hook once it is removed. Often this hook is hand placed or simply tapped to seat.

A DMM Bulldog ice hook

Never pass good runners; you may never know where the next one will be. (The author climbing, Scotland).

WARHOGS OR ICE PEGS

Pound-in protection is useful in frozen turf or mud, commonly used on some Scottish routes.

ICE SCREWS

Tests by Black Diamond have shown that an ice screw placed at a positive angle will hold better (see Fig. 20). The theory is that the surface area of screw threads is greater than the tube area and therefore provides better holding power. This is fine for perfect ice, but we rarely experience perfect ice. Placing all ice screws at a positive angle could lead to failure in some situations, especially if the ice is detached, hollow, slushy, or rotten. It may be better to rely on the lever resistance (negative) of the screw rather than the holding power of the threads.

Don't waste your money on cheap ice screws and forget "drive-in" ice pegs for pure ice. (Point Five Gully, Ben Nevis, Scotland).

The quality of the ice is more important than screw length or screw diameter, but a fully inserted (into the hanger) large diameter screw is stronger than a small diameter screw of the same length, and the longer the screw, the better it will hold.

When you are close to the ground, or belay, you have the potential to generate a greater IF on your protection so these placements should be as strong as possible. Place ripper slings on the first two ice screws of a pitch and whenever you doubt a placement. Use longer screws when close to the belay, or even equalize more placements if the quality of the ice is questionable.

ASSESSING THE QUALITY OF ICE

Ice is at its best between 0 and -5°C (32 and 23°F)—above this surface thaw reduces the strength of ice screws considerably. Colder temperatures will make the ice far more brittle and fragile. Dense ice is generally clear (glassy), bluer, and contains less air—a positive angled screw is then better. If there is a lot of seepage the ice can be dark colored. Less dense ice is greyish, opaque, and often has bubbles—a negative angled screw is better.

Look for dense, shaded ice behind pillars and other features. Clear away poor quality ice to the better stuff underneath. Only place ice screws into solid free hanging pillars; if they collapse, you do not want to be attached. Be careful using old ice screw holes as they may be too large.

You can assess ice for brittleness, plating, and layering when you place your ice axes and ice screws. Low-density ice often receives picks without creating much surface deformation, but high-density ice must be displaced as the pick enters, revealing a pit or cracking. Further information is gained as you place the ice screw: how hard is it to turn? If you do not need the handle to turn the screw, it may be better to place it at zero or a negative angle. As you turn the screw there should be even resistance to turning. If you feel the screw break through into less dense layers remove it and place at a negative angle.

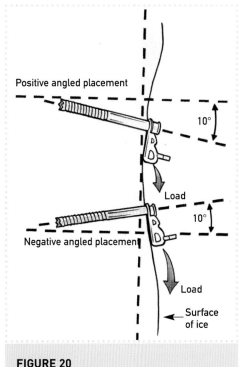

Positive angled placement

10°

Load

10°

Negative angled placement

Load

Surface of ice

FIGURE 20
Angle of ice screw placements

TYING-OFF ICE SCREWS

If the screw sticks out less than 5cm (2in), just clip the eye or use a wired runner. There are also some very short ice screws to avoid tying-off ice screws if it is more.

LOOKING AFTER ICE SCREWS

After climbing, dry your screws (inside as well as out). Using an undamaged screw as a guide, touch up any damage to the teeth with a small file. For advice on sharpening ice screws go to www.blackdiamondequipment.com.

ABALAKOV V-THREAD

See Fig. 21. Named after the Soviet climber who devised it in the 1930s, the Abalakov V-thread anchor is simple and very strong. It is useful for abseiling or top-rope set-ups, assuming that the ice is good quality. Do not blindly trust old Abalakovs. You will need two 22cm (9in) ice screws, a length of 7mm (0.3in) cord, and a wire coathanger with a hook or purpose-made puller.

FIGURE 21
The Abalakov thread anchor

- Insert the ice screws at a 10-degree angle uphill to the slope, and a 60-degree angle sideways. The greater the distance between the two holes, the stronger the thread.

- Leave the first screw or the thread puller partway in place as a marker for placing the second one.

- Once you have the tunnel, thread the cord and use the puller to retrieve it. If you have not got a piece of wire, insert the cord and try to capture it by twisting an ice screw. This involves enlarging the hole so the ice screw can turn freely.

- Move the webbing or cord back and forth to smooth out the tunnel and then tie a knot. If you are using Dyneema tie a triple fisherman's knot.

ICE BOLLARD

This can be laborious and time-consuming to create.

- Use your axe's pick to make the initial horseshoe shape. A scraping action with the pick is faster and less traumatic to the surrounding ice.

- Cut a trench at least 15cm (6in) deep, being careful not to crack the ice.

- The bollard should be 30–45cm (12–18in) wide.

- At the top, make an undercut to keep the rope from slipping off. Be very careful not to crack the horn shape you have created for the rope to rest on.

When rock anchors are not available use a waist belay (Scotland).

CLIMBING ON SNOW

"I believe in running away often so that I can come back and climb another day."

—Will Gadd, ice climber

CREATING A BELAY AND BELAYING

When a rock or ice screw belay cannot be found, a buried axe, snow stake, or deadman is best (a snow bollard is too time-consuming and is used mainly for abseiling. See Fig. 22). The anchors can be doubled up if the snow is poor, but ensure you do not disturb the snow of one anchor when placing the other.

After creating your anchor, cut out a deep bucket seat 2m (6.5ft) below the axe, with slots for your legs (at least the depth of your thighs) and a ledge for the rope to lie on. Put something down to sit on and waist belay because it is the most dynamic system. A crab clipped to the front of your harness and to the leaders rope will stop it being ripped from your body should the leader fall (see Rock Climbing, page 55). When your belay is beyond doubt it is possible to use a belay tube. If in doubt, keep to a waist belay.

It is vital with all of the belay methods to place a runner as soon as you leave the stance to prevent FF2 on to the belay.

FIGURE 22
Creating a belay on snow—a buried axe with a bucket seat. The climber's rope is on the same side as the rope to the axe.

STOMPER BELAY AND CARABINER AXE/SCOTTISH BELAY

Stomper (see photo on p. 202)—This is a quick and easy method for belaying a second climber in non-serious terrain, especially when the snow is poor. It does have serious limitations—should the second fall, and end up on steep or overhanging ground, you can do nothing to help and escape from the system is impossible. The advantage is that any forces generated in a fall pull the belayer down into the axe increasing its holding power. Use a shoulder belay with the crab slotted on to the shaft of the axe (do not put an Italian hitch onto the crab, as it will redirect the forces to the axe).

Avoid climbing through cornices whenever you can. The snow slope below the cornice is likely to be avalanche prone and they collapse on a regular basis. If you do have to tunnel through one, create a belay 10m (33ft) horizontally to the side of the lead climber. Dig deep, preferably down to rock or ice for anchors.

(1) The stomper belay—a quick belay method, but only where the climber is not going to end up dangling in space. (2) The Scottish—try both and see which you prefer.

Scottish belay—Not as reliable as the Stomper, and should only be used when the snow conditions are good. It may allow you to escape from the system more easily. Plant the axe and lark's foot a sling with a crab to the shaft. Take the rope through the crab and waist belay.

A crab clipped into the live rope and attached to the front of your harness will stop it being pulled off in a fall.

BOOT AXE BELAY

The boot axe belay is a fast method, but is bad for your back. Like the above methods, it is only suitable for bringing a second up the pitch. It should not be used for protecting someone in serious terrain, e.g., crossing a crevasse.

(3) A boot axe belay—do not use it to protect someone in serious terrain.

STEEP ICE CLIMBING

Good rock climbers do not always make good ice climbers and vice versa. While technique and fitness are important, without confidence you will not cope with the long gaps between runners that make ice climbing such a huge challenge (see Appendix, page 359, for winter climbing grades).

TACKLING A STEEP ICE CLIMB

The first question to ask is "if there are other climbers on my route, is it safe to climb behind them?" Consider the prevailing conditions: is it too warm (risk of collapse)? Is it too cold (sudden big drops in temperature can make ice falls extremely fragile and prone to collapse)?

Place yourself and your belayer away from falling ice and rack up slowly and methodically with a calm mind and put on your harness before your crampons. Whether to anchor the belayer to the ground will depend on the consequences of a fall (see Rock Climbing, page 55). Just like rock climbing, break the route into manageable sections; look for places where the white/grey ice gives way to the better plastic, blue ice. Where are the rest places? Can you bridge or get close to the rock to place a runner?

CONSIDERATIONS FOR BOTTOM-ROPING ICE CLIMBS

When using ice screws as anchors be aware that when they are left in place for a long time they may melt out, due to the heat generated by pressure. Use three equalized screws and cover them with snow/ice to protect them from the sun.

SWINGING YOUR ICE TOOLS

It is worth practicing the following techniques at ground level or on a bottom belayed rope until you have a relaxed swing that is accurate and uses the minimum of energy.

Before swinging, touch the ice with your pick at the point you want to hit. Practice swinging at a marked spot and watch the pick all the way. Do not stretch up too far because it is then hard to get the axe out from a poor placement.

Your swing should be relaxed, using the weight of the axe head to do the work, and not your shoulder or body. Your aim is to penetrate the ice enough, but not too much. Prepare the swing by dropping the head of the axe behind your shoulder far enough to hit your backpack (if you are wearing one) and relax your wrist. Start the swing with the shoulder and progressively straighten the arm, keeping your shoulder, wrist, and axe in a straight line. At the moment of impact, snap the wrist forward to increase the strike force (by up to 70 percent), and release the hand to maintain the kinetic energy of the axe head. Every time you hit the ice, open your fingers slightly to keep the blood flowing; this also stops your fist punching the ice. Your arm should be slightly bent when the pick hits the ice—that is the position of maximum power. A good placement makes a "thunk" sound. If the ice dinner plates (shards like a smashed dinner plate), there may be better quality ice underneath, so clear the shattered ice away. To improve your placements and efficiency:

- Look for depressions where the ice is more dense than on bulges and will resist fracturing.

- Hook the pick of your axe into the holes left by other climbers; if it does not feel good, try to tap it with the hammer.

- Hook between icicles where the ice is often compressed and more solid.

A steep ice route requires a cool head. (Devils Appendix, North Wales. Photo: Steve Long, BMG/IFMGA Guide.)

MISTAKES WHEN PLACING YOUR ICE AXES

- Elbows too low
- Not relaxing the wrist
- Taking your eye off the spot
- Gripping the axe too hard, preventing the natural rotation of the hand
- Arm out to the side and not in line.

Swinging an ice axe is akin to swinging a badminton racket. Keep your shoulder, wrist, and axe in line.

- To save energy on good ice, a single sure swing is better than several taps.
- When climbing brittle or thin ice, as on waterfalls, place the axe with little short swings/taps from the wrist, and not from the shoulders or the arms.
- Think ahead: cut stances for your feet to give your calf muscles a rest.
- If you have to remove ice do it carefully: take icicles off bit by bit.

REMOVING A STUCK TOOL

To remove your tools lift them out the way they went in. If they are stuck, push up on the adze or hammer to lift it out. Do not wiggle the pick from side to side as this can weaken it.

Push upward on the adze or hammer to remove a stuck tool.

PLACING YOUR FEET

Take small steps and kick from the knee, not the whole leg—let the weight of your boot do the work. Kicking too hard simply makes the boot bounce off the ice. If the ice is hard, kick twice: once to shatter the ice and the second to get to the good ice underneath. Kick perpendicular to the ice so that both front points go in. Once the front points have engaged, drop your heel so that the secondary front points make contact with the ice and keep your feet flat so your crampons remain horizontal.

Standing on your toes raises your heels, forcing the front points down, possibly causing them to sheer. Sometimes the shape of the ice forces you to kick out to the side. To do this, turn your boot to get the front and secondary points in contact with the ice. Look for natural ledges where the foot can be placed sideways, relieving strain on the calves.

Swing from the knee and not the whole leg, unless you are climbing over a bulge.

PUTTING IT ALL TOGETHER

Before embarking on an ice route, practice on a bottom belayed rope first to ensure that you are (a) fluid in axe and feet placement, (b) can shift your center of gravity around using your hips, and (c) that you understand the importance of keeping your hips into the wall when placing your axe and freeing them to move your feet.

Do not stand on tiptoes as it forces the front points out of the ice. Keeping your heels down also engages the secondary points and relaxes your calf muscles.

Climbing vertical ice has been adapted from the techniques of rock climbing. The old fashioned technique of planting your two axes above your head at the same height to create an X with your body is a slow method of climbing and can feel insecure on steep ice (see Fig. 23). It is still a reasonable technique for moderately angled ice, but has been superceded by "cycling," or the triangle position.

The basic triangle position will allow you to adopt a balanced rest position on your legs with only one axe placed. At first, the triangle technique can seem more difficult and tiring because you are only pulling on one tool instead of two. However, this technique uses half the number of swings. Additionally, having the tools placed at different heights reduces the chances of the ice dinner plating.

Start in the triangle position (see A in Fig. 24) with your crampons at the same height, knees slightly bent, and legs slightly apart. One axe should be above your head along an imaginary line that runs through your head, hips, and between your feet to form a triangle. Your hips should be pushed towards the ice and your chest and shoulders away from the ice.

Now, lower your hips and hang your chest from the highest arm (B) then make three short steps. The first foot moved should be the one furthest from the lower axe. The first step should be short, and then bigger steps can be taken. To lift a leg, shift your hips over the weight-supporting foot. The secret to moving smoothly is these continuous hip movements to the right and left as you move your feet (the same as transferring your COG in rock climbing). Move each foot up to mid-shin level then straighten the legs until you are in a new triangle position (C,D,E). The higher you take your feet the further you must move your hips.

From this position, look up for your next tool placement. Remove the lower tool and place it about a foot higher than the other tool and no more than a shoulder width away from it (F,G). Take two steps up and sideways to return to the triangle position (H,I,J,K).

FIGURE 23
Placing your ice axes and legs in an X configuration on steep ice means that when you remove one of your axes you are likely to pivot off.

FIGURE 24
The triangle position sequence

As you progress you may sometimes find it difficult to get back into a triangle position. When this occurs, use the left-right rule, flagging, and frogging (see Fig. 26), adopted from rock climbing, to stay in balance, e.g., right axe high and your left leg under the axe The other foot can be splayed to the side like an outrigger (see Fig. 25).

ADVANCED ICE CLIMBING

Even vertical ice feels as if it is overhanging, because your axes force you out from the ice. As the ice steepens and the surface becomes irregular with bulges and pillars, the more you have to move away from the basic triangle and engage rock climbing skills. Once you have mastered the basic triangle progression try bridging between pillars and bulges and even the rock out to the side. Use back steps, heel hooks (with a spike on the back of your crampon), side pulls, and underclings. The important thing is that you have mastered the fundamental triangle progression first.

As you move on to more difficult ice climbs, you will come across icicles, cauliflower ice, mushroom ice, air pockets, and fragile ice. It may be better to hook or wedge these so that swinging the axe does not destroy them.

FIGURE 25
Flagging the leg when you cannot get into the triangle position.

FIGURE 26
Frogging

COMMON ERRORS WHEN ICE CLIMBING

- Arms too bent
- Chest not far enough away from the wall
- Legs are not the same height
- Gripping the tool too tightly
- Ice axes are the same height.

On very thin or fragile ice, it is difficult to place or hook both tools. Try instead to hook one pick on the head of the other so that you can use the strength of both arms to obtain a higher placement. Practice searching for rest positions, however unorthodox, and that terrifying pitch will start to look like a reasonable proposition. You may now find mono-point crampons easier to use.

MOVING OVER BULGES

This should be done the same way as mantle-shelfing in rock climbing, but often climbers stretch too far over the bulge and cannot see or use their feet. Place an axe just below the bulge and walk your feet up, remove the lower tool and place it over the bulge at a comfortable distance (bent shafts make this easier) to keep your hips away from the ice. Kicking in the conventional manner (where your knee joint acts as a hinge) leaves your front points downward as they penetrate.

To go over a bulge, gently lock your leg and swing from the hip. This keeps your toes higher than your heels, helping to engage your front points at the moment of impact. Hang straight-armed from the higher tool and bring your feet up in small steps until you are over the bulge. Slide your hands along the shaft until you are almost standing, then remove the axe.

TRAVERSING

This is described for moving rightwards. Start in the triangle position (see A, Fig. 27); place your axe 0.75m (2.5ft) out to the side and move your weight over the right leg (B) (the other leg may end up flagged). The foot used for counter-balance then crosses in front or behind the weighted leg and is placed using the front points (C), the second step allows one to come back to the triangle position under the new placement (D). It is also possible to shuffle your feet along the wall. Continue the traverse by crossing one tool over the other (E). You will have to rotate your chest to do this and remember to pull on the axe in the direction it is placed, not straight down. Ensure that you are in a triangle position when removing a tool (see Fig. 23); otherwise you will spin off the existing tool. You can use the holes made by the previous placements. Practice it by traversing back and forth at ground level.

FIGURE 27
The sequence of movements for traversing

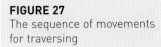

TROUBLESHOOTING PLACING AN ICE SCREW

- Your legs are not at the same height and your COG is off center.
- Your higher arm is not in a triangle position.
- Your hips are not pushed into the wall with the result that you must pull on your axes.
- Your chest is too close to the ice.
- Your axes are at the same height.
- You are placing the screw too high.

REMOVING ICE SCREWS

Clean the ice out immediately by tapping the hanger (not the threads) facing downward (most screws are tapered internally) against the ice. Do not poke them with an ice axe—internal scratches will increase the chances of the ice sticking in the future. If this fails, start another placement to dislodge the ice or place them somewhere warm until it falls out, e.g., inside your jacket.

Push from your hips when placing an ice screw. (Climber: Sam Ponsford.)

CREATING A BELAY AND BELAYING ON ICE

Think about the position of the belay for the next pitch—is the second going to be bombarded with ice? The perfect ice belay has at least two screws placed 10–15cm (4–6in) apart and 30–50cm (12–20in) one above the other.

Use slings to equalize the anchors to a single point and attach your rope to it. To improve the dynamic element, place a ripper sling between you and the belay. Do not worry about upward pulls; focus on preventing an FF2. The leader should place an ice screw with a ripper sling on it immediately upon leaving the belay to prevent this. It is also possible for the belay to have an extra ice screw, which the second's rope is passed when belaying—this can then serve as the first screw on the next pitch. With cold hands, mittens, icy ropes, and minimal rope drag, your belaying technique must be good. Take care bringing two climbers up a route at the same time because the lower one will be bombarded by ice from the first climber.

To climber

Ripper sling

Always think FF2 when creating an ice belay. (Climbers: Sam Ponsford and Chris Trull.)

A stein pull. Mixed routes are more difficult with leashed tools. Leashless mixed climbing is faster, more creative, and less painful on the wrists.

TIPS FOR BETTER MIXED CLIMBING

- File the bottom of the pick to an aggressive point for supreme hookability.
- Tape your leashes a third of the way down the shaft for reduced leverage.
- Try grabbing the axe low enough below the head to resist levering off on the placement.
- A sticky glove, a rubberized shaft, or surf wax will maximize grip.

MIXED CLIMBING AND DRY TOOLING

The pioneers of Scottish winter climbing did not have leashes on their axes and climbed steep snow and the chimney, gully, and ridge routes, because they did not have equipment to climb steep ice and the faces. It was only later with the advent of front points and drooped picks that leashes appeared, and the steep ice routes and hoar frosted buttresses and faces were tackled. Approximately ten years ago competition ice climbers started the leashless revolution, and this circle of reinvention continued.

In recent winters, mixed climbing has leapfrogged with mixed M-grade climbing developed by European, Canadian, and U.S. climbers searching for new ice or rock routes as the obvious lines ran out.

Early dry tooling routes followed dry rock to reach free hanging icicles, but the sport has developed so much that climbs are now being developed on rock devoid of snow or ice (dry tooling). It seems that this progression in the sport closely resembles the radical, challenging development of sport climbing. When such changes are afoot, the boundaries of different sub-disciplines become challenged and developed. Modern practitioners feel that bolt-protected mixed climbing could contribute much to the rich heritage of

Mixed climb uses your rock climbing skills and a lot more! (Climber: Clive Hebblethwaite, Scotland.)

traditionally protected, ground-up, and on-sight mixed climbing. Signs of this are already evident in all the major mixed venues around the world, and not least in the big mountains.

For mixed climbing get modular tools with sturdy, drooped picks. Choose leashes with wide comfortable wrist loops that lock tight. Crampons should be the step-in variety with replaceable front points. On mixed ground, mono-points do what slippers did for sport climbing—they give precision. For climbing in less than arctic conditions, leather boots—especially those with insulation—are best.

CLIMBING SNOWED UP ROCK

The fickle Scottish winters mean that eager mixed climbers often climb as soon as the cliffs have a dusting of white, and the difference between techniques for dry tooling and traditional mixed climbing becomes blurred.

Full on M-climbers use two hammers (or none at all), but for more traditional mixed climbing keep your adze (a beefy model) handy for the odd soft snow and turf section. Mixed climbing uses the full gambit of rock, ice, and even aid climbing skills, but with an axe and crampons—from heel hooks, drop-knees (Egyptians), and lay-backing, to a huge range of often devious tricks to win vertical height, such as Figure 4s, 8s, and 9s—that are beyond the scope of this book.

Look out for features to climb—there's an art to "feeling" just how good a potential hold is from below with your picks. Move up on a previously untested hold with some trepidation, keep your axe as still as possible and your elbows in, while keeping your face out of line should it break free. Axes put an enormous strain on the rock, so look for solid cracks and positive edges, but beware of flakes.

HOOKING

Ice tools can be used in a variety of ways for hooking on edges, flakes, and chockstones. Bring your rock climbing skills into play, use side pulls and underclings and remember: the axe also has an adze.

Mixed climbing often means that snow must be cleared away to reveal the natural features of the rock. However, you can also drag your axe through the snow until you feel it hook on something beneath the surface. A test pull from the shoulder will tell whether it is a placement that will hold.

Climb with your arms as straight as possible—this will require good hip and shoulder rotation. Keep your axe still and keep the shaft close to the rock to maintain a proper downward force as you try to gain height. This will require body tension between your feet and the pick. It is a difficult concept for a rock climber who is able to adjust the degree of grip.

Experiment with holding your axe further up the shaft or on the upper handle (with leashless tools) to gain extra reach towards the next placement. Such a move will change the pick balance and can send you flying. If the hold is questionable, try to move around on the axe as little as possible. Experi-

EXPERT TIP

Matt Spencely—Competition mixed climber and explorer www.greenland expeditions.com

"When pushing the boat out on mixed climbing where there's little snow about, skateboard grip tape wrapped around your axes offers a lot of purchase for your hands. On snowy ground, avoid grip tape like the plague!"

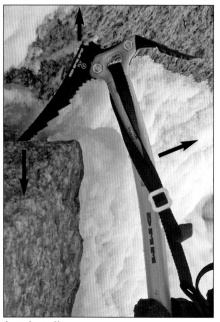

A stein pull

ment (in a safe position) with some outward pull on the axe to see what will hold. It is also possible to hook sideways on an edge.

The "stein pull," named after pulling a stein of beer, has the pick and the head of your axe working in opposition. They can be found under overlaps, but any three-dimensional feature in the rock can work as long as there is something for the top of the tool to brace against. Stein pulls are very stable because the tool is firmly wedged; you can reach further, pulling out as well as down. Be sure the hold is solid enough to withstand the leverage forces involved. Stein pulls are abundant on roofs, because the pick often slots into cracks or holes, orientating the shaft parallel to the ground like a chin-up bar (see photo, left, page 208).

Inverted stein pulls are achieved by reversing your grip on the tool, thumb towards the adze or hammer. Pulling down on the grip then cams the head firmly against the wall, which creates a stable position.

If you are climbing leashless, stein pulls can create a variety of no hands rests. The most basic stein pull rest is the arm hook, but equally effective is the leg hook. Modern ethics on the hardest routes make any use of axes for anything other than the hands a no-go area.

ICE-CHOKED CRACKS

The technique you use will depend on the amount of ice:

- When the ice is thin use controlled, gentle blows and place your thumb against the back of the tool's grip to stabilize and direct your swing.
- If the ice is super-thin, gently chip a hookable divot instead of planting the pick.
- In soft or unstable rock, dry tool thin or closed cracks devoid of ice.
- When the ice is thicker, swing hard and on target to sink the pick into the crack like a peg. If you're feeling brave you can tap the pick in further by hammering it with your other tool!

Stacking axes when the holds are limited can help you to gain height.

Use the adze and hammer as well as the pick. (Climber: Clive Hebblethwaite.)

TORQUEING

Flakes and chockstones can be simply hooked by the pick or adze of your axe, but cracks without ice often require the art of torqueing—jamming any part of your axe, including the hammer or the shaft, into a crack and levering it to stay in position (see photo bottom left). This can be practiced on old quarries and brick walls. Focus on keeping the pressure on the torque.

When there is only one good placement, you can stack your axes. Hook the pick of the good placement with the other tool, gain height, and then place your free axe.

4

ALPINISM

"Go for your dreams, but build up steadily, alpinism takes a long time."

—Ian Parnell, top U.K. climber

Alpinism is not controlled adventure like sport climbing or climbing on a roadside crag, it is real adventure where you have to rely more on your awareness and judgment than technical skills. There are challenges to suit everyone's ambitions, experience, and abilities—glacial walking, non-technical, and technical routes on low or high altitude mountains.

A non-technical peak is one where one axe will suffice, yet the ascent requires fitness and an understanding of objective dangers such as altitude, rock fall, and avalanche. It requires general crampon and ice axe skills, and rope work skills for crossing glaciers and ascending easier snow slopes. A technical peak usually involves all of the above plus the skills of scrambling, rock-climbing, and/or ice climbing.

Alpinism refers to mountaineering in areas such as the Rocky Mountains, the Cascades and the Sierra Nevada in the United States, and the Canadian Rockies. For U.K. climbers, the European Alps are a useful stepping-stone to expedition climbing, where the mountains are more remote, logistics are difficult, and rescue is largely down to the climbers themselves.

Many of the skills required for competent alpinism are the same as traditional rock climbing and winter mountaineering or climbing. They are applied here to the European Alps, but the principles also apply to alpine mountain ranges around the world.

Climbers on Peigne d'Arolla, Swiss Alps.

CLIMBING LIGHT

"Whatever safety exists in the mountains derives less from proper technique than from awareness"

—Mark Twight, *Extreme Alpinism* (1999)

Climbing quickly is the essence of safe alpinism, because you are exposed to the danger zone for less time—it enables the summit to be reached and a descent to be made before the afternoon storms catch you or a snowbridge collapses and a crevasse swallows you. Being fit and a good climber are obvious assets but climbing quickly is also synonymous with climbing light—if you carry everything you are probably going to need it!

Weight can be saved on nearly every piece of kit from crabs to your backpack.

CLOTHING

Layering has been discussed in chapters 1 and 3, but in winter, extremes of temperature will be experienced in the same day, so a flexible system is essential. Carry layers, but consider shorts and T-shirt for the walk to the hut. Use lightweight waterproof shells for emergency protection and invest in a good pair of windproof, quick-drying, robust mountaineering pants.

ALPINE BOOTS

Boots are likely to be B2 for easier, low altitude peaks with little technical rock, and B3 for everything else (see page 180). You can wear a pair of running shoes for the hut walk (leave them at the hut if you're coming back the same way or hide them somewhere obvious). A plastic boot is warmer on the higher snowy peaks, but a leather or fabric boot is cooler at lower altitude and will give greater comfort and feel.

GAITERS

(See chapter 1, page 6.)

ROCK BOOTS

Unless you are pushing your technical limits, wear a rock shoe with a thin sock, or a thicker pair with the toes cut out to act as leg warmers. They keep snow and grit out of your shoes and you can pull them down over your shoes to keep your feet warm on belays.

Alpine boots must be able to cope with walking to huts, climbing on technical rock, and snow and ice.

> **ALPINE STYLE**
>
> A pure style of mountaineering where climbers carry all the necessary equipment for a one-day or multi-day ascent. It applies to mountains all over the world.

BACKPACK

Get the simplest and lightest (1-1.5kg for a 50 liter sack) (2-2–3 lb for a13 kg sack) to carry your load comfortably. You sacrifice durability, but you will enjoy your trip much more. Light sacks rarely have a back adjustment system, so you must purchase the correct size and pack it carefully. The size can vary from 30 to 50 liters (8–13 gal) depending on your objective. Choose a narrow profile with compression straps, an extendable lid, a lightweight hip belt, and cut off anything that is unecessary. Ensure you can look up without your helmet hitting the sack.

CRAMPONS

Avoid technical crampons unless you are doing something outrageous, and buy a general purpose 12-point crampon, with toe straps and heel clip system, that is lightweight, easy to put on, and folds down small. Rigid C3 crampons are likely to "ball up" and are no good for long glacial treks. Anti-balling plates and a crampon bag are essential.

SUNGLASSES

UV radiation is extreme in the high mountains, even in winter. Create shade by wearing a wide-brimmed hat and glasses with category 4 lenses and full-wrap sides to prevent light leaking in. Avoid side shields that can impair your vision. Carry a spare pair between two climbers. Clip-on sunglasses are not adequate—if you wear glasses, get prescription sunglasses or wear disposable contact lenses. Goggles are unnecessary in summer, but they can always act as a spare pair of sunglasses.

SUNSCREEN AND LIP BLOCK

Skin cancer is the most common form of cancer. Protecting the body from UV light is simple—use sunscreen with a minimum SPF of 15 (more is better). Zinc oxide or titanium dioxide block out all the sun's rays—especially good for the nose, lips, and fair skin. Lips are particularly vulnerable because they lack melatonin, the skin's natural shield against the sun.

Sunscreen alone does not offer enough protection—clothing is as important. The higher the composition of synthetic fiber, the tighter the weave of the fabric, and the darker the colors, the greater the protection will be. For a simple test at home, hold up your clothes in front of a light source. The more light visible through the fabric, the more UV light will pass through.

Combined with a handkerchief around your neck, a good sun hat will protect you from the worst of the sun, but ensure it fits under your helmet.

Snow reflects 85 percent of UV and the intensity increases by 10 percent every 1000m (3280ft).

FLASHLIGHT

(See chapter 1, page 13.)

GLOVES AND HATS

(See chapter 3, page 179.)

ICE AXE

For non-technical routes, one general mountaineering axe is best (see chapter 3, page 184).

HELMET

Stonefall is a real problem in the Alps, so wear the best, but lightest helmet (see chapter 2, page 62), but also realize that rocks can hit you anywhere on the body.

HARNESS

Get the lightest available, but ensure it will fit over all of your clothes. The actual design will depend on the type of Alpine climbing—rock climbing requires a fully specified harness (four gear loops etc.), whereas non-technical mountaineering needs minimal features. An adaptation to allow you to drop the leg loops from the rear makes it easier to go to the bathroom, and gear loops that hang from the bottom of the waist belt extend below your backpack giving easier access to your gear.

A DMM alpine harness; simple and lightweight and can be put on when wearing crampons.

HARDWEAR

Success on an Alpine peak usually depends on climbing much moderate ground fast. Safety depends on judgment and confidence, not on placing a runner every foot. The hardest thing is making your rack light enough to move quickly, yet large enough to be safe—researching your route should help you to decide what to take.

ROPES

Use two 60m (197ft) of 9mm, dry coated ropes for technical climbs. If you are climbing on a single rope use a 9.5-9.7mm rope to save weight. If you know the route well you can carry very specific lengths, and in some cases as little as 30m (98ft) of 9mm for non-technical climbs. With so many sharp edges around avoid super-thin half ropes.

EMERGENCY KIT

Take a two-person group shelter and a small, foam pad to sit on. Also carry a small stove, pan, windshield, and some instant soups. Jet boil and MSR Reactor stoves do not require separate pans and work in the wind.

The Fedchenko Glacier, Pamir Mountains. It is the longest glacier in the world (77km/48mi) outside of the Polar Regions.

215

FIGURE 1
The features of an Alpine peak

1 Gendarmes	15 Glacier
2 Horn or aiguille	16 Truncated spur
3 Cornice	17 Avalanche debris
4 Ridge	18 Hanging glacier
5 Couloir or gully	19 Crevasses
6 Rognon	20 Medial moraine
7 Rock arête	21 Lateral moraine
8 Bergschrund	22 Roche moutonnée
9 Cirque or bowl	23 Snout
10 Firn line	24 Moraine lake
11 Sercas	25 Outwash plain
12 Ice fall	26 Terminal moraine
13 Nunatak	27 Erratic boulder
14 Snow field	

THE ALPINE ENVIRONMENT

For the purpose of this chapter, Alpinism takes place in mountain ranges where access is not too difficult, but the approaches to climbs involve crossing glaciers. The routes can be long, and success requires a high level of commitment, judgment, and fitness. Along with altitude problems, stonefall, and violent electrical storms, this is an environment with many potential hazards.

You cannot remove the hazards, but you can reduce the risk by understanding what they are and when they might happen.

ALTITUDE (with thanks to Dr J. Duff)

The percentage of oxygen in the air at sea level is 21 percent and the barometric pressure is around 760mm Hg. As you go higher, the percentage of oxygen remains the same, but the pressure drops and the number of oxygen molecules per breath is reduced. At the summit of Mont Blanc (4810m/15,771ft) the partial pressure of oxygen is half that at sea level. The lower air pressure not only makes it more difficult for your lungs to absorb oxygen, but also affects your brain and digestive system, and can cause fluid to leak into the lungs and brain.

ACCLIMATIZATION

The good news is that, as you ascend progressively to higher altitude, your body's chemistry and physiology adapts to the lower oxygen levels by:

- Increasing the depth of respiration

HIGH ALTITUDE

High altitude: 1500-3500m (4921-11,483ft)

Very high altitude: 3500-5500m (11,483-18,045ft)

Extreme altitude: above 5500m (18,045ft)

- Producing more red blood cells to carry oxygen
- Increasing pressure in pulmonary capillaries, forcing blood into parts of the lung that are not normally used when breathing at sea level
- Producing more of the enzyme that triggers the release of oxygen from red blood cells.

Everybody can acclimatize—it is a matter of allowing enough time. However, if you have been slow to acclimatize on previous trips the same pattern is likely on subsequent trips. You can only fully acclimatize to about 5000-5800m (16,404–18,045ft); above this there is a trade-off between acclimatization and deterioration due to prolonged lack of oxygen. Above 8000m (26,247ft) a prolonged stay is incompatible with life. Some experienced mountaineers say you should stay at 5500-5800m (18,045-19,029ft) until you can move like you do at sea level, and then go to higher altitudes.

Acclimatization takes time, and if you ascend too fast you risk potentially lethal acute mountain sickness (AMS), or high altitude pulmonary oedema (HAPE), and high altitude cerebral oedema (HACE). AMS can occur as low as 2500m (8202ft), but is more common over 3000m (9843ft). Virtually all climbers will experience some of the symptoms of AMS. Your chance of being affected is not dependent on age, gender, or fitness, although there is some evidence that older people are less affected as their brain shrinks and they travel more slowly than fit people.

To acclimatize you must gently stress your body—too little and you will not adapt, too fast and you will become ill. The actual altitude is not important; it is how fast you ascend to that altitude that matters. It is safer (and more enjoyable) to climb gradually and slowly, and you can descend as fast as you like! Above 3000m (9843ft) you should make a slow and gradual ascent with an ideal height gain of 300m (984ft) from the last place you slept to your next place of sleep. The sleeping altitude is particularly important—it is fine to go higher each day as long as you descend to sleep lower. Maintaining 300m (984ft) is not always possible, but you should be aware of the problems it can bring if you make that jump too quickly. A rest day after every three days or after 1000m (3281ft) of ascent is recommended.

Only 40 percent of climbers who attempt Mount Kilimanjaro ever reach the summit, and each year ten people die trying. This is a trekker being dragged upward, despite his AMS; the mountains will always be there, will you?

AMS

The symptoms of AMS are due to your body's failure to acclimatize. The incidence depends on the altitude, speed of ascent, and individual susceptibility. Symptoms usually start twelve-twenty-four hours after arrival at altitude and tend to worsen at night when respiratory drive is decreased. AMS can vary from mild to severe. HACE is considered to be the extreme end of the AMS spectrum.

There are no signs of mild AMS, only symptoms. A diagnosis of AMS is made when there is headache (typically throbbing and becoming

AMS SCORING

Symptom	Score
Headache	1
Nausea/loss of appetite	1
Insomnia	1
Giddiness	1
Headache after painkillers	2
Vomiting	2
Difficulty breathing at rest	3
Abnormal or intense fatigue	3
Decreased urination	3

1-3	light AMS painkillers
4-6	moderate AMS painkillers, rest and no ascent
>6	descend

EXPERT TIP

Kenton Cool
www.dream-guides.com

"Acclimatising properly not only helps to prevent serious oedemas, but allows you to climb faster, better and efficiently, which is safer and more fun."

worse when lying down or bending over) plus one or more of the following: nausea, vomiting, loss of appetite, dizziness, fatigue or weakness, poor sleep (periodic breathing).

Do not hide your symptoms from your friends because you will not recognize when you are slipping into HACE or HAPE.

The symptoms of severe AMS are more acute and you must carefully check for HACE and HAPE. If the patient is not improving, administer oxygen and medication and descend (600m/1966ft). HACE, HAPE, and the treatments for both are examined in more detail in chapter 6, page 314.

TREATMENT

AMS is treated with rest at the same altitude, rehydration, warmth, food, and painkillers (if pain relief is needed Ibuprofen is preferred, although paracetamol is a safe option). Giving acetazolamide (Diamox)—125 to 250mg every twelve hours—and oxygen speeds up the process of acclimatization. Painkillers and acetazolamide will not mask the symptoms of altitude illness.

Mild AMS is not life threatening, but as it progresses it will start to interfere with normal activity. You have acclimatized when the symptoms disappear and sleep becomes settled. Ascent to a higher altitude will require further acclimatization, but on descent to lower altitude the beneficial effects only last eight days.

ALPINE WEATHER

The weather in the European Alps is dominated by similar weather systems to the U.K., with depressions and fronts coming from the Atlantic. The weather patterns affecting the Alps are also affected by the Azores High that pushes the Atlantic depressions north resulting in longer, stable periods of good weather. The Alps do, however, make their own weather, which is extreme and unpredictable with thunderstorms, gusting winds, and torrential downpours.

Huge temperature variations can cause wet snow avalanches, snow bridges to collapse and large stonefalls. Alpine air is so dry that the lapse rate is 1°C per 100m (33.8°F per 328ft), but when it is raining it drops to 1°C per 200m (33.8°F per 984ft). See chapter 1, page 33.

The Alps make their own weather. (A thunderstorm approaching.)

THUNDERSTORMS AND LIGHTNING

Intense heat in the Alps generates huge thunderstorms and lightning, which usually appear in late afternoon and form suddenly, even in good weather.

Warnings of lightning are thunder; a sudden cloudburst of raindrops or hailstones; signs of highly charged air, such as hair standing on end; crackling noises or buzzing in the air; equipment humming; and small sparks around metal objects.

Lightning strikes are rare; you are more likely to be hit by a side flash or a ground current as it arcs to find an easy way to ground. Ground pathways include cracks and crevices filled with water, wet rock, wet climbing ropes, and root systems, so taking shelter at the opening of a cave may be more hazardous than being out in the open.

If you are caught in a thunderstorm, get off the highest location (see Fig. 2). Stay away from taller trees and out of depressions, gullies, and water. Avoid caves and overhangs unless dry or large. If you cannot get down, remove metal objects, occupy as little area as possible, and sit, crouch, or stand on your pack with your hands and feet off the ground. (See also chapter 1, page 32.)

AVALANCHES

The warmer temperatures, greater speeds of metamorphism, and settling of the snowpack mean that avalanches are less likely in summer. In very hot weather, or if soaked by rain, old snow can peel off in layers, and full-depth wet avalanches are not unheard of. The problem for summer alpinists is that you have fewer options to travel. The best tactic is to be up and down your route before the sun can warm the snow. Snow pits and shovel tests will not tell you more than you already know and are rarely performed in summer.

FIGURE 2
Dangerous places to shelter in a lightning storm

STONEFALL

Due to global warming the mountains are loose and becoming looser. Rock in the high mountains should always be treated with caution because it is subject to a constant freeze/thaw cycle. The orientation of the climb to the sun will affect the route, and on popular routes other people can present considerable objective dangers.

- Wear a helmet, but remember that the rest of your body is vulnerable.
- Avoid gullies when it is warm or has just rained.

- Ask for local advice about the conditions on your route.
- Start early and climb quickly.
- Be careful cleaning loose rock from routes.
- Rest where you are not exposed.

CORNICE COLLAPSE AND ICEFALL

The dangers of icefall are much the same as in winter, but the greater temperature changes in the Alps make it more likely.

NAVIGATION DIFFERENCES

An alpinist with great technical skills, but poor route finding technique is in more danger than if his skills were reversed. Alpine navigation is mostly done by map reading alone—the geographical features are large and easily identified. A compass is rarely used, but may be useful to orientate yourself for a descent or when it is dark or misty. Altimeters are useful to identify your location on the route and the distance to the summit (see Navigation, chapter 1).

A cornice on the Monch, the Alps, which collapsed not long after this photo was taken, taking a climber with it...luckily he survived.

MAP VARIATIONS

U.K. maps of mountainous areas use a 3D shading effect to indicate relief. French maps have very few grid lines and Austrian maps don't have any at all.

The French use a 10m (33ft) vertical interval that changes to 20m (66ft) when you cross into Switzerland, Germany, and Austria, sometimes on the same map. The magnetic variation is very small and is largely ignored. Also be aware that glaciers are largely retreating and change shape yearly and the snout may be further back; marked routes may be impassable and crevasses shown on the map may not be there.

Climbers on the Jungfrau, Bernese Oberland, Switzerland

WHEN AND WHERE TO GO

The summer season is from June to September, but for easier routes and valley rock climbing the season is longer. Winter conditions in the European Alps occur anytime between October and May, with the "official" winter season from December 21 to March 20. It is best to avoid popular areas in August, especially in France during the annual holiday period. However, there are always quiet places in the Alps for the truly adventurous climber.

There is rarely enough snow in winter and spring to maintain the condition of the steeper snow and ice faces throughout summer. Spring may be a better time for snow routes, but then skis or snowshoes may be needed for approaches and the avalanche danger is real! Conversely, technical rock routes are better when the snow has melted later in the season.

Global warming and the fickle nature of the weather require you to be flexible with your goals until you have a sense of what the climbing is like. Some mountains have a small window of opportunity that opens and closes erratically during the season, e.g., the Matterhorn.

The Dent du Geant, Chamonix, France

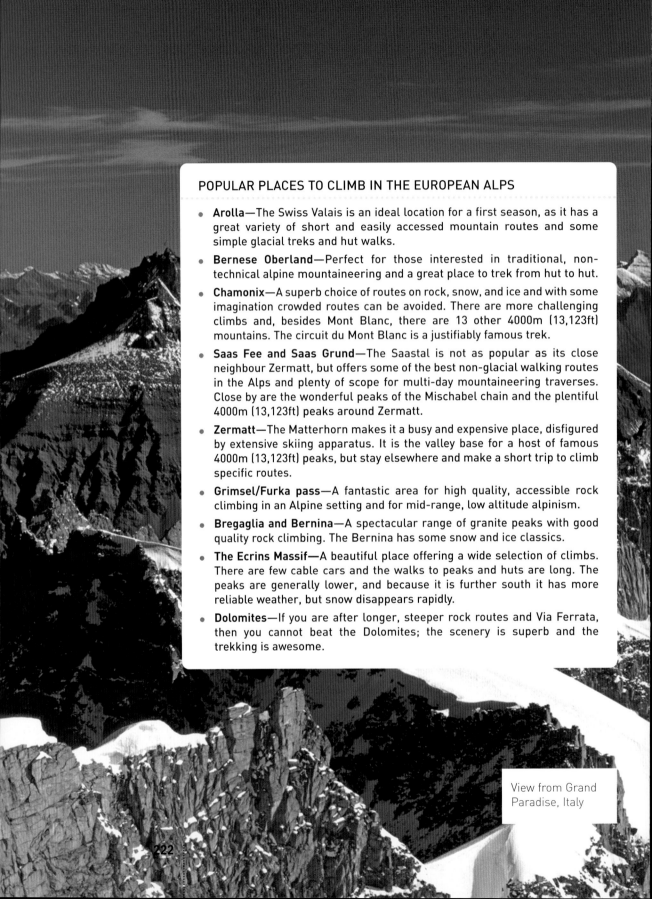

POPULAR PLACES TO CLIMB IN THE EUROPEAN ALPS

- **Arolla**—The Swiss Valais is an ideal location for a first season, as it has a great variety of short and easily accessed mountain routes and some simple glacial treks and hut walks.
- **Bernese Oberland**—Perfect for those interested in traditional, non-technical alpine mountaineering and a great place to trek from hut to hut.
- **Chamonix**—A superb choice of routes on rock, snow, and ice and with some imagination crowded routes can be avoided. There are more challenging climbs and, besides Mont Blanc, there are 13 other 4000m (13,123ft) mountains. The circuit du Mont Blanc is a justifiably famous trek.
- **Saas Fee and Saas Grund**—The Saastal is not as popular as its close neighbour Zermatt, but offers some of the best non-glacial walking routes in the Alps and plenty of scope for multi-day mountaineering traverses. Close by are the wonderful peaks of the Mischabel chain and the plentiful 4000m (13,123ft) peaks around Zermatt.
- **Zermatt**—The Matterhorn makes it a busy and expensive place, disfigured by extensive skiing apparatus. It is the valley base for a host of famous 4000m (13,123ft) peaks, but stay elsewhere and make a short trip to climb specific routes.
- **Grimsel/Furka pass**—A fantastic area for high quality, accessible rock climbing in an Alpine setting and for mid-range, low altitude alpinism.
- **Bregaglia and Bernina**—A spectacular range of granite peaks with good quality rock climbing. The Bernina has some snow and ice classics.
- **The Ecrins Massif**—A beautiful place offering a wide selection of climbs. There are few cable cars and the walks to peaks and huts are long. The peaks are generally lower, and because it is further south it has more reliable weather, but snow disappears rapidly.
- **Dolomites**—If you are after longer, steeper rock routes and Via Ferrata, then you cannot beat the Dolomites; the scenery is superb and the trekking is awesome.

View from Grand Paradise, Italy

222

HOW TO TACKLE AN ALPINE PEAK

"The greatest test of a climber's judgment is his willingness to turn back."
—George Alan Smith, *Introduction to Mountaineering* (1957)

Alpine routes are generally long and involve a lot of height gain and loss, for example, the standard route on Monte Rosa (4632m/15,197ft) is 1830m (6004ft) from hut to summit, with the hardest part at the top. However, access via téléphériques and railways has made certain routes an easy day out, but only when you can move swiftly.

Alpine climbs are exposed, and even easy climbs have big drops. There can be several types of climbing in the same route, and the weather can change the grade overnight. Add to this big boots, a backpack, long run outs, loose rock, crevasses, moving together, the altitude and the descent when you are tired, and it can all seem a tall order!

PREPARE AND PLAN

The Club Alpine Français found that 85 percent of accidents are due to poor preparation. If you plan and prepare, choose and research your route, practice specific skills at home, watch the weather, build your experiences gradually, and travel lightly, the Alps are a much less daunting place.

PHYSICAL PREPARATION

Climbing with big boots and a backpack is the best training for Alpine peaks. Do not leave it to the last moment; start training several months in advance.

MENTAL PREPARATION

Fear is natural; the mark of a good alpinist is how they cope with it. Your state of mind is as important as your technical ability for avoiding accidents. Three factors have been found to frequently contribute to accidents:

- **Ignorance**—You will never know everything and you can learn something from everyone. Practice as much as possible, e.g., do not leave Prusiking until you are down a crevasse.

- **Casualness**—Most accidents occur on easy ground or when your guard is down. Be vigilant, become self-sufficient, and do not climb expecting to be rescued.

- **Distraction**—Anxiety, sore feet, euphoria at the summit and forgetting that the climb is only half over, relying on a more experienced partner, etc., can take your mind off the climb. Keep your mind on the big picture.

DEVELOP GOOD JUDGMENT

Safe mountaineering requires judgment, but remember: what worked well in a given place at a given time may not be appropriate in the same place at a different time. Judging any situation by protocol or rules invites disaster. Aldous Huxley said, "Experience is not what happens to you. Experience is what you do with what happens to you." Listen to the messages your body and

Knowledge without understanding is dangerous. (Climbers study the map and guide at a hut.)

Wisdom in the mountains is not about being absolutely correct, but correct enough.

EARLY START

Starting early is essential because you will climb with the sun for longer.

the environment is giving you—the weather, temperature changes, speed of the team, your kit, etc.—and choose the appropriate course of action. Ultimately safety and risk reduction is being aware of danger—but remember: what is dangerous for one team may not be dangerous for another, so do not simply follow what others are doing.

KNOWLEDGE IS POWER

The Alps are in a constant state of change, and much planning and preparation at home can save time. Check your route description in local guidebooks and magazine articles, and seek up-to-date information from other climbers and local guide offices. Internet sites provide up-to-the-minute Alpine climbing conditions with climbing forums. Professional Mountain Guides provide good information, even if they do err on the side of caution.

Guidebook times are averages for acclimatized, fit, competent parties who know where they are going and how to climb quickly. Climbing in the Alps rarely depends on what grade you can climb, but what grade you can climb fast! Start with a climb two technical grades inside your technical limits, so that you perceive how quickly you move. The harder and more committing the climb, the finer the line you will have to tread, and the greater judgment and experience you will require.

Ask the following questions about your route:

- How long is the approach and what type of approach is it?
- How long is it—can you move fast enough?
- Does it stay safe all day?
- Is it in condition?
- How do you get down?
- Is there a hut, or is a bivvy better?
- What is the weather forecast?
- What equipment do you need to take and what can you leave behind?

ALPINE GRADING

The grading of Alpine climbs is fundamental to selecting a route. The most common grading system in the European Alps (except for the Bernese Alps and sometimes the Eastern Alps) is the International French Adjectival System (IFAS). This system is sometimes used to grade climbs in the Andes and Himalaya. The overall grade describes the difficulty of the route and is combined with the International Mountaineering and Climbing Federation (UIAA) or French rock grading system to describe the rock pitches. The technical ice rating numbers are roughly the same as in the U.S. or Canada.

The overall grade combines:

- Altitude and length
- Length and difficulty of approach and descent

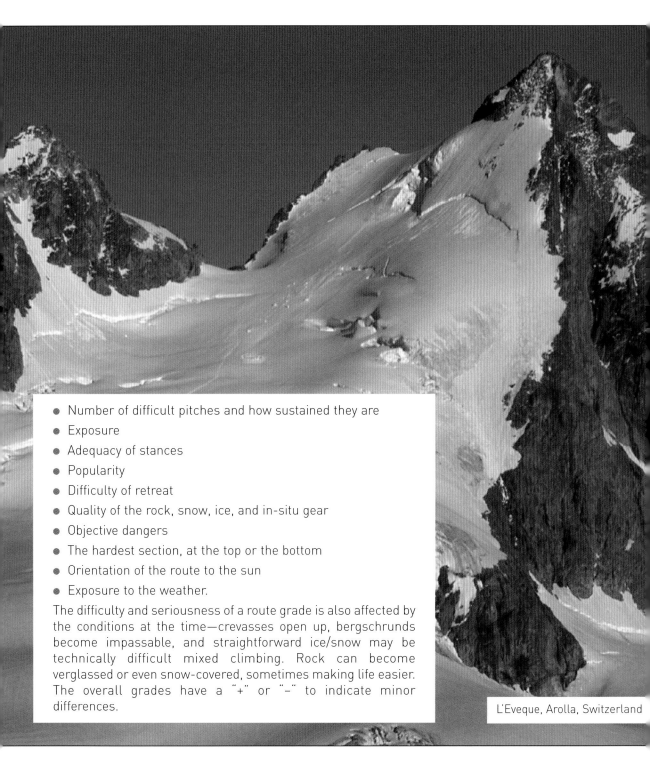

- Number of difficult pitches and how sustained they are
- Exposure
- Adequacy of stances
- Popularity
- Difficulty of retreat
- Quality of the rock, snow, ice, and in-situ gear
- Objective dangers
- The hardest section, at the top or the bottom
- Orientation of the route to the sun
- Exposure to the weather.

The difficulty and seriousness of a route grade is also affected by the conditions at the time—crevasses open up, bergschrunds become impassable, and straightforward ice/snow may be technically difficult mixed climbing. Rock can become verglassed or even snow-covered, sometimes making life easier. The overall grades have a "+" or "–" to indicate minor differences.

L'Eveque, Arolla, Switzerland

Grade	Description
F Facile	Easy. Straightforward, possibly a glacier approach, and very simple scrambling. The snow or ice will be of an easy angle, e.g., Allalinhorn, West Ridge and Aiguille du Tour.
PD Peu Difficile	A little difficult. Routes may be longer and at altitude with snow and ice slopes up to 45 degrees. The glaciers are more complex, the scrambling is harder, and there are more objective dangers, e.g., Mont Blanc, Goûter Route (PD-), Jungfrau (PD+) SE Ridge, and the Gran Paradiso (PD-).
AD Assez Difficile	Fairly hard. Snow and ice at 40-55 degrees. Rock climbing up to grade III, but not sustained, e.g., Matterhorn Hornli ridge (AD-); Aiguille du Chardonnet Forbes Arête (AD).
D Difficile	Hard. More serious with rock climbing at IV and V and snow and ice slopes at 50-70 degrees, e.g., Eiger Mittellegi Ridge, Aiguille du Chardonnet, North Buttress (D-), and the Aiguille du Midi Frendo Spur (D+).
TD Tres difficile	Very hard. Routes at this grade are a serious undertaking with high levels of objective danger. Sustained snow and ice slopes at 65-80 degrees. Rock climbing at grades V–VI, with possible aid, e.g., Mont Blanc du Tacul Gervasutti Pillar TD/TD+; the Matterhorn North Face.
ED Extremement difficile	Extremely hard. Exceptional objective danger, vertical ice slopes and rock climbing VI-VIII with possible aid pitches, e.g, Eiger, North Face 1938 Route (ED2); Grandes Jorasses, Walker Spur (ED1).
ABO Abominablement difficile	Self-explanatory!

TECHNICAL DIFFICULTY

Technical grades also inform you about a route's seriousness. If the technical difficulty is low compared to routes of a similar grade, the route is likely to be long and/or serious. The opposite is true of a route with high technical difficulties when compared to similarly graded routes; it is likely to be short, unserious or have a short, difficult crux section.

TECHNICAL DIFFICULTY OF THE ROCK

The UIAA scale (Roman numbers) or French sport grade is given. Generally, the longer the route the less severe the rating. Therefore, if a pitch is 6a in the valley, the same pitch on a mountain route would possibly be given 6b. Add to this no bolts, heavier clothing, footwear, and a sack and the climbs will feel harder than an equivalent route in the valley.

Point du Vausson, Arolla—Facile

Mont Blanc—Peu Difficile

Top of the North Face of the
Tour Ronde—Difficile

Swiss route, Grand Capucin—
Tres Difficile

The Eiger North Face—ED2 (Climber:
Phil Thomas.)

TECHNICAL DIFFICULTIES ON SNOW AND ICE

Some guidebooks give the steepness of the snow/ice sections, but for longer routes only an average angle may be given and steeper sections missed out. On genuinely steep routes, the ice grading system is often used, most commonly WI-grade, but sometimes the Scottish grade is given.

TECHNICAL DIFFICULTY OF MIXED SECTIONS

The normal rock grading system is often used, even though it does not tell you much about the actual difficulty, but sometimes the WI-grade system is used (M-grade).

THE APPROACH

The advantage of many European Alpine bases is their ski infrastructure, with cable cars to shorten the walk to the hut or the route, but this can also destroy the feeling of remoteness.

USING A CABLE CAR

Téléphériques (or cable cars) are often crowded, but there is no need to rush to be sure of a space. Good etiquette will prevent injuries. Remove your backpack and put it on the floor with the waist belt wrapped around it to prevent buckles being broken. Carry your ice axe and ski poles in your hand and keep your crampons inside the backpack.

HUTS AND BIVOUACS

Huts enable walkers and climbers to get an early start without carrying heavy bivouac (bivvy) gear and lots of food. National Alpine clubs own most of the huts, but some are privately owned. They vary, from small bivvy huts with no facilities or guardian to large mountain hotels with showers and single rooms.

Following paths to huts. Walking routes in the Alps are marked on rocks and trees with white/red/white stripes. When the track ahead is difficult, the marks become white/blue/white.

The average hut has dormitory beds and a guardian who provides a good three course evening meal and breakfast. The guardian makes their living from supplying the food and drink, but in France you can bring and cook your own food in a separate area of the hut; elsewhere it is forbidden or you must give your food to the guardian to cook for a small charge.

Huts are open from mid-June to mid-September and some popular ones during the ski touring season, but even outside these times a winter annexe without a guardian is always open. Huts can be crowded and some, such as the Mont Blanc huts, are booked months in advance. Book early by phoning the hut, and tell them if you decide not to go—you may be charged, especially in Switzerland.

Wild camping is officially frowned upon, and in some countries it is against the law. Bivvying, however, is acceptable in certain areas from sunset to sunrise, but not in the vicinity of a hut.

BIVVYING

There are two reasons to bivvy. The first is an emergency or unplanned night out and the second is a planned bivvy, because the route is too long or you just wanted to enjoy a night on the mountain. The problem with a planned bivvy is carrying enough equipment to allow a reasonable nights' rest. The problem with an unplanned bivvy is that they are miserable.

Bivvying on a route is something all climbers should experience at least once. (Dave Williams, The Walker Spur, France.)

BIVVY SITE

Your first task is to select a sheltered bivvy spot. Keep in mind the mountain features, which are above you, but are not visible in the dark. Ridges may be exposed to wind so move down the side. Be aware of chimneys, which may be large enough to accommodate you, but can transform into a rock waterfall.

PLANNED BIVOUAC

The difference between a good and bad night is often down to the details.

Remain tied into your anchors and wear your harness inside your sleeping bag. To prevent water wicking along the rope, keep it lower than you before it enters your sleeping bag, and tie a couple of knots between yourself and the anchors. You should have enough rope to reach the furthest points on your ledge, but also be easily adjustable—a Prusik from your harness to the attachment rope via a 60cm (24in) sling will allow you to stay tight on the rope wherever you are. A handrail between two anchors is useful for clipping gear.

Take a warm bottle to bed to keep you warm and force any moisture out (see chapter 6, page 341).

SLEEPING MATS

Closed cell foam is bulky, but inflatable mats puncture. If you are planning to bivvy, cut a closed cell foam pad into three or four sections and rejoin them by sewing and taping; this will allow the mat to lie flat against the side of your backpack. Alternatively, use the pad from your backpack and stuff your jacket and top pant under your legs. Your fleece jacket can act as a pillow.

BIVVY BAG

A breathable material is essential, but avoid heavier models with hooped poles. A bivvy bag with a cowl keeps spindrift and rain out and helps to seal you into the bag without having to zip yourself in completely. Try not to breathe directly into your bag, and if forced to seal yourself in, leave a gap that you can breathe through.

SNOW CAVES

These provide much more shelter than bivvy bags or small tents, but it is rarely possible to dig them in the Alps.

EATING

You will sleep warmer if you are well-fed and watered because digestion releases heat. Carry a small gas stove. A small, steel cup with a lid can be used instead of a pot, or alternatively use a Jet Boil stove. For an ultra lightweight bivouac carry ready-to-eat food and only use the stove for melting water. Heating several small quantities of water is more fuel-efficient than one large quantity.

EMERGENCY BIVVY

Bivvying without a sleeping bag is usually miserable! An alternative to carrying a bivvy bag is to use a Blizzard Bag, which is smaller, lighter, and warmer, although condensation is a problem and the bag is difficult to pack small again. If you do not have a closed cell pad, sit on your climbing ropes or your sack.

   If you are stuck on a steep, small ledge improvise a seat from your backpack or a padded rope to ensure blood can flow to your limbs. If you can abseil down to a ledge and jumar back up, do it. If you are carrying food, have a bite to eat once in a while, and perhaps brew up a hot drink. You can still get into your bivvy sleeping bag, even on a standing bivvy, but stay tied to the anchors.

(Left) Alpine huts are often busy and the guardians work hard looking after you. (The Vignettes hut, Arolla, Switzerland.)

(Right) Approaching the Vignettes hut, Arolla, Switzerland.

HUT LIVING

When you arrive, leave your sack, boots, crampons, and ice axes in the entrance room (sometimes they are left outside). You can keep your crampons inside your sack as long as they are in a protective bag. Check in immediately and carry ID. In most huts backpacks can eventually be taken to the dormitories. Boots are banned inside the hut, but slippers are supplied. To help you organize your gear, many huts have small baskets. You can hang gear up to dry, but do not spread it out all over the hut. Gear is rarely stolen, but in the morning rush things are often picked up by mistake so ensure it has your name on it.

After checking in, the guardian will assign you a room and bunks. The hut will have a number of wake-up calls, depending on the route you are climbing, and you are likely to be in a dorm with people rising at the same time. It is normal practice to mark your bunk with some clothing.

Being organized is important; keep out your headlamp, water, earplugs, toothbrush, and toiletries for the evening only. People will try to sleep at anytime, so be quiet in the dormitory—if you must talk, go outside. Do not pack or fiddle with gear in the dorm. Use your headlamp if necessary, but avoid shining it into sleeper's eyes.

Dinner is usually served at about 6:30 PM. On crowded days there may be multiple sittings. After dinner, clear the table and wipe it with a cloth kept near the kitchen. During the evening you may have to tell the guardian what drink you want for breakfast. Cold water is only sold in bottles due to health concerns, but hot water is available and cheaper. If you take tea bags, etc., you can make your own drinks.

Typically the bill is paid in the evening just after dinner (some huts take debit/credit cards, but ask when you book). If you are staying multiple nights in one hut, you can usually pay the bill on the last night. Water bottles and Thermos flasks are usually gathered the evening before and filled that evening or by the following morning for a small charge.

THE ROPE

For glacier travel, a UIAA half rope is enough. But beware: the thinner the rope the more stretch it has and the harder it is for a Prusik to grip the rope.

GETTING UP IN THE MORNING AND DEPARTING

Departing early is often a manic rush as you try to get ahead of other teams. After rising, check your sleeping area for anything left behind and fold your blankets neatly. The skill to departing quickly is to pack your backpack the night before and have the items you will need for the morning at the top. On many routes you will be wearing your harnesses all day, so wear it from the start.

GETTING TO YOUR ROUTE

Most routes, especially snow and ice faces, look much steeper in the dark and when looking straight on. Spend the evening before looking at your route. Find prominent features that you can identify en route, and take a photograph with a digital camera and review it later. Do the same for the descent. It is advisable to walk the start of the approach in daylight to avoid wandering aimlessly around in the dark. Start the approach slowly and speed up later; a stop-and-go tactic uses energy inefficiently, leaving you sweating. Eat and drink on the move, or when you stop, for example, to put on crampons.

PRACTISING CREVASSE RESCUES

Place a good set of anchors to back up the rescuer. Wear a helmet, but remove your backpack, ice axe, and crampons.

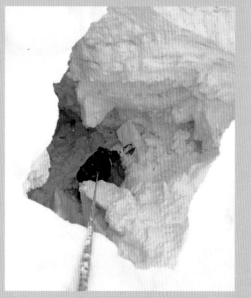

Crevasses are cold places. (A climber after a fall through a snow bridge.)

TRAVELING ON GLACIERS

There are about 160,000 glaciers in the polar regions and high mountains of the world, and 75 percent of Earth's fresh water is locked up in glaciers—but they are disappearing fast.

A glacier is formed by the accumulation of snow at high altitude. Gradually, the force of nature converts the snow to ice, and the glacier is pushed downhill on a layer of water.

There are two types of glacier: wet and dry. Wet glaciers are snow-covered, resulting in the crevasses being hidden. A dry glacier is bare ice. Travel on dry glaciers is usually easy, but crampons are sometimes required. The best advice for travel on wet glaciers is to rope up, know how to avoid falling into a crevasse, and understand rescue techniques should the worst happen, as rescuing someone from a crevasse is difficult.

GLACIAL MORAINES

Glacial moraines appear after the glacier has retreated, usually as linear mounds of rock, gravel, and boulders within a fine, powdery material (till). The moraines at the end of the glacier are called terminal moraines. Lateral moraines are formed on the sides of the glacier. Medial moraines are formed when two different glaciers flowing in the same direction meet, forming a moraine in the middle of the merged glacier. Walking on them can be safe, but there is often rockfall from above on lateral moraines.

SPOTTING HIDDEN CREVASSES

Crevasses usually form when the ice comes under tension.

- **Over a drop**—Crevasses appear perpendicular to the glacier's flow. On steep drops, the glacier breaks into a chaotic jumble, with huge blocks of ice (seracs) that can tumble without warning.
- **On a bend**—The faster-moving ice in the center pulls away from the slower ice along the sides, leaving radial cracks.
- **As the valley base widens**—The ice spreads out and vertical cracks may appear running parallel to the direction of the glacier's flow.

There are a few indicators to help you identify crevasses hidden under snow. Look for dips in the snow as snow bridges sag—especially after a long, warm period—and changes in surface color—after a snow-free period, duller, wind-blown snow tends to collect in the small dips. Conversely, after fresh snowfall without wind, brighter and lighter coloured fresh snow may collect in the dips.

ROUTE FINDING

Alpine maps show likely crevassed areas, contour lines, and even suggested routes to help you plot your route, but remember that glaciers change rapidly. Take advantage of the times when you are high above a glacier to check your planned route, but do not assume that a trail or previously traveled route across a wet glacier is safe. The snow changes constantly and new crevasses can open up at any time, to the point where what was safe in the morning may not be so in the afternoon.

Never travel un-roped on a wet glacier—you will be playing Russian roulette.

WET GLACIERS—THE ESSENTIALS

Cover your arms and legs from the cold and wear gloves. Crampons are essential unless there are many climbers on the rope. Everyone must carry rescue kit that is easily accessible, but ensure it is neat and does not hang below your knees. Keep your ice axe in your hand. If you are walking with ski poles just use one. Use a rope, and ensure that there is a minimum of slack rope between you—do not carry hand coils. Don't gather together when stopping for a break; your combined weight may prove too much for a crevasse bridge. The most experienced member leads to allow for the best route finding and pacing, but when descending on hard snow or ice, the most experienced and/or largest should be at the rear. When crossing a crevasse the rest of the team should move backward.

Where possible, the line of travel is perpendicular to the crevasses and the lead person should call out or mark the crevasse. In certain circumstances, echelon travel (see Fig. 3 overleaf) can be useful when the crevassed area cannot be avoided, on steep terrain when the snow is firm, or a traverse parallel to the crevasses is required. This does have drawbacks, forcing each climber to break their own trail, slowing down the group, and making control of the rope more difficult.

CREVASSE RESCUE KIT

3 Prusik loops
Petzl mini traxion or Wild
   Country Ropeman
2 slings, 220cm (87in)
1 revolver crab
2 long ice screws
1 abseil device
2 screwgate crabs

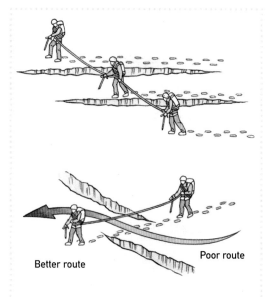

Better route

Poor route

FIGURE 3
Echelon formation and traveling perpendicular to crevasses

ROPE USAGE

A rope is essential when:

- in summer on wet glaciers.
- you are skinning on unfamiliar wet glaciers in poor visibility.
- you are skiing downhill when the snow cover is shallow, low density, or variable (particularly early or late winter).
- visibility is poor.

Travel without a rope may be acceptable when:

- the glacier is free of snow, crevasses are clearly visible, and visibility is good.
- skiing downhill when winter snow cover is deep, high density, and consistent, and the terrain and crevasse patterns are known and/or easy to access.
- it compounds other problems, e.g., avalanche terrain.

HOW MUCH ROPE IS REQUIRED?

The amount of rope between each climber depends on the terrain and the number of people on the rope. Have enough rope available for a rescue, plus a few extra meters to allow for rope stretch. However, when there are large crevasses, when you are carrying heavy loads, or where you may have difficulty arresting a fall, you might need to increase the distance between climbers. This does, however, increase rope stretch, which can compromise communication making it difficult to negotiate obstacles. It may also leave

CALCULATING SPACING ON THE ROPE

This system assumes that there are 30 arm spans in a 50m (164ft) rope, but you must work out how many of your arm lengths it is and how many arm spans you have between people. If you are tying knots in the rope you must allow more arm spans to allow for the tying of knots.

A—Two people on the rope. Spacing between the climbers is eight arm spans. Thirty arm spans, less two for tying in and eight between the climbers leaves twenty arm spans, ten on each person.

B—Three people on the rope. Six arm spans between climbers (a total of twelve), three for the knots, leaves fifteen for chest coils on the first and last person.

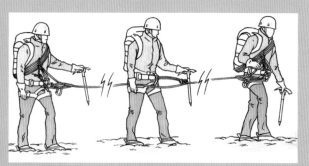

FIGURE 4
Rope calculating system for travel across glaciers

less rope for a rescue, but it is more important to prevent someone falling into a crevasse in the first place. When there are long distances between climbers, it may be prudent for the rear person to carry a separate section of 7mm rope for a rescue.

For two climbers using a 50m (164ft) rope there should be eight to ten arm spans between the climbers; for three it is six arm spans. The remainder is taken as chest coils or kept in your backpack. For four or more climbers the distance is rarely more than four arm spans.

Make sure you give enough rope! (Jumping a crevasse, Alpamayo, Peru. Climber: Gareth Richardson.)

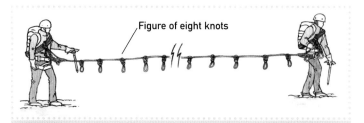

Figure of eight knots

FIGURE 5
Tying four or five knots at each end of the rope can make it easier to hold a heavier climber but can make rescue more difficult.

USE OF KNOTS
To increase the chance of holding a substantially heavier climber, tie four or five large knots, 1m (3.3ft) apart, close to each climber or just the heavier one. This is especially useful when the snow is hard, and/or on steep slopes, where self-arrest is difficult. Using knots may complicate certain types of rescue, but the most important thing is to be able to stop someone falling (see Fig. 5).

CONNECTING TO THE ROPE
With two climbers you have two options:

- Tie-in normally and take chest coils. This is particularly suitable when the terrain is changing constantly and the rope needs to be shortened then lengthened or you are carrying a heavy load.

- Both mountaineers attach to the rope at just over one-third of its length using a figure of eight knot on a bight and back-to-back screwgate crabs or a re-threaded overhand knot. Carry the extra rope in the sack.

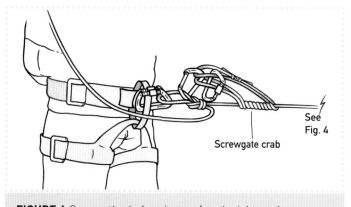

See Fig. 4

Screwgate crab

FIGURE 6 One method of roping up for glacial travel

When there are more than two climbers, two should attach at the ends and

Taking coils around the chest for glacier travel (see Chapter 2, page 109)

An alternative method for tying into the end of the rope—the remainder of the rope is carried in your backpack.

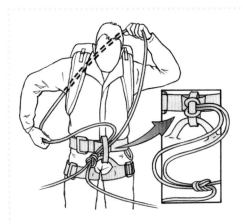

FIGURE 7
Using a lark's foot to attach to the middle of the rope. It creates a small attachment knot, but makes it difficult to escape the rope quickly.

take coils, and the rest should attach to the rope using a figure of eight knot with two back-to-back screwgate crabs (to allow for easy escape), a re-threaded overhand knot or a lark's foot (see Fig. 7).

In all situations, a French prusik should be attached to the tie-in loop or carabiner on the harness via an open gate crab. An extra crab (screwgate) is then attached to the prusik to enable easy transfer of the load to an anchor (see Fig. 6). If the terrain is serious, the middle person should then attach two prusiks, one on each side.

Attaching a prusik will ensure the load will come on to the pelvis and not the chest and can make arresting a fall much easier. If you do fall down a crevasse slide the prusik backward to direct the forces higher up the body.

TOWING SLEDS OR CARRYING HEAVY LOADS

In remote areas the victim is often accompanied into the crevasse by a heavy backpack and/or sled. It is unlikely the victim and the backpack or sled can be pulled out together, and the rescuers should consider hauling the packs or sled out first.

It is important to attach the sled from the rear to the safety rope via a prusik. This will prevent it from crashing on top of the victim. The hauler must also ensure that it is possible to detach from the sled when down the crevasse (see chapter 6, page 347).

USING ANCHORS AND BELAYS

A fall into a crevasse generates small forces due to minimal acceleration and the friction of the rope cutting into the snow. This makes routine anchors and belays unnecessary, except on hard snow and steep slopes or when large suspect bridges have to be crossed. Any belay system must be strong enough to use for a subsequent rescue.

ARRESTING A FALL

Holding a fall into a crevasse is usually not difficult, but it can happen very quickly! When the climber falls, drop backward and stamp your feet well in or hit the snow in the ice axe arrest position (see chapter 3, page 192, Fig. 15A). If you are minimizing the slack in the rope the chances are that they will only have fallen a very short distance into the crevasse and can get themselves out. If this is not the case follow the method below.

CREATING A RESCUE ANCHOR

Where the victim has fallen down the crevasse and cannot communicate, the rescuers must create an anchor strong enough to transfer the loaded rope to (see Ice anchors and snow anchors, page 197). Crevasse rescue anchors are generally built at the location of the climber nearest the crevasse to reduce rope stretch. The closest climber can create the anchor, but in a team of three or more this is best done by another climber moving forward along the rope, using their prusik to keep the rope taut to assist the climber closest to the crevasse should they start to slide.

TRANSFERRING THE LOAD TO THE ANCHOR

Once an anchor has been created the loaded rope is transferred to it by rolling towards the sling attached to the anchor (see Fig. 8). The spare screwgate crab from the French prusik is then clipped into the anchor. Gently load the anchors by moving towards the crevasse. When you are confident the anchor is holding, remove the open gate crab from your harness and back-up the prusik by immediately clipping the rope to the anchor with a locking crab and a tied-off Italian hitch.

In crevassed areas with a big backpack it may be prudent to wear coils or a chest harness. (Climbers: Clive Hebblethwaite and Adrian Wilson, Alaska.)

PRINCIPLES OF CREVASSE RESCUE

1 Arrest the fall
2 Create a rescue anchor
3 Transfer the load to the anchor
4 Assess the situation
5 Attend to the victim
6 Prepare the edge of the crevasse
7 Rescue the victim

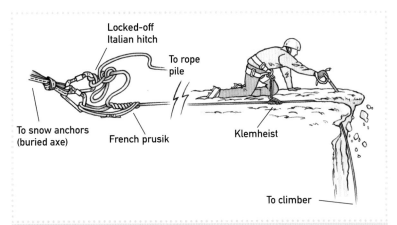

FIGURE 8
Approaching the edge of the crevasse with care.

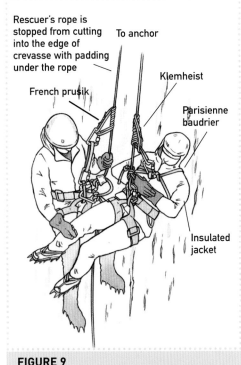

FIGURE 9
Descend to the victim and make them comfortable.

ASSESSMENT OF THE SITUATION

The rescuer can now move to the edge of the crevasse, protected by a prusik or ascender probing the snow to find the true edge of the crevasse (see Fig. 8). The edge will probably have to be prepared, no matter what the next step (the exception may be if the victim's life is threatened, and speed is essential, or if the collapsing snow will injure them).

Remove overhanging snow to free the loaded rope, but take great care—a rope under tension is easily cut. A backpack, ski pole, or ice axe is placed under the loaded rope or rescue rope at the edge and secured.

Once the edge is prepared you have a number of options in order of preference:

- lower the victim to somewhere they can climb out, or to take the load from the rope.
- it may be possible for the victim to climb out of the crevasse while being belayed from above.
- simply pull the victim out.
- perform a two-team pull.
- hoist the victim…the last resort!

The worst-case scenario is a seriously injured victim—the rescuer will then need to abseil to them using the other end of the rope. Pad the lip of the crevasse under the abseil rope and take a first-aid kit and warm clothing, or a sleeping bag, to treat and bundle the victim. The process of hauling out an unconscious victim can easily take over an hour (see Fig. 9).

After treatment, make an improvised chest harness and clip it to a prusik on their rope to keep them upright. To prevent the victim from suffocating by being dragged through the snow, turn them so that their back is against the wall of the crevasse. Retrieve any climbing gear the victim has with them, particularly prusiks, before ascending.

PRUSIKING OUT

To prusik out remove your coils and undo them. Clip your backpack into the loop of rope below you or attach it via a knot. Attach a foot prusik to the rope and ascend. It may be prudent to drop the other end of the rope so the victim can prusik up the second line, rather than the line jammed into the snow.

SIMPLE PULL

If there are enough rescuers, simply pull the victim from the crevasse (rescuers should not walk backward unless they are certain that they will not fall into another crevasse). The rope to the victim should be belayed or protected via a prusik or ascender. If you feel resistance, do not pull anymore; the victim may be at the lip of the crevasse.

TWO-TEAM PULL

If another team is available, the first team arrests the fall and holds the victim while the second approaches the edge and sends a rescue rope to the victim. If this team can do this quickly it may not be necessary for the first team to build an anchor and transfer the load. If an anchor is not built, the first team belays the victim by moving backward in the self-arrest position as the second team hauls the victim usually using an assisted hoist (see Fig. 10).

HOISTING USING PULLEYS

Now things get serious; any pulley system will put an enormous load on to anchors and, because of friction at the lip of the crevasse, all hoisting is difficult and bad for your back. The rope will usually have cut deeply into the snow at the lip of the crevasse; whether this can be freed, how far the victim is in the crevasse, and whether the victim can help the rescuer will all dictate the method used.

All of the methods for hoisting have pros and cons. Figs 10–11 show three I have found to work—they all follow the same principles as hoisting systems for rock climbing. (See chapter 2, page 120.)

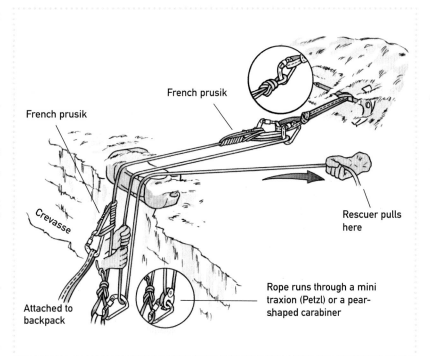

French prusik

French prusik

Crevasse

Attached to backpack

Rescuer pulls here

Rope runs through a mini traxion (Petzl) or a pear-shaped carabiner

FIGURE 10

An unassisted hoist. If the loaded loaded rope has cut in too deep, leave the Italian hitch tied off or tie a double figure of eight and lower a Petzl Mini Traxion or Wild Country Ropeman to the victim (ensuring it is the correct way round to pull), and use this as the assisted hoist. This is the fastest method for getting someone out of a crevasse. (The circled diagrams show alternative methods of hoisting from a crevasse.)

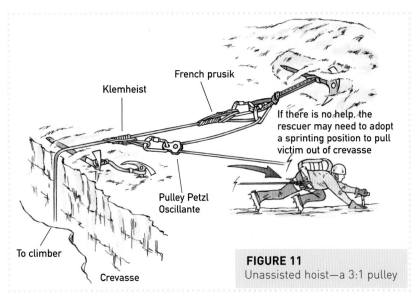

Klemheist

French prusik

If there is no help, the rescuer may need to adopt a sprinting position to pull victim out of crevasse

Pulley Petzl Oscillante

To climber

Crevasse

FIGURE 11
Unassisted hoist—a 3:1 pulley

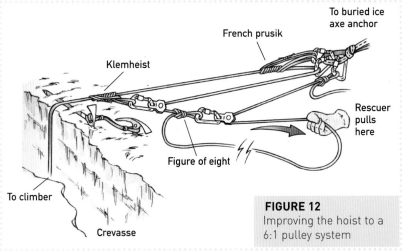

To buried ice axe anchor

French prusik

Klemheist

Rescuer pulls here

Figure of eight

To climber

Crevasse

FIGURE 12
Improving the hoist to a 6:1 pulley system

ALPINE CLIMBING

"Going fast is a relative idea, which depends on your experience level, objectives, and fitness."

—Will Gadd, ice climber

The alpine climber must be versatile, efficient, and capable of climbing quickly, placing protection rapidly (few routes have bolts), and belaying while performing other tasks. The techniques are similar to those used for scrambling and winter mountaineering, but what makes alpine mountaineering a unique skill is that decisions must be made and the skills used much faster. Being fit and acclimatized and minimizing the gear you carry will go a long way to improving your speed on all sorts of terrain. Whom you climb with is also important—a solid partnership where you can trust each other to do the right thing at the right time and where you can pick each other up when the one is down is something to be celebrated. Falling off has become the norm for many crag climbers, but you should realize that alpine routes are rarely vertical, the run-outs are long, the rock loose, and wearing a backpack increases the chance of falling upside down—taking a leader fall in the mountains is not recommended.

ROUTE FINDING

Preparation at home, on the approach and at the hut will simplify route finding, but be careful of blindly following the marks of other climbers, although they may give you some clues. Does the trail become fainter? Do scratches disappear? Treat cairns with scepticism; they may be placed to help mountaineers retrace their steps, and not to show the way upward. Fixed protection can be a good indicator that you are "on route," but an abseil point may also show that you have gone the wrong way! Eventually you will develop a "feel" for the right way as you absorb information subconsciously.

MOVING TOGETHER ON SNOW

Moving together on steep slopes with a short rope between you is a judgment call. It can give you an illusion of safety and a false sense of confidence. If you come from a rock climbing background it is probably hard to accept that soloing in the Alps is a legitimate and often necessary practice.

If you do decide to use short roping, beware that should one of you slip the other is likely to be pulled off, unless they are very quick and alert. It may be preferable and almost as quick to run the rope out and belay.

A solid partnership is essential for safe alpinism

MOVING TOGETHER ON EASIER, ROCKY TERRAIN

Alpine routes have much exposed, yet straightforward, ground that is too risky to solo, but pitching it would take too long. Learning to move quickly on this terrain is the key to climbing quickly. The skill of "moving together" enables you to keep the risk acceptable and allow you to move rapidly. Moving together is a skill composed of many techniques and improves greatly with experience (see chapter 2, page 110).

Your rock climbing level and confidence will dictate the standard of ground you are prepared to move on together, and the nature of the terrain will dictate the length of rope between climbers.

MOVING TOGETHER ON DIFFICULT TERRAIN— SIMU-CLIMBING

This is a risky procedure, and both climbers must climb within their grade and understand the consequences of a fall.

Simu-climbing is when two (or occasionally more) climbers move together (at the same rate to reduce slack in the system) on ground that would normally be pitched. Protection should be placed sparingly, but each one should be bomb-proof, which requires a consideration of the direction of the force on the gear.

When the leader is down to a few pieces of protection, stop, set-up a belay and, when the second arrives, exchange the gear.

To lessen the chances of the second pulling the leader off, a Ropeman or Tibloc can be placed on protection above crux

Moving together quickly and safely is the key to alpine success. (Climber: Maria Newton).

Learning to climb pitches efficiently will speed you up.

sections. This will hold the second should they fall—and prevent the leader being pulled off. This largely untested technique requires much practice to perfect it, and care should be taken to prevent rope damage. It is a useful technique to use on snow or ice climbs, as there are no rope drag problems. An example would be reaching the top of the difficulties on a steep snow/ice route: the leader places protection, places a Ropeman on the protection, and romps up the easy ground with the knowledge that the second cannot pull them off should they fall.

TIPS FOR MOVING FASTER ON PITCHED ALPINE ROUTES

- Improve your personal climbing standard on rock and ice and climb within your technical limits, enabling you to cruise through the harder sections. The second should follow rock pitches in half the time of the leader and ice pitches in a quarter of the time!
- Be fit enough for the climb you are tackling.
- Practice climbing wearing big boots and a sack.
- Practice climbing on rock with crampons.
- Practice your rope work until it is second nature, and keep it neat and slick.
- Use direct belays whenever possible.
- Do not waste belay time. On pitched ground eat, drink, and look at the guidebook while belaying. Using a Petzl Reverso on a direct belay means you can belay a second, but safely take your hands off the rope.
- Make changeovers at belays speedy and efficient. Three minutes saved on every belay on ascent and descent will save half an hour over ten pitches.
- Eat and drink frequently to keep your energy levels up.
- When you stop to put gear on, work together—one flake the rope out, the other sort the rack.
- Organize your pack so that the gear you need first is on top.
- Swap gear quickly—bandoliers can be useful.
- Carry plenty of long extenders to reduce rope drag.
- On granite rock climbs with many smooth cracks cams are faster to place and remove.

- Look for fixed runners and belays, which can be used quickly, but check in-situ gear and tack before using it.
- Place enough gear to keep you safe, but as little as possible.
- Climb without your backpack on a difficult pitch, pulling it up afterwards.
- Pull on gear—ethics are great unless they kill you!
- If the route is at your limits, carry three rung etriers—do not rely on making them from slings, and understand aid climbing.
- Maximize the strengths of the team. Plan ahead and ensure you and your partner lead on the ground you like best.
- On routes that are climbed in pitches lead in "blocks" (see Big walling). Breaking the climb down into blocks means:
  - The leader can get mentally "into the zone" for their four or five pitches.
  - The second can chill out and rest, rather than move straight into leading.
  - The leader can study the next pitch while belaying, which can help to speed up route finding.
  - You both stay warmer because no one person is sat on a belay ledge for too long.
- If leading in blocks, stack the ropes so that the leader's ends come from the top of the pile. You can start to restack the ropes once your second is just below you with the help of a Petzl Reverso on a direct belay.
- Climb light. Use twin ropes or a full-weight rope on very technical routes and carry a 5.5mm Dyneema line for pulling on abseils. This is a specialist technique, but has advantages when you have to haul, aid climb, or jumar.

Getting to the top is only halfway!

Descents from Alpine peaks often involve down-climbing intricate ground with the rope on.

GETTING DOWN

"What more could he possibly want as he stood on top of the world? There was nowhere else to go. Nowhere else to go? Oh, but there was! Down again..."

—George Alan Smith, *Introduction to Mountaineering* (1957)

The summit is only the halfway point, and the descent is invariably the most trying part of an Alpine climb. Tired minds and bodies have to cope with the most serious aspects of mountaineering— abseiling and loose rock. Route finding is difficult from above, so spying out the descent before you start your climb will pay off.

Descents from Alpine peaks often involve down-climbing intricate ground with the rope on (see chapter 2, page 113).

At some point an abseil may be required. If you are not absolutely sure it is the correct way down, it may be quicker to lower your partner to check the route. If incorrect, they can then be belayed back up. There are often in-situ abseil anchors on standard descents from classic routes. Always check the condition of both the tape and the anchors and, if in any doubt, back the system up with a good nut for the first abseiler. Do not throw the whole rope down as it can get snagged (see chapter 2, page 96), and always clip the ends of the abseil rope into the belays upon arrival to possibly prevent a catastrophe should the abseil belay fail.

It is crucial to have an efficient and speedy system for a descent involving many abseils. Hours can be saved in the day if the descent is slick and quick. Crucial points include:

● Using a cow's tail to clip into belay stations quickly.

● Using a French prusik as a back-up for the first person abseiling. Subsequent abseilers can be protected by the person at the bottom holding the rope.

● Keeping communication simple. Some teams use a loud whistle to mean "rope free, come on down." Two-way radios can be useful.

● Working together is the key to speedy abseiling—one pulls the rope, the other can thread the next anchor. As soon as the knot arrives, the first man down can attach the abseil plate, etc., while the remainder of the rope is pulled down.

RESCUE

Accidents can happen! Highly professional rescue teams that may work alongside voluntary rescue teams serve all Alpine areas. Guardianed mountain huts have radios; these and mobile phones are the most common methods of alerting rescue services. The usual international signals of six whistle blasts or six light flashes may also be used, but should not be relied upon.

Mountain police, gendarmes, and fire officers provide the French rescue service for free, but Swiss and Italian mountain rescue is private and reimbursed by insurance fees. Insurance is a necessary evil, but it can lead to a false sense of security, evident in the increasing number and severity of accidents and rescues in the Alps.

Search and rescue experts are almost uniformly opposed to charging for their services, even in cases of negligence and stupidity, because it is evident that charging for rescue has actually encouraged more risky behavior. They also believe charging could delay requests for help, leading to worsening injuries, weather or other conditions, and ultimately to more difficult, dangerous rescues.

HELICOPTERS

Helicopters can rescue injected climbers quickly, but they should not be relied upon, because they may not be able to fly or may be on another rescue mission.

They pick up a casualty by landing or hovering just off the ground while the patient is taken on board or placed in a basket or stretcher. They can also hover and winch the casualty on board.

If you are waiting for a rescue:

- The downdraft can reach 100kph (62mph), so clear the landing area of all loose objects including vegetation, clothing, and sacs. If you cannot do this, tie them down.

- Helicopters cannot land on slopes of too much angle. A flat area of about 5m (16ft) square is ideal, but there must be enough clearance for the helicopter's blades and tail in a 180 degree arc. A helicopter tilts forward on take-off, so high ground that slopes away under the tail is best.

- If the helicopter is light enough to descend vertically or horizontally it only requires enough room to hover. If it is heavy, the helicopter needs a clear flight path.

- Mark your location with bright objects.

- If it is steep the helicopter may hover with the skids touching the ground. It is likely the helicopter will drop off a rescuer and then depart until told to return. Hovering is risky when close to the ground.

Peigne D'Arolla,
French Alps

Helicopters can rescue injured climbers quickly, but should not be relied upon.

- Helicopters perform better if they can take off and land into the wind.
- Indicate the wind direction using streamers or stand with your back to the wind, arms pointing in the wind direction.
- Stay clear of the landing zone.
- If visibility is poor, a reference, such as a person or pack, on the pilot's side of the helicopter can be useful. Disturb the snow to allow the pilot to see you.
- Do not try to touch the helicopter or cable before it has made contact with the ground. Static charges build up in a helicopter when it is flying and this is discharged when the helicopter or a cable touches the ground
- Helicopters are noisy—protect your eyes and ears.
- Only approach from the front when signalled to do so in single file.
- Drag, rather than carry, equipment such as skis.

THE ALPS IN WINTER

The Alps in winter are an entirely different experience to summer. Temperatures fall to –25°C (–13°F), and you need to carry a heavy backpack and wear big boots and thick clothing. You must learn how to move around efficiently and quickly, often on skis or snowshoes. The weather can change suddenly, and you must be able to recognize avalanche terrain. Alpine winters are not the place for first time alpinists and self-reliance is paramount. Your gear should be similar to that used for standard winter climbing, but with some additions:

- A powerful flashlight and extra batteries, because you will be operating in the dark for longer periods.
- A balaclava or face mask.
- Plastic boots (essential).
- Spare socks and foot powder to dry your feet.
- Avoid sleeping in wet socks or inners, unless sitting in a bivvy with your feet in contact with the snow. Use an old sock to dry the inners.
- Mittens and a duvet jacket (essential).

ALPINE WATERFALL ICE

During winter the Alps are riddled with frozen waterfalls. In good years, the season runs from November to April, with the most reliable conditions found in January/February. In March, the longer, sunny days can quickly ruin icefalls, but if you aim high then routes can still be found in condition.

Streams and melting snow create many of the ice climbs, but this means that there are often large snow bowls above the climbs that can create dangerous avalanche conditions after bad weather. North-facing bowls keep their

EMERGENCY NUMBERS

Emergency services telephone numbers are usually on maps and guidebooks, but should be checked at the tourist office or guides office.

U.K.	999
Norway/Sweden	112
Italy	113
Switzerland	117
(Wallis)	144
Austria	133
U.S./Canada	911
Japan	110
New Zealand	111

avalanche conditions for a long time, so seek local information and look at the weather history. Scottish ice is predominantly snow ice, while Alpine waterfall ice is often harder and more brittle. Temperature plays a big part in this however, and warmer days can result in perfect, soft, first-time placements.

European water ice grades range from 1-7 and are offset from Scottish grades by roughly one grade: a 4 in the Alps equates to Scottish grade 5 and French 5 is a Scottish 6. Several areas have gained worldwide acclaim due to a combination of quality climbing and ease of access. Below are a few ideas for climbing in Europe:

- **Chamonix**—A wide variety of grades, with the most popular at Servoz, Les Houches, the Mont Blanc tunnel entrance, le Chapeau, Col de Montets, Chatelard, and Argentière.

- **Cogne**—A wide variety of grades an hour's walk from the car. Situated on the Aosta Valley side of the Gran Paradiso National Park, it has a huge variety of over a hundred waterfalls.

- **Kandersteg**—The ice climbing mecca of Switzerland. Easy access and a wide variety of grades.

- **La Grave and the Argentiere la Besse** on the fringes of the Ecrins National Park—Some are among the longest ice falls in Europe, but the south-facing routes quickly lose condition.

- **L'Alpe d'Huez**—A ski resort great for novice/intermediate climbers.

- **Argentera Valley, Italy**—Good for beginners and intermediate ice climbers, but the approach is long unless the road is still open.

- **Gressonay, Italy**—A wide variety of accessible routes, but can be crowded.

- **Val Varaita**—Convenient, easy access, and many routes.

- **Bardonecchia, Italy**—The climbs are low altitude, therefore the season is pretty short (December to February).

- **Ceillac**—High up, so the conditions are usually good, plus there is only a short walk in.

- **Fournel, France**—Most routes are grade 4 or above, but there are some easier climbs. During snow, access is difficult and avalanche danger becomes a reality.

Alpine ice (photo: Mike "Twid" Turner)

5

SKI MOUNTAINEERING AND SNOWSHOEING

"Skiing is the pleasurable part of alpinism—way more pleasurable and fun than alpine climbing."

—Michael Kennedy, former Editor of *Climbing* magazine

For the ski mountaineer, leaving a tent as the sun creeps up over the mountains, with the prospect of a four-hour ascent and a one-hour ski back down untracked snow is the stuff of dreams. It is the most wonderful way to get away from the crowded pistes and experience the mountains in their winter clothes.

Ski mountaineering (alpine touring/ski randonnée) is a complex pastime combining the skills of alpinism and skiing. You must have the ability to ski off-piste, navigate, choose a safe line, be aware of the mountain environment in winter, assess and test snow conditions for avalanches, use an avalanche transceiver, probe and shovel, travel safely on glaciers, and use the rope, ice axe, and crampons for descending and ascending steep snow slopes.

HOW WELL DO YOU NEED TO SKI?

Ask a mountain guide whom they would rather take ski mountaineering out of a skier or a mountaineer, and they will always say the skier. Ski mountaineering is not for novice skiers, but you don't have to be an expert either. If you can combine mountaineering skills with the ability to link controlled parallel carved turns, on-piste, while wearing a small backpack, you can probably attempt some very easy tours in good snow conditions. However, do not overestimate your skiing ability with more serious tours.

Chamonix, Mont Blanc, skier: A. Perlins

For most skiers contemplating ski mountaineering the problem is that the snow off-piste can vary from deep powder to crust. Mountaineering experience will not compensate for lack of skiing ability but, as long as you can traverse, sideslip, snowplough turn, and perform a downhill kick turn, you will be able to find your way down most slopes, albeit more slowly and with less fun. The opposite is also true: losing a ski or fracturing a limb in a remote area is serious and falling should be done carefully!

EQUIPMENT

Ski mountaineering differs from downhill (alpine) skiing in that the bindings free the heel for walking along the flat and up snow slopes. Equipment designed for ski mountaineering is always a compromise between the two disciplines: for instance, ski mountaineering bindings do not have all the release possibilities of the best downhill bindings. However, the gap in safety and performance is becoming smaller.

There are two forms of skiing in the mountains to consider, each with its own band of faithful followers.

There is a saying that goes "free the heel and free the mind," but mine is "fix the heel and fix the problem." (Skier: Owen Cook.)

NORDIC OR CROSS COUNTRY SKIS

Nordic ski bindings leave your heels free all the time, so you don't have to change between uphill and downhill modes. The boots flex at the toe for more natural walking, and have front-toe bindings and a spring-loaded cable that fits around the heel of the boot.

Nordic skiing is sometimes referred to as "telemark" skiing, but the Telemark is actually a type of turn, not a ski. There is no doubt that on gently rolling terrain Nordic skis have the advantage but, unless you are an advanced Nordic skier who has mastered the Telemark turn with a pack on, do not consider using Nordic skis for tours that have substantial steep descents. A further drawback is that the boots are difficult to use with crampons and useless for kicking steps in snow.

ALPINE TOURING (AT) SKIS

For ski tours with serious downhill sections there is no doubt in my mind that AT gear is the superior choice; it is more robust and will allow an average skier to cope with a wider variety of snow conditions. You can use any alpine ski to ski mountaineer, however, it must be light enough to allow you to travel quickly, yet still be able to perform well on the descent.

Your choice of ski depends on the type of ski touring you do, how heavy you are, and how aggressively you ski (stiffer skis need to be bent). The first thing to decide is whether traveling between huts is a priority, or making better and safer turns is more important. For the former, buy a lighter, purpose-built touring ski. If you are a skier at heart buy an all-mountain ski. Choose a ski equivalent to your own height and up to 10cm (4in) shorter, but ensure it is compatible with the combined weight of you and your backpack.

SKIS: WHAT TO LOOK FOR

Tip width—Wide compared to waist width = greater pull in the turn.

Waist width—Narrow = quick edge change and better edge grip on hard snow. Wider = more speed and tracking stability on off-piste snow, but a poorer edge grip on hard snow.

Tail width—Wide compared to waist width = greater guidance at end of turn and support in tight turns; narrower = easier ski slides.

Radius—Smaller = tighter carved turns. Larger = wider turns.

Surface area—Bigger = more lift in deep soft snow, and more speed stability on off-piste terrain.

SKI BOOTS

Normal alpine ski boots can be used for simple day tours, but they are uncomfortable on long walks and may let snow in when loosened for walking. Purpose-built ski mountaineering boots are a compromise. They are generally lightweight, more flexible and have a Vibram sole for walking. They are also suitable for kicking steps in snow and are compatible with crampons. Very lightweight models are great if you are a good skier, but for an average skier a sturdier version will hold the feet more firmly on descents. The Scarpa Spirit 3 and 4 buckle models are the favorite among ski mountaineers who also want good downhill performance. Fit is important, and it is worth having your inner boot and outer shell custom-fit to your feet (Scarpa are broader, Garmant narrower).

BINDINGS

An AT binding has two positions—hinged for climbing, and fixed for the descent. Modern AT bindings are almost as safe as standard ski bindings when used properly, but no AT binding has the safety release of the latest alpine bindings. The consequences of injury are more serious, so start with a low setting and increase it by small increments if you find that you pre-release too often. Use ski brakes rather than safety straps; if you fall, it is best not to have a ski flailing around your head.

Leading AT bindings include the Fritschi "Explore" and the Fritschi "Freeride." The latter is a good choice for heavier, more aggressive skiers. Brakes are included with these bindings. The Dynafit Tourlite bindings are the lightest and strongest available, but having such a small binding does take some getting used to.

The binding best suited to approaching climbs in mountaineering boots is the Silvretta 500 model. The wire toe bail accepts standard plastic mountaineering boots without risk of damage to the lip of the boot. To prevent injury, keep your heels free, even when skiing downhill, because mountain-

Purpose-built ski mountaineering boots are a cross between a plastic mountaineering boot and a ski boot.

eering boots will not release reliably when locked down.

Specialist skis, e.g., Karhu Karva and Meta, have an integrated climbing skin embedded into the base and full metal edges. Their universal binding allows you to use any winter boots, and the skis' wide footprint and short length make them great for first-time skiers accessing climbs.

SNOWSHOES

Skis are better in deep snow, but in poor snow, and when carrying a heavy pack, less skilled skiers may prefer the convenience of snowshoes. They are, however, slower and are not as much fun on downhill sections, but they are lightweight, compact, and the easiest form of snow travel. Snowshoes have distinct advantages—avoiding difficulties in deep snow; approaching or retreating from ice and alpine climbs; ascending or descending non-technical mountaineering routes; and for winter approaches that are difficult to ski when narrow and steep.

When choosing snowshoes, remember that all properly designed snowshoes work—it's just that some will work better in certain conditions than others. A larger snowshoe will float on loose snow, but is it heavier and less maneuverable. Stay with a smaller snowshoe for climbing and mountaineering, because of the increased maneuverablity and traction. Your combined body and backpack weight, plus the type of snow, will determine the size of the snowshoe needed.

Modern snowshoes have technical bindings and crampons for difficult terrain. Look for steel crampons that rotate on a door-type hinge; vertically orientated metal blades that run the length of the snowshoe's underside and a binding that fits well and stays on all day without adjustment.

Neoprene straps are easier to use with mittens on, and nylon often absorbs water and freezes.

TECHNIQUE

Many of the techniques are the same as walking in crampons and skinning for skiing (*see* page 270). Lift your feet higher than normal, roll your feet slightly, and slide the overlapping inner edges over each other to avoid the unnatural and tiring "straddle-gait." It is difficult to reverse in snowshoes.

On steep descents it is best to seek soft, unconsolidated snow, which gives you control. If you must descend a steep icy section, be prepared to sidestep, making sure to plant each step firmly using "flat foot" technique, just like walking with crampons.

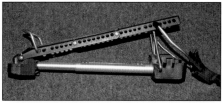
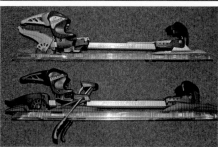
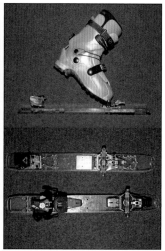

Top left: You can ski mountaineer using standard bindings with a removable insert that allow walking, but they are heavy, stiff, and uncomfortable uphill.

Bottom left: Fritschi AT bindings

Right: [Dynafit] Tourlite Bindings

Snowshoes

Don't step on the snowshoes and don't place them over a gap as they may break; instead, step on top of rocks or logs. When jumping across streams keep the shoes low so that the heels do not land first.

If the terrain is such that a slip or fall could cause serious injury or death, remove your snowshoes, put on your crampons, and get out your ice axe.

OTHER EQUIPMENT

SKI POLES

Use non-collapsible poles for most tours. Telescopic poles are useful if you need to leave your skis behind and climb the mountain on foot. They do, however, have a tendency to collapse when you don't want them to, the locking mechanism can jam and they can break. They must have padding below the handles, so that you can grip the pole lower down on traverses, but you can add this yourself.

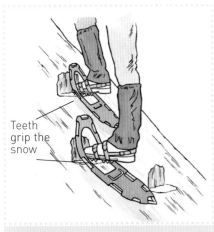

FIGURE 1
Snowshoe technique—step-kicking up a soft snow slope

Teeth grip the snow

CLIMBING SKINS

Climbing skins are temporarily glued to the base of the skis, allowing them to glide forward, but not backward. They are made from nylon or mohair fibers, or a mixture of both, and vary in width and length. Nylon is cheaper and lasts longer, but mohair glides better—this difference is more marked at cold temperatures. The amount of grip a skin has depends on the length of the fibers rather than the material it is made from; the longer the fibers, the more grip. However, given that mixed skins last three to four times longer, they may be the best compromise, but for ultimate speed and glide use mohair.

Skins can be full length and hooked on to the back of the ski (a notch in the tail is useful) or they can be cut 15cm (6in) shorter than the length of the ski (because the back plays little part in the skinning process). The full length system is heavier and produces more drag, but may stay on the ski more effectively. If you are cutting your skins shorter than the ski, ensure that you round off the end of skin to prevent it from lifting off.

Skins should be narrow enough to leave the ski edges uncovered (old, narrow skins do not work well on modern, broad skis). You can buy shaped skins, or wide, straight skins to cut into shape. After cutting, fold them in half and re-cut them so they are perfectly symmetrical tip to tail and the glue is not visible; this makes them easier to store. Most modern skins come with plastic sheets attached to the skin making it much easier to peel them apart.

Climbing skins are glued to the base of the skis.

SKI CRAMPONS: HARSCHEISEN (GERMAN); COUTEAU (FRENCH); AND RAMPONI (ITALIAN)

Crampons must match your bindings, and should be attached when the snow is hard and your skins are not gripping. Crampons fit between the boot and

Harscheisen

the plate of the binding and allow a row of metal teeth to protrude downward on either side of the ski. When the foot and plate of the binding are raised, the ski glides forward; when the foot is lowered, the teeth bite into the snow. If you are flexible enough, the Diamir Explore binding and the Dynafits let you fix crampons without removing your boots from the skis—a distinct advantage.

TRAVELING LIGHT

You can use most of your usual alpine gear, but reduce the weight of every item. Use lightweight waterproofs; divide food into individual portions; take sample-sized or half-full tubes of toothpaste and sunscreen; and use lithium batteries for electronic devices (**except transceivers**, see page 254) as you won't require spares. Avoid doubling up on personal and group equipment, and if something can serve two purposes, use it rather than carry two items, e.g., spare sunglasses versus goggles. Seal your maps and leave the map case behind.

The amount of equipment carried will also dictate the type of tour, because with heavier backpacks and tents you are unlikely to choose steep descents. You may even resort to Nordic skis and towing a sledge.

Shovels—buy a sturdy one, as cutting into avalanche debris is difficult.

BACKPACK

Skiing with a light backpack is more fun, uses less energy, and is safer. A heavy backpack will accentuate any shoulder rotation, increasing your chances of twisting something in a fall and making it strenuous to get back up. For day tours, 30 litres (8gall) is large enough, but 50 litres (13gall) may be needed for more serious tours. Look for good ski attachments, and when you try the backpack on, ensure it has minimal side-to-side movement on your back when it is loaded.

SHOVEL

Buy a sturdy, brightly colored metal shovel with a handle that will not break when digging in hard-packed avalanche debris (plastic or composite shovels are unable to efficiently cut through it). You may find it easier to keep the extendable handle retracted when digging—-kneeling is a better position to avoid back injury anyway.

AVALANCHE PROBE

These are lightweight, sectional probes used for locating avalanche victims. The sections are connected by a wire or cord and assemble quickly to form a 2.4-3.2m (8-10ft) probe with a hardened tip, which easily penetrates avalanche debris. Tent poles do not work!

Adjustable ski poles, which can be joined to form a probe, are useful when a sectional probe is unavailable. However, it takes time to remove the baskets and assemble. A good solution is for all members of a party to carry probe-convertible ski poles, with several sectional probes carried as group gear.

Avalanche probes—take care; they break easily.

Clothing—wear the same as you would to go mountaineering.

A shovel with the avalanche probe or snow saw inside the handle is a useful innovation. However, the probe is too thin for adequate rigidity and too short (1.8m/6ft) for locating deep burials. A snow saw is a much better item to store in a shovel handle, as it is useful for a number of tasks, including cutting snow blocks for igloos and wind barriers, and for rutschblocks or snow columns for avalanche stability tests.

CLOTHING

Pack just like any other remote mountain venture. Use layers and try to keep yourself dry during and after exercise. Cut as much weight as you can from your upper body layers, but carry a lightweight duvet jacket, such as the Mountain Equipment Trango, or an extra fleece in case of emergency or bad weather.

Use lightweight, breathable waterproofs, as normal ski clothing is too warm and not flexible enough. The rest of your clothes should be the same as you use in the Alps for summer mountaineering.

ICE AXE

Specialist ski mountaineering models weigh about 230g (8oz) and have light alloy heads. They are useful if you don't use them on ice, but otherwise consider a lightweight axe with a sturdier head.

CRAMPONS

Specialist lightweight, aluminum alloy crampons are suitable for most ski tours, but they are only designed for use on snow slopes, not ice or rock, and are not suitable as a general mountaineering crampon. For more technical tours a more robust pair is preferable.

HARNESS

A harness is vital, unless you are sure that you won't need to abseil or cross glaciers. You can improvise a lightweight harness from slings, but they are uncomfortable, especially when you are down a crevasse. Compromise by using a simple, lightweight, adjustable mountaineering harness with a chest harness made from a sling for carrying a heavy backpack.

Carry the same rescue kit as for summer alpinism, but have two 30m/8mm (98ft/0.3in) dynamic ropes to share the load (such as the "Randonee") but a full 50m (164ft) rope may be required for abseils on some tours. Some ski mountaineers carry 8mm Dyneema cord.

AVALANCHE TRANSCEIVERS AND BEACONS

John Lawton developed the first avalanche transceiver, the Skadi, in the U.S. in 1968. They are worn on the body and emit a radio signal. If someone is buried in an avalanche, other transceivers can be used to pick up the signal. The receiving transceivers change the signal into a visual or audible display that guides the searcher towards the transmitting beacon. They are essential for anyone ski mountaineering or off-piste skiing, and can make finding a buried victim much quicker.

Wear an avalanche transceiver at all times, and know how to use it. (The Pulse Barryvox transceiver.)

All modern transceivers operate on the 457kHz frequency and are compatible with one another. Models operating on only 2.275kHz and dual frequency models should be retired. Transceivers should be used with high quality alkaline batteries—not rechargeable batteries, as their performance degrades rapidly at low charge. Mobile phones can interfere with the signal when very close to each other.

There are two types of transceiver—analog and digital, and both emit signals that can be detected by other transceivers.

- Digital transceivers light up or show the direction on a display panel.

- Analog transceivers respond by emitting audible beeps that get louder as they get closer to the buried transceiver. Some have a visual indicator.

- Visual indicators are useful when there is high wind or when more than one transceiver is buried.

The range covered is usually around 50m (262ft) for analog and slightly less for digital. Range is, however, completely dependent on the orientation of the transmitting transceiver to the receiving transceiver. In transmit mode, a transceiver creates an elliptical electromagnetic field. If a second device is set to search mode, it will detect this field—if it is in range. The maximum signal is obtained when the two antennae are parallel (the antenna is usually situated on the longest side of the transceiver). Conversely, the signal is weakest when the two devices are at right angles. By moving the transceiver through an arc a searcher can pick up the strongest signal and follow this directly to the victim. This is easiest with digital devices that give a visual indication of signal strength and approximate distance to the victim.

The burial time refers not only to the time spent locating a victim, but also how long it takes to dig them out. Therefore, all search devices are effective only when shovels and probes are carried.

The excellent Tracker avalanche transceiver

DIGITAL OR ANALOG?

The digital unit is easier to learn and to use, especially with a single burial. However, they are less effective with multiple burials, as the task of separating and identifying the different signals becomes more difficult with a digital readout than with an audible signal. Some versions allow you to mask the signal from an identified transceiver. For this reason, many professionals trained in the use of avalanche transceivers prefer an analog model. But, for the recreational user who cannot invest a lot of time learning to use a transceiver, the digital, dual antenna technology is a better choice, because the lack of range is compensated by the increased search speed.

MISCELLANEOUS ITEMS

You will need the following items, which have been covered in other chapters: altimeter; small LED headlamp, spare batteries and bulb; map and compass; GPS; goggles; sunglasses; sunscreen; lip balm; and food. Also take the following:

TRECCO OR SIMILAR PASSIVE SYSTEMS

Passive tags are designed to perform a similar function to transceivers. You need specialist bulky equipment to search for one, which few ski resorts keep and no one carries off-piste. They are, therefore, of questionable value.

Water—Hydration bladders freeze up. A flask may be useful, and you can always pack snow into a mug and melt it with the hot water.

Velcro ski strap—Useful for tying skis together on your backpack.

Repair and emergency kit—In remote areas, an EPIRB (Emergency Position Indicating Radio Beacon) or PLB (Personal Location Beacon) is recommended.

Mobile phones—Useful in emergencies, but in mountain valleys you may not receive a signal. Phones are easily damaged in a fall, expensive to run, and difficult to use for "intercom" talk. New satellite phone technology may change this, but currently the expense and weight count against mobile phones.

Two-way radios—Have been proven to save lives, especially in avalanche terrain and poor visibility when you can direct the group in another direction. They can be rigged with a microphone that is clipped to your jacket or backpack strap, so you don't have to dig for your radio.

AVALANCHE

See also chapter 3. The first rule is, if you feel uncomfortable about the level of risk, go home. The second is that a great downhill run produces a feeling of euphoria that can cloud your judgement during and after the run. The third is get caught in an avalanche and your chances of survival are slim.

- Ski mountaineers are in greater danger than walkers, because the cutting action of skis readily releases unstable snow.
- Many avalanche accidents occur just after new snowfall, but clear skies, little or no snowfall, and light winds do not mean the avalanche danger is low.
- The victim or members of the victim's party trigger most avalanches.

Nearly all avalanche terrain can be avoided. (Col des Ecandies, The High Level Route, Chamonix, to Zermatt, France.)

- Seventy percent of avalanches start on 30–40 degree, often convex slopes, and often near the crest of a ridge. Most red runs average 20 degrees and black runs are seldom steeper than 35 degrees, although on both there may be steeper sections. Carry an inclinometer or measure the angle using ski poles (see page 260).
- Only 6 percent of avalanches happen on slopes of less than 25 degrees and they are usually wet snow avalanches. They travel slowly, but often over considerable distances with great force, and set solid.
- Almost all victims survive if they are not seriously injured and not buried deeper than 2m (6.6ft) for up to 18 minutes. U.S. research indicates that the survival rate of victims buried 2m (6.6ft) or deeper is only 4 percent.
- After eighteen minutes, survival declines rapidly, and after thirty-five minutes, only victims that have a good air pocket survive. It is therefore crucial that the victim is located and dug out as quickly as possible. In perfect conditions, finding someone with an avalanche transceiver and probe takes three–five minutes and digging to a depth of 1m (3.3ft) with a shovel takes ten–fifteen minutes.

Several devices increase your survival chances. The danger is that they may give you a false sense of security.

ABS AVALANCHE AIRBAG
This is a backpack with two plastic balloons built into it. When a cord is pulled, the balloons inflate in seconds, helping to keep you on top of the avalanche. Currently they are only for use by off-piste skiers and ski mountaineers doing short day tours.

AVALUNG™
Creating an air pocket in front of your mouth and nose can prolong survival. The AvaLung™ safety vest from Black Diamond contains a breathing system that creates an artificial air pocket. There is as yet no statistical evidence to show it increases survival, but tests have shown that a completely buried person can survive for up to an hour.

Black Diamond Avalung

AVALANCHE TRANSCEIVERS
Help your friends to find you, but whether that is alive is another matter!

PRACTICE AVALANCHE SEARCHES
- Real avalanches often happen during bad weather, which limits visibility and group communications. Practice in poor weather.
- Real avalanches occur when you are tired, cold, hungry, and dehydrated. Often it is the very presence of these human factors that caused you to get caught in the first place.
- In a real search there is often shock, disorganisation, disagreement, and outright panic.
- Avalanches set like concrete, making digging tough and reducing the transceiver range.

SAFE ROUTE FINDING

"Europeans may lead the world in transceiver technology and guide training. They also lead the world in avalanche and climbing accidents and fatalities."
—David Spring, Ski Patrol Rescue Team (SPART), Washington State, U.S.

Nearly all avalanche terrain can be avoided. The process starts at home (read guidebooks and maps to find the safest route) and continues when you leave your car, hut, or tent, and throughout the day, both on the ascent and descent!

When conditions are potentially dangerous, follow gentle slopes without steep ground above them. You could set absolute limits when planning your tour depending on the snow conditions:

- 30° in NW-N-NE facing slopes when the danger is moderate
- 30° on all slopes when considerable
- 25° or less when the danger is high.

When planning your route, you can deduce the slope angle from the separation of the contour lines on the map—use 1:25,000 maps for greater accuracy. The French Alps have a 10m (33ft) vertical interval, which changes to 20m (66ft) when you cross into Switzerland. However, maps do not show all the bumps and hollows, and there might be steeper sections on the ground.

When the conditions are dangerous you can use the terrain to help you find a safe route. Densely packed, mature trees may increase the stability of the slope and provide some protection from a slide. Think about which side of the valley to ascend according to the sun's direction, the temperature, and where the avalanches are most likely to fall. Try to use high points, such as ridges, knolls, or the tops of small hills, and wide valleys, to travel along (see Fig. 7). There are a number of terrain traps to avoid:

CONVERSION

For 20m (66ft) vertical intervals between contours (on Swiss maps) this equates to:

Gradient	Scale 1:25,000	Scale 1:50,000
15°	3.0mm	1.5mm
20°	2.2mm	1.1mm
30°	1.4mm	0.7mm
45°	0.8mm	0.4mm

- **Drop offs**—Even a small slide could have dire consequences if it carries you over a cliff or on to rocks.
- **V-shaped valleys or gullies**—The snow from a slide is forced into a confined area and could bury you to a great depth.
- **Old moraine areas**—You could sustain damage sliding over rocks and boulders. Be wary of avalanche cone slopes—avalanches fall there regularly.
- **Convex slopes**—See chapter 3, page 147.
- **Ridge crests**—Avalanches are more likely to be triggered where the depth of the weak layers of snow are shallow (50cm/20in or less below the surface) such as near ridge crests or at the edges of gulleys and hollows.

Get an avalanche bulletin and a weather forecast and consider the following:

ASSESSING POTENTIAL AVALANCHES

QUESTION:	THINK:
Can you see fresh avalanches?	Which slopes and in which orientation?
Is it the first good day after heavy snow?	Loading (see p. 165)
Was it very cold when the snow started falling?	An icy layer under new snow
Does the snow settle under your skis or make a "wumph" sound?	Slab avalanche (see p. 164)
Is snow breaking up and sliding away at turns?	Slab avalanche
Are there cracks in the snow?	Pack moving
Is there a lot of new snow on trees?	Loading (see p. 161)
Is a lot of snow still falling?	Loading
Can you see to assess the steepness of the slope?	30 degrees or more (70 percent of avalanches occur at this steepness)
Is it a lee slope?	Slab avalanche
Is it a convex slope?	Stress at the top of the slope
Are you close to the ridge crest?	Small slab on a leeside
Can you see fresh snow ripples or rime or sastrugi?	Wind direction
Is the wind strong?	Where are the lee slopes?
Can you see plumes of spindrift?	What direction is the snow blowing?
Has there been a sudden rise in temperature?	Pack instability and cornice collapse

CONSIDER THE ASPECT OF THE SLOPE

The aspect of a slope affects the temperature of the snowpack. A cold snowpack tends to develop more persistent weak layers. Therefore, the majority of avalanche accidents occur on colder north- and east-facing slopes.

In warm, wet snow conditions the opposite occurs, and south- and west-facing slopes produce more wet avalanches than the more shady slopes. However, during prolonged cloudy or stormy conditions, when the sun seldom shines on the snow, there is little difference between sunny and shady slopes.

Kate Scott skiing in deep snow, Chamonix, France

CHECKING THE STABILITY OF THE SNOW —SNOWPACK TESTS

You should have built a picture of the snow's probable stability from the avalanche report, the prevailing weather, and as you travel, but there are times when you must assess the risk of skiing a particular slope. If the slope is greater than 25 degrees with new snow, it's always going to be a risk. If you have any doubts do not ski, whatever the following tests tell you.

The problem with the observations gained from snowpack tests is that they only provide partial information about existing avalanche conditions. You must mix this information with what has occured beforehand in order to make a reasonable evaluation of the hazards and risks.

If you find a weak layer you must consider the strength and depth of snow on top of it. Is the air temperature cold or warm? When did the last snowfall take place? Have you seen any avalanches down to the weak layer you found in your pit? Is the snow above the weak layer loose or bonded together?

It is important to practice these tests so that you can match previous and current observations. Dig your pit and test in the most representative spot on the slope you want to ski. If you release something on a 30 degree slope it will release more easily on a 40 degree slope!

SKI POLE TEST

Push your pole into the snow at a consistent rate and feel for changes in resistance as layers are encountered. This should never be used as the sole judge of stability, but rather as an indicator that snow conditions have changed and further testing is required. The main advantage is that it is quick.

THE "SHOVEL" TEST

Adapt the standard shovel test (see chapter 3, page 168) by isolating the column of snow completely, inserting a ski behind it, and pulling on the ski. Some people feel this gives a better result.

THE LOADED COLUMN TEST

This must be done on a slope of 30 degrees or more, and indicates how much weight must be applied before the snow fails. Isolate a column, as with the shovel test above, but cut the column down to the bottom of the pit, and not just to the suspect layer. Flatten the top of the column and load it with blocks of snow of the same size until it fails or holds enough snow to give you the confidence that it won't fail.

RUTSCHBLOCK TEST

This is the snow pit test of choice for skiers who dig many snow pits. On a slope of at least 30 degrees, which is representative of the slope you are about to ski, isolate a block of snow about a ski-length across and a ski-pole length up the slope. Do this by first cutting the face of the block using your shovel, then cutting out the back and sides of the block using a ski tail (a snow saw can make the job quicker). Next, step on to the block with your skis and jump progressively harder until the block fails.

The advantages of the Rutschblock test are that the larger sample size gives a more reliable reading, it duplicates what happens with a skier on the slope, and it is easier to quantify and interpret. Most people rank the test on a scale of one through seven; the higher the number, the more stable the conditions are. Ideally, you're looking for a score of five or more:

1 Fails while isolating the block

2 Fails while stepping on to the block

3 Fails with a light weighting of the skis

4 Fails with one light jump

5 Fails with one hard jump

6 Fails with several hard jumps

7 Doesn't fail

After doing the test, edge towards the slope, probing with a ski pole to check that the consistency of the snow is the same as the test area.

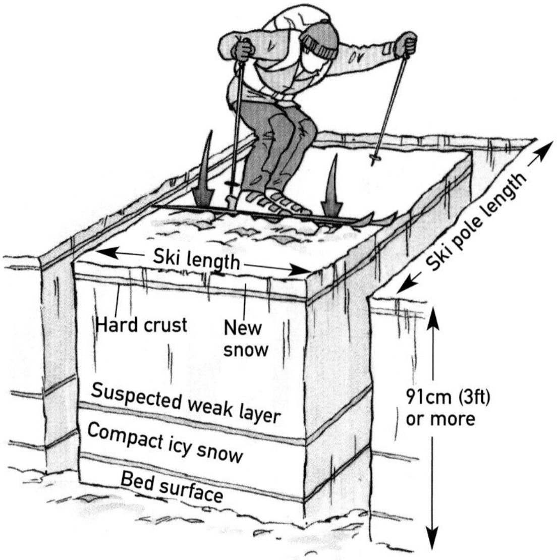

FIGURE 2
The Rutschblock test—first apply pressure with your own weight, and then use hard jumps.

WEAK SPOTS

Snow slopes are not uniform and the depth of snow varies. There may be buried rocks or vegetation where the temperature gradient and snow depth is different to your test area, which can trigger an avalanche. They are, however, rarely generated when the weak layer is greater than 1.5m (5ft) deep. Ski where the snow is deepest and avoid rocks or vegetation protruding through the snow.

CROSSING A SUSPECT SLOPE

If you must cross a dangerous slope, ask yourself if it can be avoided. Lower someone on a rope to examine it. If you have to go ahead, remove ski straps, zip up clothing, take your hands out of ski pole straps, and, if you are roped up, remove it, unless the risk from falling is greater than that of an avalanche.

Keep a minimum of 10m (33ft) apart on traverses and 50m (164ft) on descents or ascents. If the risk is serious, cross one at a time, with everyone observing the person at risk—it is better to have four people searching for one, than one person searching for four! Spacing out also reduces the stress on the slope. Maintain contact with each other, especially in poor visibility.

Use the same track—do not overtake other groups. Do not stop until you reach a safe haven such as a ridge, behind a very large rock buttress, within the shelter of large trees, or simply on a flat slope away from potential avalanche danger. Ensure that you watch the last person across the slope.

IF YOU ARE CAUGHT IN AN AVALANCHE

Start fighting for your life! (See page 170.)

- Do not release your bindings immediately—ski out of the avalanche to the closest edge. Should you fail, try to remove skis as they will drag you down.
- Try to remain on the surface using swimming movements.
- Try to protect your face with your hands before the avalanche stops.
- Try to maintain an air pocket in front of your mouth and nose, clearing snow away from your mouth.
- When it starts to slow down, fight to the surface and poke a ski pole or arm out.
- Remain still and do not give up hope.

RESCUING A VICTIM

Around 95 percent of survivors are rescued by their companions. The several minutes it will take to call for help is better spent searching.

DURING THE AVALANCHE

Watch and note where the victim was last seen, using landmarks such as rocks and trees. This can eliminate a whole section of the slope from your search.

AFTER THE AVALANCHE

- Start searching immediately.
- Be disciplined: someone must take charge and panic helps nobody.
- How many are missing? Spot clothing, equipment, and body parts protruding from the snow (remember that equipment may not necessarily indicate the victim's position).
- Appoint searchers to find the victims and rescuers to dig out and attend to victims. Switch searcher's transceivers to "search."
- While transceivers are switched off, there is a high risk that if a subsequent avalanche buries someone they will not be found. Place guards high enough up the slope to give adequate warning of further avalanches and to determine a safe way out of the avalanche area.
- People not involved in the search must stay high in a safe region and keep their skis on.
- Switch off all other transceivers.

AVALANCHE SEARCH PHASES

(Thanks to the Alpine Ski Club for help with the diagrams, see www.ASC.co.uk.)

The techniques used are broadly the same for any transceiver. There are three phases to every search:

1) PRIMARY SEARCH

The aim is just to find the signal from the victim's transceiver. If you switch your transceiver to "search" and you have a signal, you have done the primary search.

Switch the rescuers' transceivers to receive/search mode. Do a sweep search, from the level of the party, side-to-side down the track of the avalanche, traverses, and kick turns, with the line of each traverse ending no more than 20m (66ft) from the previous line, until the transceiver starts to beep. Turn no more than 10m (33ft) from the edge of the avalanche track.

During the primary search, slowly rotate your beacon in all orientations (i.e., twist your wrist 360 degrees) to increase the likelihood that your antenna will align with the victim's. This rotation is especially important if you have a single antenna transceiver.

If the avalanche is large, it may be appropriate for two or more searchers to make parallel searches. When a signal is received, home in on the nearest (strongest) signal. If there is more than one victim, continue the primary search, even after the first contact, in order to discover victims who may be elsewhere in the avalanche.

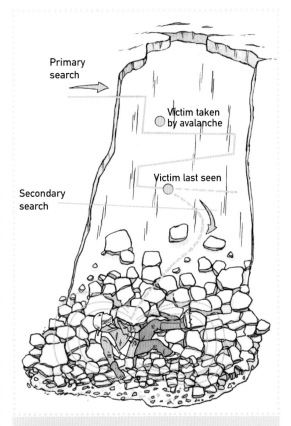

FIGURE 3
Primary, secondary, and pinpoint search

2) SECONDARY SEARCH

After you have found a signal, the aim is to get within 3m (10ft) of the victim. The secondary search technique varies depending on whether you have a single or multiple-antenna transceiver. Here, I only consider the multiple-antenna approach.

When you have a signal, you may be up to 35m (115ft) from the nearest victim. If the distance numbers increase (or the audible signal decreases), turn around and follow the direction indicator (or audible signal) in the opposite direction. As you follow, slowly re-orientate the transceiver so the arrow is pointed in line with the transceiver. The indicator lights of the transceiver point along the curved magnetic field lines. The range display shows how far away you are along the field lines from the target transceiver.

If there is more than one victim, the transceiver finds signals for all of them and the lights indicate their directions more or less alternately, depending on how fast each target transceiver sends its "beep." Head for the closest victim. As you come closer, the transceiver locks to the strongest signal so only one

victim is indicated. Transceivers beep at roughly one-second intervals and the receiving transceiver can only display one at a time, so identify the victim positions accurately. If you are descending, this should be the highest victim on the slope. If weaker, more distant signals are lost, mark the point (split point) so you can return there later to resume the search. The line followed will curve, since the transceiver follows the field lines of the victim's transceiver.

As you get closer, the beeps become more frequent, and then the tone will change, until a high-pitched, rapid beeping indicates you are very close. Ensure the range indicated is always getting smaller and is not increasing again.

3) PINPOINT SEARCH

Once you are within 3m (10ft), the aim is to get as close to the victim as possible. If there is more than one rescuer, only one should do the pinpoint search. The other should get ready to probe and dig. If there is more than one victim, additional rescuers should start a multiple burial search.

At about 3m (10ft) from the victim, tip the transceiver towards the ground at about 45 degrees, but do not swing your arms around. As you come close or cross the victim, stop, and search slowly with the device close to the snow surface. The victim might be buried deep below your feet. Tipping the transceiver gives a better indication of the victim's position in the snow, with the display indicating how deep they are buried. If you overshoot, the range will start to increase and the direction indication might become erratic (and then you will have to backtrack).

When it is time to dig, do not put the transceiver down on the snow; instead, loop the strap around your neck and stuff the unit down your sleeve or the front of your trousers.

MULTIPLE BURIAL SEARCH PATTERN

If there are more victims buried and you can't turn off the transmitter of the victim just found, use the "three circle" search method to locate nearby victims or return to the "split point" to resume the search for more distant victims. The three circle method searches in three concentric circles around the victim who was just found, and it works for all types of transceiver.

- Step away 3m/10ft (the length of an avalanche probe) from the victim already found.
- Search in a circle of radius 3m (10ft) round the victim already found, slowly scanning the transceiver across the slope as you search, until you find the next victim.
- If no victim is found on this search increase the circle radius to 6m (20ft) and repeat the search.

- Should no victim be found again, increase the circle radius to 9m (30ft) and repeat the search. The diameter of this circle (18m/60ft) approximates to the 20m (66ft) search track interval used on the initial search.
- Do the pinpoint search.
- Resume new primary, secondary, and pinpoint search for any remaining victims.

DIGGING AND PROBING

Using an avalanche probe limits the amount of snow that has to be excavated. Since the pinpoint search is done along the snow surface, insert your probe perpendicular to the surface, not straight down. Probe in a grid—not randomly—at 30cm (12in) intervals. After striking the victim, leave the probe in place and start shovelling downhill of the probe. Dig out victims that are close to the surface first; the shallow buried victim might be able to help dig out the deep burial.

- Keep your transceiver attached to your body when digging—don't lay it on the snow. Use it to frequently confirm the position of the victim.
- Do not trample on the victim's air space.
- Start digging 1.5 times the burial depth on the downhill side towards the probe. The slot you are digging should be 2m (6.5ft) wide to enable the victim to be rolled on to their side into the recovery position, or on to their back for artificial respiration.
- Throw snow to the side, and when waist-deep, throw it downhill.
- If there are two diggers, dig side by side.
- Dig in relays and rotate diggers every few minutes.
- Slice the snow in to blocks; do not try to lever it out as the handle of your shovel may break.
- If the burial is deep, dig in tiers. Diggers on each tier remove snow dug from lower tiers.
- Clear space around the face and the chest as soon as you can, and snow from the mouth and the airway.
- Resuscitate (mouth to mouth) if necessary.
- Turn off the victim's transceiver.
- Insulate the victim from the snow, but leave them in the hole until proper insulation and evacuation can take place.
- Keep the victim warm.

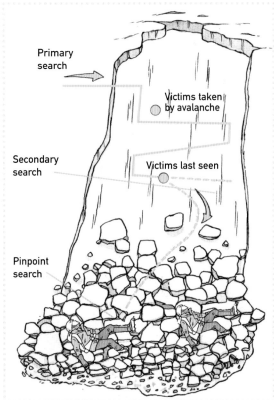

FIGURE 5
Multiple burial search

WHEN YOU HAVE NO SIGNAL

Probe in likely burial spots—the fall line below where the victim was last seen; around the victim's equipment on the surface; above and below rocks and trees; in depressions and curves, and at the toe of the debris pile. Because victims rarely survive more than 2m (6.5ft) down, probe multiple shallow areas rather than probing deeply.

AFTER THE RESCUE

When all victims are found, switch back to transmit and check the transceivers before setting off. Return everyone to a place of safety and account for all members of the group. Decide a safe evacuation route, which may even be down the avalanche.

If professional help is required:

- Use a mobile phone in preference to sending someone for help. Alpine huts and ski lifts have telephones and emergency equipment.
- Ensure the rest of the group are safe and stay put until required.
- Identify your position clearly.
- Identify injuries and the help required clearly.
- Find a safe, level helicopter landing position. Mark it clearly. Trample the snow to compact it (see chapter 4, pages 245–6).

PUTTING IT ALL TOGETHER

To avoid avalanche risk entirely you would rarely venture into the mountains on skis. If you follow advice about choosing a safe route, the mountains can, however, be visited at almost any time with relative safety. Start by skiing

Searching for an avalanche victim. *"The best way to get out of an avalanche is to wait until the spring thaw."* —Bob Brinton, 1938

easier angled slopes and work towards steeper ones. Enter a slope from the top, not the sides (especially under a cornice), and ski the edge of slopes before running the center.

BEFORE LEAVING
You have planned your route, checked the avalanche conditions, and packed your backpack and food. In addition, remember the following each day:

- Wear your transceiver under your outer layer where it cannot be torn off. If you remove clothing due to warm weather, move your transceiver under your remaining clothes.

- Test that all transceivers are transmitting; it isn't good enough that the light is blinking. One member should ski away with his transceiver in receive mode and on maximum volume (range). Each member should then ski slowly past (not quickly, and 10m (33ft) away). If the signal is weak, replace the batteries.

- Turn all mobile phones off.

- Check that everyone has a shovel and that there are probes in the group.

- Ensure that everyone knows where they are going, because they might need to find their own way out.

- Wear your harness unless you are definitely on un-glaciated terrain—you never know when it will be needed.

Find the best snow by finding the right slope for the time of day. (Skier: Andy Perkins, IFMGA Guide.)

SNOW TYPES

On a typical ski tour you will encounter several types of snow depending on the prevailing weather conditions and orientation of the slope to the Sun.

- **Corn snow**—Produced by repeated daily thaws and nightly refreezing of the surface. This alters the snow crystal shape, producing snow similar to wet granular snow, but larger. It is a delight to ski.
- **Crust**—A hard surface on top of softer snow, created by freezing rain, direct sunlight, or wind loading, which packs down the upper layers of the snowpack, leaving lower layers generally unaffected.
- **Firn/neve snow**—Snow that has undergone freeze thaw cycles and solidifies.
- **Granular snow**—These crystals are small pellets that may be wet, indicating a high water content, or drier, loose granular snow. Wet granular snow will form a snowball; loose granular snow will not. Wet granular conditions are often found in springtime.
- **Ice**—True ice conditions are comparatively rare. Much of what is perceived to be ice is actually a frozen granular condition—wet granular snow that has refrozen to form a very dense surface.
- **Powder**—Light, fluffy snow, found during and immediately after a snowstorm—the stuff of dreams.

FINDING GOOD SNOW

Finding the best snow is a case of finding the right slope for the time of day; a question of aspect, angle, and elevation.

ASPECT

The changes in the snowpack are related to how much sun the slope receives and the air temperature. Just after snowfall, powder is found on all slopes.

- North-facing slopes keep their snow conditions for longer.
- East-facing slopes catch the morning sun when the air is cold.
- West-facing slopes catch the sun in the warm afternoon.
- South-facing slopes soften first, then west-facing slopes generally soften by midday. South- and west-facing slopes have a crust, but it will melt. Crust on north- and east-facing slopes lasts longer.

If conditions are cloudy there may be no overnight refreeze and slopes will be skiable, but there is a greater risk of wet snow avalanches. Rock and serac (falling colomns of ice) fall is also a danger, and snow bridges over crevasses will be weaker. When the wind is strong the snow is stripped from windward slopes leaving a hard, icy surface, often with small ridges that are difficult to ski. When the wind-blown snow lands on lee slopes, soft or hard slabs may form.

ANGLE

Generally, steeper slopes that face the sun will melt and freeze quicker than lower-angled slopes so the snow will change faster. In deep snow there can be a fine line between having a slope steep enough to turn on, yet shallow enough to be safe. Lower-angled slopes are better in crusty conditions, because you stay on the top. Steep slopes can make 20cm (8in) of fresh snow feel knee-deep.

Use two identical ski sticks to measure the angle of the slope (mark halfway to make life easy):

- Place the first pole vertically in the snow.
- Hold the second pole at a right angle (90 degrees) to the first, so that it is horizontal.
- Adjust the height of the second pole until it touches the slope.
- Using the major angles and these easy-to-estimate ratios, estimate the angle of the slope:

$$1:\tfrac{1}{2} = 27°$$
$$1:\tfrac{3}{4} = 37°$$
$$1:1 = 45°$$

- For slopes greater than 45 degrees, do the opposite and move the vertical pole along the horizontal one.

Using ski sticks to measure the angle of the slope (this slope is approximately 30°).

ASSESSING GRADIENTS FROM A DISTANCE

Observe the climbing tracks of others. Most skiers tend to start doing kick turns when slopes reach 30 degrees. Some people are uncomfortable skiing down a slope steeper than 30 degrees and may do kick turns in descent.

You can also estimate minimum slope angle from avalanches. Loose snow avalanches often start spontaneously on slopes greater than 35 degrees.

ALTITUDE

It is colder the higher you go and slopes without wind at altitude will hold powder longer. Lower altitudes are generally warmer, so the melt freeze can make them safer earlier.

EXPERT TIP

Eric Pirie BMG/IFMGA
Mountain Guide
E_pirie@talk21.com

"Always keep your skis flat on the snow when you are skinning—more surface area contact means more grip. Should you feel them starting to slip back, stand up tall and feel you are pushing down through your heels."

The high A-frame carry.
(Skier: Owen Cox.)

The diagonal back sling
carry. (Skier: A. Perkins.)

HOW TO CARRY SKIS

When the slope is too steep to ski up, or there is not enough snow, you will have to carry your skis. Here are several techniques:

- **The high and low A-frame**—Loading the skis high up is best for most situations, especially abseiling, but beware that it does raise your center of gravity. Loading the skis lower down is better in high winds or when scrambling, because it lowers your center of gravity. However, skis do catch the backs of your legs.

- **Loosely tied**—Load your skis individually on each side, as low as possible and with the tips free. This is useful when traveling through trees, as the skis are unlikely to catch on overhead branches.

- **The diagonal back sling**—Bind your skis together. This is useful when you are removing the skis regularly.

SKINS AND SKINNING

Skins are the equivalent of a Vibram sole on a walking boot. They should not come off the ski, unless the ski is wet or your skinning technique is poor. You must maintain the stickiness of the glue by keeping the skins as clean, warm, and dry as possible. After use, fold each end into the middle so that the skin sticks to itself, or attach them on to the clear, plastic sheets that they are supplied with.

- **Care at a hut or tent**—Hang the skins up folded so that the glue cannot attract dust. If you are camping, take them into your sleeping bag at night. Do not leave them drying on your skis, especially in the sun or a warm room, because the glue can transfer to the ski base, making skiing downhill difficult.

- **Preparation**—Dry the ski base and ensure the skins are stuck on by firmly smoothing them down the length of each ski. Pay particular attention to the front and back, where most problems occur. Start moving as soon as possible; the pressure will help the skins to stick.

- **Looking after them when skiing**—Keep your skins warm when skiing downhill by placing them under your clothes or, if it is warm, carrying them in the top pocket of your backpack.

- **When a skin comes off**—Stick it back on with duct tape as soon as possible. Once a skin has totally unpeeled you have a real problem, because the glue must be free of snow and water to stick again. If the skin has completely detached, first rub the glued side across your thigh to get as much moisture off as possible, or plant a ski firmly in the snow, wrap the skin around the ski with the glue towards the ski, then drag the skin over an edge, back and forth. If possible, hang the skin up with the glue facing the sun. In extreme circumstances you can use a lighter to warm the glue. Dry the ski, and if all else fails, try Colltex quick glue spray.

- **Balling up**—On hot days, particularly after fresh snowfall, skins can collect snow. Pre-treating them with Colltex skin wax, standard ski wax or, at a push, candle wax, will help to reduce the problem and enhance their glide properties. At the first sign of balling, stamp your feet with each stride. If it all gets too much, de-ball skins by rubbing a ski pole up and down the bases. If you have a block of wax, use it now to prevent it happening again a short while later. Various glide sprays that do the same thing are available, but the skin must be dry and they do not last as long or work as well. After going through water, stop and use the edge of the other ski to scrape excess water off before it turns to ice.

- **Longer-term maintenance**—Store skins in airtight bags to prevent the glue drying out between trips. To check the glue, fold your skins together, and then try to pull them apart. If it is easy to do, especially around the tail, re-glue the skins before your next trip. New glue can be easily applied on top of the old glue a few times but, if you have time, remove and put on new glue. Remove glue with a solvent and scraper, or a soldering iron modified with a flat blade scraper and thermostat controller. Alternatively, place newspaper over the glued surface and warm it with an iron—the glue transfers to the paper. Repeat with clean sheets until it has all come off. Glue should be applied thinly and left to dry overnight in a warm room. It is also possible to buy iron-on glue.

Balling up is a problem after fresh snowfall followed by a hot day.

SKINNING TECHNIQUE

A ski, binding, and boot can weigh a combined 5kg (11lb), so good skinning technique will keep your legs fresh. Glide the ski forward smoothly and rhythmically, without lifting. Rolling your hips slightly can help to put pressure on each ski. The heel on your rear boot should rise until the sole is almost vertical, but you can still maintain pressure. Then push forward with your rear ski by applying slight pressure on the center, so that the skin maintains contact with the snow as it glides forward. Keep the tip of your ski a foot or two between the tails of the person's skis in front of you.

As the slope steepens, more pressure must be applied to keep the skins in contact with the snow. Look ahead, not at your ski tips, and keep your chin up and your shoulders back, which will ensure your weight stays at the rear allowing you to maintain more pressure on the center of your ski. You can lessen the strain on your calf muscles by taking shorter strides, pushing with the sticks behind you, and using the heel lifts to maintain a more level ski. Heel lifts also reduce blistering and chafing. When the slope angle becomes greater than 30 degrees you should zigzag, following the line of least resistance (see Selecting a line and kick-turning, page 273).

On hard snow, edging your skis soon leads to strenuous side-stepping. Instead, roll your ankles and knees slightly downhill, so that the skin is in contact with the snow, rather like flat footing when wearing crampons. Using heel lifts makes this difficult, so keep them low in these conditions. If the slope is too steep, and the snow too hard to do this, use harscheisen.

When skinning on a hard snow surface, avoid edging your skis, because this will soon lead to strenuous sidestepping. Instead, roll your ankles and knees slightly down the hill. (Skier: Bruce Goodlad.)

Using heel lifts can reduce calf strain on steeper slopes.

Harscheisen are useful on moderate slopes of hard snow.

USING HARSCHEISEN

Harscheisen are not worth wearing all the time or on easy-angled slopes, as they reduce glide and restrict the stride; nor are they designed for use on water-ice or rock, which can bend the soft, metal teeth. If the consequences of a slip are serious remove your skis and use crampons.

On moderate slopes of hard snow, harscheisen make skinning easier by reducing the need to keep skins flat. Like crampons, they are best fitted at the bottom of the slope. With the Fritschi Diamir bindings, when you raise your heel the harscheisen come off the snow. This means that you get minimal penetration when you are using heel lifts. Lower your heel lifts to improve crampon contact. Do not be tempted to ski downhill with your ski crampons folded upward, or still in place; they will bend.

DESCENDING ON SKINS

The additional drag created by skins can give increased control when descending very steep slopes, but they do reduce the maneuverability of the ski, which creates its own problems.

USE OF YOUR POLES WHILE SKINNING

Efficient use of your ski poles saves energy. Keep your hands out of the leashes to save time on turns. On uphill traverses, the uphill hand will have to hold the pole lower down and the downhill hand will have to push on the top of the pole.

When skinning uphill, keep your arms close to your sides. When you reach forward, plant your pole with straight rather than bent arms—your poles will naturally tilt slightly. This will propel you forward, directing your energies to moving uphill, and not side to side. The basket of the ski poles should plant near the middle of your back foot.

TRACK SETTING WHEN SKINNING

An effective track minimizes kick turns, reduces the ups and downs, avoids areas where grip may be poor, such as ice, and minimizes exposure to hazards.

In deep snow, the track will feel very steep to the lead skier, but the followers will find the angle quite comfortable as the snow is flattened, so change the lead skier frequently. It is best to choose a line where you can make a smooth walking turn that does not require a kick turn. Look for softer snow, flat areas near trees, bumps, or other terrain irregularities that will allow a smooth, easy turn rather than a sharp, hard one.

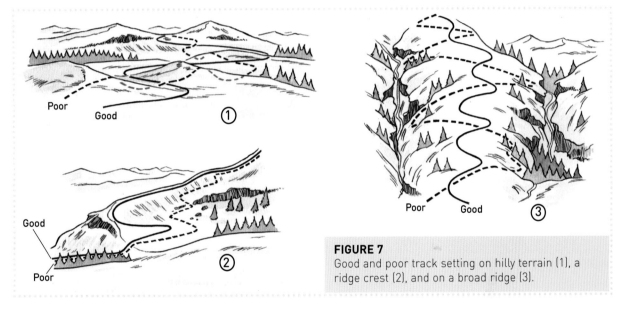

FIGURE 7
Good and poor track setting on hilly terrain (1), a ridge crest (2), and on a broad ridge (3).

Experienced skinners seek a balance between efficiency and safety and know how to set a track that takes the path of least resistance.

TURNING ON STEEP SLOPES

You will eventually ascend slopes so steep that you cannot easily walk around the turn. There are a number of turns you can use.

THE DOWNHILL KICK TURN

This is useful when snow conditions are too horrible to ski. It can also be used when ascending, but you do lose height and, if you are using a rope, it can make life difficult. This technique is done more easily with the bindings in "downhill mode:"

1 Face downhill with your skis perpendicular to the slope.
2 Place your poles behind you on the uphill slope to provide support.
3 With your weight on the ski poles, lift the downhill ski and rotate it to face in the new direction.
4 Move the ski in close to the uphill ski and stamp to set it in the snow.
5 Move the uphill ski into the new direction.
6 Point the tip downhill to help the tail clear the uphill snow.

In hard or crusty snow, the downhill kick turn can be modified by removing the ski on the downhill foot, making a kick turn with one ski, and then replacing the ski on the uphill side after the turn is finished. If all else fails, remove both skis.

The downhill kick turn
(skier: A. Perkins)

STEP AROUND TURN (CLOCK TURN)

The next stage if the slope is too steep to walk around in a gentle curve. As you approach the turn, stamp the lower ski to make a good platform, lift the uphill ski and place it in the new direction, weight it, and then bring the lower ski into the new direction. You can do this turn in a series of smaller changes in direction, like the moving hands of a watch. Try to do this turn without a break in rhythm.

The clock turn (skier: B. Goodlad)

THE UPHILL KICK TURN

This is the most common method for changing direction uphill:

1 At the corner, stamp out a flat platform, perpendicular to the fall line and position the poles as shown in photo 1 below.

2 Move the uphill ski forward, lift the tip, and turn it to the new direction.

3 Move the feet close together. Be sure the uphill ski is nearly level.

4 Reposition the outside pole for better stability, leaving enough room for the next ski to come around.

5 Transfer your weight to the uphill ski.

6 Once you have the uphill ski in position and can balance on it, pick up the downhill ski and, in one continuous motion, "clack" your heel against the ski to bring the tip up and push the tail down, while pivoting it into the new direction. You need to do the "clack" with your foot behind you and your ski still pointing in the original direction.

7 Slide the ski into the track, and off you go.

Uphill kick turn for changing direction while traveling uphill. (Skier: B. Goodlad.)

THE ALTERNATIVE UPHILL KICK TURN

When the track is in deep snow and the slope is steep or there is an obstacle above you at the turn, it can be difficult to get the first ski around to face the new direction.

1 At the corner, stamp out a flat platform, perpendicular to the fall line. Place both poles on the uphill slope.

2 Lift the uphill ski and drop it downhill, behind you.

3 Pivot the tail downhill as the ski tip clears the downhill ski boot.

4 Turn it 180 degrees into the new direction, and place it below what was originally the downhill ski.

5 Transfer your weight to your new downhill ski and stamp it to be sure it won't move. The poles are moved slightly for better balance, as the right foot (uphill ski) is un-weighted.

The alternative kick turn in deep tracks.
(Skier: B. Goodlad.)

6 Pick up your uphill ski, clear the tail past your other boot, then "clack" and follow through as per the regular kick turn.

GENERAL TACTICS FOR SKIING SLOPES

The following assumes that all skiers are equal ability:

- Ski with a partner, maintaining voice contact by leap frogging or skiing in formation.
- It is easy to lose contact in trees (whistle frequently to maintain communication with your group).
- Stop at the bottom (most experienced skiers stop).
- Look for hazards such as sudden drops and crevasses.
- Stop well above a hazard and do not gather together.
- In poor visibility, or when the terrain is serious, shorten the sections skied and follow the tracks of the more experienced skier to give you a reference point.
- Use yellow goggles or glasses in flat light.

SKIING SIGNALS

A clear set of signals may be important to direct the following skiers to the best snow or the safest line past a crevasse. Do not follow each other too closely, and on suspect slopes you should descend one at a time. To indicate it is safe to ski put your poles in a Y shape above your head (see photo below for other common signals).

Alway ski with a partner!
(Skier: John Taylor.)

Common skiing signals:
1 Move to the right before skiing until the poles are put into a "Y"
2 Do not ski the slope;
3 Ski, but stay right of me.
(Skier: B. Goodlad.)

CONTROLLING SPEED IN STEEP TERRAIN

When the terrain become too steep to ski in control, try the following:

- Drag your ski poles on a traverse
- Side slip
- Kick turn
- Push your ski poles across your body into the slope
- Fan turn in soft snow—kick the tail of the skis into the snow and walk them

You can ski mountaineer wherever and whenever there is snow and mountains. (Lorenz Frutiger, Greenland.)

round into a new direction.

FALLING ON SKIS

Falling on steep ground is the second most frequent cause of serious off-piste accidents. Sit, rather than fall—the added weight of your pack can cause a sudden fall. But if you do fall, and the consequence of a slide is serious, here are several methods to try.

THE HIP CHECK FALL

Fall on to your hip sideways and uphill (keep your knees clear). Try to use your momentum to bounce immediately back up on to your skis, so you do not begin sliding.

THE SHOULDER ROLL

If you fall face first, tuck into a somersault, roll, and land back on your skis. If you want to stop, land with your skis across the fall line. If you want to recover, angle your skis down the fall line and stand back up. Practice this on steep slopes with no serious consequences.

FALLING IN DEEP SNOW

If your skis have stayed on, get them across the fall line below you; pack a platform and place your ski poles flat on the snow by your hip. Push down on the poles with the uphill hand and stand on to your skis. Someone can help by standing downhill of you and pulling on your downhill hand.

If your skis have come off, create a platform, stick the tails of your skis into the snow, keep them flat, clean snow from your boots and put the downhill ski on first.

If you have lost a ski, try to determine the trajectory by looking for tracks. The ski is often higher than anticipated. Begin your search below the suspected point, and use your ski poles to slice through the snow perpendicular to the line of travel.

THE SELF-ARREST

Conventional self-arrest technique has two basic steps:

1 Get your skis below you quickly. Shoulder-roll or drag your hand or ski pole grip out to one side, like a canoe paddle. With some effort, the skis will circle below you.

2 A natural response is to sit on your rear or lay flat on your stomach, but your clothing is likely to be slippery. Arch your back and rear towards the sky; push your ski pole grips, fingers, and ski edges into the snow. Try to get everything off the snow except for your hands and skis.

The value of using ski pole self-arrest grips is questionable; they tend to rotate in your glove and then face toward your body. If you use them to arrest, you must drive your shoulder into the grip head to help bury the pick, just as you would do with an ice axe.

SKIING IN CREVASSED TERRAIN

Ensure you understand glacial travel and rescue techniques before venturing into glaciated terrain, and wear a harness (see chapter 3, page 232). During the winter there is often enough snow to allow you to ski over crevassed terrain with safety and it is rare that teams rope-up. Attach a sling and a crab to your harness and the shoulder of your backpack to make it easier to attach a rescue rope should you end up down a crevasse.

Ski perpendicular to crevasses

The safest method is to ski straight across crevasses. It is important that you give yourself time to react. Keep every-one in sight, and follow the tracks of the lead skier. Be wary of any new snow cover on glaciers. Keep your eyes open; don't just look down the fall line, but spot crevasses out to the side of your descent line. If you crash and both skis have released, stay put and get someone else to retrieve them.

If you must take a break in crevassed terrain, avoid walking around without your skis.

ROPING UP

Skiing roped up is a nightmare, even for experienced skiers. It slows you down, and rope management on turns is difficult. However, it is necessary when poor visibility is combined with skinning uphill on unfamiliar wet glaciers, especially during warm conditions, or when skiing downhill with shallow, low density or variable snow cover (particularly in early or late winter).

ROPING UP WHEN SKINNING

On uphill sections, all members of the rope team need to pause and manage the rope when any other member does a kick turn. The technique for roping up is the same as for summer alpinism (see chapter 3, page 234). Two 30m (98ft) Dyneema cords are often carried, which prevents one person taking all the weight, but means that only three or four people can attach to each rope. Three to a rope is better than two for holding a fall, but it makes managing the rope on turns more difficult.

The second strongest skier should be at the front and the strongest at the rear. Each member should carry at least one Wild Country Ropeman mk 2, Petzl Mini Traxion, or similar device that will grip a thin icy rope more effectively than a prusik. Do not allow slack to develop in the rope and do not carry hand coils.

FIGURE 8
Managing the rope when descending

DESCENDING ROPED UP

The only practical way to descend roped up is in a very slow snowplough (see Fig. 8). The second and third skiers should not turn at the same place as the first: the second turns shortly after the first, and the third shortly after the second, preferably in the same direction! The lead skier skis with a pole in each hand, while the second and third skiers carry both poles in one hand or stowed on the backpack and manage the rope with the other (a sling attached to the rope can help). Take particular care not to speed up and catapult the other skiers off their feet. The strongest skier, or the one with the biggest thighs, should be at the back.

When conditions allow, a preferable option to roping up the whole group is for the strongest skiers to rope up 25m (82ft) apart and the rest of the team to follow in their tracks.

HOLDING A FALL

The aim of the skier holding the fall is to get their skis parallel to the crevasse. It is advisable to have your ice axe available by slotting it down your back in case you cannot remove your skis to make a belay.

PERFORMING A RESCUE IN CREVASSED TERRAIN

Everyone should wear a harness and carry a crevasse rescue kit when skiing in crevassed terrain. (Skier: A. Perkins.)

The two people carrying the ropes must not be together at the front of the group. If the party is divided into two roped teams, the other team should quickly come forward and attach their rope to the victim's loaded rope via a Wild Country Ropeman or equivalent. This will allow the team holding the victim to create an anchor more easily. Once the anchor has been created it is important for the rescuers to see the victim and, if possible, to use another rope to remove their backpack and skis.

WHEN DOWN A CREVASSE

Release your skis and backpack, and then attach them to the rope. Hopefully, rescuers are on the way and can haul your skis and backpack to make your escape easier. Without skis you may be able to crampon out, but it is important that you communicate first with the rescuers so that, should you fall, the belay system is not shock loaded. If all else fails, prusik out.

THE RESCUERS

The rescue principles are the same as for summer alpinism (see chapter 1, page 237) but, whenever possible, use the spare rope to get the victim out, because the loaded rope (if the victim is wearing one) will have bitten into the snow on the edge of the crevasse. An assisted hoist with a Ropeman, or better, a Petzl mini traxion, is probably the fastest option when the victim is able to pull. Use an unassisted hoist as a last resort (see Fig. 11, page 240).

SKI ANCHORS

The amount of snow in winter increases the difficulty of creating a secure anchor, and the extra snow increases friction in any crevasse rescue system. However, your skis can be used to create an anchor. There are two methods, depending on what the anchor is to be used for and the quality of the snow. The first is adequate for rescue when the snow is firm or for an abseil or "lower off", but if the last person must also abseil, a snow mushroom (see chapter 3) may be better. If the snow is softer, method 2 is best.

Creating a ski anchor using the rope (note the orientation of the ski edge)

Method 1

Best used in firm snow. Plunge the tails of your skis slightly back from the direction of pull and into the snow as far as you can, at least to the bindings. Ensure they are approximately 45cm (18in) apart, perpendicular to the direction of pull (the metal edges should be facing downhill).

To link the skis, attach the rope to the rear ski with a bowline, and then attach it horizontally to the front ski using a clove hitch. Leave some slack rope and attach the rope as low as possible on the front ski using a figure of eight on a bight. The same can also be created using slings. The combination of two skis with their camber resisting the direction of pull make a very strong anchor that is quick to set up. It is difficult to do when you are holding someone down a crevasse.

Method 2

Preferable when the snow is softer and the anchor is to be used for a hoist. Bury your skis horizontally, the same way you would bury an ice axe (see chapter 3, page 197). Ensure the sharp metal edges are pointing towards the crevasse. You can also place a buried ice axe uphill of the skis.

Creating a ski anchor using slings

6

EXPEDITIONS TO REMOTE AREAS OF THE WORLD

"We do not deceive ourselves that we are engaging in an activity that is anything but debilitating, dangerous, euphoric, kinaesthetic, expensive, frivolously essential, economically useless, and totally without redeeming social significance. One should not probe for deeper meanings."

—Allen Steck, mountaineer

Most expeditions to remote parts of the world are lightweight, with a small team, and minimal equipment. The size and/or remoteness of mountain ranges and the lack of huts, however, mean that you cannot just turn up and climb—you must research where you are going, organize food and equipment, plan and prepare the logistics, get visas and vaccinations, and possibly organize permits.

The location does not necessarily have to be exotic or the venture extreme to be called an expedition—you can make it anything you want it to be. Although much of the information in this chapter is about organising an expedition to the Himalaya, it applies to wherever you are going.

HOW TO CLIMB IN REMOTE MOUNTAIN RANGES

There are many different tactics that can be used to tackle a remote or large mountain, which are often interlinked during the same trip. For instance, you may set up a base camp and trek from it, or camp one and two may be established and the rest of the route climbed alpine or capsule style (see opposite). To determine the tactics that best suit your experience and objective start at the summit or end of your trek and work backward. How fit are you? Do you want to

Mount Everest

be part of a small team or a large expedition? Can it be done in one push? How cold is it? Do you need porters? How long is it? Can you acclimatize on another peak? How much equipment do you need? What risks are you willing to take?

These are common terms describing expedition tactics:

Himalayan (conventional) style—The biggest single factor that demands this style is the use of oxygen at extreme altitude (8000m+/26,247ft). Himalayan style is usually conducted from a base camp with high camps progressively established. Fixed ropes are often used to make sections safer and easier for carrying loads. However, it is expensive and requires the involvement of many. It does not fit into the lightweight approach.

Capsule style—Climbers ferry loads to establish a higher camp. The lower camp stays in place so that the climbers have somewhere to retreat to sleep. The lower camp is then leapfrogged higher up the mountain. The process is repeated to a point where the summit can be tackled quickly and lightweight (alpine style). Because you climb high and sleep low, you can acclimatize on the same mountain. This style is also used when it is inefficient to break camp each day, so it is common on routes where it may take days to cover enough ground to move camp e.g., big walls. The advantage is that you can push out the next section in marginal weather, as your camp and security is closer.

Lightweight alpine style—Alpine climbing without huts. From a base camp, and sometimes not even that, minimal equipment is carried for a single ascent to a summit. It is a committing and riskier style, because should bad weather come in, you may have to sit it out on the mountain instead of retreating to a lower camp. The advantages are that planning is easier, fewer people are needed, and, as you are moving faster, you should get up and down before bad weather strikes. If the mountain is at altitude, acclimatization is usually done on smaller peaks first.

Trekking—Either "unsupported," where you carry everything including your food, or "assisted," where pack animals or porters carry some or all of your loads. You may camp or stay in hostels, huts, and/or teahouses.

Alpine style on Alpamayo

Left: Capsule style on Aconcagua

Right: Trekking to Everest Base Camp

WHERE TO GO?

"You know, Alf, going to the right place at the right time, with the right people, is all that really matters. What one does is purely incidental."
—Colin Kirkus to Alf Bridge

Sadly, the wild places of the world are increasingly being turned into theme parks, as tourism tries to make them accessible to all, but there are still places for the intrepid traveler who wants to experience the world, and not just see it. The inspiration for an expedition destination can come from many sources including books, articles, and other climbers.

Coping with the unforeseen is part of any expedition, but if you don't research your trip you must be prepared for the frustrations, delays, and challenges that inevitably occur. Start your expedition career with a small objective, where the weather, logistical, and communication problems are not too great, or consider a commercial trip first to see if it is for you.

ASIA

Asia contains some of the most spectacular mountain ranges in the world. There is great trekking in all areas—circuit routes are plentiful and routes into mountains are great treks in their own right. (Thanks to www.peakware.com for providing some of this information.)

Himalaya (Afghanistan, Bhutan, China, India, Nepal, Pakistan)—Contains nine of the world's highest peaks. Sikkim, Kumaon, Garhwal, Kulu, Lahul-Spiti, Padar, Zanskar, and Ladakh all have many 5000-7000m (16,404-22,966ft) peaks. Look also at the Kangchenjunga, Mahalungur, Langtang, Rolwaling, Ganesh, Manaslu, Annapurna, Dhaulagiri, Nilgiri, and Kanjiroba ranges of Nepal. West Nepal is also opening up, but the approaches are quite long.

Pamirs, Congling Mountains (Afghanistan, Kyrgyzstan, Pakistan, Tajikistan)—Wild and remote, with many peaks above 6000m (19,865ft). The highest point is Communism Peak (7495m/24,590ft).

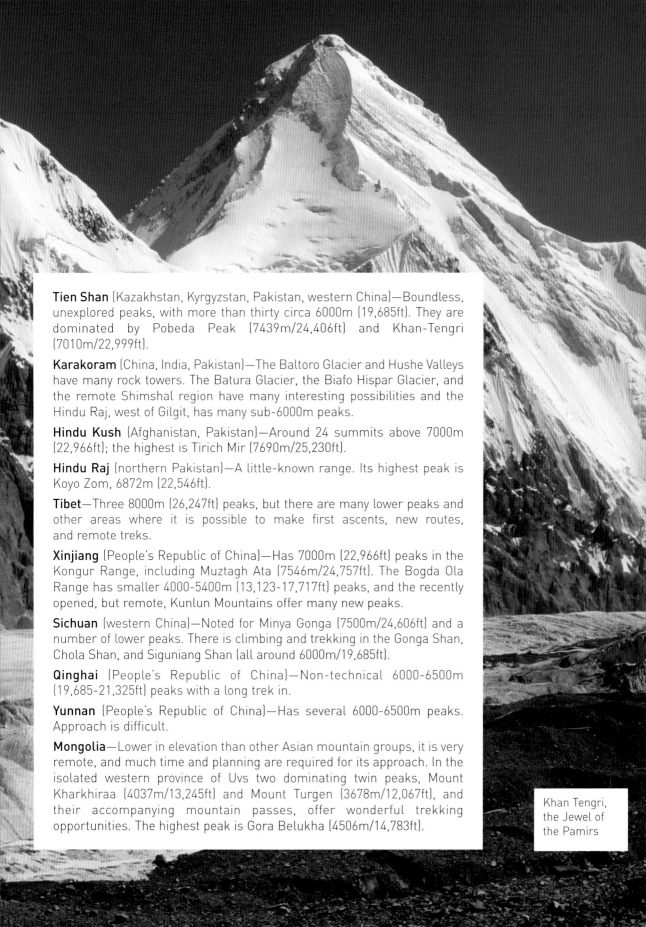

Tien Shan (Kazakhstan, Kyrgyzstan, Pakistan, western China)—Boundless, unexplored peaks, with more than thirty circa 6000m (19,685ft). They are dominated by Pobeda Peak (7439m/24,406ft) and Khan-Tengri (7010m/22,999ft).

Karakoram (China, India, Pakistan)—The Baltoro Glacier and Hushe Valleys have many rock towers. The Batura Glacier, the Biafo Hispar Glacier, and the remote Shimshal region have many interesting possibilities and the Hindu Raj, west of Gilgit, has many sub-6000m peaks.

Hindu Kush (Afghanistan, Pakistan)—Around 24 summits above 7000m (22,966ft); the highest is Tirich Mir (7690m/25,230ft).

Hindu Raj (northern Pakistan)—A little-known range. Its highest peak is Koyo Zom, 6872m (22,546ft).

Tibet—Three 8000m (26,247ft) peaks, but there are many lower peaks and other areas where it is possible to make first ascents, new routes, and remote treks.

Xinjiang (People's Republic of China)—Has 7000m (22,966ft) peaks in the Kongur Range, including Muztagh Ata (7546m/24,757ft). The Bogda Ola Range has smaller 4000-5400m (13,123-17,717ft) peaks, and the recently opened, but remote, Kunlun Mountains offer many new peaks.

Sichuan (western China)—Noted for Minya Gonga (7500m/24,606ft) and a number of lower peaks. There is climbing and trekking in the Gonga Shan, Chola Shan, and Siguniang Shan (all around 6000m/19,685ft).

Qinghai (People's Republic of China)—Non-technical 6000-6500m (19,685-21,325ft) peaks with a long trek in.

Yunnan (People's Republic of China)—Has several 6000-6500m peaks. Approach is difficult.

Mongolia—Lower in elevation than other Asian mountain groups, it is very remote, and much time and planning are required for its approach. In the isolated western province of Uvs two dominating twin peaks, Mount Kharkhiraa (4037m/13,245ft) and Mount Turgen (3678m/12,067ft), and their accompanying mountain passes, offer wonderful trekking opportunities. The highest peak is Gora Belukha (4506m/14,783ft).

Khan Tengri, the Jewel of the Pamirs

Siguniang Mountain,
Sichuan Province of China

Siberia (Russia)—Ranges are small compared to Central and Southern Asian counterparts, yet are remote and rugged, with some spectacular isolated peaks. Major ranges include the Cherskiy Range, Kamchatka Peninsula, Kinghan Range, Sayan Mountains, Sikhote-Alin, Stanovoi Range, Ural Mountains, and Yablonovyy Range.

Bhutan—Sandwiched between India and Tibet, and almost entirely mountainous. Climbing and trekking is very expensive—this is not a place for expeditions on a shoestring.

Mustang (Nepal)—Elevation of more than 2500m (8202ft). Has been completely untouched by modern life for centuries.

SOUTH AMERICA

Andes (Argentina, Bolivia, Chile, Colombia, Ecuador, Peru, Venezuela)—One of the world's great mountain ranges, rising to well over 6500m (21,325ft). The Andes fall somewhere between the mountains of Europe and the wild peaks of Asia in height, difficulty, and access, making them ideal for experienced mountaineers aspiring to more remote peaks without the bureaucratic problems of a Himalayan expedition. There are easily ascended volcanoes in Ecuador, Chile, and Argentina, and many desperate ice faces in the Cordillera Blanca, and Huayhuash and Vilcanota of Peru.

Bolivia is an ideal country for a first visit, with a very stable climate and both hard and easy peaks. The rugged range of Cordillera Quimsa Cruz, south of Bolivia's capital La Paz, comprises more than eighty peaks above 5000m (16,404ft). From the range's northern edge, multi-day treks lead to remote and striking rock spires and snow-capped peaks.

Beyond the Andes, the mountaineering possibilities in South America are limited to the coastal ranges of Brazil, isolated mountains in Venezuela, such as Roraima (inspiration for Sir Arthur Conan Doyle's *Lost World*), and the sub-Andean ranges, e.g., the Sierra de Còrdoba.

Alpamayo, Peruvian Andes:
"the most beautiful
mountain in the world"

Patagonia (Argentina and southern Chile)—Probably the most famous region of the Andes, with some of the most difficult big walls in the world, such as Fitzroy and the Torres del Paine. However, much of it is unknown and unexplored. The mountain-sides are densely covered in rainforest, and numerous glaciers—some 80km (50 miles) long—flow through the forests, coming to rest in a complex system of lakes and narrow fjords. The entire range is blanketed by two long, narrow ice caps. Access is difficult, but Patagonia is great for anyone willing to brave the weather, which becomes worse as you travel south, changing from Mediterranean in the north to "Scottish" in the far south.

EUROPE

Masses of mountains, but only several can be considered "remote."

Caucasus (Armenia, Azerbaijan, Georgia, various parts of Russia, and several other "territories")—Stretching from the Black Sea to the Caspian Sea, and comparable in character to the European Alps, peaks average 1830-2743m (6004-8999ft), with Mount Elbrus at 4413m (14,478ft). The weather is seldom settled, particularly in the west, where the climate is affected by the Black Sea.

Iceland—Several volcanic peaks and ice fields, which make a great first ski crossing. Expect very cold, wet, and windy conditions year-round.

NORTH AMERICA

North America has a fantastic choice of mountains with some more similar to climbing in the European Alps, but there are many areas that definitely come into the realms of remote expeditions.

Alaska Range (United States)—Some of the longest mountain routes in the world. Starts in south-central Alaska and continues southwest as the Aleutian Range. The highest peak is Mount Denali at 6,193m (20,320ft). Harsh weather and heavy snowfall has created large glaciers.

The Brooks Range (Canada, U.S.)—Remote range stretching across Northern Alaska, from the Chukchi Sea, to the Yukon border. The mountains are not especially high, the highest peak being Mount Isto at 2762m (9062ft). The higher slopes are snow- and ice-clad for much of the year.

Wrangell Mountains (U.S.)—In southeast Alaska, they rise above an immense snowy wilderness, and average around 3660m (12,008ft). The region is best known for several higher peaks, including Mounts Blackburn at 4995m (16,388ft), Sanford at 4950m (16,240ft), and Wrangell at 4560m (14,961ft). They are mostly non-technical, but serious, requiring long expeditionary approaches in often challenging weather.

Saint Elias Mountains (Canada, U.S.)—The highest coastal range in the world, with hundreds of sharp, ice-clad peaks rising above sea-level glaciers. The dominant mountains are Mount Logan (5960m/19,554ft)—the highest mountain in Canada—and Mount Saint Elias (5488m/18,005ft).

The Fairweather Range (U.S.)—The southern continuation of the Saint Elias Mountains. The mountains tower near the sea and form extensive glaciers. The highest is Mount Fairweather (4663m/15,299ft).

Baffin Island (Canada)—An Arctic wilderness

The inappropriately named Mount Fairweather, Alaska

Torres del Paine, Patagonia (Photo: John Biggar.)

Cotapaxi, the highest active volcano in the world, Ecuador

located in the extreme northeast. Towers with sheer rock walls give excellent climbing. The finest peaks are located on the Cumberland Peninsula, at the head of the South Pangnirtung Fjord. Access is by boat, dog sleds, float-planes, or ski-planes. The highest peak is Tête Blanche (2156m/7073ft), but the most famous is Mount Asgard (2011m/6598ft).

British Columbia Coast Range (Canada)—An immense snowy massif, filled with glaciers that stretch for miles with many steep faces rising up to c.1500m (4921ft). Mount Waddington is the highest at 4019m (13,186ft).

AFRICA

Atlas Mountains (Algeria, Morocco, Tunisia)—The most northerly of Africa's mountains, extending in a broken chain across three countries. The highest peaks (twelve over 3960m/12,992ft) are in the western range, the High Atlas. The highest peak is Mount Toubkal (4165m/13,665ft). They maintain their snow caps for much of the year, but there are no glaciers. There is good trekking in the Rif Mountains.

Rwenzori (Democratic Republic of Congo, Uganda)—A group of six high glaciated massifs, including Africa's third-highest peak, Mount Margherita at 5109m (15,762ft).

The Virunga Mountains (DR Congo, Rwanda, Uganda)—Includes eight volcanoes. The highest is Mount Karisimbi (4507m/14,787ft).

The Aberdare Range (Kenya)—Heavily forested uplands with an average elevation of 3810m (2367ft). Oldoinyo la Satima 4001m (13,120ft) is the highest. Mount Kenya (5199m/17,057ft), the second-highest mountain in Africa, lies several kilometres to the east.

Simien Mountains (Ethiopia)—A vast, hilly plateau rising occasionally to form higher groups, separated by broad river valleys. A number of peaks rise above 4000m (13,123ft), including Ras Dashen at 4533m (14,872ft).

Cameroon Mountains (Cameroon, Central African Republic, Chad, Nigeria)—An isolated volcanic mass, towering higher than any other mountains in Western Africa. On the island of Malabo, Pico de Santa Isabel rises to 3008m (9869ft). Cameroon is home to some of the heaviest rains on Earth.

The Tibesti Mountains (Chad)—The largest and highest range in the Sahara desert, formed by a group of dormant volcanoes—with Emi Koussi the highest

Mount Baker, Rwenzori Mountains, Africa

Mount Kilimanjaro—contender for the most dangerous mountain in the world according to the number of people who die on it.

at 3445m (11,302ft).

Madagascar—A large island off the southeast coast of Africa. Its granite peaks have many big walls, the highest being Maromokotro (2876m/9436ft).

NEW ZEALAND

The Southern Alps—Run along the western side of the South Island, with many smaller peaks with complicated access. Aoraki/Mount Cook is the highest point 3754m (12,316ft). Sixteen other points in the range exceed 3000m (9843ft).

AUSTRALASIA/OCEANIA

The Malay Archipelago—A number of interesting destinations such as Borneo, Java, Sulawesi, and Sumatra.

NEW GUINEA

The Owen Stanley Range (Papua New Guinea)—Part of the central mountain chain. The highest peak is Mount Victoria at 4072m (13,360ft).

Pegunungan Maoke (Irian Jaya, Indonesia)—Formerly known as the Central Range, many peaks lie above 3660m (12,000ft).

The Bismarck Range (Papua New Guinea)—In the central highlands, the highest point being Mount Wilhelm at 4509m (14,793ft).

Sudirman Range (Province of Papua, Indonesia)—The western part of the Maoke Mountains. Includes Oceania's highest peak, Puncak Jaya (Mount Carstensz) at 4884m (16,024ft).

ANTARCTICA

The world's fifth-largest continent. It is the coldest, windiest, highest and driest continent on earth.

The Queen Maud Mountains—A major mountain range lying between the Beardmore and Reedy Glaciers. The highest peak is Mount Ellsworth at 2925m (9596ft).

The Sentinel Range—Forming the northern part of the Ellsworth Mountains and lying north of the Minnesota Glacier. Many peaks rise over 4000m (13,123ft), with the highest, Vinson, at 4897m (16,066ft).

Greenland: the future of remote mountaineering, with no altitude problems.

GREENLAND

Greenland provides unlimited potential for remote mountaineering and trekking with both large and small objectives. Greenland's highest mountains are in the Watkins Range on the east coast. Large pack ice limits the sea approach, so expeditions typically require airlifts. Smaller peaks can be climbed all year round if accessed by dog sled or ski.

The three primary peaks are all nunataks (nunataqs), high mountains protruding through glacial ice. The highest peak is Gunnbjorn's Fjeld (3700m/ 12,139ft). The Schweizer Land Mountains are located south of the Watkins Range; the highest is Mont Forel (3360m/11,024ft).

A more accessible alternative to both are the smaller mountains in the far south, just north of Cape Farewell, with a longer climbing season and easy access from Narssarsuaq. The highest is Mount Patuersoq (2740m/ 8989ft). The west coast mountains are also reasonably accessible, as much of the coast is approachable year-round by sea. Godthaab, Greenland's capital, is located on the west coast and has a large subsidiary ice cap from which rises the west coast's highest peak, Mount Atter (2189m/7185ft).

THE ARCTIC

Only 1125km (699 miles) from the North Pole, a cluster of Arctic islands make up the Norwegian archipelago of Svalbard. The west coast is ice-free during the summer months. The largest and most mountainous island is Spitsbergen, which has sharp peaks averaging 1000m (3281ft), though some exceed 1500m (4921ft), rising steeply above long ridges, numerous glaciers and a heavily indented coastline.

AND THE REST...

Don't forget the following mountain ranges: Altay Mountains (Turkey); Sulaiman Mountains (Pakistan); Safed Koh (Afghanistan-Pakistan border); Zagros Mountains (Iran, Iraq); and several ranges in Yugoslavia and Poland.

PLANNING A LIGHTWEIGHT EXPEDITION

"Any worthwhile expedition can be planned on the back of an envelope."
—Eric Shipton, early explorer and mountaineer

Expedition planning is not rocket science, but it is easy to underestimate the time and effort involved—forget a stove or get the wrong visa and your trip could be over.

As soon as you have decided where to go, you must consider every aspect of the trip. Do you all have the necessary technical skills? Do you require special visas, permits, and permission? Do you need to be immunized? What insurance do you need? Will you require a driving license? Do you need customs clearance for equipment? The list is endless!

SOURCES OF INFORMATION

There are many sources of information on past expeditions:

- **The Alpine Club (AC) library**—Numerous reports, journals, and an extensive collection of mountaineering books. It has a computerised index of Himalayan peaks above 6000m (19,685ft) from which, for a small charge, all known references to a peak can be obtained.

- **Journals**—The most useful are *The Alpine Club Journal*, *The American Alpine Journal*, and the *Himalayan Journal* (all available at the AC Library).

- **Magazines**—The "Mountain Info" section in *Climb* magazine is very useful.

- **The Expedition Advisory Center**—Based at the Royal Geographical Society, London, the center produces tailor-made information packs for mountain areas, keeps a library of expedition reports, and runs lectures and seminars.

- **The British Mountaineering Council**—A range of information sheets on permits, etc., and reports from BMC-supported expeditions.

OTHER TREKKERS, EXPLORERS AND CLIMBERS

Talk to other climbers. However famous they are, I can guarantee they will help—they are, first and foremost, trekkers and mountaineers.

OTHER COLLECTIONS

- **Alan Rouse Memorial Library (Sheffield City Library)**
- **Fell and Rock Climbing Club Library (Lancaster University Library)**
- **Graham Brown Memorial Library (Scottish National Library, Edinburgh)**
- **Backpack Club Library (Manchester Central Library)**
- **Scottish Mountaineering Club Library (SMC members only)**
- **Yorkshire Ramblers Club Library (Leeds Central Library).**

View of Everest from Kala Pator

WHEN TO GO?

It is possible to climb or trek at any time of the year, but by choosing the right time you maximize your chances of success. **Note**: This table does not cover the possibilities for ski mountaineering.

BEST TIME TO GO

	January	February	March	April	May	June	July	August	September	October	November	December
Best time												
Possible												
Afghanistan/Kyrgyzstan/ Pakistan/Tajikistan (Pamirs)												
Alaska												
Algeria/Morocco/Tunisia (Atlas Mountains)												
Antarctica												
Argentina												
Bhutan												
Bolivia												
Canada (Baffin Island)												
Canada (Coast Range)												
Canada (Saint Elias)												
Chile												
China/Kazakhstan/ Kyrgyzstan (Tien Shan)												
DRC/Uganda (Rwenzori Mountains)												
Ethiopia (Simien Mountains)												
Greenland												
India												
Kenya												
Mongolia												
Nepal												
New Guinea (Carstensz Pyramid)												
New Zealand												
Svalbard												
Patagonia												
Peru												
Tanzania (Mount Kilimanjaro)												
Tibet												

HOW LONG WILL IT TAKE?

Give yourself enough time; bad weather, bureaucracy, illness, and flight delays can all result in some members having to return home early. If your schedule is tight, members with more time can leave early to resolve customs/permit problems, hire staff, and buy food. Alternatively, use an agent or commercial company at home (see page 300). Some mountain ranges are accessible by plane or helicopter, or at a low altitude to reduce acclimatization time, both of which decrease the time needed. Total the following to deduce how long your expedition will take:

- How long it takes to travel to the country
- How much time is needed to get organised when you arrive (i.e., paperwork, food, a visit to an agency, domestic flights, etc.)
- How many days are required to trek to or reach the mountain
- How long it takes to climb the mountain and acclimatize
- Spare days for bad weather, bureaucracy, illness, sightseeing, etc.

RECOMMENDED TIMESCALES FOR COMMON EXPEDITIONS

Examples		Timescale including travel (days)
Mountain	**Range and country**	
Mont Blanc	The Alps, France/Italy	10–14
Trek at low altitude	Nepal	10–14
Mount Kilimanjaro	Tanzania	14–16
Rwenzori Mountains	DRC/Uganda	16–18
Trek to Everest Base Camp	Himalaya, Nepal/Tibet	20–25
Mount Vinson	Sentinel Range, Antarctica	20–25
Mount McKinley (Denali)	Alaska Range, Alaska	25–30
Khan Tengri	Tien Shan, Kyrgyzstan/Kazakhstan border	25–30
Aconcagua	Andes, Argentina	25–30
Mustagh Ata	Pamirs, China	30-35

WHO SHOULD YOU GO WITH?

"The best climber in the world is the one having the most fun."
—Alex Lowe, top U.S. climber

Gaining the summit is rewarding, but what matters in life is the journey, and not the destination. Expeditions can make or break friendships; on one memorable trip we did not even reach the mountain, but still returned home as friends, and on other expeditions I have watched friendships tainted by lack of thought.

EXPERT TIP

John Biggar
www.andes.org.uk
info@johnbiggar.com

"Tired of your yeti gaiters popping off at the toe? Use skin glue, as used by ski mountaineers, to fix them into place, as its better than superglue."

Adrian Wilson, Dave Williams, and Richard Townsend packing food, Alaska.

A team of three or four increases safety (Peruvian Andes)

It would be nice if every expedition consisted only of climbing mates, but work, family, and money often get in the way. There is also the possibility that your friends do not have the necessary skills, such as the ability to ski, or experience. But on lightweight remote expeditions, technical skills are often less important than the ability to survive and remain relaxed.

Difficulties can arise when team members do not agree on what they are there for. It is important to therefore discuss the trip and for everyone to agree on the aim and how it is going to be achieved before you go. A few warm-up trips to discover each other's idiosyncrasies are a good idea, because finding yourself locked in a tent in a five-day storm with someone you don't like or trust might cost someone their life!

It is also important to realize that some will find the technical, psychological, and physical demands of a remote expedition hard to cope with, whatever grade you climb at home. Homesickness is common during the first weeks, and lack of privacy and isolation from family and loved ones will cause fluctuating moods. Recognize when someone is having a rough day, when they need support, or when they just need a bit of space. If you want to be "the best climber in the world," as defined by Mark Twight, then people skills are just as important as technical ability.

An expedition can be a life-changing experience, but for some it is something never to be repeated. Your expectations and possibly your views on life will have changed, yet life at home will have continued without you. It can be difficult to get back into the groove of work and family responsibilities, but be reassured that it is the same for every mountaineer. You will be tired, possibly for weeks; you may not recognize that you are, but those around you will! You will want to tell friends and family about your experiences and adventures, but mountaineering is an inherently selfish pastime, so try not to be disappointed if some are bored by your stories.

THE SIZE OF THE TEAM

The style of the expedition and the size and complexity of the objective will often dictate how many people are required. It will also rely on the transport you are using, e.g., the payload of the aircraft or helicopter.

Larger teams will increase safety, and spread fixed costs such as permit fees and helicopter hire (there is often a maximum number allowed on a single permit). A large team also creates a dynamic social mix, so there is less chance you will be forced to share a tent with someone you don't get on with. Large teams do, however, have disadvantages, and they can fragment through problems arising from sharing equipment, food, and tents between individual members. A small team of two or three is easier to manage and can be adaptable but, should someone fall ill, the whole team may have to descend. A two-person team can work on technical routes with an easy approach, but a team of three or four is not much slower and safety is greatly increased in many circumstances, especially if it is your first trip.

LEADERS

All permit granting bodies in the developing world demand to deal with a leader. The first priority of all leaders is to become good at delegating, because a large part of the organization will be on their shoulders.

Choose carefully: leaders are not born—it is an acquired skill. The leader is not necessarily the best climber, they are the person in the group who has the ability to ensure that the group works together well and stays motivated.

VISAS, TREKKING PERMITS, CLIMBING PERMITS, AND PERMISSIONS

"Challenge is the core and mainspring of all human activity. If there's an ocean, we cross it; if there's a disease, we cure it; if there's a wrong, we right it; if there's a record, we break it; and, finally, if there's a mountain, we climb it."
—James Ramsey Ullman, climbing historian

The enjoyment of an expedition largely depends on the people you meet and travel with, and not necessarily on reaching the summit.

Access to many mountains ranges is governed by rules and regulations, especially in Asia and other developing countries. It is vital that you read, understand, and comply with the rules and regulations to avoid unexpected costs or disappointments. In addition, you may require a permit or need to pay a national park and conservation fee. Do not leave it too late; you may need to apply a year ahead, since the applications have to be processed through a multitude of government departments.

You may also require special visas, and not just ordinary tourist visas. Most notable in this respect is India, who demands that each team member has a special "X" visa for areas normally restricted to mainstream tourists, especially border areas. Tibet has special visa requirements which are distinct to those required for China. Frequently, visas are only granted after the expedition permit has been issued; this can take up to three months for some regions in India.

The rules do not only govern access to the mountains; on some trips you may have to take a liaison officer (LO) who you feed, pay, insure, equip, and clothe. Also, study the restrictions and permits for two-way radios, filming,

You may think that mountain climbing and trekking are the last expressions of individual freedom, but bureaucrats often have other ideas.

helicopter rescue bond, satellite telephones, insuring and equipping staff, and permits for guns and ammunition (for Polar Regions). Consider hidden costs such as environmental fees and staff/porter insurance.

Keep an eye on civil unrest, as permission can change rapidly. The Expedition's Commission of the International Climbing and Mountaineering Federation (UIAA) offers up-to-date information about fees, regulations, etc., on www.uiaa.ch. The site is updated each time the Commission receives information about significant changes. At present, they only supply information about Himalayan countries, but they are gradually covering others, notably the U.S.

The following table provides Internet contacts for many countries around the world.

Country/area	Climbing permit required?	Useful websites
Asia		
Afghanistan	Yes	www.afghanconsulate.net
Bhutan	Yes	www.bhutan.gov.bt
China	Maybe	Mountcma@sports.gov.cn
India	Yes	www.indmount.org/index.htm
Kazahkstan	Yes	www.kazakhstan-ecotourism.org
Kyrgyzstan	Yes	www.kac.centralasia.kg
Nepal	Yes	www.nma.com.np and motca@mos.com.np
Pakistan	Yes	www.pakmission-uk.gov.pk
Tibet	Yes	*See* China
The Americas		
Alaska	Yes	www.travelalaska.com
Baffin Island, Canada	Maybe	www.baffinisland.ca
Bolivia, Columbia, Ecuador, Peru, Venezuela	No	www.andes.org.uk
Argentina, Chile, Patagonia	Maybe	www.andes.org.uk
Other		
Antarctica	Yes	www.fco.gov.uk
Greenland	Yes, in the northeast	www.greenlandexpedition specialists.com
Russia	Yes	www.Mountainguides.ru

GETTING THERE

Often the most expensive part of any trip is traveling to the destination country, but the cheapest flights are not always the best. The return flight is usually fixed; you cannot change passenger's names should someone pull out; and you can't cancel or change dates without a penalty. If your return date is not certain, ensure your ticket has a flexible return date. You will, however, still be required to select a return date when you book your ticket—the added flexibility costs more and it is also subject to the availability of seats.

On international trips, most airlines require that you reconfirm your return reservations at least 72 hours before the flight. If you do not, they may be cancelled. E-tickets allow someone at home to confirm your return flights online, but always leave your real tickets with someone in-country who can confirm your flight in person. This will avoid you having to return to the destination city three days before you fly just to ensure you get a seat.

Surprisingly, consumer protection laws do not apply to airlines. Therefore, if you buy a flight ticket direct from an airline you won't be protected in the same way as you would be if you bought the same flight from a tour operator.

Today's flights can appear "cheap," but airlines recoup their money by nearly always collecting excess baggage charges. At approximately £27/kg ($26.92/lb) between London and Kathmandu, for example, it may be cheaper to leave some items at home and to plan an extra day in Kathmandu so you can buy them there.

If you have not secured your return flight and it is canceled due to bad weather, you could find yourself at the back of a very large line (Lukla Airport, Nepal).

To reduce the impact of baggage charges, consider booking in as a team, but be aware that all luggage is allocated to one person's boarding card, which can cause problems if luggage is lost in transit. It may also be worth negotiating extra baggage allowance directly with the airline. Keep in mind that on stopover flights the baggage allowance may change on the next flight.

It is no longer possible to take climbing gear on to an airplane in your hand luggage. You can still wear big boots, but you will be asked to take them off to be scanned. Do not take large water bottles with you on to the plane—they are confiscated even if they are empty.

In Autumn 2004, the U.S. Transportation Security Administration announced that all luggage traveling through U.S. airports—whatever the airline—must be either unlocked or locked with approved padlocks. Put your backpack into a separate bag; otherwise it will be sent through the special baggage section and can take longer to emerge on to the baggage carousel on arrival.

For in-country flights ensure that you have a secured seat when you book; flights into the mountains are often canceled due to bad weather, meaning when the weather clears and flights resume there will be a backlog of passengers to clear. If you have a confirmed booking, and you arrive just as the weather clears, you will fly as scheduled and not join the line.

The air operator will question you about your flight to the mountains (unloading bags, Mount Fairweather, Alaska).

Using helicopters is expensive (The Tien Shan)!

USING HELICOPTERS AND AIRPLANES TO ACCESS MOUNTAINS

Private flights are usually charged on an hourly basis to the nearest tenth of an hour. You cannot expect the helicopter or airplane to wait at pick-up points, so arrive on time and ready to go.

To reduce costs, combine the flight with picking up another team or traveling part-way by car and using a staging post, where supplies and people are taken to reduce the ferrying distance. Flights into and out of the mountains are easily delayed by the weather, so be prepared to sit it out before and after your expedition.

Beware of baggage allowances on small airplanes, such as those used to access glaciers—in some cases the passengers are also weighed. Pilots in Alaska are used to carrying climbers, so you will probably manage to take 60kg (132lb).

The questions an air operator will ask are:

- Exactly where, when, and what are you doing?
- How many days will you be there?
- How many passengers?
- Total weight of equipment?
- Size of the largest item?
- Exactly where and when do you want to be picked up?
- How much luggage is returning?
- Do you have insurance to cover an emergency evacuation?

PERSONAL AND RESCUE INSURANCE

See www.dh.gov.uk. There it states that travelers from the U.K. to most other European countries, including countries in the former Soviet Union, can get urgent medical treatment, either at reduced cost or—in some cases—for free. If you travel to the U.S., Canada, the Middle East, Asia, Africa, and some other countries you require private health insurance. In the U.S. see www.insubag.com

Whatever reciprocal medical agreements exist, it is essential to have adequate rescue and repatriation insurance. The cost of a helicopter search for a missing person in Nepal, Alaska, or Greenland does not really bear thinking about. However, it is also worth considering that there is no helicopter or light aircraft rescue available in some countries, such as China and Tibet.

Always carry a copy of your insurance policy, and leave another copy with your agent or embassy. Even with adequate insurance it is wise to have a contingency fund (a credit card may do)—if one of your party requires emergency evacuation by helicopter you may have to pay upfront, regardless of insurance. You must also try to contact your insurance company, as they may not pay for the rescue if you have not called them first.

Read your travel insurance policy carefully. Does it cover everything you need? If you have household insurance you may be covered for possessions taken abroad for a limited time, or you may need to take out an "All Risks" policy.

THE BUDGET

An expedition may seem like a lot of money, but it is usually excellent value compared to a package holiday.

Beer talks! Ask everyone to provide a large financial deposit to ensure commitment. If you manage to get a grant or raise money through sponsorship, you can always reduce the contributions later.

A separate, high interest, tax-free bank account is usually required when applying for grant funding. An account with limited access (two signatures) not only helps to prevent accidental spending, but they also have higher interest rates.

There are many ways of taking money overseas, but traveler's checks are difficult to cash in remote places. Debit/credit cards can be used in most countries, but they are charged at official exchange rates which are high, especially in countries with high inflation. They also charge a phenomenal interest rate on cash withdrawals, which start immediately. My preferred way is to take U.S. dollars to exchange for local currency and several credit and debit cards as back up.

REDUCING THE COST

GRANTS

The grand title "expedition" opens the door to funding from a wide variety of sources. Before applying, find out what the grant-giving body requires—they may ask you for your application well in advance, to provide references, and they may even request a presentation. Do not expect grants to cover the cost of your whole trip; most entail personal contributions from each expedition member.

SPONSORSHIP

This is where a company gives you money or equipment (sponsorship in kind), to increase awareness of their company and improve their public image. Gaining sponsorship is usually difficult and has associated hassles that should not be underestimated.

Writing speculative letters is usually a waste of time; phone the company first to find the name of the person to contact and, before calling, think about what you can offer the company. Does your expedition have a unique aspect? Are you exploring an unusual part of the world? Is it a difficult expedition? Is it a first? Offer free advertising, publicity, written articles, or supply photographs, etc., but do not offer what you cannot do and—for the sake of other expeditions—if you do offer to do anything, then do it.

Spiti Valley, Ladakh

Be realistic: you may have more success obtaining small amounts from local companies than a small amount from a large company. If team members come from different parts of the country target the relevant regional sections of a larger company.

When a company is interested, meet them, taking pictures, and written material. Make your presentation short and be clear about what you want—equipment is always easier to obtain than cash. You can largely forget about asking outdoor equipment companies, because they are regularly asked for free gear and they are essentially small business ventures with little spare funds. However, you may be able to obtain a discount or there may be a pool of equipment you can borrow. Also try to barrow equipment, such as tents, etc., from local outdoor activity centers or schools, but remember that they are likely to be heavyweight items.

Getting media interest improves your chances of gaining sponsorship. Tackle the local press first; the national media search local news for stories of interest. A short, well-written press release, sent to a named individual, is the best way of communicating. Give facts, statistics, history and current events to describe your expedition and your aims.

RAISING MONEY FOR CHARITY

Using your expedition to make money for a charity gives some people justi-fication for their trip and a purpose beyond just enjoyment, but it can be a lot of hassle. Do not confuse sponsorship with fund-raising, and be honest and clear about whether you are approaching a business for funding or a charit-able donation, or both. It is probably better to get donations sent direct to the charity, because processing and keeping track of them is time-consuming.

Record all monies received together with details of who made the donation and when. The charity uses this information when reporting to the IRS. The RGS expedition handbook has advice for gaining sponsorship fund-raising for charities (www.rgs.org).

ASSISTANCE WITH ORGANIZATION

It is common for many expeditions to short circuit the gaining of permits and logistical support by using a commercial company at home or in-country agents. The amount of assistance they give varies, from logistical support (including flights) to a full-blown expedition service including leadership and all shades between. A team of experienced climbers may want to ensure they get the best support from people who know the specific country or range, and who can organize flights, freight, food, and have a stock of equipment within the country making the enterprise cheaper. If you are new to expeditions, you cannot find anyone to go with or you have a specific objective, like Mount Kilimanjaro, a commercial operation in your own country or an agent can be a good way to find out if a remote expedition is for you.

COMMERCIAL COMPANIES

Home commercial companies can provide a total expedition package or essential logistical arrangements including all or any of the following: porters, a guide, a cook, food, tents, sleeping bags, mattresses, transport to and from starting points, flight arrangements, permits, staff insurance, etc. Booking with a reputable home-based operator (Jagged Globe and Andes Expeditions, for example) can give you peace of mind, but select carefully, as low budget companies may be unregistered, poor at planning, provide poor provisions and use inexperienced leadership/guiding.

An important safeguard that a commercial company gives over a local/domestic agent is financial guarantees on all your fees, as they are bound by consumer protection law. In addition, a reputable commercial company uses domestic agents that aspire to a high level of service. This not only ensures you get what you have paid for in terms of food and equipment, but that local staff are also well looked after.

As well as this safeguard, if you don't get what you think you've paid for, or some part of the service has let you down, you can resolve the issue at home with the organization direct, rather than trying to haggle with someone overseas that does not speak your language, and is not bound by any consumer laws.

When you speak to an employee at a commercial company, ensure that they have intimate knowledge of the mountain range you are interested in and can offer real advice.

LOCAL AGENTS

Domestic agents in your destination country can provide a similar service to home commercial companies. It is advisable to use an agency that comes recommended by friends or is government-approved, as you don't know how reliable they are with your money, or how concerned they are for their employees' welfare. You may find yourself on steep, exposed, avalanche-prone slopes accompanied by porters without the correct gear! If you intend to organize an agent when you arrive, ensure you allow time to visit several agencies and for them to organize permits, etc.

DOING IT YOURSELF

Visiting countries where porters, visas, permits and much more is required can be frustrating and, if you don't know what you're doing, you are more vulnerable to being "ripped off." However, this can be part of the challenge. If you are going to hire equipment, guides and porters yourself ensure that you have someone who can speak the language (we hired an interpreter on one trip to China). If you are climbing a peak that requires a Liaison Officer, they may be able to help organize the porters and other staff when you arrive. You could also hire an experienced English speaking head guide and get them to organize some aspects of the trip for you.

Your reason for going it alone may be to cut costs, but it doesn't always work out cheaper unless you know exactly what you are doing. You may also

EXPERT TIP

Simon Lowe
www.jagged-globe.co.uk

"Look beyond impressive brochures and websites to find out about the people who run and work for an organization. Speak to someone who has been to the mountains you want to go to, so that the advice they give you is relevant and up-to-date. Ask them about their policy for clothing and equipping local porters, especially if you are going to any unusual or remote mountain."

believe that doing it yourself cuts out the middlemen and, therefore, puts money into the hands of those that need it most. However, good expedition companies and agencies may employ their guides and cooks all year-round and provide for their family should he/she get injured or killed.

LEADERSHIP AND QUALIFICATIONS FOR GUIDED EXPEDITIONS

Looking after someone in remote mountain terrain requires very different skills to those used by recreational climbers. There are few countries where laws apply as to who leads an expedition. You should, therefore, satisfy yourself that the person leading your trip has the experience and ancillary training to make the correct decisions in a tight situation, and can look after you. Holders of an American or International Federation of Mountain Guides Association (AMGA/IFMGA) qualification, or a Mountain-eering Instructor Certificate (MIC) are a good place to start, as they are more likely to be experienced and technically competent within the remit of their award (*see* Appendix, page 353). However, leading an expedition requires skills beyond those assessed by these awards, and top commercial providers select their leaders on the basis of a whole host of attributes.

Ask to see their CV and make sure you have the opportunity to discuss it with them before committing to taking them on. If you are employing a leader through the services of a U.K. operator, meet the leader before you go, take the chance to climb or visit the hills with him/her, and only go on the trip if you have confidence in them. You should ensure that they can operate legally in the necessary country by contacting the guide's organization in that region. Only registered companies can guide on Mount Denali and only IFMGA Guides are legally entitled to work in Europe, Canada and New Zealand.

LOCAL GUIDES

Local guides may know the mountains intimately, but the concept of a mountain guide is different in developing countries, so you cannot assume you will get the same level of technical competence, judgment, and decision-making as an experienced home country or IFMGA guide.

PORTER, SHERPA, GUIDE, SIRDAR—WHAT'S IN A NAME?

Sherpa is a term commonly used for anyone who carries (porters) loads or helps on an expedition, but strictly the Sherpa are an ethnic group from the mountainous region of Nepal. They are very different to porters in Africa because they probably porter for a living.

A Head Guide in Nepal Himalaya is a Sirdar—a Persian word meaning commander. They keep everything running smoothly, organize porters, and guide you in the correct direction. They usually start off as porters, and by virtue of their organization skills, willingness to work, and often their command of another language, rise through the ranks of Porter, Cook, and Assistant Head Porter to Head Guide.

The porter carries the loads and, in a small expedition with only one or two people, can also be the guide and even the cook. Trekking porters are found mainly in Nepal, but also in Pakistan, Peru and other South American countries, Tanzania, and Papua New Guinea.

There are three types of porter in India, Pakistan and Nepal:

1 **High Altitude (Expedition) Porters**—Carry the loads from the base camp to the summit.

2 **Trekking Porters (Kuli in Nepal)**—Carry the loads for trekkers and expeditions to base camp.

3 **General Porters (Dhakre in Nepal)**—Carry the loads/goods for the hotels, stores, and local market.

Organising porters,
Himachel Pradesh, India

LIAISON OFFICERS (LOs) AND INTERPRETERS

The UIAA believe that LOs should not be mandatory, but they are still required in China, India, Nepal, and Pakistan for certain areas and mountains of a certain height. LOs are usually a civil servant or army officer—rarely a mountaineer—and won't go above base camp.

LO regulations vary. In some countries you pay the national body to equip them, in others you must provide them with clothing of the same standard as other climbers. Ensure you know what you have to provide before you arrive.

You may view LOs as an unnecessary burden, but it is better to view them as a team member and an asset—if they feel unwanted they can create difficulties. Only the leader should liaise with the LO. They come from a different culture and may seem authoritarian, so explain and agree upon their role and function. They may be inexperienced in understanding the problems of expeditions and might even be frightened. Patience and politeness pays off.

Yaks carrying loads, Nepal

303

Nepalese porters use a headstrap (namlo) to support a basket (doko) and a T-shaped stick (tokma) to support the load while taking rests.

PORTER BACKGROUND

We should be careful not to put all porters around the world into the same category. For example, the famous Sherpas of Nepal and Balti porters of Pakistan still carry loads for a living outside of expedition work, but porters in Eastern Africa are impoverished subsistence farmers who travel from lower elevations in search of work. The way you recruit porters and use them should reflect these issues.

Ensure that they are provided with suitable food—Muslims do not eat pork or pig products, Hindus and Sikhs do not eat beef, and Buddhists and many Hindus are vegetarian. The LO may, therefore, be nervous about the content of tinned or dehydrated foods.

THE ETHICAL DILEMMA OF EMPLOYING TREKKING GUIDES AND PORTERS

(I am indebted to Simon Lowe of Jagged Globe and Dr Jim Duff and the International Porter's Progress Group for their comments and help with the following sections (www.IPPG.net).) Most major mountains are in countries with a poor transport infrastructure. This not only exacerbates the problem of poverty, but also means that many expeditions must use porters or pack animals, especially in the Himalaya. The use of humans to carry equipment is an emotive and complex issue, requiring a deep understanding of a country's culture, history, and economy to understand it fully. Porters are not essential if you are traveling lightweight, but deciding not to employ porters because you find it distasteful doesn't solve their poverty.

Hiring a porter and/or a guide to help you not only aids the rural economy, but can also add greatly to your expedition experience. They know the area and its culture, where to stop, stay, and eat. Maps are often poor in remote areas, and having a guide/porter can remove much of the stress of navigating.

Portering is a respectable occupation and is as essential to rural areas in Nepal, Pakistan, and India (there are no roads) as truck drivers are in the U.K. and U.S. So use them, but treat them well. Ensure that they are well clothed, have good footwear and insurance if available, and enough food and adequate shelter.

RECRUITING TREKKING PORTERS, GUIDES, AND COOKS

You can recruit guides, porters, horsemen, etc., yourself; large well-run lodge/guest houses should be able to refer you. Always hire in the presence of others not on the trail. Hiring a guide can help you to overcome language barriers and reduce the stress of buying food and hiring porters, especially in countries where local customs dictate the proportion of porters that can be taken from each village.

There are other benefits to hiring staff—taking a cook in Asia, even if you are staying in lodges and tea-houses, can be safer as you have someone who can supervise the cooking and preparation of food.

In popular expedition areas guides, porters, yak, and horsemen assemble at road-head villages, such as Lukla and Pokhara in Nepal and Gilgit, Chitral, or Skurdu in Pakistan, but this is not always the case in less popular areas and you may have to hire lower down the valley. If you are using large numbers of porters, try to distribute employment opportunities and consider using staff from lower villages. In East Africa and Peru the best way to hire porters is at the town from which you depart, but beware of rogue guides and porters.

It is always worth hiring staff that come with recommendations from previous employers, either by word of mouth or by a written reference that they carry. The referee's identity is important, of course. Failing this, you can sometimes employ staff on a provisional basis, but this must be clearly spelled out, which is not easy if there are language problems. The majority of Head Guides and porters have a reputation to maintain and can usually be left to get on with the job of recruitment and organizing the porters. However, sometimes it may be wise to talk directly to the porters—you may find that things are not always as good as the Head Guide portrays. Theft is rare, and a Head Guide will prevent it.

INSURANCE FOR GUIDES AND PORTERS

Independent guides in some countries are registered and sometimes covered by insurance, but this is not always the case. Hiring through a reputable home-based company or registered overseas agency generally means they are insured, but do not simply trust your agent to do every-thing properly.

Clothing appropriate to season and altitude must be provided to porters for protection from cold, rain, and snow.

Getting insurance cover for guides and porters is no longer as difficult as it once was. Insurance information can be obtained at the Porter's Progress offices in Kathmandu. In India, insurance for the headman, cooks and porters can be gained from the Indian Mountaineering Foundation, and in Pakistan by a government-approved insurer.

LOOKING AFTER HEAD GUIDES, TREKKING PORTERS, YAK, AND HORSEMEN

Whatever country you are in, the porter's, guide's, yak, and horsemen's welfare is your responsibility, whether they are booked through an agency or not.

Porters and guides from an agency should come with adequate clothing and equipment; otherwise it's your job to ensure they are adequately supplied. This may include a windproof jacket and pants, a fleece jacket, long johns, suitable footwear, socks, a hat, gloves, and sunglasses. It has become standard practice for experienced climbing porters to supply their own gear as it solves problems with clothing sizes.

To reduce loss, only issue the kit when required and collect it back when it is no longer needed. Alternatively, make the porters responsible for clothing and equipment loaned to them. Some guides may prefer extra money instead of kit, but if money is to be paid, be absolutely sure that they bring their clothing and sunglasses.

Porters at altitude are more at risk from AMS due to their extra exertion, and have a higher tendency to become dehydrated as they sacrifice the weight of extra water. Keep an eye on them and carry extra water and food to give to those that are struggling. Brief the porters on the symptoms of altitude sickness, but don't expect to dislodge deeply held beliefs or superstitions. A

ORGANIZING PORTERS

Have a defined stop-off point during the day. Ensure that the final stop is not too late—you won't have easy access to your bag or tents until the porters arrive.

porter with no previous experience of altitude and with a headache is more likely to believe the cure is to be found in placating the gods of the mountains than in taking Diamox!

Above the tree line porters should have a dedicated shelter, either a room in a lodge or a tent (the mess tent is no good as it is not available until late evening), and a sleeping pad and a blanket (or sleeping bag). They should be provided with food and warm drinks, or cooking equipment and fuel.

Sick or injured porters should be given the same standard of treatment and rescue facilities as you. The person in charge of the porters must let the leader know if a sick porter is about to be paid off. Failure to do this has resulted in many deaths. Sick/injured porters should never be sent down alone, even on popular treks, as the path can rapidly become difficult or impassable. They should be accompanied by someone who speaks their language and understands their problem, along with a letter describing their complaint, and sufficient funds should be provided to cover the cost of rescue and treatment.

HOW MUCH SHOULD GUIDES AND PORTERS BE PAID?

National and local governments sometimes have set rates, but they are often difficult to enforce when competition is high. If you are the only expedition you may find yourself paying much more. You or the agent should pay a fair rate, judged in terms of local pay (ensure your agent is paying enough). Find out in advance what the going rate is; information from recent parties is useful. Underpayment is exploitation, but receiving wages four times greater than a farmer or teacher may also have a destabilizing effect on the local economy.

Equally, some expeditions unknowingly exploit porters. They pay a fair wage, but do not provide insurance or proper clothing. They expect the porter to pay for his own food and lodging, which may amount to at least 50 percent of his daily pay.

Every traveler to a developing country should try to improve the conditions for those involved in their trips.

Agree the amount you will pay for each stage or day, including extras such as the unloaded return journey home, food allowance, clothing, and equipment, and ensure all porters are aware of what they will get. To avoid misunderstandings, write a list and get the guide to sign it. Give porters a basic allowance for each day; a food allowance to cover their costs getting to base camp and the rest when the job is completed. Agreement about what happens if the trip is delayed by bad weather is difficult, but you could offer half-pay. Negotiate how far they will carry each day and for how many days. Do not allow the number of porters to be reduced as the loads get lighter—let it be a perk of the job (but this is a perk that you or the local agents may not be willing or able to afford).

In a wider sense, if you wish to support mountainous peoples and porters make a donation to a charity that is trying to support them (such as www.ippg.net). Giving to individuals may disturb the local economy, expectations, and the recipient's self-worth. Giving to an organization avoids such disturbance and guarantees that your money is put to good use.

HOW MUCH SHOULD PORTERS CARRY?

To us the loads that experienced professional porters carry are unimaginably heavy, but then we weren't brought up carrying our siblings on our backs from the age of three. This does not mean that they do not require care and that heavy loads do not damage their backs. A good Head Guide ensures that porters do not carry too much or too little and that the loads are packed correctly. Some countries have legal limits that range between 15-30kg (33-66lb) maximum, but it varies with the country and the type of trek or expedition, and it is often difficult to enforce these limits. Any load carried may need to be adjusted for:

Using humans to carry equipment is a necessity for many expeditions, because there are no roads.

- The porter's personal kit and food
- Altitude
- Difficulty and duration of the trek
- Trail conditions
- Weather conditions
- The porter's physical ability.

A difficult issue arises when there is a shortage of porters or young, fit porters want to carry double loads to maximise their earnings in a short season. I don't have the answer, but common sense should prevail.

Just looking at the size of the load carried by the porter is no way to assess the weight. Some porters loaded high with sleeping bags and foam sleeping pads may only be carrying 15kg (33lb) while porters carrying the stainless steel cutlery and gas bottle in a small pack may be carrying 40kg (88lb)!

There are few weighing stations, and ground agencies often find their way around the law. Conduct frequent checks on your ground agents to ensure that they are not exploiting porters.

EXPERT TIP

Kit Spencer
summitreck@trekking.
wlink.co.np

"Be ruthless in reducing the amount of gear you take. Freight and excess baggage charges are steep. Import duties can hurt, and once in the country you still have to move it to the mountain. Round barrels are difficult for both porters and yaks. Square barrels take up less space and are easier to carry."

Below are the load criteria for several countries:

LOAD CRITERIA FOR VARIOUS COUNTRIES		
	Employment criteria	Weight (including personal allowance)
Nepal	Judged fit to work by physical appearance alone	Above 4000m (13,123ft): 25kg (55lb) Below 4000m (13,123ft): 30kg (66lb)
Peru	Must produce a certificate from the Ministry of Health to work	Adult male: 25kg (55lb) Adult female or adolescent: 20kg (44lb)
Tanzania	Climbing experience	25kg (55lb)

PACKING PORTER LOADS

Some porters may be experienced at carrying heavy loads, but you must ensure they are packed carefully to protect the load and the porter's welfare.

- Protect the porter's back from sharp corners and edges. Ensure that wax/gas containers do not leak.
- Protect the contents from rain and any knocks.
- Keep the load secure—sacks should be sewn and kitbags and barrels should be locked. A good porter won't resent this, as it puts him beyond suspicion should something go missing.
- Number the loads, keeping a list of porters' names against load numbers and contents, or give porters numbered tickets/tags.
- Pack sufficient food and all other requirements for the approach walk in a small number of loads for easy access. The majority of loads can then be left intact until base camp.

TIPPING

Tips have become expected as a right in many developing countries, but rewarding bad service is not a good idea. Decide what the tip is going to be from the start and make it clear that tips are for good service and not guaranteed; a bonus system could be organized beforehand with the agency. The amount of tip varies, but in Nepal, India, and Pakistan it is usually around 10 percent of the fee and is distributed at the end, often during a celebratory dinner. Tips for guides, cooks, and head porters are normally treated separately, as they have a more permanent basis of employment and more responsibility.

Our head guide in Africa receives a tip for excellent service.

Ensure that the tips are distributed fairly to each person. If you are using a Head Guide you could entrust them with the job, but only after you have agreed what each person is to be paid. Note the porter's names so that if any leave the expedition early you can tip them in person when they leave. Take extra sweaters and good socks that you no longer need as gifts.

Take care that the promise of a tip does not encourage porters to carry more than necessary or undertake unsafe tasks, and only pay bonuses to high altitude porters if they reach the summit.

PACK ANIMALS

In many areas, pack animals are used to carry loads instead of, or in addition to, porters. Traditional pack animals include camels, yaks, reindeer, water buffalo, llama, donkeys, and mules. Pack animals are cheaper than porters, but do not necessarily cover more distance.

Life in developing countries is hard for pack animals; they are often beaten and hobbled (legs tied together) so that they cannot run away. You may find the treatment of animals disturbing, and the locals won't understand your concerns, but there are things you can do:

- Pack equipment carefully and pad sharp edges.
- Ensure the animal has a saddle blanket to reduce sores and padding to keep the load off the spine.
- Ensure the load is evenly balanced.
- Carry enough animal food.
- Refuse to use an animal that looks sick.

MAXIMUM LOADS

Mules and horses can carry up to 60kg (132lb); yaks 40-50kg (88-110lb); donkeys (burros) up to 40kg (88lb); llamas up to 30kg (66lb).

Pack animals do not necessarily cover greater distances

A team of ten sled dogs can carry up to 300kg (661lb) in soft snow.

COPING WITH A DIFFERENT CULTURE

"Travel is fatal to bigotry, prejudice, and narrow-mindedness. Broad, wholesome, and charitable views cannot be acquired by vegetating in one tiny corner of the globe."

—Mark Twain, author

You may feel helpless at times, but realize that you cannot solve the world's problems alone, and by being there you are bringing money and employment to their country. (A leper, Kathmandu.)

Adjusting to the different culture and poverty in the developing world can be difficult. We may not always agree with, or understand, the way people in other countries live their lives, but we are guests and we should not expect them to have the same attitudes or philosophies as Westerners. Neither should we expect their culture to stand still just for our enjoyment. The world is not a theme park and all countries are constantly evolving under influences from around the world, including expeditions.

To better understand the country and the people in it read about its history, society, political structure, environment, art, and religion before you go. Develop basic language skills: forms of greeting, please and thank you, days of the week, time, and numbers. This improves the quality of communication and often breaks down any barriers. If you demonstrate traditional human values of honesty, trust, and friendship and treat the people you meet and employ with kindness, tolerance, and respect, it is returned.

Acquaint yourself with socially acceptable ways of doing things. Something as simple as shaking hands is considered offensive in some countries. If people don't look you in the eye, don't worry—it may be considered rude in their culture.

Avoid displaying bare skin in countries where it is unacceptable for religious or social reasons and dress conservatively. Women especially should cover their arms, legs, and cleavage (and their hair in Muslim countries). You can find out more about worldwide dress codes for women at www.Journeywoman.com.

A lone Western woman may be considered fair game, so prepare yourself mentally for propositions, suggestive comments, or catcalls and ignore them. Be careful of eye contact or even smiling, as it may suggest that you want a person's company. Some women solve this problem by wearing dark glasses and being formal with everyone. In some regions, "respectable" women do not go out alone after dark. It can be very useful to have photos ready of your "husband" and "children" (even if you don't have any), and perhaps consider wearing a ring on your wedding finger, if you do not already.

BARTERING

In developing countries and much of Mediterranean Europe, bartering is expected. Only start to bargain if you intend to buy and pay what you think is a fair price. Bartering should be fun, but common politeness should prevail—for the seller it amounts to a lot more than a casual amusement.

Some people believe they are being scrooges by bartering. The opposite is actually true— traders think you are stupid if you do not.

COPING WITH BEGGING

In the developing world you are much richer than the locals, but handing out money to individuals does not help. Giving sweets, pens, and paper to children is of equal dilemma. Begging often keeps them out of school, sweets rot their teeth, and pens and pencils are often sold at the local market. By giving you are perpetuating the problem, and possibly undermining the parents, who are unable to give their children these things. Many travelers carry writing paper, chalk, pencils, and sharpeners to give to local schools, but give them to the teachers, and only in less popular trekking areas as schools in popular areas are becoming inundated with pens and pencils.

You can help more people if you buy locally made goods, use local services, and eat local food, rather than bringing things with you. Developing countries can be corrupt and money has a habit of finding its way to the richest and most unscrupulous people. Charities like Oxfam and Comic Relief are highly trained and experienced in getting money and resources to the right people in the right places.

Begging—can you make a difference?

IS IT ACCEPTABLE TO TAKE PHOTOGRAPHS?

Joe Simpson in his book *Dark Shadows Falling* (1997) pointed out that just because you have a camera, it does not mean that moral decency disappears. You do not have the right to photograph just because you are on an expedition. However, you will want something to remember and show your friends.

Try not to intrude on private ceremonies, and spend time sitting with the locals to gain their trust before you snap them. Smile and show them the camera to deduce whether they are happy for their photograph to be taken. Don't pay children for photographs, as it can encourage them to beg and miss school. Be cautious when taking photos of bridges, official buildings, people in uniform, airplanes, and airports, as you may end up with your film or digital card confiscated, which happened to me once.

Be patient, polite, and friendly—locals work to different timescales from you. (The author playing Neil Young to the locals in Ladakh.)

Explain why you take photographs and show locals the shots on your digital camera, but only promise to send them a copy if you really intend to.

311

TRAVELING SAFELY

Many travelers worry about tropical illnesses, but the most likely source of medical problem is an accident. However, you also need to protect yourself from crime.

FAKE POLICE

Be suspicious of anyone who asks to see your money or ID. Check their documents first, or ask to be taken to the nearest police station before they search you or your belongings.

THIEVES

Do not create temptation by being ostentatious with your property. Be suspicious if somebody slows you down (i.e., by falling over), and especially if the same person was behind you for several minutes. Use a decoy wallet and spread your money around your luggage and person.

Backpacks can be easily opened, even while you are walking. Leave expensive gear and jewelery at home. Avoid showing how much cash you are carrying; hand over a small amount. Many pick-pockets use an accomplice—often women and/or children—to distract you. If you are robbed do not chase the thief; follow the person who generated the disturbance as they are probably an accomplice. Do not try to stop them unless there are police near by.

Crowded public transport is also a thief's paradise, so protect your pockets and backpack.

Beware of crime (Delhi— a busy town).

DRUGGED FOOD/DRINK

Do not accept food or drink on a bus or train, as it may be drugged.

MONEY CHANGERS

Do not exchange money on the black market; the rates in hotels and banks are good enough. A common way of swindling you is to show you a roll of banknotes, then switch it with another roll of worthless notes while they take your dollars.

TAXIS

Be wary of taxis you hail on the street. Use a reputable taxi service recommended by your hotel. Always bargain the price of a taxi before entering it, even if it has a meter.

RENTING CARS

Carry a mobile phone and an emergency phone number in case your car breaks down. Never pick up hitchhikers. Never get out of your car if another vehicle bumps into it, as thieves sometimes fake accidents. Instead, wait for the police to arrive.

WHEN DRIVING

Keep your luggage hidden and windows closed, especially at traffic lights in busy towns. Do not rely on public telephones. Use the car trunk for luggage and avoid using roof racks, unless the roof is high enough to be out of reach of casual thieves.

ACCOMMODATION

Arrive in daylight so you can see where you are staying and ask to see the room first. Do the door and windows lock properly? Trust your instincts; do not stay anywhere unless you feel comfortable.

Ask that your room number and location be kept private, and never accept a room if the check-in clerk calls out your name or room number. Never open your door to anyone without taking the necessary precautions. Even if your visitor claims to be a member of staff, you should check with the front desk to verify the person. Consider carrying a small, lightweight, portable smoke detector, and a rubber doorstopper that can be easily installed on an inward-opening door. A rape alarm taped between the door and the frame can be a great deterrent.

LOOKING AFTER YOURSELF

"When all the dangerous cliffs are fenced off, all the trees that might fall on people are cut down, all of the insects that bite have been poisoned ... and all of the grizzlies are dead because they are occasionally dangerous, the wilderness will not be made safe. Rather, the safety will have destroyed the wilderness."

—R. Yorke Edwards, conservationist

Before leaving home visit your doctor and obtain extra of any regular medication. Inform all team members that you are taking medication—should you fall ill, there will be no danger from conflicting drugs. Have a dental check-up three months before departure to allow time for any work. You will be exposed to new bugs on a daily basis; depart as healthy as you can and ensure your gut flora are well balanced by eating probiotic yoghurt regularly.

Don't worry about tropical illness, as the most likely source of medical problem is an accident. (Beware of over-loading!)

GLASSES AND CONTACT LENSES

Contact lenses can be used successfully, but as everyone is constrained to wear sunglasses once above the snowline, it is easier to wear sunglasses with prescription lenses. Opticians regularly make them, but it is not always easy to get a pair suitable for mountaineering, i.e., those that have been designed to ensure little light enters from the sides, bottom, or around the nose.

Close-fitting, wraparound style glasses are common, but these don't always come with the option of taking prescription lenses. The easiest and most cost-effective solution is to buy standard mountaineering sunglasses from an outdoor shop and then to have them reglazed by an optician with prescription lenses, darkened with your referred tint, and other flens coatings, such as extra UV filters.

IMMUNIZATION

Check that you are properly vaccinated against polio, tetanus, typhoid, and hepatitis and seek advice on the risks of malaria and other diseases. Mandatory immunizations are much less frequent than they used to be—yellow fever is still required for parts of Africa, South America, and Asia. A certificate of vaccination is often required on entering a country from another country where yellow fever is endemic. This might not be an issue if traveling from the U.K., but if you pass through one of these countries en route, you might not be allowed to continue without a certificate.

Travel companies and embassies may tell you that you don't require vaccination, but be warned; this could mean that no vaccination certificates are required for entry into that country, and not that you don't require immunization.

Vaccinations take time to become fully effective so consult your doctor at least eight weeks before departure. Information on immunization is available from the London School of Hygiene and Tropical Medicine, as well as several commercial companies, including www.masta.org, www.tripprep.com, and www.cdc.org.

MEDICAL ISSUES

(With thanks to Dr J. Duff.) Traveling in developing countries or remote places is risky—it could be days before help or evacuation is possible. Be self-sufficient and do not expect rescue or help. Be quick to spot signs of illness in yourself or your team. Expedition members may be unwilling to admit they are ill for fear of having to go down or return home so encourage an atmosphere of openness and be quick to spot signs of illness in your team. Dr Jim Duff summed it up when he described the symptoms to look for when someone is not feeling well: "grumble, mumble, stumble, tumble."

Serious medical mishaps are rare, but the entire team should have a plan of what to do in case of emergency. Each member should carry a small personal first aid kit, in addition to a more substantial expedition kit, and know how to use it. Carry a small, easy-to-read first aid manual, such as *First Aid and Wilderness Medicine* by Dr Jim Duff 2001. The UIAA Mountain Medical Center also produces a range of excellent information sheets covering issues such as acclimatization and injury, etc., available at www.thebmc.co.uk/ world.htm. Information on high altitude illness and acetazolamide, a drug often used to avoid or treat it's milder symptoms, can be found at www.treksafe.com.

The information below should not be construed as medical advice—consult your doctor before taking any medication. Much of this information on insects, spiders and animals is taken from the excellent travel website www.bugbog.com.

ALTITUDE

Chapter 4 examined how to acclimatize and avoid AMS. This section covers the more serious altitude illnesses of High Altitude Pulmonary Oedema (HAPE) and High Altitude Cerebral Oedema (HACE). Both of these conditions occur more frequently above 3500m (11,483ft) and are brought on by ascending too rapidly. HAPE is twice as common as HACE and is more likely to kill. They may occur together, so if you find one, check for the other. If you feel unwell at altitude, it is altitude sickness until proven otherwise.

HAPE

This is the leakage of fluid into and around the lungs, reducing your ability to absorb oxygen. Having a respiratory infection increases the risk of HAPE, and it is made worse by cold temperatures and exercise.

Symptoms—AMS can precede HAPE. Early symptoms include loss of energy or feeling tired. This proceeds, either rapidly or slowly, to recurrent breathlessness while exercising, through to breathlessness at rest. If there is a cough, it usually starts off dry, becoming bubbly and wet with frothy sputum, which may be bloodstained. Once the disease is advanced, rate of breathing (breaths per minute) and heart rate rise disproportionately at rest, and it is sometimes possible to hear crackles in the lung fields with a stethoscope. There may be a mild fever making it difficult to distinguish HAPE from pneumonia (infection of the lungs), which has sometimes led to fatal misdiagnosis. The lips and nail beds take on a bluish tinge (cyanosis), as the fluid in the lungs prevents oxygen getting into the blood, and unconsciousness occurs.

Treatment—Early recognition and treatment saves lives. If available, give oxygen immediately, either from a bottle or by using a portable hyperbaric chamber (but remember that descent is the definitive treatment and should not be delayed once the patient has recovered sufficiently). Exertion worsens HAPE—carry the patient (they may feel worse lying flat and so may need to be sitting or propped up), assist them, or at least carry their pack. Keep the patient warm and hydrated and give them food or a sugary drink. The drug Nifedipine is used to prevent recurrence during descent.

HACE

HACE is the end-stage of AMS. It can develop very quickly. Death is due to the accumulation of fluid in and around the brain, which increases the pressure within the skull. While AMS and HACE may be linked, do not expect casualties to necessarily exhibit mild symptoms of AMS before presenting with clear symptoms of HACE (or HAPE). Depending on the rate of ascent and any one person's ability to acclimatize, symptoms of HACE and HAPE can present very quickly, for example, in someone who only the evening before appeared quite well.

Symptoms—The patient may complain of a severe headache and may be vomiting, but absence of a headache must not be taken as absence of HACE. If someone is hallucinating near the summit of Mount Kilimanjaro, then headache or not, they are one symptom short of being close to death.

EXPERT TIP

Dr Jim Duff
www.treksafe.com.au

"If someone is very ill at altitude and you can't figure out why, the patient should be re-warmed, rehydrated, re-sugared, and re-oxygenated (using descent, bottled, or hyperbaric means)."

Climbing at altitude is hard work. (Climber on Pik Korzhenevski, Pamirs (7150m/23,458ft).)

315

The earliest sign is lack of physical coordination (clumsy with their hands and unsteady on their feet), and, as the condition progresses, they may not be able to walk at all, and stagger or fall when asked to stand upright (especially when they close their eyes). Mental symptoms can be any or all of the following: confusion, disorientation, irrationality, uncooperativeness, unusually quiet or noisy, and hallucination. Eventually they become sleepy and lethargic before slipping into coma and dying.

Treatment—If available, give oxygen immediately, either from a bottle or by using a portable hyperbaric chamber (but remember that descent is the definitive treatment and should not be delayed once the patient has recovered sufficiently). Dexamethasone should be given and the patient must be carried or assisted to descend. If descent cannot proceed immediately, then oxygen and Dexamethasone must be administered regularly. It should be noted that the clumsiness can persist for some days or weeks even though the person has otherwise recovered.

USE OF DIAMOX

AMS is best prevented by sensible acclimatization, but acetazolamide (Diamox) can be used in an attempt to make the process of acclimatization more comfortable or to minimize the symptoms of AMS. It works by increasing your rate of breathing, thereby improving oxygenation during sleep. It does have side effects, but these are not harmful and include an increased need to pass water, tingling in the fingers and toes, and making carbonated drinks taste flat. It has not been shown to have an effect above 7000m (22,966ft).

The use of acetazolamide should be considered when the ascent is a forced rapid ascent, e.g., flying or driving to very high elevations or when rescue is needed, and in people who have a proven susceptibility to AMS.

Try the medication at home: half of one tablet (125mg) should be taken twice daily for two days, several weeks before a visit to altitude. Assuming no unpleasant side effects are experienced, take the drug in the same dose for three days before staying at 3500m (11,483ft) and thereafter for two or three days until you feel acclimatized (for approximately five days in total). **Note**: Acetazolamide is a sulfonamide medication, and those severely allergic to sulfa medicines should not take it.

SLEEPING PILLS

Everyone has trouble sleeping at high altitude, but most sleeping pills can be dangerous and actually predispose you to altitude sickness, as they depress your respiration, reducing your oxygen uptake. If you are acclimatizing, acetazolamide can help with the periodic breathing that disturbs sleep. Melatonin is a sleep aid that helps many and has no contraindications at altitude. It is also worthwhile spending time and money on a good mattress, staying warm, and relaxed.

PORTABLE ALTITUDE CHAMBER (PAC)

It is unlikely that a lightweight expedition will carry one, but a PAC can be a lifesaver. There are two types available: the PAC, which is cheaper and easier to use, and Certec. Used correctly at 6000m (19,685ft), the pressure inside can be increased to an equivalent altitude of 3250m (10,663ft) (put an altimeter inside the chamber).

Add oxygen (4-6l/min) (1-1.6gall), but over-oxygenation is a problem as CO_2 stimulates the reflex to breath. If the bag can effectively take someone down to a height below that at which the patient was last well, you don't need to add bottled oxygen.

If it is cold add a warm sleeping bag; conversely, if it is hot put the bag in the shade. Include a vomit bag, water bottle, and pillow, and maintain eye contact during treatment. If you have to inflate a PAC on a slope ensure it is anchored and flat. The pressure and air supply is maintained by continuous pumping at a rate of 1 pump per 5 seconds. Treatment varies from half an hour for AMS, 3-4 hours for HACE, and 6–8 hours for HAPE, but can be prolonged indefinitely.

As pressure increases, the patient needs to be warned to equalize their ears. Reduce the pressure slowly. The zip can be opened slowly when the bag starts to collapse. Patients with breathing difficulties may need to have the head-end of the bag elevated, and unconscious patients should be propped on their side.

Once removed from the bag, HACE or HAPE may "rebound." This is unpredictable, but be ready to restart treatment at any time. Check the patient frequently and place them in the bag if they deteriorate. The point about using a PAC is not to cure the casualty, but to ensure they can walk down more quickly and so reach safety sooner.

Igor Gamow designed the first commercial PAC in the late 1980s.

OTHER PROBLEMS AT ALTITUDE

High altitude can also lead to the following conditions:

- **Retinal hemorrhages**—If they interfere with vision, descend.
- **Snow blindness**—Caused by UV light damaging the cornea. Wear eye protection, even if the sky is totally overcast and the day appears dark, as the UV still penetrates and rebounds off the snow. Snow blindness is excruciatingly painful and serious.
- **Sleeplessness**—If you can lie for eight hours at rest with a relaxed mind and body it is supposedly the equivalent of six hours' sleep, so do not become distressed about lack of sleep.
- **Weight loss**—The gastrointestinal system is affected, and on a three- to six-week expedition to altitudes over 3600m (11,811ft) climbers can expect to lose 5–8kg (12-17lb).
- **Dehydration**—Lowered oxygen levels and AMS stimulate urine flow. Everyone's fluid needs vary, so the golden rule is to drink just enough to keep your urine pale and plentiful.
- **Sunburn**—Your skin at altitude is at risk from increased UV, the cold, and

You are often days away from a hospital and medical treatment, so come prepared.

the wind (see chapter 4, page 214).

- **Peripheral oedema** (the swelling of hands and feet)—Symptoms usually diminish after a few days, and they are not an indication of HACE or HAPE.

DIARRHEA

Diarrhea is common in developing countries, but your bowel habits may also change due to other factors, including altitude and dietary changes. However, the passage of three or more loose stools within 24 hours, possibly accompanied by nausea, vomiting, abdominal cramps, or fever, should be considered as diarrhea resulting from an infection.

Diarrhea is most commonly contracted through taking contaminated food or water. Therefore, avoid the following:

- Drinking untreated water—see Purifying water (page 334)
- Ice cubes (alcohol does not provide protection)
- Chang (rice beer, usually made with untreated water)
- Raw vegetables and salad
- Uncooked or rare-fish and meat
- Unpeeled fruit
- Fresh fruit juice
- Cheese
- Ice cream
- If you are sampling locally cooked foods, choose well-cooked hot, spicy meals.

Travelers' diarrhea is best resolved without medication; overuse of anti-diarrhea agents, such as Imodium or Lomotil, can cause "rebound" constipation. However, if the frequency of diarrhea is severe or causing tiredness, then take Imodium to slow it down. Discontinue if symptoms persist beyond forty-eight hours. If they do, you won't want to spend a week of your expedition running to the toilet, and treatment with antibiotics is necessary.

The following tips will help you to decide on treatment:

- As soon as diarrhea occurs use oral rehydration solution (ORS). If this is unavailable, use a flat soft drink or any clean fluid (dirty water can be given via an enema)!
- Bacterial infections are ten times more common than protozoal, so assume that the onset of watery diarrhea is a bacterial infection.
- Protozoal (Giardia, amoeba) diarrhea takes at least a week

to develop from the time of infection and usually comes on slowly. The famous "rotten egg burps" are not an indicator of Giardia as they also occur in bacterial diarrhea.

- For bacterial infection take Ciprofloxacin (500mg twice a day for three days), while for Giardia take Metronidazole (800mg three times a day for four days). Relapse is not uncommon, so be prepared to treat again. If you are not sure of the cause, start with Ciprofloxacin. But if no improvement is seen within twenty-four hours, switch to Metronidazole.
- Nausea and vomiting without diarrhea should not be treated with anti-biotics, but consider an anti-emetic (Buccastem) if vomiting will not stop.
- Uncontrollable dehydration, vomiting that will not stop, high prolonged fever, or severe abdominal pain lasting more than six hours usually require hospital referral so that intravenous fluids can be administered.

None of the above drugs should be given to children, and pregnant women should discuss the risks of adventure travel with a well-informed doctor before departure.

Ensure that food is well-cooked at street stalls.

KHUMBU COUGH

Khumbu Cough is a non-serious, persistent, annoying dry cough, caused by cold air especially above 4,000m (13,123ft). It should not be confused with bronchitis, asthma, pneumonia, or HAPE. Repeated examinations should be made to check for these more serious problems. Warming and humidifying the air, by using a scarf or mask, and sucking cough sweets and throat lozenges may help.

HEARTBURN

This is very common at altitude, probably because you drink a lot more tea than at home, and tannin is abrasive and irritating to the stomach. Heartburn is also a side effect of acclimatization. Drink more herbal tea and take antacids.

TOOTHACHE

Toothache can put an end to your expedition, and visiting a village dentist is frightening. Take care eating hard things like popcorn, and beware of small stones in local rice. Try paracetamol or ibuprofen for a severe toothache and use an antibiotic if swelling or fever occurs. If you are allergic to penicillin, use Erythromycin. Do not put painkillers directly on to gums, as they may burn. Antiseptics containing Benzocaine applied directly to the tooth and gum temporarily relieve pain. Oil of cloves also helps.

Ice cream is particularly dangerous.

The tooth pain may be due to a sinus infection, which puts pressure on the gums from above, and you will need to use antibiotics. Some temporary relief is possible if you can clear the sinuses by inhaling the steam from a bowl of boiling water. Carry a temporary filling kit, but they won't last. If you do have to visit a dentist in a developing country, check that they are using gloves and sterilized modern tools.

319

Keep any cavity clean by washing frequently with saline water. Make a simple pack from cotton wool soaked in oil of cloves, replacing as necessary.

COLDS AND SORE THROATS

Becoming run down is common, and crowded places such as airports, tea-houses, and dusty trails are great places to catch a cold, sore throat, and influenza. These infections (and also diarrhea) are easily spread through touching handrails, doorknobs, and taps, so to reduce the risks pay scrupulous attention to hand washing/drying and use alcohol gel (wipes are not adequate).

Colds and sore throats are easily treated by rest, drink, avoiding alcohol and smoking, and taking medication to relieve the symptoms.

Antibiotics treat secondary bacterial infections and don't cure viral infections, which are common. Obvious signs of bacterial infection are a foul smelling breath on exhalation or coughing up of yellow, green, or rust-coloured sputum. But, if any sputum is coming up from someone's lungs, you must assume it is HAPE, and treat with immediate descent. Once at low altitude, treat with antibiotics if it persists.

Travelers to countries experiencing avian influenza should avoid areas with live poultry.

HEAT EXHAUSTION AND HEAT STROKE

Temperatures at altitude can reach 30°C (86°F). Heat exhaustion is the result of salt and water loss through sweating accompanied by dehydration. Symptoms are profuse sweating, dizziness, and fatigue.

Heat stroke can be fatal when body temperature rises above 40°C (104°F). Sweating may cease, the body is very hot to touch, and headache and mental disturbance are possible. Get the patient out of the sun, fan them, give them water, and cool the body surface with liquid—even snow or ice—followed by evacuation to hospital.

PANIC ATTACKS, ANXIETY, AND DEPRESSION

The technical, psychological, and physical demands of an expedition can be difficult to cope with, and anxiety and poor sleep are common. Lack of privacy and isolation from home can change people's moods daily. Fear of the unknown and worrying about the climb can induce acute panic attacks. The breathlessness, headaches, and dizziness caused by panic attacks can resemble AMS.

All team members should look for changes in moods and be encouraging and supportive while excluding physical problems. At altitude it is worth using the buddy system where you pair off to sleep and look after each other. In my experience admitting that everyone is apprehensive, tired, fed up, cold, or nauseous helps tremendously! Descending to base camp or lower can be a great help, but if the problems persist then a return home may be in order.

Recognize when someone is having a rough day, when they need support, or when all they need is space. (Abby Harrison)

WOMEN'S ISSUES

THE PILL AT ALTITUDE

Oral contraceptives do not affect acclimatization, although there is a theoretical risk (except for progesterone alone) of blood clots forming in the deep veins of the legs, in the lungs, or in the brain during long stays at high altitude.

Actually, very few incidents have been reported, but if you are to spend greater than one week higher than 4500m (14,764ft) you should discuss the risks of continuing to take the oral contraceptive with a doctor who has experience of travel or expedition medicine. Smoking increases the risk of thrombosis at high altitude.

Occasionally women do stop menstruating or their cycle becomes irregular when traveling for extensive periods, so don't worry. If in doubt, get a pregnancy test. Tampons and sanitary towels are unobtainable in parts of Africa, Asia, and South America, and they are scarce luxuries in many former Eastern Bloc countries.

ABOVE 7000M (22,966 FT)

Even when you are fully acclimatised, you should avoid spending more than three or four days above 7000m (22,966ft), as you experience weight loss, worsening appetite, poor sleep, increasing apathy, a sore throat, and a chest infection. If you are going to extreme altitude, you should site the base camp at or below 5000m (16,404ft) in order for proper recovery to take place between sorties to higher elevations.

THINGS THAT BITE, STING, OR SUCK YOUR BLOOD

It is rare to be bitten on an expedition by something that can kill you directly.

INSECTS

Insects can be divided into venomous, which sting in defence, and non-venomous, which bite to feed on your blood.

Venomous stings are painful, red, and can swell up to 30cm (12in) around the sting site. However, in sensitive individuals a whole body reaction (anaphylactic shock) can occur, with redness, hives (itchy, raised skin lumps), and swelling remote from the sting site. These systemic reactions can be life threatening. Those with a known allergy to stings should carry an emergency syringe with 0.1 percent adrenaline and the team should know how to use it.

Biting insects are not generally dangerous because allergic reactions are rare. They do, however, spread diseases such as malaria, yellow fever, Lyme disease, typhus, and encephalitis. For most of us the bites just cause itching.

MOSQUITOES AND MALARIA

Malaria kills 2 million people every year. The malarial parasite cannot survive above 2000m (6562ft), however, if you are below this altitude you should take precautions, even if it is only for a few hours at the airport.

YEAST INFECTIONS

Yeast infections are more likely to recur in warm, moist climates. Wearing loose-fitting cotton underwear and skirts may help. Carry appropriate medication in your first aid kit, as it might not be available.

To reduce your chances of suffering from cystitis, drink lots of water, especially in hotter climates, and carry your own antibiotic treatment.

INSECT REPELLENTS

- **Deet** (Diethyl-toluamide)—Very effective, but unfortunately it is not kind to your skin, so only use it on clothes or nets. Check with your doctor about using Deet, especially if you are pregnant.
- **Mosiguard**—Relatively natural (citrodiol and eucalyptus) and often effective. Start with this and save Deet for heavy duty mosquito attacks.
- **NeemCare Herbal Insect Repellent**—Neem tree oil is burned in India to repel insects. It is available as a general repellent, and testing has shown it to successfully repel the voracious midges that plague the Scottish Highlands, as well as mosquitoes.

Do not rely on anti-malarial drugs alone, but also avoid being bitten. Wear long-sleeved shirts tucked into your pants, and pants into socks, especially in the evenings. Apply repellent to clothing, shoes, tents, mosquito nets, and other gear.

If you decide to chance passing quickly through a malarial area en route, take a course of treatment with you, as developing malaria on a mountain is potentially fatal. Talk to an experienced doctor about your needs and the potential side-effects of anti-malarials. If you suffer fever or flu-like illnesses up to one year after travel, inform your doctor of the possibility of malaria.

TICKS

Ticks are small, blood-feeding parasites found in tall grass and shrubs. They carry many diseases, including Lyme disease, Rocky Mountain Spotted Fever, and encephalitis. Tick bites are common, but serious illnesses are rare—but a circle of pink skin around the bite may indicate infection.

Keep covered in tick-infested areas and search for ticks daily. If they are removed early they have very little effect. Take them off with fine tweezers or a noose of dental floss while avoiding squeezing the body. If the head is left behind, cut it out.

LEECHES

These are blood-sucking worm-like creatures common in wet, warm areas, especially jungles and rainforests in monsoon season. Leeches do not carry diseases but can cause secondary infections if they are not carefully removed. To detach a leech gently pull it off, allow it to bleed, inspect your skin for remaining mouth parts, and then apply antiseptic. Cover the area for several days to prevent scratching, which is the cause of most infections.

SNAKE BITES

You are unlikely to come across snakes at altitude or when the ground is continually frozen, but you may when approaching lower-altitude mountains or walking in the foothills. Very few snake attacks are accidental; like most animals, they only attack if threatened or surprised.

If a snake is within striking distance stay still and move back very slowly. Snakes on the ground hardly ever bite higher than 30cm (12in), so wear stout boots and long, tough pants or gaiters. When walking in snake territory, look down either side of where you tread. Many snakes are nocturnal, so take a light.

If you are bitten, and the snake can be safely killed, bring it into hospital with the victim. In Australia, wounds should not be cleaned unless the snake has been firmly identified, as venom on the skin can help with detection.

Insect repellent gets leeches and ticks off your skin without the risk of separating them from their mouth parts, making it the cleanest means of removal.

DEALING WITH A SNAKE BITE

- Keep the victim calm and get them to hospital.
- Allow the bite to bleed freely for thirty seconds.
- Remove any jewelery or tight-fitting clothing.
- Immobilize/splint the bitten limb and keep it at heart level (gravity-neutral); too high causes venom to travel to the heart, too low causes more swelling.
- The victim should not exercise or take any medicine, alcohol, or food.
- Maintain hydration of the victim and be prepared to give CPR.
- Sucking the venom out of the wound is not normally recommended as the cut may do more damage (through secondary infection) and may increase blood flow, which can accelerate the flow of venom to the heart. (See www.bugbog.com.)

Be careful with snake charmers; although they remove the fangs, snakes re-grow them and they can have venom even after they have been removed.

SPIDERS

There are only several very dangerous spider species in Australia and South America. Take care at night as many spiders are nocturnal; check and shake out bedding, bags, clothes, and shoes. In high risk areas, keep bedding off the floor and walls allowing access only from the supports.

Most spider bites are non-fatal but can be very painful.

Bites from truly poisonous spiders, such as Funnel Webs, should be treated like snakebites—seek medical assistance as soon as possible. If you are bitten, try to kill the insect for identification purposes—do not panic; very few people die of a spider bite. Ice can be applied to the bite site and antihistamines and painkillers may also be used to treat symptoms. Remove any jewelery or tight-fitting clothing.

DOG BITES

Few wild animals attack humans unless cornered, surprised, rabid, or to defend their young or food, but dogs are different. Carry a big stick in towns and cities and use it. Apart from the obvious injuries, a bite can spread infections like tetanus or rabies.

Everyone should be adequately covered against tetanus, but rabies is another matter. If you are bitten, clean the wound with soap or detergent and running water for thirty minutes. Apply antiseptic such as iodine, chlorhexidine, or alcohol. If you suspect the animal has rabies, seek medical assistance immediately. Immunization should be administered within twenty-four-forty-eight hours, and rabies immunoglobulin infiltrated around the wound. Vaccination within days of exposure is 100 percent effective in preventing the progression of the infection to encephalitis. If you have been immunized against rabies prior to being bitten you will still require further doses of vaccine.

Few wild animals attack humans, but dogs can and often do.

Yaks are adapted to the high altitude plateaus of the Himalayas.

LARGE WILD ANIMALS

Never walk closer than 100m (328ft) to wild animals, unless you are forced to do so, and never feed a wild animal as it learns to associate humans with food, and can later become aggressive towards humans if they do not provide it (it can also make them ill).

Yaks—True yaks are rarely used for load carrying, as they have less stamina, are more irritable, and are uncomfortable at low altitudes. Technically, the yaks you may come across are a yak-cow crossbreed (or nak/bull, since the term yak only strictly applies to the male of the species). They are dzopkyo, rather than true yaks. Like all animals they are unpredictable, so stay clear of the front horns and the back end and stay on the uphill side of them. They should never be used to carry a casualty.

Sled dogs—They are bred to attack polar bears, so you should never approach them without their handler. If you must approach, kick them if they come close; they may want to test their dominance by fighting with you. Take care not to be trapped by an approaching sled, and do not feed them.

Wolves and foxes—Only dangerous if they are trapped, threatened, or carry rabies. Avoid animals that seem to lack the normal shyness of wild animals, as this may be a sign of the later stages of rabies.

Buffalo—Rogue male buffalo separated from the herd are among the most dangerous animals you can encounter and are known to charge without warning. Walk close to an armed ranger in danger areas.

BEARS

With the exception of polar bears, larger carnivores are not known to attack parties of four or more people.

Polar bears—Their main habitat is sea ice, from which they hunt seals. In several areas they appear on land, but usually only on the beaches or in bear corridors between beaches. The polar bear is is agile on rough terrain and an excellent swimmer. It is curious, and investigates any strange object, smell, or noise—they are programmed to kill!

Brown or grizzly bear—Found only in the north-west and Alaska in the U.S. and in Alberta, British Columbia, the Yukon, and the Northwest Territories in Canada. They can be dangerous if with their young and disturbed or startled.

Black bear—Smaller relatives of the brown bear, they rarely attack humans but will if they are starving.

There is no 100 percent defence from a bear attack—avoidance is best. Attacks occur for two reasons: defence or hunger. Starving bears are particularly dangerous, as they see you as meat on two legs. When a bear is hungry it may stalk you without displaying anger, but its intent is deadly. Bears standing on their hind legs are probably just curious rather than planning on lunch, so be cool and slowly back off.

Only Greenland residents who are full-time hunters are allowed to hunt polar bears. Report all catches, including struck-and-lost polar bears, to the relevant authorities. (Swiss Guide Lorenz Frutiger practising his aim.)

AVOIDING ATTACK

- Arrange the tents in lines or semi-circles so that you have a free view of approaching bears at a distance of at least 200m (656ft).
- All "smelly" areas should be placed downwind from the sleeping area and do not bring food or anything else with a strong smell into your tent.
- If bear visits are likely, always have a watch schedule.
- Pack food in airtight containers, and store it at least 20m (66ft) from your campsite.
- Avoid areas where bears feed such as fruit groves and streams with fish.
- Make noise, on the move so a bear is not surprised by you.

WHAT TO DO IF A BEAR ATTACKS

If a bear approaches slowly, experts suggest talking calmly and firmly and then backing away. Don't make eye contact with the bear, don't threaten it, and hopefully it will lose interest. If this doesn't work, be aggressive, make a noise, and wave your hands.

If a bear does run at you on its hind legs puffing, teeth chomping and snarling, then try one of the following:

Don't take any chances if a polar bear approaches. (Photo: istockphoto.com)

- It may be a "bluff" charge, which is not uncommon. The bear will veer off or stop at the last moment if you stay still, which is not easy to do! Then slowly back away.
- Run for safety—if you are absolutely sure that you can reach it before the bear! Running may trigger a chase response from an animal that otherwise would not bother.
- Trees are not a good refuge—all bears can climb or shake a tree.
- Water is equally useless. Brown and polar bears are excellent swimmers and don't get hypothermia or drown (unlike you).
- Spray repellent "pepper" spray in its face (this is apparently effective 75 percent of the time). Wind and other factors may reduce the spray's effectiveness, and a bear's tolerance for pain may be such that after just a few seconds they shrug it off and attack again, with even more anger. But it may buy you time.
- Fight back. This may work with a black bear, but don't try it with a polar or grizzly unless you have a weapon.
- When a grizzly or polar bear attacks, roll up in a ball, protect vital organs, and pretend to be dead. Bears with no interest in eating you may roll around on you for a short while, or just depart, but if the bear is hungry this may not be a good choice!

SHOOTING A POLAR BEAR

- Polar bears are good at ducking from flares and the results are often disappointing. One member should use the flare and another should be ready with the gun.

- Shooting a polar bear is a criminal offense if you haven't tried to scare it off first. The decision to shoot a polar bear is a personal one. Whatever you do make the decision quickly! The shotgun should be 15 calibers and not greased. Carry it with you at all times and test fire it occasionally.

- Although it is a difficult thing to do, wait until the bear is within 10–15m (33–9ft) before shooting. The first shot is the most important one. To kill a bear, kneel down; if the bear is broadside aim for the low neck area, if the bear is facing you aim for the low, center neck between the shoulders. If the bear goes down, keep shooting at vital areas until it is still.

A REMOTE EXPEDITION FIRST AID KIT

What to put in a kit depends on your skills, experience, environment, preference, and the purpose of your expedition. Deduce the common diseases, injuries, and logistical and medical support—and adapt your medical kit to fit. Even if you do not know how to use some of the kit, someone else on another expedition might.

There are several items to carry at all times in remote places:

- A roll of zinc oxide tape for taping injuries and bandages
- Ibuprofen, especially useful for musculoskeletal injuries and altitude headaches
- Tin of iodine, used to purify water and as an antiseptic for wounds
- Triangular bandage
- Bandage for simple bandages of wounds
- Compeed or similar bandage, which adds padding to nasty blisters
- Plastic wrap—useful for absolutely everything
- A roll of duct tape for covering blisters.

The remainder of the kit depends on how far from help you are.

Painkillers—Paracetamol, ibuprofen, and codeine phosphate are simple analgesics for mild to moderate pain. Reassurance, warmth, and splinting are also effective.

Severe pain relief is complicated by customs restrictions and delivery methods (severe pain, especially when associated with shock, means medication cannot be taken orally and is best given intravenously, intra-muscularly, or rectally). Stronger painkillers, such as morphine and tramadol, should be discussed with a doctor who may advise on administration of the medication and on how to obtain the correct customs clearance.

Penthrox is an inhaled vapor from a simple plastic device. It is useful for short-term pain relief and when splinting broken bones and reducing dislocations. It is available on prescription from Australia where it is used extensively by mountain rescue teams and the armed forces, etc.

Fracture management—The simplest way of immobilizing a fracture is ingenuity using tape or plastic wrap. Sam splints (a thin core of aluminum alloy sandwiched between two layers of closed-cell foam) are versatile, while a Kendrick Traction Device is lightweight and essential for lower limb fractures, as it reduces internal bleeding and shock.

Antibiotics—Should cover as wide a variety of infections as possible from dental abscess to traveler's diarrhea—co-amoxiclav, ciprofloxacin, metronidazole, and flucloxacillin are all recommended. Note that some people are sensitive to antibiotics.

Lotions and potions—Irritating skin conditions are common, especially in tropical regions. Take an antifungal, an antihistamine, a steroid, and an antibiotic, Clotrimazole, Anthisan, 1 percent hydrocortisone, Fucidin, and an antiseptic spray or liquid. High altitude expeditions should carry dexamethasone, nifedipine, acetazolamide, and, if possible oxygen, and a PHC (see page 317).

Bandages and wound closure—Simple bandages, possibly impregnated with Betadine, are useful, together with dry bandages and crepe bandages. Wounds can be closed with steristrips, sutures, or even superglue (applied across the skin outside the wound, and not inside). Take care not to trap infection on the inside.

Medical emergencies—Carry a salbutamol inhaler, an assortment of syringes and needles, and treatment for anaphylaxis (adrenaline), Piriton, and hydrocortisone. Be sure to know how to give an enema and practice it!

COPING IN AN EMERGENCY
Having a plan of action when things go wrong is essential.

- Stay calm.
- Assess the situation slowly and methodically. Many crises quickly go from bad to worse because of poor decision-making at the start.
- Establish a plan to resolve the situation quickly and efficiently. Do not forget the rest of the team.
- Never hesitate to bring out the emergency equipment, put up a tent or get some warm food in time. You can easily pack the tent again and the food is replaceable!

WHEN TO EVACUATE QUICKLY

HEAD INJURIES—Can result in uncontrolled brain swelling. The duration of unconsciousness tells you roughly the severity of injury, but if bleeding occurs inside the skull, a patient may recover batter become unconscious later. If a person has been unconscious for more than five-ten minutes, has significant facial trauma, a severe headache which is getting worse, altered mental status, a

A climber with frostbite evacuated from Aconcagua on an improvised stretcher.

WARNING

To signal distress stand with both arms raised in a "Y," meaning "yes." A person with only one arm raised and one arm straight down means that all is well; imitating an "N," meaning "no." Other conventional distress signals are six whistling signals (you can whistle for much longer than you can shout), shots, or fires.

!

deteriorating level of consciousness, or uncontrolled ongoing nausea and vomiting, then evacuate.

SPINAL INJURY—Can result in significant localized pain or neck or back tenderness should be presumed to be an unstable injury until proven otherwise. Keep the victim still and gently move them into a neutral position (flat with arms by sides and legs straight) once a primary survey has been completed. If the victim is unconscious and/or vomiting turn them on to their side using a log roll. If evacuation has to be made without medical help, splint the victim's back and neck, place them on a stretcher, and keep horizontal.

OPEN FRACTURES—Where the bone penetrates the skin, it is exposed to contamination. Place pressure bandages to keep the bone ends clean, and any gross deformity should be minimized and splinted if possible. Transport time is critical to reduce the risk of infection. Evacuate quickly to the nearest medical center.

SIGNALLING FOR HELP

All shiny material can act as signal mirrors, and flashing lights always attract attention. Distress signals should be at least 3m (10ft) high, visible, and in contrast with the background. If you can, make a fire, or if you have flares or signal rockets use them, but only when you hear a helicopter or plane.

EXPEDITION COMMUNICATION SYSTEMS

TWO-WAY RADIO SYSTEMS

A two-way radio can be used anywhere and allows more than two people to have a discussion. VHF radios are better for outdoor use than UHF, because VHF radio waves travel twice the distance on open ground. However, UHF waves are better at penetrating solid objects, hence their use in avalanche transceivers.

Two-way radios can operate on different frequencies, although they usually have pre-selected channels so that you need not tune to a particular frequency. Each country allocates radio frequencies to different two-way services. VHF radios are either licensed or license-free. In the United States, the General Mobile Radio Service (GMRS) requires a license and the Family Radio Service (FRS) is free. In the U.K., there are License-Free 446 radios and more powerful Professional Licensed Radios with similar channels.

Radio licensing rules vary from country to country and you should be sure that you have permission to use your VHF radio. License-free radios are fine for occasional use in close contact, e.g., for skiers, but because of the low power, their range is severely limited, sometimes to several hundred meters. They are also fragile, and do not hold their charge well.

When choosing a channel for your team to operate on, privacy and range are your primary concerns. All radios in your group should be set to the same channel before you can communicate.

Signalling "yes" to a helicopter. (Photo: Steve Long.)

POWER

The greater the power the greater the range—a 1-watt radio is enough for 1.5km (0.9 miles) and a 2-watt radio up to 3.5km (2.2 miles). Some radios have high and low power options—high power to transmit long distances. However, the best method to improve the range is to have a taller antenna. Once the maximum range is exceeded, the only way to communicate is through the use of a repeater. A repeater is an intermediate receiver and transmitter located to relay messages to an out of sight location. They are not simple to use, because they receive and transmit on different frequencies. You must transmit on the frequency the repeater listens on and vice versa.

TALKING ON THE RADIO

Keep conversations short and simple. Press the "Push To Talk" (PTT) button to talk and release it to hear. The squelch control regulates speaker hiss when not transmitting, but too far and you will not hear anything. Hold the microphone close to your mouth, but do not shout.

Start with the person you are calling and then, to avoid confusion, introduce yourself twice before you say anything. It is useful to repeat the message back to the sender to ensure you heard it correctly. Use the phonetic alphabet and write things down so that you can get the message across clearly. There are accepted ways of getting an emergency message across e.g., the "May Day" call, but as you are likely to be communicating within your group, it is probably not necessary. Below is a typical radio conversation.

> "Base camp, base camp this is Alun, Alun, over."
> "Alun, Alun, this is base camp, base camp, go ahead."
> "Base camp, base camp, this is Alun ... we are running low on fuel, over."
> "Alun, Alun this is base camp ... fuel will be sent up this evening with Tom, over."
> (If you require an answer say "over"; if you do not say "out.")
> "Base camp, base camp, this is Alun, Tom is bringing fuel this evening, thanks, out."

SATELLITE PHONES AND PAGERS

There is often a significant time delay on satellite phones, so be patient and use voice procedure, as with two-way radios.

There are a number of different satellite phone systems:

Inmarsat—Developed for intercontinental and marine communication. The position and height of geo-stationary satellites, and the fact that radio waves move in straight lines results in "dead ground" in Polar areas—communication is dependent upon the local topography above 70° latitude.

BGAN (Broadband Global Area Network)—A satellite, Internet, and telephone service provided by Inmarsat. The service is currently accessible throughout Europe, Africa, the Middle East, Asia, North and South America.

Two-way radios make life so much easier, even on a lightweight expedition. (Richard Townsend arranging a pick-up in Alaska.)

WARNING

Never try to transmit on any radio-transmitting device if the antenna is not connected, as it may destroy the transmitter.

!

Iridium—Uses orbiting satellites, providing global coverage.

Globalstar—The signal is only routed through more expensive satellites when a ground-based connection cannot be made.

SELECTING A SITE

Establish a line of sight between the antenna and the satellite and get into the open (the closer you are to the Poles the lower the angle of the satellite and the more room required).

SATELLITE PAGERS

Log on to www.iridium.com and send a message to the pager, which almost instantly receives the message.

MOBILE PHONES

Mobile phones work in most places (but rarely in remote mountains) and newer models incorporate GPS type technology so they can be traced to within 100m (328ft).

Some phones may not work in other countries, but you can easily rent one, which is often cheaper to use. Communication between a mobile phone and a satellite phone requires a specific "number" sequence, which differs between brands of phone.

EMERGENCY POSITION INDICATING RADIO BEACON (EPIRB)

EPIRBs are used to alert search and rescue services. They send a distress signal on 406 MHz, which contains a unique code, allowing a registered EPIRB to be matched up to your details and approximate position. If the EPIRB incorporates a GPS it can give a precise position. The beacons also transmit on the 121.5 MHz homing frequency so that Search and Rescue aircraft can accurately locate you when they are near by. Once set off, there is no way of stopping a major rescue or transmitting information about the severity of an emergency. Therefore, use beacons as a last resort in real emergencies only—misuse can carry heavy penalties.

PERSONAL LOCATOR BEACONS (PLB)

Essentially mini EPIRBs, registered to an individual.

TRACKING AND MESSAGING SYSTEMS

Argos is a system of Low Earth Orbiting (LEO) satellite. When switched on, it regularly sends a ground position to a control center. A series of numbers with pre-arranged meanings give the expeditions' location and status. Note that the Argos system is operated on a cost recovery basis.

Satellite phones can make a remote expedition feel less remote, Greenland. (Swiss Guide Lorenz Frutiger.)

POWER SUPPLIES

BATTERIES

Batteries are divided into two types: disposable and rechargeable. Mixing them can cause leaks and a battery inserted the wrong way can explode. For fixed radio or communications equipment consider using a leisure battery, as used in caravans. Some types of larger batteries may require special packaging on airplanes.

Disposable batteries

- Zinc-carbon—cheap and drain quickly.

- Alkaline—Best for emergency devices: inexpensive; temperature range specified down to –20°C (alkaline-manganese batteries can be used down to –30°C); low discharge rate, giving a long shelf life (6-8 years); high capacity, and dim slowly.

- Lithium—Most powerful batteries you can buy—expensive, and the contents are toxic. Designed for high-drain devices like digital cameras. Last for 10+ years when not used and excel in cold weather, but when done, can quit without warning. Can cause LED lamps to overheat and possibly damage the bulb—check suitability to your device. Not to be used for emergency devices.

Rechargeable batteries

Rechargeable batteries lose some of their charge everyday and are poor in cold weather. They are not recommended for emergency devices, as the remaining battery life is difficult to ascertain, and the power quickly drains on storage.

- Alkaline—Some can be recharged ten times, but buy a special charger as this can cause them to explode. Great for high voltage, giving a brighter light in LED torches.

- Nickel-cadmium (NiCad)—Cheap, but superceded by NIMH batteries.

- Nickel metal hydride (NIMH)—New generation of re-chargeable batteries that can be recharged up to 900 times! Two to three times the capacity; more environmentally friendly; do not suffer from memory effect, and cheaper than an equivalent NiCad. Discharge continues, even when not in use, so do not use for emergency devices.

- Lithium ion—Not to be confused with standard lithium batteries. Low weight and high power = suitable to high-drain devices. Their unique drawback is that they age from the time of manufacturing, regardless of whether they are charged. When using a laptop, the battery should be removed and stored in a cool place as it is affected by the laptop's heat.

SOLAR CHARGING

Some portable solar power devices produce enough power to charge a laptop, others are useful only for smaller devices such as cameras (although they can often be connected together to generate more electricity). Solar charging is

---

RECHARGING BATTERIES

For best performance buy a "smart" charger that can discharge the battery before charging it. Always mark rechargeable batteries and charge those that have similar amounts of discharge simultaneously. Try to buy batteries with the highest possible mAh rating.

Solar chargers can charge devices directly or charge the devices' separate battery (see selectsolar.co.uk).

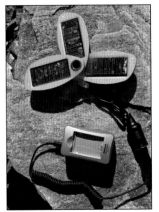

Solio Charger: a great small charger.

CARING FOR SOLAR PANELS

Most are manufactured on robust backing materials, but treat them carefully and protect them from sharp edges and flexing. Ensure that the inter-connecting wiring, plugs and sockets are suitable for cold climates. *See* www.selectsolar.co.uk for further information.

generally slow, and the amount of electricity generated depends on the cell's size/surface, the sun's strength, any cloud/mist/dust obstruction, and the length of exposure.

Solar panels have differing wattage—the higher the rating, the faster the device charges. To find out how much power you need, look at the output rating of the charging adapter on the device. If it doesn't show the wattage, it should show the ratings for amperes (amps) and volts (amperes x volts = watts).

FOOD AND COOKING

"An army marches on its stomach." —Napoleon Bonaparte

Insufficient intake of energy for more than two days, especially when combined with inadequate fluid intake, leads to a serious deterioration in performance. Food keeps you going, maintains warmth, and adds to your enjoyment. You use more energy at altitude and in the cold. You must therefore increase your intake of calories to in excess of 4000 per day. However, gaining calories is not that simple and you will often find it difficult to eat and prepare food. Your stomach is also not as efficient at absorbing nutrients; for every 1000m (3281ft) climbed your basal metabolic rate increases by almost 10 percent and you will develop a craving for specific foods (that you left at home!). A diet high in carbohydrates (65 percent) and lower in fat is best during periods of maximum exertion, because a high fat diet requires more oxygen to burn, which can hinder the process of acclimatization.

On any long expedition, especially to altitude, it is a major challenge to provide meals that you can stomach; snacks that do not freeze keep your fuel levels up and taste nice for weeks at a time. However, a small amount of effort can transform a simple meal into a culinary delight and, the greater the variety of food, the better chance of getting the nutrients your body requires. Make food colorful, interesting, and familiar. Ask expedition members for ideas, finding their likes and dislikes. Try recipes at home—expeditions are not a good time to experiment (expect a recipe for six to serve four after a day's walking or climbing). Develop a menu with a day-by-day ingredient list that turns into a shopping and packing plan. Do not forget drinks to accompany each meal.

Supplementing your diet with multivitamin tablets or mineral supplements is only necessary when eating inadequate, vitamin-deficient, or low-salt food over a period of several weeks; just eat well-balanced food.

Do not create menus around daily energy requirements, as you will probably end up taking rations that are boring and inedible. You may also have to supply food for local employees who may have religious issues or find digestion of some western foods difficult.

If you are taking food with you, balance the cost of transporting it against the cost of buying it in the destination country. Check what food is banned, e.g., it is illegal to take freeze-dried meat into Alaska and do not try to export beef to Nepal and India, or pork to Pakistan!

Meal times should not be just refuelling stops; they are a time to talk and gather together.

Take a large, insulated plastic mug, a plastic (not metal) spoon (a 'spork' is great), and a sharp knife. Tie them together to prevent them becoming lost. Larger pots and stoves, a pressure cooker, and Thermos flasks make life easier, especially at base camp.

LOCAL FOOD

Small villages can have a wide variety of food when they have good road connections, however, we were once the first to arrive at a village after the road was opened and they had not had a delivery for three weeks!

VEGETABLES AND FRESH FRUIT

Choose those that are un-bruised/un-blemished. Most vegetables in developing countries are grown with human feces as fertilizer and fruit is often contaminated by pesticide. If you eat raw fruit or vegetables, wash them in sterilized water, wipe, and peel. Choose cucumbers or tomatoes for salads, and avoid lettuce, unless you can soak it in potassium permanganate for thirty minutes and rinse it.

MEAT

Cook all meat until well done. Dried meats are great for long trips (specialized rations for the mountain usually have to be taken with you). Salami keeps for up to five days in summer.

FISH

Fish and shellfish are hazardous at certain times of the year, even if well cooked. Take local advice about seafood, but if in doubt, avoid it.

Buying food locally helps local economies. The food is also fresher and lasts longer.

Ensure meat is freshly killed and eaten within a few days or take it live with you! Top: Gareth Richardson packing live chickens for later in the trip.

Bottom: Yak meat for sale in China.

MILK, ICE CREAM, AND FRUIT JUICES

Milk should be boiled, unless you are sure it has been pasteurized or sterilized. All bottled drinks are environmentally unfriendly so do not buy them, even water! Bottled drinks with metal caps should be safe, although the necks should be rubbed well before consuming. Avoid bottled waters—they have often been refilled. Cheese is often made from un-pasteurized milk so should only be bought from larger, well-established companies where quality can be assured.

DIFFICULT FOODS TO SOURCE	FOOD USUALLY AVAILABLE IN DEVELOPING COUNTRIES
• Instant "Cup-a-Soups" • Packets of spiced couscous • Bags of drinking chocolate/luxury coffees • Instant white/cheese/bread sauce mixes • Oatcakes/fruit cakes • Tubes of vegetarian herb and mushroom paté • Marmite/Vegemite • Packets of "veggie burger" and "soya mix" • Instant custard • Energy bars • Sandwich and freezer bags	• Powdered fruit drinks • Teabags/dried milk/coffee/Ovaltine • Sliced/tinned/processed cheese • Cream cheese spread • Packet soups (limited flavors) • Quick noodles and egg noodles • Basmati rice • Pasta • Muesli/porridge • Peanut butter • Tinned tuna • Chocolate bars • Dried fruit • Salted nuts • Boiled sweets

SPECIALIST EXPEDITION FOODS

Designed for saving weight, specialist foods are nutritionally and calorifically poor. Add fresh produce to improve them. There are three main types—dehydrated, accelerated freeze-dried, and pre-cooked meals in a bag.

1 **Dried**—Cheapest, but often don't taste or look anything like they do on the packet and need a lot of cooking, except for pre-cooked and dehydrated cereals, rice, and some vegetables. Avoid unless the budget is tight.

2 **Accelerated freeze-dried**—A less harsh preservation technique, maintaining the flavor and texture. Most expedition foods available in the U.S. are freeze-dried. There is a large selection of exotic meals available. Look for "rehydrate in the bag" brands.

3 **Pre-cooked meals in a bag**—Taste better, do not have to be reconstituted, do not dirty the pan, and can be eaten un-heated in an emergency. But they are heavy.

CONVENIENCE ENERGY FOODS

Any food with calories is energy food. Energy bars, gels, and powders for drinks are convenient, light, and compact, but they are expensive, have a strange texture and taste, and do not always provide the correct type of energy (a sudden hit of glucose triggers your insulin response, telling your body to store the energy). Avoid high glucose foods unless it is the end of the day or you need a short-term boost for the final hour. Complex carbohydrates raise blood glucose levels more slowly, so are better consumed during the climb. If you are using high glucose bars or drinks nibble or sip them to prevent a glucose overload and subsequent glucose crash.

PACKING AND STORAGE

Plan the packing so you know where everything is and who has what. Discard unnecessary packaging, but keep the instructions in a separate zip-lock plastic bag. Pack day ration packs; each containing breakfast and dinner, plus lunch and trail mix, and mark with the menu. Pack seven daily rations into a weekly pack and store in sturdy stuff bags such as Ortlieb. Assign each bag a particular week. Store extras, such as drinks, treats, and spices, in separate bags; oils, cheese, butter, and meat in another.

Gareth Richardson eating one of the excellent dry tech meals.

Keep food away from fuel, toiletries, soap, and other smelly items, and keep strong-smelling foods separate, for instance coffee and peppermint tea. Avoid squeeze tubes and tinned food when it is very cold as they freeze solid and thawing them uses valuable fuel.

Protect soft fruit and vegetables by packing in round, plastic containers that can later be used as mixing bowls. Keep fruit and vegetables in a cool place at camp where air can circulate, e.g., hung in a net. Regularly sort them and discard those badly bruised, eating the less damaged fruit immediately. Green vegetables do not keep well—eat as soon as possible.

Some foods change state after exposure to large temperature variations. Olive oil, cheese, butter, some biscuits, and chocolate tend to freeze solid, or melt. Eggs last a week or longer if coated with grease or wrapped in plastic wrap. Keep meat as cool as possible, raising it to allow air circulation, and protecting it from flies with muslin. Use any spare containers for waste.

Pack so you know where everything is!

335

Be scrupulous about cleanliness. Stomach problems are all spread through the fecal/oral route.

HYGIENE

Cover all food and avoid buying uncovered food in villages. Wash your hands with water containing a disinfectant before eating or handling food and always after using the toilet (antibacterial wipes are not enough). Check that employed local cooks wash and rinse their hands and dishes and use clean drying cloths. Carry antibacterial wash or potassium permanganate.

Be meticulous about washing pans—even with minimal fuel or water it is possible to be fastidious. Use your pasta/rice water for the first wash and rinse with clean water or wipe dishes clean with soft paper before they are washed in hot water. Detergent is unnecessary; a green scourer is sufficient.

Dispose of kitchen and human waste well away from cooking areas and water sources. Consider taking solid waste away with you, especially in cold places where grease, etc., doesn't break down easily. Dig a small hole for wastewater, straining food out first. Burn and bury rubbish, which attracts scavengers, but remove cans and bottles for disposal elsewhere.

WATER

Do not drink water without boiling, iodine treatment, or using a reliable filter, unless you are certain it is clean. Tea and coffee, bottled beer, and wine (wipe the tops) are usually safe. Be fastidious; keep your mouth closed in showers and clean your teeth with dry toothpaste.

PURIFICATION

Prior to any purification, let the water stand for one hour to remove suspended particle matter, improving the effectiveness of purification methods and the taste.

One fast method of removing suspended particles is to add ¼ tsp/gal of aluminum sulphate (pickling powder), mix, and wait for five minutes. When the "floc" has settled, remove the clear water by pouring it through a coffee filter.

BOILING

Boil water for several minutes to kill bugs. At higher altitudes, boil water for at least twice as long because of the lower boiling point. Boiling gives water a flat taste—aerate by pouring it from container to container for several minutes. If fuel and time is available, choose boiling.

FILTERS

Filters remove sand, clay, and other matter, as well as organisms, by means of small pore size, membranes, adsorption, exchange resins, and osmosis. They effectively remove protozoa, bacteria, and parasites, but not viruses, unless using an iodine resin that might give protection. However, as contact time is short, filters are not entirely reliable, and so water must also be chemically treated or boiled. However, filters do not require fuel, are fast for small quantities of water, and give a better taste.

Water left in the filter after use can freeze and crack it, rendering it inoperable or, worse, if it goes unnoticed, allowing it to let harmful bugs through. When dealing with a lot of silt the filters can fillup very quickly, making filtration impractically slow and therefore not useful as a group solution. Filters are great at altitude or in countries where the chance of viral infection is minimal and Giardia may be present (as in snow melt).

IODINE

Iodine is effective against viruses, bacteria, and protozoans, except crypto-sporidium cysts, and is available in tablet, liquid, crystal, or resin form. Iodine works well if the risk of cryptosporidium cysts is low.

Iodine's effectiveness depends on the water's temperature, the concentration, and the contact time, which should be one hour with cold water (as it takes much longer to kill Giardia cysts, it may be better to warm the water first). Clean the bottle's neck after iodine is added.

Iodine is easy to carry and fast to use, but leaves a taste. Eliminate it by adding a small amount of powdered vitamin C to the water after treatment is complete (not before!). Iodine has been used safely for periods of several months; however, those with a history of thyroid disease or iodine allergy, the pregnant, and the very young should avoid it.

CHLORINE

When used correctly chlorine destroys most bacteria, but it is less effective against viruses and cysts (e.g., Hepatitis A, Giardia, and amoebic cysts). Organic matter deactivates chlorine and its effectiveness varies with acidity—iodine is safer.

UV PENS

Ultraviolet (UV-C) radiation breaks down the DNA of viruses, bacteria, and cysts, rendering them harmless. It is a fast and safe system for purifying clear water and is used to purify water in hospitals and water-bottling plants. However, discoloration, solids, and debris limit the penetration of UV light. Ensure you use clear, unfrozen water or that it is pre-filtered beforehand. Tests at the University of Maine, U.S., show that two doses of UV light kill 99.99 percent of all harmful bugs. A set of four regular AA alkaline batteries lasts for about 20–40 uses, each for 0.5l (1pt) of water at room temperature (the LED flashes red quickly when the batteries are running low). The UV light tube wears after approximately 5000 uses. It gives an error signal and the unit must be returned to the manufacturer to replace the light tube. UV pens are excellent, but better suited to hut-to-hut tours and short trips.

WATER FROM SNOW AND ICE

Melting snow for water uses energy; to save fuel, dig a hole in a frozen lake or stream or use a "solar water collector." Spread a dark plastic bag over a 0.3m (9ft) hole, packing clean snow over the raised margins. Punch a small hole in the center and place a large pan underneath. The sun heats the dark plastic and water collects in the pan. Alternatively, hang a black stuff sack in the sun.

WARNING

It is important to filter or allow dirty water to settle—too much organic material uses up the iodine.

Melting 10l (21pts) of clean snow makes 1l (2pts) of water. It is more efficient to heat a small amount of water in a pan and slowly add snow to it, but it can draw up water, leaving the pan-base dry. Snow draws salt out of underlying first-year sea ice, resulting in brackish drinking water, whereas salt leeches out of multi-year sea ice, leaving good drinking water.

Bury the water pot (or bottle) overnight under 0.5m (2ft) of snow for insulation. Even if it freezes, it is more efficient to melt ice than snow.

EQUIPMENT AND TECHNIQUES

"Anybody with the will and the drive to climb will do so regardless of what food and equipment they take. They will overcome their own problems and learn from their own experiences."
—Brian Hall, 1984

Much of the equipment is the same for alpine climbing, but if you are going to high altitude or operating in especially cold environments, choose equipment carefully. Equipment routinely fails, so know everything about it; be able to take it apart and re-build it. If you are using a commercial company or agent to organize all/part of the expedition, whatever they say, take your own mug, sleeping mat, possibly a spare stove, nice food, and extra hats and gloves for porters. Some equipment is best bought or hired in the host country, e.g., large cook tents, base camp stoves, cooking utensils, and fuel.

The wind is more problematic than the temperature. If you are going to the Polar Regions—even in the summertime—prepare for temperatures as low as –30°C (–22°F) combined with strong winds.

CLOTHING AND FOOTWEAR

Technical mountaineering equipment should be balanced between the close-fitting clothing and boots that make climbing easier and the need to stay warm in cold conditions. Plastic boots have a liner that can be removed and dried, so are better for multi-day trips. On skiing expeditions, a boot that is soft and large enough to flex the toes with each stride helps to avoid frostbite.

In remote mountains the temperatures often remain low, even during the day—add a shadowy mountain face and you require extra layers. Loose-fitting outer layers over several light- to medium-weight base layers are usually sufficient for pulk-hauling skiing expeditions. Whether climbing or skiing, wear just enough to stay dry and comfortable when moving. Avoid starting out warm, then sweating. When taking a break or standing still, immediately put on layers of insulated clothing before you get cold.

Rain is unlikely to be an issue at altitude or in the Polar Regions, so consider windproof clothing, rather than a waterproof. Choose black items to aid heat absorption from the sun. Avoid open-face fabrics (fleece) as outerwear, as frost build-up causes problems. Pay particular attention to extremities; exposed skin can freeze in minutes.

Climbers attempting peaks such as Vinson in Antarctica require a one-piece down suit or a down jacket and down skipants, in addition to all the accoutrements necessary for ultra cold weather climbing. A neoprene mask that covers the mouth and nose, and wraps around the neck (commonly worn by skiers and snowboarders) is essential wear in all Polar Regions and on peaks of over 7000m (22,966ft). Avoid sunburn by wearing a neckerchief, using it over the mouth and nose on hot glaciers.

SLEEPING BAGS FOR THE COLD

It may sound obvious, but to be comfortable a sleeping bag should cope with temperatures below what you are expecting. Take a close-fitting, mummy-style bag with a hood, a baffle over the zip, and a draft collar at the neck (see chapter 1, page 17). You have three options and each has advantages and disadvantages in terms of price, weight, and volume:

- An expedition bag, e.g., Mountain Equipment range.
- A three-season bag augmented with a vapor barrier liner, or a GORE-TEX bivvy bag that gives an extra operating range of 5–10°C (41–50°F).
- Two smaller bags—combine a two-season down bag with a two- or three-season synthetic bag. Ensure the extra bag fits over the down bag without compressing it. The synthetic bag protects the inner down bag from damp. This does, however, increase weight and bulk. The actual combination you use depends ultimately on how cold it is.

The wind is often more of a problem than the cold.

On prolonged trips in very cold places, perspiration from your body condenses and ice crystals slowly build up inside the bag's insulation, wetting the bag and reducing its loft. It is important, therefore, that you wear as few clothes as possible to generate heat inside your sleeping bag, which drives the moisture out. Whenever you can, drape your bag in the sun to dry it out, but be sure to tie it to one of the guy lines to ensure it doesn't blow away in a sudden wind gust (do this even when it is below freezing as moisture is removed by sublimation of the ice).

VAPOR BARRIER LINERS (VBL)

A VBL is an impermeable layer designed to trap moisture close to the skin, shutting down the body's sweating response. This prevents evaporative heat loss, slows dehydration, and keeps moisture out of your insulation layer. They are useful on extremely cold dry trips, when it is difficult to dry equipment. They should not be used directly against the skin, as evaporation at the skin surface cools you down.

In remote mountains, temperatures often stay very low, even during the day. (Coping with the cold in Greenland.)

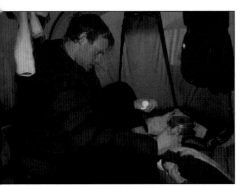

Look after your feet in cold places (Gareth Richardson).

FOR SLEEPING BAGS

Sleeping in a VBL is miserable, as you end up being damp, but as your bag remains dry, you are at least warm and damp, rather than dry and cold. An added disadvantage is that you cannot dry clothes next to your body.

FOR YOUR FEET

With plastic boots, the closed cell foam liner and plastic shell prevents water from escaping; therefore, above 7000m (22,966ft) and in polar climates VBLs can be very useful. The drawback is that many purpose-built socks are slippery and tempt you to tie your boots tighter, which restricts blood flow. You must wear a lightweight sock inside them, yet wet socks next to your skin will increase your chances of blisters, trench foot, and infection. It is therefore important to use foot powder and to rub in antiperspirant gel each morning (this also works equally well for non-VBL sock users). RBH Designs have designed a thick and thin fleece with a VBL in between, which seems to overcome these problems (www.rbhdesigns.com). They are worn without liner or outer socks and removed at the end of the day to dry. They have proved comfortable and versatile, with the only downside being the lack of stretch.

GORE-TEX SOCKS

GORE-TEX socks are very useful in continually damp conditions, such as the Rwenzori, but not much use in dry cold, as they let moisture pass to the insulating layers.

LIVING ON EXPEDITIONS

Most mountain areas, with a few exceptions like Borneo, have well-defined trails through villages and across mountain passes—even at high altitudes there are often isolated settlements. Once you are away from the towns, you can camp, but on many popular trekking trails, especially in Nepal, accommodation is readily available in teahouses. The standard of food and hygiene varies tremendously, so pay attention to personal hygiene and bring your own mug and toilet paper. Cooking meals is slow in teahouses, so get up early, have a hot drink ("bed" tea is common in Nepal) and walk for several hours before stopping for breakfast. Carry gear for all eventualities (it does rain, it does get cold, and it does get dark!). You rarely need ice axes and crampons during a trek, but some passes can be tricky when it is snowy or icy.

BASE CAMP

The benefit of a pleasant base camp, whatever the size of your expedition, should not be underestimated. It should be a place to relax, recuperate, and celebrate special occasions, but it should not be so comfortable that you don't want to leave. A mess tent or a large sheet of polythene to make a communal area can be invaluable, especially if it is high enough to stand up in, with a lightweight table and chairs.

A pleasant base camp can make or break an expedition (Ladakh).

Fortunately for mountaineers and trekkers there are still only several roads into some remote mountain areas. (Trekking into Aconcagua, the Argentinian Andes.)

A mess cooking tent is highly desirable at a base camp.

If there are enough of you, use a cooking tent, which can be combined with the mess tent. However, keep fuel away from the tents and consider carrying a fire blanket or a sand bucket. Ensure stoves are well ventilated—smoke aggravates everyone's eyes, noses, and throats, which will already be suffering because of the dry mountain air.

BATHROOMS

Human waste does not degrade easily at altitude or low temperatures. Erect a bathroom tent with a deep trench 50m (164ft) away from the cook tent and all water sources.

If you are a large team, dig a hole 2–3m (7–10ft) deep, which should last several months. Carry a bucket and a toilet seat if you want luxury and you are at base camp for extended periods. Cover the deposit each time with earth or ash from a fire; you can "flame" it periodically by pouring in kerosene and igniting. Do not pour disinfectant down the hole as it kills the bacteria necessary for decomposition. Have a bin for the disposal of toilet paper and sanitary towels (you can carry it out later), and remember bears and other scavengers are attracted by smells.

Asian cooks and porters will not often use a Western toilet.

In popular trekking areas it might be regulation to carry all rubbish and bathroom waste away with you in a leak-proof receptacle (e.g. any North American National Park, the Antarctic, and the Sagamartha National Park, Nepal).

CAMPING ON SNOW

Three-season tents do not stand up to high winds or the weight of snow build-up, and they may be too ventilated to provide much shelter from a storm.

Four-season tents usually have stronger poles, often snow avalances, and a roofline that sheds snow. However, they are heavy, and for a short stay in sheltered mild winter conditions a three-season tent may be enough.

Camping on snow is the ultimate "no trace" campsite—a good storm after you have left and all signs of your camp disappear (unless you have left a mess, which will be revealed when the snow melts). (Camp 3 on Pik Korshenyevskya, Pamirs.)

Freestanding geodesic dome tents, with the poles running through the inner, are better than tunnel tents, as they shed snow well and provide efficient interior space. Consider a single skin, center-poled, pyramid tent without a floor, e.g., Mountain Hardwear "Kiva," but they should be collapsed. They also require staking out and can be cold. Seal it by using a space blanket as flooring and covering the edges with snow.

When choosing a tent, remember that you require lots of internal space for all your bulky gear, and if you get snowed in, you may need to stay in the tent for a long time. Bring extra poles and pole splints for any pole breaks. Regular tent pegs are useless unless buried horizontally. For overnight camping use ice axes, skis, and trekking poles to guy the tent. For longer stays, use snow stakes and sections of bamboo, or bury stuff sacks full of snow. Use Abolokov threads or ice screws on bare ice.

Condensation is a problem when camping on snow. During the night moisture from expired breath hits the inner tent wall and condenses into ice. These fine particles can cover you and your gear. Brush them off the tent in the morning and sweep them outside. A frost liner hung inside the tent allows moisture to pass through, providing a layer between you and the ice, but I have never used one. Venting the tent decreases ice build up, but makes for a colder night. A small brush is essential to clear snow off your clothes, gear, and boots before getting into the tent, while a sponge cleans up spills and frozen condensation that has melted.

A PERFECT CAMP SITE

The perfect site is sheltered from the wind and avalanches, avoids low-lying areas where cold air settles, and faces south, meaning longer days and more direct sunlight. In the Polar Regions the sun is very low and dips behind mountains, flinging you from −20°C (−4°F) outside, yet warm inside the tent, to −20°C (−4°F) both inside and outside.

A lake or stream prevents you having to melt snow. If the site is on a glacier, probe the entire area for crevasses while still roped up. Establish paths around the tents to be used by everyone. Dig or stamp out a tent platform (leave your snowshoes or skis on to do this), otherwise the melting and refreezing of snow under your mattress is uncomfortable as a trough slowly forms. In warm conditions, a tent left in one place for days ends up on a pedestal and has to be moved.

If you cannot find shelter, dig a hole 1m (3ft) deep to reduce wind impact. Build a thick wall as high as the tent and as far away from it as it is high—a teardrop shape reduces the amount of snowdrift over the wall. Pulks are a quick means of building (or forming the foundations) of a wall, which also stops them from blowing away. An alternative method is to build snow mounds up the tent sides, but someone should push from inside the tent to prevent it collapsing and the inner and outer meeting. As the snow thaws and

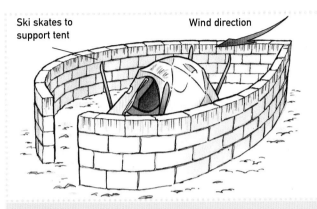

FIGURE 1 Build a wall to protect your tent from the winter winds.

refreezes, you get a hybrid tent-snow shelter, which is better insulated than the tent alone. Even with a wall, during a storm you still have to shovel (keep it handy) wind-blown snow away from the tent to prevent the poles breaking or leading to asphyxiation. If your tent starts to disappear, move it!

Dig a deep, rectangular pit in the tent porch to make it easier to take boots off, store gear, and possibly cook in. When you leave the tent mark it with a large wand and take a GPS waypoint to find it.

A COMMUNAL TENT

Use a Kiva-type tent to create a roomy mess/kitchen tent. Mark out a circle using a ski or rope. Dig down approximately one meter, pile the excavated snow around the perimeter, and pack it down. This provides at least a 2m (7ft) deep area protected from the wind. Carve out a table for the stove, seats and benches. Erect your tent over the hole (see Fig. 2).

FIGURE 2 A communal cook tent is great for a long camp in one place. (Mountain Hardwear Kiva, ski touring trip, Greenland.)

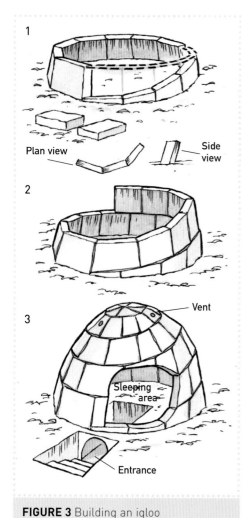

Plan view

Side view

Vent

Sleeping area

Entrance

FIGURE 3 Building an igloo

BUILDING AN IGLOO

Snow holes or igloos are much quieter places in a storm, but it takes around two hours to build one (see Fig. 3). Draw a circle 2m (7ft) across and pack the snow. Set up a quarry area close to the circle, dig for the best snow, and don't underestimate the number of blocks required.

Cut blocks 75cm (30in) by 30cm (12in)—bigger blocks do not necessarily make a stronger igloo due to the extra weight. Create a circular ramp with a snow saw (see Fig. 3.1). Start the second row by placing the first block on the ramp's lowest point (see Fig. 3.2).

Each round of blocks is laid ensuring the slope of the top block points to the center. Each new block is supported both by the blocks beneath and its neighbor to one side (this allows you to lean each row of blocks inwards a little further).

One group member should stay inside to support and trim each block while the other members cut, carry, and place them. Lay the remainder close to horizontal overhead. Finally, excavate into the ground, digging a tunnel under the wall to create an entrance (see Fig. 3.3). Fill the cracks with snow to create a very strong structure. Once it's completed, dig the floor out at an outward angle to increase the floor area.

MARKER WANDS

While GPS does well on a featureless glacier, you are reliant upon screen legibility in poor light and the batteries operating in the cold. Marker wands guide you confidently and quickly through any intricate maze of crevasses. They are also essential for marking tents, toilets, food stores, crevasses, and the route back in poor visibility, after a storm, or in a crevassed area. Bamboo sticks with a fluorescent tape are best. Take 20–200, depending on your trip. Mark danger areas with two wands in an X shape. If you are in a popular area, mark them with your initials to ensure you follow your wands. Use them to mark the line of ascent across a glacier, ensuring they are no more than a rope-length apart, which allows you to find the next pole safely before leaving the last one.

BATHROOMS ON SNOW

Lack of sunlight and cold temperatures slow down the decomposition of fecal material. Each person should therefore make a personal hole as needed. You can dig a wall for privacy around a group toilet area, using a marker wand to indicate when it is occupied.

Kick snow over urine stains to prevent "yellow snow" effect (urination on snow is forbidden in Antarctica as the stains remain on the ice for a very long time, given it never melts and there is virtually no precipitation to cover it. Along with feces it has to be "packed out."

Toilet paper is a problem, so try burning in a tin can or packing it out. On a glacier find a safe crevasse to situate the toilet. Take care when gathering snow for water if camping in an area that has been used before.

STAYING WARM AND DRY

Change into dry socks and layers as soon as camp is set up. Insulated booties with closed-cell foam insoles keep your feet warmer than boots. Carry a small closed-cell foam pad to sit on and don't use your sleeping mat outside as it gets wet. A large flask keeps water/soup hot, and insulated mugs heat drinks for longer.

Limit alcohol intake, as it thins your blood and inhibits the body's ability to warm itself. Avoid caffeinated drinks before bed, as, with 10+ hours in the tent, you are likely to need to urinate. Do not wait to urinate until morning, as your body wastes energy keeping the extra fluid warm and you won't get back to sleep. You can get out and back in to a tent surprisingly quickly, but a pee bottle is easier (keep it in your bag for warmth and to stop it freezing).

DRYING BOOTS

To help you to put frozen boots on the next morning, open them as wide as possible when you remove them. Put them in a breathable stuff sack and place a bottle of warm water inside them (clear Nalgene bottles are best for hot water) or put the inners inside your sleeping bag. Remove the insoles and put them on your chest. You could also put the inners in a breathable sack and place them between your sleeping bag and pad as a headrest.

SLEEPING

Put your sleeping mat and bag immediately into the tent so it can expand. Snack before bed so that your body has enough fuel to generate heat during the night and get warm by exercising for several minutes before getting into the bag.

Avoid wearing layers (unless your sleeping bag is poor), as they hold body heat close, rather than warming up the inside of the sleeping bag, leaving hands and feet cold. If your feet are cold, raise them to allow warm air to flow to them. Put a bottle of warm water in the foot of your sleeping bag an hour before you get in to warm your feet. Use two sleeping pads on snow, as insulation from the ground is more important than insulation from the cold air.

Keep at least one water bottle in or under the sleeping bag. Put others that don't fit in your extra wool socks, upside down to prevent the top freezing.

The author wearing full protective snow gear.

John Russel
www.greenlandexpedition.com

"Pitched well, lightweight single-skin pyramid tents with a single center pole (even a trekking pole), are surprisingly robust and provide a lot of space. On snow, dig a pit with seats to create a spacious communal tent and cooking area. It is good for morale, and will also cut down on condensation in your sleeping tent."

Dropping equipment, Spizbergen. (Photo: Steve Long.)

Sleep with your face outside the bag to reduce moisture build-up. The sleeping bag neck draw cord can be claustrophobic, so use a neck scarf. It is normal in cold conditions to frequently change position and allow circulation to compressed tissues. If you wake up cold, eat some food; have a Thermos of hot drink in your tent and exercise.

IN THE MORNING

Vent your tent as much as possible at night to reduce condensation on the inside of the tent walls (the few degrees of warmth trapped by a sealed up tent increase condensation, causing wet clothes). Stay in the sleeping bag as long as possible while cooking breakfast, packing, etc. If you have left your boots outside your sleeping bag, remove the insoles and warm them in your sleeping bag or next to your body.

PECULIARITIES

There are some techniques unique to expeditions that are not usually required in general climbing.

AIRDROPS

It may help to airdrop supplies into position, thus avoiding the need to haul or carry large loads. In some Polar Regions, e.g., Greenland National Park, advance airdropping of supplies is not permitted.

Pick the drop zone carefully to ensure it is suitable for the aircraft and for you to locate it. A team member on the plane/helicopter can mark the spot with a GPS. If you are to receive an airdrop, simply trample or mark a cross on the ground at the drop zone a minimum of 100m (328ft) from campsites.

Pack supplies so that everything survives the impact. Use 50l (11gal) plastic drums painted brightly for easy location. Fill each barrel with items of similar density and hardness; for example, glass and tins do not mix. Individually bubble wrap every tin and packet and triple bag every portion of food.

SEA ICE

Sea ice forms from seawater when the temperature drops below −1.8°C (35.24°F) for a long time. There isn't room for salt molecules to collect in its close-knit structure and they are rejected back into the sea as the ice forms.

"Land-fast" ice, or simply "fast ice," is flat sea ice that has frozen along coasts extending out from land into sea. "Drift" ice floats on the water's surface. When packed together in large masses, it is called "pack" ice, which may freely float or be blocked by "fast" ice while drifting past. Icebergs form out of chunks of fresh water from ice shelves or glaciers that have "calved" into the sea.

The actual coastline may be tens of miles inland from the ice shelf

(glacier's snout), which can drop down quite steeply to meet the sea ice. Be careful in poor visibility when you are close to the shelf edge. Furthermore, the sea's tidal movement creates cracks between the sea ice and the ice shelf—always consider them as fresh.

Interpreting sea ice quality is difficult—treat all of it with suspicion, particularly when buried under fresh snow. However, surface ice is often supported by the water and can take more weight than you would imagine. In general, opaque, "white" ice that resists several hard hits is weight bearing; black ice is highly dangerous, as is sea ice thinner than 75cm (30in). When walking, beware that cracks and seals' breathing holes may be covered with snow. Wind and sea currents constantly affect sea ice and it is important that you check with the locals about the condition before wandering on to it.

Sea ice occupies about 7 percent of the world's oceans.

SLED HAULING

Sleds (pulks) vary from a child's plastic sled to purpose-built fibreglass models. Inexpensive plastic sleds, made from very thin polythene, flex or crack.

Purpose-built pulks around 1m–2.6m (3–8.5ft) are available, dependent upon the trip length, the number of crevasses, and the snow consistency. In soft snow it should be 2m (6.5ft) or longer to prevent it from sinking and to make crossing crevasses safer. The bottom should be ridged (on plastic models) or have runners (on more expensive composites) to maintain a straight line and prevent sideways sliding while traversing slopes. However, they have limited effect on hard snow or ice. In this situation, crampons and a course directly perpendicular to the slope are the best strategy.

There are several excellent companies that supply sledges—Snowsled Ltd. (U.K.), Wilderness Engineering (U.S.), and Fjellpulken (Norway).

PROTECTION AND PACKING

Keep heavyweight items at the bottom of the sled to stop it tipping over. Purpose-built covers can have a zip along the length of the sledge. You can also use watertight canoe gear bags for items inside the sledge. In wet areas, be sure to empty any standing water in the bottom of the sledge every day. If it rains at night, tip the sled over to prevent water from entering. You can secure the load with a zigzag of rope or bungee cord, but with the latter you must have the right length to create the correct tension. Leaving with a poorly packed sled only means time consuming problems later.

Be fastidious about protecting the base of the sled, even when loading them on to helicopters.

EXPERT TIP

Shaun Hutson
shaun@sphutson.com

"Just because you have had very cold feet and hands in oxygen-rich lower altitudes without frostbite, don't think you can apply the same approach to higher altitudes. Frostbite is often the result of ignoring a bit of the body."

TOWING SYSTEMS

Ropes are lighter and fine on flat surfaces, whereas poles (traces) give you more control when traveling downhill and guiding the sled through difficult sections. Poles can be made of bamboo, aluminum, or fiberglass.

A sled harness distributes the strain between the waist, chest, and shoulders; a waist belt will not do, but a comfortable, well-padded, large volume backpack with a chest strap is almost as good. Clip directly into the strap that ascends over your shoulder, just above the waist belt or have purpose-made loops sewn in. Alternatively, thread the rope around the backpack, just above the waist belt. Create an X in the ropes by tying them together one-third of the way from the sled to maintain a stable pull. Do not attach the haul line to loops on the back of the backpack, as this tends to hunch the hauler over. Bungee cord can stop the sled from jerking.

PULLING THE SLED

Your legs are strongest, so use them. Leaning forward enables you to overcome many small obstructions. Placing weight in your backpack increases your effective hauling mass. In dangerous terrain and crevassed areas, keep close to your partner, but not so close that you would fall into the same crevasse. Use a rope and carry rescue gear. Attach the sled to the trailing rope via a prusik to prevent it following the skier into the crevasse. The last person can't do this and is, therefore, more vulnerable to being hit by a sled should they fall. In serious terrain lighten their sled or eliminate it.

To keep the sled tracking on hard snow attach steel fins to the base with pop riveting or butterfly bolts. On a steep slope with deep snow, make a rising traverse, which is less strenuous.

Descend steep slopes in a straight line with the sled in front if possible. Alternatively, fit a rope brake under the front of the pulk for descent of long or steep slopes. When sideslipping, use someone at the back to prevent the sled running too far forward or down the slope. Attach a rope from the rear of the sled to the person behind, as for crevassed terrain. If you need two people to pull, one behind the other works better.

KITES AND SAILS

These range from ex-military parachutes to purpose-made, highly sophisticated adjustable kites. Designed for hauling loads, they work best when the wind direction is blowing towards where you wish to go. In reality, some designs will work up to 45 degrees off the wind direction. Easy to raise in light winds they are usually attached to the hauler's harness. Under the right conditions, they can give very fast traveling times.

The use of kites has become popular, but the risk of injury and accident are higher than with standard hauling. Spider (South Wales, U.K.) are expedition-proven providers of kite/parafoil traction systems. Others include Parawing from Wolf Beringer of Germany and Skiseil of Norway.

FIXED LINES

Fixed lines allow mountaineers to cross or ascend dangerous or steep terrain quickly. Pre-stretched rope is better than dynamic rope for avoiding stretch, and kernmantle is better than hawser-laid. Not all ascenders perform well on all rope types. The grip is affected by the rope diameter, the way it is made (hawser laid or kernmantle), the material (nylon or polypropelene), and how icy it is.

Anchors for fixed ropes use the same principles as for winter/summer climbing (chapter 2, page 134). Mark the anchor points with wands to locate them after heavy snowfall and protect the rope from abrasion on edges. Place intermediate anchors to permit more climbers to use the line and lessen the weight of rope on one anchor (there should only be one climber between each fixed section). Positioning of anchor points depends on the terrain, but it is essential they are placed at a change in direction and at the top of any difficulties. Always bury anchors and check them frequently. There should be some slack between points to reduce vector forces, allow movement of the climber and minimize side-loading of the anchor. For fixed ropes on the flat (crevassed ground) you need two cows' tails (for ascending a steeper fixed line, see Fig. 5). Old or damaged lines should be inspected for damage.

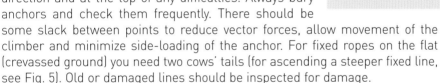

Fixed anchor

FIGURE 4
Ascending fixed lines. Lark's foot on ascender and a sling and crab on to your harness. If you are carrying a heavy backpack on steep sections, it may be useful to pass the slings through a chest harness. To descend, use a figure of eight descender or reverse going up.

RIVER CROSSING

It is best to find a bridge or camp until the river subsides. The next best thing is to carry an inflatable raft, or at least an inner tube. Rivers fed by glacial melt water drop during the night but may be impassable by midday. Even a shin-deep fast flowing river can build up in front of you as you are crossing—wait for morning, after the cool night has reduced the river flow, or for a suitable time after a storm.

Use the map to gauge where best to cross. The river may divide around islands and the widest part is usually the shallowest—upstream there may be less water flowing into the main river. Cross below any dangers, such as waterfalls, and beware of bends, as the outside banks can be undercut and the water deeper and faster.

Unbuckle backpacks to make them more buoyant in preparation for a potential ducking or remove and bring them across on a rope. It may be possible to strip off and wear your waterproofs to keep your clothes dry, but keep boots on as loosing your footing is dangerous.

If you are crossing alone, use a pole or stick. However, it is safer to cross as a team. Use the strongest person to break the flow away from the weaker members and to support the stronger person. Keep the strongest and biggest people at the wedge apex to create an eddy behind them.

Ascending fixed lines on Mramornaya Stena, Pamirs. (Climber: Petur Adalsteinson.)

349

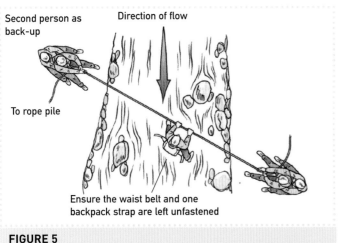

Crossing swollen rivers is dangerous (Nepal).

FIGURE 5
Find a bridge, rather than take the risk of crossing a river.

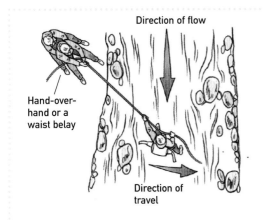

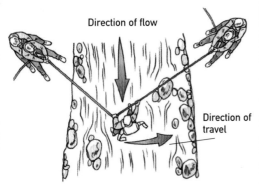

FIGURE 6 Ropes and water do not mix.

USING A ROPE

Ropes and water do not mix, and the security offered by a rope is often illusory. Never fasten someone into a rope, as they may be dragged under the water and you may not be able to bring them to the bank. If the planning for the trip reveals the potential for river crossing, practice beforehand and ensure you are equipped with a throw-line.

If the crossing is non-serious, but a slip will get you wet then place a tensioned hand line angled across the river to help you (see Fig. 5).

FROZEN RIVERS

Like avalanches, ice can give way under the first person, or the last, or not at all, so they are best avoided. If you must cross, it is safer in the morning. As a rough guide, 2.5cm (1in) of black or white ice probably holds you up if you lie down and crawl, 5cm (2in) probably holds you up walking, while 15cm (6in) is safe.

Spread the group out or cross one at a time. The lead person should probe with a ski pole. Poke the ice fairly hard. If the probe goes through, turn back and find another route. Solid ice produces a different sound (tick) versus thin ice over an air pocket (tock). Release all backpack straps to allow a rapid jettison and keep a knife handy.

Should you go through, extend your arms forward over the ice, kick your legs up to get the body level in the water, and work forward on to the ice by kicking and carefully pulling with the arms. Use a knife to pull on. If the ice breaks keep doing it until firm ice is reached. After pulling the entire body on to firm ice, carefully roll or edge toward shore, distributing body weight as widely as possible.

Throw a rope to the person who fell through. Do not approach the hole. Lie down and extend objects towards the hole using skis poles or anything you can grab hold of. Erect a tent and warm and dry the person.

ENVIRONMENTAL CONCERNS

"They paved paradise and put up a parking lot..."
—Joni Mitchell, singer/songwriter

The group wedge system needs the strongest and biggest people at the wedge apex to create an eddy behind them. (Crossing a river in Ladakh.)

Most of the world's mountains are in special places. Rubbish is not particularly environmentally damaging in the high mountains and the only other people who see it are other mountaineers, but how many of us like climbing through a rubbish heap? Mountains require special treatment in order to preserve the qualities that make them attractive to us. Learn to tread lightly, take responsibility for your actions, and think of the overall good of the area, and those who follow you. Minimum-impact techniques take extra time, effort, and occasionally money, but it is worth it—or better, have fewer kids!

The present mood against flying must be balanced against the positive impact of going to impoverished nations and spending money there. There is no need to burn fuel to holiday on a beach in the U.S., but for travel to developing countries, the benefits outweigh the environmental costs. If you disagree, buy carbon offsets, or support a local environmental project such as KEEP, in Kathmandu, who plant trees for you. Below are some ideas to help you leave no trace of your passage.

- Travel in smaller teams to lessen your impact, not only on the environment, but also the local people.
- Educate your cooks and porters to look after the environment. Explain that, without a clean environment tourism will decline.
- Remove your own and other people's waste.
- Burn only burnable or non-toxic waste (not plastic), but be considerate about burning things in the Himalaya as smoke is used to purify. Only burn things in base camp after having spoken with your Sirdar, and ask him to arrange the fire. Separate the waste and burn whenever the weather allows.
- At altitude it is not easy, so ensure there is fuel left at the end of the trip for the final fire and that everything is thoroughly destroyed.
- Throwing waste into a crevasse is not acceptable—all non-burnable and toxic waste should be carried out. Unless extenuating circumstances prevail, there are few excuses for not removing all your non-human waste. Ensure that removed waste reaches its destination—porters may dump their load as soon as they realize what they are carrying.
  - Empty glass bottles rarely make it back to recycling centers in

Polluting water and stressing wildlife are two of the greatest impacts in remote areas.

Porters burning wood

The scientific community is in doubt that global warming is occurring, but whether it is the fault of humans is another matter, and whether we are doing enough is doubtful. (Sunrise over Kanchenjunga.)

the valley (if they exist at all), and plastic bottles are tossed into open pits. Reduce your dependence on sugary drinks and purify stream water rather than buying bottled water; you reduce your impact on the environment and save money.

- Dispose of human waste at least 200m (656ft) from water sources or carry it away. Full containers are heavy and may require animals to transport them. Lime is required to sterilize the waste, and proper disposal lower down the mountain requires planning. Deep pits are by far the most practical option for most expeditions.

- Do not build cairns or walls and, if you do, take them down afterwards.

- If you fly with a lot of batteries think about their safe disposal or take them home.

- Consider using cotton sacks for holding food rather than plastic bags.

- Stay on tracks, never cut corners, and take care not to collapse riverbanks. When traveling cross-country, spread out so you don't wear a groove in trackless terrain.

- Whenever possible use established campsites. Choose a location that conceals your presence from the sight of others.

- Do not wash dishes directly in streams.

- Using wood for fires has apparently devastated many mountain areas. Reduce the impact by ensuring that only deadwood is used (but beware: good trees are sometimes cut down out of season so they can use the deadwood the following year); supply enough stoves and encourage their use, particularly at lunch stops and early evening where warmth is not an issue.

- Keep food away from wildlife, and never feed animals—it alters their natural foraging habits.

APPENDIX

APPENDIX 1: AWARDS AND TRAINING (GUIDE/COACH/INSTRUCTOR/EXPEDITION LEADER)

BODY	OPERATION
The International Federation of Mountain Guides Associations (IFMGA, or UIAGM in France)	Consists of National Guiding Associations of 17 member countries. All work to same strict syllabus and assessment standards.
The British Association of Mountain Guides (BMG) or the American Mountain Guides Association (AMGA)	Train candidates for the IFMGA/UIAGM International Mountain Guides Carnet
The AMGA and Mountain Training U.K. (MTUK)	Set standards of training and assessment for instructor qualifications valid within U.S. and U.K., respectively

THE INTERNATIONAL GUIDES CARNET (IFMGA GUIDE, USED TO BE UIAGM)

The highest award in mountaineering and climbing. It is the only internationally recognised professional qualification. Members are some of the most experienced and talented climbers and mountaineers in the world. In their home countries, qualified guides are members of their respective professional association, which trains and assesses members.

Becoming an IFMGA Guide is very difficult, with only several people each year making the grade. They are assessed in rock (E1), ice (grade 5), Alpinism, and skiing. They are also trained in a wide range of professional topics, including first aid and rescue training, sports physiology, coaching, the law, professional standards, environmental issues, mountain weather, snow science, avalanche forecasting, mountain history, and flora and fauna.

The essential differences between the IFMGA Carnet and other qualifications are the greater level of experience and higher climbing standard required to start the scheme and the broader range of areas covered. You can be assured that anyone holding this award is seriously passionate about climbing. IFMGA Mountain Guides are widely respected for their quality of work, attention to detail and client safety.

AMGA AWARDS

MTUK AWARDS

AWARD	DESCRIPTION
Top Rope Site Manager	Prepares climbers to safely teach top rope climbing and to manage group climbing sites
Rock Instructor Course	Introduces aspirant guides to multi-pitch guiding skills on rock routes up to grade III in length and with relatively simple approaches and descents
Advanced Rock Guide	Further prepares and evaluates guides on difficult terrain above grade III

CHOOSING A GUIDE/ COACH/INSTRUCTOR/ EXPEDITION LEADER

- Beware: there is no law requiring a person to be officially trained or qualified to work in the U.K. or U.S. As a result, anyone can claim to be a competent Mountain Guide, climbing instructor, or coach!

- To properly teach and protect someone in a new environment requires techniques different to those used by recreational climbers. Therefore ask questions of the person leading you. What qualifications, training, and experience do they have, and do they have relevant insurance?

- Find out whether they are breaking the law when working abroad.

GUIDING IN EUROPE AND THE ALPS

Strict laws apply to professional guiding in the Alps, with only IFMGA guides allowed to work legally in many countries with ice fall climbing and via ferrata. If your instructor is working illegally, his insurance is likely to be invalid and so may yours!

CLIMBING EXPEDITIONS

There are few countries where laws apply to expedition guiding. To help differentiate professionally led expeditions from other trips, there is a new standard that guides may adhere to in order to use the IFMGA logo to advertise their expeditions. Any expedition meeting the IFMGA standard must be professionally planned, staffed by IFMGA guides and have thorough medical safety and evacuation contingencies, as well as radio and satellite communications at base camp and on the mountain.

AWARD	DESCRIPTION
CWA	Supervising sessions on climbing walls, with an optional module for abseiling and climbing towers
SPA	A low-level award intended for leaders supervising groups top roping and bottom roping on single pitch rock climbs on crags and indoor walls. Although individuals may be highly experienced climbers, there is no way of knowing that from the award
Walking Group Leader (WGL)	Leading groups in non-mountainous terrain, e.g., Dartmoor
Mountain Leader Summer	Holders of this award are highly competent at leading walking trips in the U.K. in summer conditions. It is not a climbing award.
Mountain Leader Winter	Holders of this award are highly competent for leading walking trips in the U.K. in winter conditions. It is not a climbing award.
International Mountain Leader (IML)	Leading walking groups in Europe in all areas, except on glaciers and where the techniques or materials of Alpinism are required. Can also operate on easy, snow-covered terrain – including using snowshoes – providing it is of a gentle, Nordic type in the "middle" mountains. In such cases, they will not spend consecutive nights outside, unless they use refuges with uardians.
Mountain Instructor Award (MIA)	The holder is trained and assessed to lead up to VS multi-pitch rock climbing and hill walking in summer conditions. Designed for the specific types of situations/conditions found in the U.K.
Mountain Instructor Certificate (MIC)	The holder is trained and assessed as for MIA, but also at grade 3 for winter mountaineering and climbing. Designed for the specific situations found in the U.K.

OFF PISTE SKIING

Only IFMGA guides are qualified to work off-piste in glacial terrain in the Alps. Some ski instructors are allowed to take groups off-piste too, so long as there are no glaciers involved, but definitely not the tour hosts and reps that commonly show skiers around the pisted runs within large resorts (check the insurance situation with anyone taking you out). Guides are trained to look after groups off-piste and on glaciers and find the best snow for their clients: i.e., give you a great days' skiing. They are not trained as professional ski instructors.

APPENDIX 2: CLIMBING GRADES

The problem with climbing grades is that they are really grading a climber – what one person will find easy another will find hard, depending on their strength and physical characteristics. Grades can vary from country to country and venue to venue, and in reality it is difficult to compare. For instance; the French sport climbing system only rates difficulty, whereas the U.K. system grades traditional climbs. Just because you can climb a French 7a does not mean that you can climb E5!

COMPARISON OF ROCK CLIMBING GRADES

U.K.	SPORT	AUSTRALIA	U.S.	UIAA
E1 5a/5b	6a	18	5.10b	VI+
E2 5b/5c	6a+	19	5.10c	VII–
E2 5c	6b	20	5.10d	VII
E3 5c	6b+	21	5.11a	VII+
E3/E4 6a	6c	22	5.11b	VII+
E4 6a	6c+	23	5.11c	VIII–
E5 6a	7a	23	5.11d	VIII
E5 6a	7a+	24	5.12a	VIII+
E5 6b	7b	25	5.12b	VIII+/IX–
E6 6b	7b+	26	5.12c	IX–
E6 6b	7c	27	5.12d	IX
E6 6c	7c+	28	5.13a	IX+
E7 6c	8a	29	5.13b	X–
E7 6c/7a	8a+	30	5.13c	X/X–
E7/E86c/7a	8b	31	5.13d	X
E8 6c/7a	8b+	32	5.14a	X+
E8 6c/7a	8c	33	5.14b	XI–
E9 7a/7b	8c+	34	5.14c	XI
E9/E10 7a/7	9a	v	5.14d	XI+

COMPARISON OF BOULDERING GRADES

U.S. (V-SCALE)	FRANCE
V0	2/3
V1	4
V2	5
V3	6a/b
V4	6c
V5	7a
V6	7a+
V7	7b
V8	7b+
V9	7c
V10	7c+
V11	8a
V12	8a+
V13	8b
V14	8b+
V15	8c
V16	8c+

SCRAMBLING GRADES

U.K. scrambles are usually rated using Steve Ashton's system of grades 1, 2, 3, or 3S (S for serious), with the grade being based around technical difficulty, the need to use a rope, and exposure.

Some books on scrambling rate the routes:

GRADE	DETAIL
Grade 1	Straightforward for experienced hill walkers. It may be necessary to use the hands occasionally for progress. The exposure is not too daunting.
Grade 2	This grade is more sustained and requires more use of the hands. The exposure is significant and retreat difficult.
Grade 3	The rock becomes very steep and is exposed at times. Most people will prefer a rope, and there are occasional moves more akin to a full rock climb. The ability to abseil may be important.

In the U.S., the Yosemite Decimal System (YDS) is used. The system consists of five classes indicating the technical difficulty of the hardest section:

LEVEL	DETAIL
Easy	Just off-trail hiking with minimal exposure (if at all), and perhaps a handhold or two. UIAA Class I.
Moderate	Handholds frequently needed, possible exposure, route-finding skills helpful. UIAA Class II.
Difficult	Almost constant handholds, fall distance may be fatal, route finding-skills needed, loose and down-sloping rock. Less experienced parties may consider using a rope for short sections.

CLASS	DETAIL
Class 1	Walking with a low chance of injury or fatality
Classes 2 and 3	Steeper routes with increased exposure and a greater chance of severe injury, but falls are not always fatal
Class 4	Can involve short, steep sections where the use of a rope is recommended, and un-roped falls could be fatal
Class 5	Considered true rock climbing, predominantly on vertical or near vertical rock

THE U.K. GRADING SYSTEM

COMBINED GRADES

These are combined to give the overall grade for the climb. The table below outlines the usual range of technical grades that you would expect to find combined with the different adjective grades, but there are many routes that fall outside this range.

The interplay between the two parts of the U.K. grade is rich and provides a lot of information about the difficulty of a climb, and what type of difficulty this might be. Climbs of a particular adjectival grade will often have an associated average technical grade (see the table below). For example, if for a particular adjectival grade the technical grade is high (e.g., VS 5a, E1 5c), then you can expect the route to be technical, with a single, hard, well-protected move. If the technical grade is low for the adjectival grade (e.g., HVS 4c, E3 5b), then expect either a very sustained and strenuous struggle, or a route with relatively easy climbing, only in a serious situation. Whether a route/pitch is bold or sustained is usually described in the guidebook or obvious when you look at it, i.e., an overhanging hand crack could reasonably be supposed to be sustained and well protected, a blank slab could be supposed to be serious.

NATIONAL CLIMBING CLASSIFICATION SYSTEM (U.S.)

ADJECTIVE GRADE	TECHNICAL GRADE	ADJECTIVAL GRADE	TECHNICAL GRADE
D	N/A	E3	5c–6a
VD	N/A	E4	6a–6b
S	4a–4b	E5	6a–6c

HS	4a–4c	E6	6b–6c
VS	4b–4c	E7	6c–7a
HVS	4c–5b	E8	6c–7a
E1	5a–5c	E9	7a–7b
E2	5b–6a	E10	7a–7c

NCCS grades, often called "commitment grades" indicate the time investment in a route for an "average" climbing team.

GRADE	DESCRIPTION
I and II	Half a day or less for the technical (5th class) portion of the route
III	Most of a day of roped climbing
IV	A full day of technical climbing
V	Usually requires an overnight on the route, or done fast and free in a day
VI	Two or more days of hard climbing
VII	Remote walls climbed in alpine style

FRANCE

French sport climbs are graded for a redpoint ascent. The grading system is used only where routes are fully bolted. It is also assumed that the quick-draws are in place. A route of grade f7a ("f" indicates a French sports route) could be very long and sustained with no hard moves, or short with a powerful, technical crux move. The grade does not help you decide.

The grades are as follows: 5, 5+, 6a, 6a+, 6b, 6b+, 6c, 6c+, 7a, 7a+, 7b, 7b+, 7c, 7c+, 8a, 8a+, 8b, 8b+, 8c, 8c+, 9a, 9a+, 9b.

This system is used to grade sports climbs in the U.K., but a direct comparison is difficult.

AID GRADES

Original Aid Rating System (when the letter "C" replaces "A," the rating refers to climbing without a hammer).

GRADE	DESCRIPTION
A0	Occasional aid moves often done without aiders (etriers) or climbed on fixed gear; sometimes called "French Free"
A1	All placements are solid and easy
A2	Good placements, but sometimes tricky
A3	Many difficult, insecure placements but with little risk
A4	Many placements in a row that hold nothing more than body weight
A5	Enough bodyweight placements in a row that one failure results in a fall of at least 20m (66ft)

New Wave Aid Ratings:

GRADE	DESCRIPTION
A1	Easy aid. No risk of a piece pulling out.
A2	Moderate aid. Solid gear that is more difficult to place.
A2+	10m (33ft) fall potential from tenuous placements, but without danger
A3	Hard aid. Many tenuous placements in a row; 15m (49ft) fall potential; could require several hours for a single pitch.
A3+	A3 with dangerous fall potential
A4	Serious aid. 30m (98.5ft) ledge-fall potential from continuously tenuous gear.
A4+	Even more serious, with even greater fall potential, where each pitch could take many hours to lead
A5	Extreme aid. Nothing on the entire pitch can be trusted to hold a fall.
A6	A5 climbing with belay anchors that will not hold a fall

WINTER CLIMBING GRADES

Be wary of old guidebooks, old timers, and unrepeated routes; in the early 1990s the grading system was overhauled.

SCOTLAND

GRADE	DESCRIPTION
Grade I	Snow gullies (no more than 45 degrees) or easy ridges, that can sometimes have scant protection, and cornices can cause a problem. They are often used as descents and can usually be climbed with a single axe.
Grade II	Steeper with short icy or technical bits. Ridges are easy scrambles in summer. It is likely that two axes will be essential.
Grade III	Sustained ridges, or gullies, with short, but steep ice 60–70 degrees, or easier buttresses and snowed-up rock routes.
Grade IV	The start of real technical difficulties. Snowed-up rock routes will be sustained, and sometimes steep and more advanced techniques will be required. Ice routes will be 70–5 degrees or have short vertical steps.
Grade V	Sustained steep ice at 70–5 degrees. Mixed routes could be up to VS summer routes and may require the linking of multiple advanced moves.
Grade VI	Long vertical sections of ice, with little chance of rest. Mixed routes will be as for grade V, but harder and more sustained. Mixed routes will be at least VS summer routes.
Grade VII	Ice climbs are very serious with poorly protected steep ice. Snowed-up rock routes could have overhanging sections, even roofs.
Grade VIII	Only two ice climbs reach these heights, both are in Torridon, west coast of Scotland, and both are potential chop routes. Snowed-up rock routes follow the lines of E1s and 2s.
Grade IX	The realms of fantasy, but one has been climbed

TECHNICAL GRADE

This refers to the technical difficulties of the pitch and takes into account the angle of the icefall, whether the climbing is sustained or not, the nature of the fall's formation, and the nature of its protection.

GRADE	DESCRIPTION
1	Easy angled ice that has no particularly hard sections
2	Easily protected pitch on good ice
3	Some 80° sections, but on thick, compact ice, with comfortable, well-protected belays
4	Sustained and near-vertical pitch, or a short pitch with a short, vertical section. Good ice and satisfactory gear.
5	Sustained and nearly always-vertical pitch up discreet ice, or a less sustained pitch that is technically more demanding. Few rests.
6	Very sustained pitch that offers no rests at all. Difficult ice; some overlaps and other formations requiring good technique. Protection is difficult to place and often of dubious nature.
7	Very sustained pitch that offers no rests at all. Is extremely fragile and technically difficult ice. Protection is run-out or non-existent.

WATER ICE AND ALPINE ICE GRADES

GRADE	DESCRIPTIONS
WI 1	Low angle ice; ice axe required. General angle: 50 degrees.
WI 2	Consistent 60-degree ice with possible bulges; good protection and anchors.
WI 3	Sustained 70 degrees with possible long bulges of 80–90 degrees; reasonable rests and good stances for placing screws. Generally good protection, and screws can be placed from comfortable stances. The ice is usually of good quality.
WI 4	Sustained climbing with some vertical sections, separated by good belays. The ice may have some technical features like chandeliers, but generally the quality of ice is good and offers secure protection and belays. General angle: 80 degrees.
WI 5	A long, steep, strenuous, columnar pitch of ice. Sustained with little opportunity to rest. Expertise in dealing with the different ice formations is required (e.g., chandeliers, cauliflowers, candled sections). Adequate protection, but requires effort to place. The climb may sometimes be run-out above protection. Belays may be difficult to create or hang. General angle: 90 degrees.
WI 6	A serious lead on severe or thin ice. Long vertical or overhanging sections, which leads to extremely sustained difficulties. There are few, if any, resting sites. Ice may not be of the best quality; often thin, chandeliered, and hard to protect. Hanging belays of dubious quality may be required. General angle: 90+ degrees.
WI 7	Ice is very thin, long, overhanging, or very technical. There are free-hanging columns of dubious adhesion. Protection may be non-existent. The pitch is very physical and emotional. Belays require a very high level of expertise, and may be marginal. This grade applies to only a handful of routes led by an even fewer number of world-class climbers. General angle: 90++ degrees.

ICE CLIMBING RATINGS

Ice climbing ratings are highly variable by region and are still evolving. The WI acronym implies seasonal ice; AI is often substituted for year-around Alpine Ice and may be easier than a WI grade with the same number. Canadians often drop the WI symbol and hyphenate the technical grade after the Canadian commitment grade's Roman numeral (example: II-5).

MIXED ROUTES/DRY TOOLING GRADES

GRADE	DESCRIPTION
M1–3	Easy. Low-angle and usually no tools.
M4	Slabby to vertical with some technical dry tooling.
M5	Some sustained vertical dry tooling.
M6	Vertical to overhanging with difficult dry tooling.
M7	Overhanging; powerful and technical dry tooling; less than 10 m (33 ft) of hard climbing.
M8	Some nearly horizontal overhangs requiring very powerful and technical dry tooling; bouldery or longer cruxes than M7.
M9	Either continuously vertical or slightly overhanging with marginal or technical holds, or a juggy roof of two to three body lengths.
M10	At least 10m (33ft) of horizontal rock or 30m (98ft) of overhanging dry tooling with powerful moves and no rests.
M11	A rope length of overhanging gymnastic climbing, or up to 15m (49ft) of roof.
M12	M11 with bouldery, dynamic moves and tenuous technical holds.

INDEX